1 MONTH OF
FREE
READING

at
www.ForgottenBooks.com

By purchasing this book you are eligible for one month membership to ForgottenBooks.com, giving you unlimited access to our entire collection of over 1,000,000 titles via our web site and mobile apps.

To claim your free month visit:
www.forgottenbooks.com/free922601

ISBN 978-0-260-01880-9
PIBN 10922601

REPORTS

OF

CASES ARGUED AND DETERMINED

IN

THE SUPREME COURT

OF THE

STATE OF VERMONT

———

BY

JOHN W. REDMOND.

———

VOLUME 76.

NEW SERIES - - - VOLUME 1.

———

BURLINGTON:
FREE PRESS ASSOCIATION,
1904.

JUDGES

OF THE

SUPREME COURT OF VERMONT

DURING THE TIME OF THESE REPORTS.

Hon. JOHN W. ROWELL, Chief Judge,

Hon. JAMES M. TYLER.

Hon. LOVELAND MUNSON.

Hon. HENRY R. START.

Hon. JOHN H. WATSON.

Hon. WENDELL P. STAFFORD.

Hon. SENECA HASELTON.

A TABLE

OF THE

CASES REPORTED IN THIS VOLUME.

Aldrich (Fulton v.).......... 310
Allen (Equitable Mfg. Co. v.). 22
Angell v. Fletcher et al....... 359
Ayers (Coolidge v.).......... 405
Bailey v. Bailey 264
Bailey's Admx. v. Gleason..... 115
Bankers' Life Ins. Co. v. Fleet-
    wood et al............... 297
Barre, etc. Power Co. (City of
    Montpelier v.) 66
Barre, etc. Power Co. (Roeb-
    ling's Sons Co. v.)........ 131
Barrett v. Tyler et al........ 108
Bartholomew's Est. (Walworth's
    Est. v.) 1
Bass v. Rublee 395
Belknap v. Billings 54
Bellows Free Academy v. Sowles
    et al. 412
Bell et al. v. St. J. & L. C. R.
    Co. 42
Billings (Belknap v.)......... 54
Bostridge (Mossman v.)....... 409
Brock (Scoville v.)........... 385
Brownell v. Russell 326
Brunnell v. Carr 174
Buck v. Troy Aqueduct Co..... 75
Bugbee (Hartford Woolen Co.
    v.)......... 61

Burlington Shoe Co. (Hilliard
    v.) 57
Canadian Pac. R. Co. (Morris-
    ette v.) 267
Capital Sav. Bank (Templeton
    v.) 345
Carr (Brunnell v.).... 174
Carter v. Carter 190
Chase v. Soule 353
Cheney's Exr. et al. v. Stafford
    et al. 16
City of Montpelier v. Barre,
    etc. Power Co. 66
Cochran (King v.) 141
Collins (McKinstry v.) 221
Congregational Church of Ches-
    ter v. Cutler............. 338
Congregational Society of Fer-
    risburg (Hare v.) 362
Coolidge v. Ayers 405
Constantino (State v.) 192
Costa (Kimball v.)........... 289
Currier et al. v. Town of Brigh-
    ton 261
Cutler (Congregational Church
    of Chester v.)............. 338
Davis (Grand Trunk R. Co. v.) 187
Davis et al. v. Moyles......... 25
Deavitt v. Ring 216

Delphia v. Rutland R. Co...... 84
Dodge (State v.) 197
Equitable Mfg. Co. v. Allen... 22
Fish v. Olin 120
Fleetwood et al. (Bankers' Life
   Ins. Co. v.) 297
Fletcher et al. (Angell v.).... 359
Fletcher (Richardson v.) 206
Foss v. Smith 113
Foss v. Stanton 365
French v. Grand Trunk R. R.
   Co. 441
Fulton v. Aldrich 310
Grand Trunk R. Co. (French
   v.) 441
Grand Trunk R. Co. v. Davis. 187
Grand Trunk R. Co. (Tracy v.) 313
Gleason (Bailey's Admx. v.).. 115
Hall (People's Bank v.)...... 280
Hammond's Admr. v. Ham-
   mond 437
Hare v. Congregational Soc. of
   Ferrisburg 362
Hartford Woolen Co. v. Bugbee 61
Hassan (Luce v.) 450
Hilliard v. Burlington Shoe Co. 57
Hooker (Reynolds v.)........ 184
Hunt (Jackson v.) 284
Hunt v. Rublee 448
Hunt (Weed v.) 212
In Re Joslyn's Est........... 88
In Re Mather's Will.......... 209
In Re Wheelock's Will........ 235
Jackson v. Hunt 284
Jangraw v. Perkins.......... 127
Jewett (State v.) 435
Joslyn's Est. (In Re)........ 88
Joslyn v. Taplin & Rowell..... 422
Kennedy (Rice v.) 380
Kimball v. Costa 289
King v. Cochran 141
Klondike Machine (State v.).. 426

Lawrie v. Silsby et al........ 240
Leonard v. Sibley 254
Luce v. Hassan 450
Lyndonville Bank (Metropoli-
   tan Stock Exchange v.)... 303
Martin (Sowles v.) 180
Mason v. Mason's Exrs....... 287
Mather's Will (In Re)....... 209
Metropolitan Stock Exchange
   v. Lyndonville Nat. Bank. 303
McCloskey v. Springfield F. &
   M. Ins. Co. 151
McKannon Bros. & Co. (Parker
   v.) 96
McKinstry v. Collins 221
Miller v. Wilbur 73
Morrisette v. Canadian Pac. R.
   Co. 267
Mossman v. Bostridge........ 409
Moyles (Davis et al. v.)...... 25
Newport (Stiles v.) 154
Olin (Fish v.) 120
Parker v. McKannon Bros. &
   Co. 96
Peaslee's Est. (Vitty v.)...... 402
People's Bank v. Hall & Buell. 280
Perkins (Jangraw v.)........ 127
Raymo (State v.) 430
Reynolds v. Hooker.......... 184
Rice v. Kennedy 380
Richardson v. Fletcher........ 206
Ring (Deavitt v.) 216
Roebling's Sons Co. v. Barre,
   etc. Power Co. 131
Rublee (Bass v.) 395
Rublee (Hunt v.) 448
Russell (Brownell v.)........ 326
Rutland R. Co. (Delphia v.).. 84
Sartwell (Sowles v.)......... 70
Scoville v. Brock 385
Sibley (Leonard v.) 254

Silsby et al. (Lawrie v.)..... 240
Smith (Foss v.) 113
Soule (Chase v.) 353
Sowles (Bellows Free Academy
    v.) 412
Sowles v. Martin 180
Sowles v. Sartwell 70
Spencer v. Stockwell 176
Springfield F. & M. Ins. Co.
    (McCloskey v.) 151
Stafford et al. (Cheney's Exr.
    et al v.) 16
Stanton (Foss v.) 365
State v. Constantino 192
State v. Dodge 197
State v. Jewett 435
State v. Klondike Machine.... 426
State v. Raymo 430
State v. Tague 118
St. Johnsbury, etc. R. Co. (Bell
    et al. v.) 42
Stiles v. Newport 154
Stockwell (Spencer v.) 176

Tague (State v.) 118
Taplin & Rowell (Joslyn v.).. 422
Templeton v. Capital Sav. Bk. 345
Town of Brighton (Currier v.) 261
Town of Essex v. Town of Jeri-
    cho 104
Town of Readsboro v. Town of
    Woodford 376
Town of Searsburg v. Town of
    Woodford 370
Tracy v. Grand Trunk R. Co... 313
Troy Aqueduct Co. (Buck v.). 75
Tyler et al. (Barrett v.)..... 108
Vitty v. Peaslee's Est......... 402
Walworth's Est. v. Bartholo-
    mew's Est. 1
Waste (Wilmington Sav. Bank
    v.) 331
Weed v. Hunt 212
Wheelock's Will (In Re)..... 235
Wilbur (Miller v.) 73
Wilmington Sav. Bank v.
    Waste 331

A TABLE

OF THE

CASES REPORTED IN THIS VOLUME ARRANGED BY COUNTIES.

ADDISON.

Delphia v. Rutland R. Co...... 84
Fish v. Olin 120
Hare v. Congregational Soc. of
    Ferrisburg 362
Mather's Will, In Re......... 209

BENNINGTON.

Mason v. Mason's Exrs....... 287
State v. Klondike Machine.... 426
Town of Readsboro v. Town of
    Woodford 376
Town of Searsburg v. Town of
    Woodford 370
Wheelock's Will, In Re....... 235

CALEDONIA.

Bailey v. Bailey 264
Bell et al. v. St. J. & L. C. R.
    Co. 42
Foss v. Smith 113
King v. Cochran 141
Metropolitan Stock Exchange
    v. Lyndonville Nat. Bank. 303
State v. Constantino 192

CHITTENDEN.

Brownell v. Russell 326
Chase v. Soule 353
Hilliard v. The Burlington Shoe
    Co. et al. 57
Parker v. McKannon Bros.... 96
People's National Bank et al. v.
    Hall & Buell 280

Rice & Co. v. Kennedy........ 380
State v. Dodge 197
Town of Essex v. Town of Jeri-
    cho 104

ESSEX.

Currier v. Town of Brighton.. 261
French v. Grand Trunk R. Co. 441
Grand Trunk R. Co. v. Davis. 187
Tracy v. Grand Trunk R. Co... 313

FRANKLIN.

Bellows Free Academy of Fair-
    fax et al. v. Sowles et al.. 412
Hunt v. Rublee 448
Sowles v. Martin et al........ 180
Sowles, Admr. v. Sartwell.... 70

LAMOILLE.

Carter v. Carter 190
Jackson v. Hunt 284

ORANGE.

Barrett v. Tyler and Chadwick. 108
Bass v. Rublee 395
Equitable Mfg. Co. v. Allen... 22
Fulton et al. v. Aldrich et al. 310
Kimball v. Costa 289
Reynolds v. Hooker.......... 184
Walworth's Est. v. Bartholo-
    mew's Est. 1

ORLEANS.

Buck v. Troy Aqueduct Co..... 75
Joslyn v. Taplin & Rowell.... 422

Morrisette v. Canadian Pac. R.
Co. 267
Mossman v. Bostridge........ 409
State v. Raymo 430
Stiles v. Village of Newport.. 154

RUTLAND.

Cheney's Exr. et al. v. Stafford
et al. 16
Coolidge v. Ayers 405
Hammond's Admr. v. Ham-
mond 437
McCloskey et al. v. Springfield
Ins. Co. ....·........ 151

WASHINGTON.

Angell v. Fletcher et al....... 359
Bailey's Admx. v. Gleason.... 115
Bankers' Ins. Co. v. Fleetwood
et al. 297
Brunnell et ux. v. Carr et ux.. 174
City of Montpelier et al. v.
Barre, etc. Power Co...... 66
Deavitt v. Ring, Admr., et al.. 216
Foss v. Stanton 365
Jangraw v. Perkins.......... 127
Lawrie et al. v. Silsby et al.. 240
Leonard v. Sibley, Admr...... 254

McKinstry v. Collins 221
Roebling's Sons Co. v. Barre,
etc. Power Co. 131
Scoville v. Brock 385
State v. Jewett 435
State v. Tague ....·..... 118
Templeton v. Capital Sav. Bk.
& Tr. Co. ..·.............. 345
Weed v. Hunt 212

WINDHAM.

Davis et al. v. Moyles........ 25
Miller v. Wilbur 73
Spencer v. Stockwell 176
Wilmington Sav. Bank v.
Waste 331

WINDSOR.

Belknap v. Billings 54
Congregational Church of Ches-
ter et al. v. Cutler....... 338
Hartford Woolen Co. v. Bugbee
et al. 61
In Re Joslyn's Est........... 88
Luce v. Hassan 450
Richardson v. Fletcher........ 206
Vitty v. Peaslee's Est..·....... 402

A TABLE

CASES CITED IN THE OPINIONS OF THE COURT.

Abbott v. Coburn, 28 Vt. 664.. 91
Abbott v. Winchester, 105 Mass.
  115 178
Adams v. Smilie, 50 Vt. 1...... 186
Adams v. Warner, 23 Vt. 395.. 64
Aiken v. Smith, 21 Vt. 172.... 449
Albee v. Fairbanks, 10 Vt. 314 450
Albee v. Huntley, 56 Vt. 454.. 64
Alexander v. School Dist., 62
  Vt. 273 312
Allgeyer v. Louisiana, 165 U. S.
  578 202
Anderson v. R. Co., 37 Wis. 321 272
Arbuckle v. Ward, 29 Vt. 43.. 247
Arel v. Centebar, 73 Vt. 238... 318
Bailey v. The Mayor of New
  York, 3 Hill 531........... 166
Baldwin v. Skeels, 51 Vt. 121.. 367
Bank v. Beattie, 32 Vt. 315.... 260
Bank of Selma v. Colby, 88 U.
  S. 609 124
Bank v. Downer, 29 Vt. 332...232
Bank v. Freency, 12 So. Dak.
  156 294
Bank v. Hyde, 13 Conn. 279.. 294
Bank of Metropolis v. Ken-
  nedy, 84 U. S. 19........ 124
Bank of Bethel v. Pahquio-
  que Bank, 81 U. S. 383.... 125
Bank of Middlebury v. R. Co.,
  30 Vt. 169 81
Bank v. Tucker, 7 Vt. 134.... 234
Bankers', etc. Ins. Co. v. Ins.
  Commrs., 73 Vt. 48....... 299
Barney v. Parsons, 54 Vt. 623. 12
Barre Water Co. v. Carnes, 65
  Vt. 626 252
Barrett v. Copeland, 18 Vt. 67. 232
Bartelott v. Bank, 119 Ill. 259 400
Barton Nat. Bank v. Atkins, 72
  Vt. 33 147
Bates v. Rutland, 62 Vt. 178.. 166

Batchelder v. Boston & Maine
  R. Co., 57 Atl. 926 446
Batchelder v. Jenness, 59 Vt.
  104 425
Bigelow v. Rising, 42 Vt. 678.. 39
Bigelow v. Stilphen, 35 Vt. 521 24
Blaine v. Ray, 61 Vt. 566...... 247
Bliss v. Smith, 42 Vt. 198.... 312
Blodgett's Est. v. Converse's
  Est., 60 Vt. 410.......... 8
Bradish v. Bliss, 35 Vt. 328.. 283
Branson v. Wirth, 17 Wall. 32. 37
Brazeale v. Brazeale, 9 Ala. 491 8
Breed v. Pratt, 18 Pick. 115... 240
Brock v. Bruce, 59 Vt. 313.... 234
Brooker v. Armstrong, 93 Mo.
  49 8
Brusckerhoff v. Bostwick, 88 N.
  Y. 52 125
Buchanan v. Barre, 66 Vt. 129 166
Bullock v. Guilford, 59 Vt. 517 95
Bullock v. Dean, 12 Met. 15.. 320
Bullock's Admr. v. Rogers, 16
  Vt. 294 91
Burlington v. Traction Co., 70
  Vt. 491 319
Bushnell v. Leland, 164 U. S.
  688 125
Butler v. Ives, 139 Mass. 202.. 178
Butler v. Viscount Mountgar-
  ret, 7 H. L. Cas. 633...... 41
Cal. Bank v. Kennedy, 167 U. S.
  362 308
Carlisle v. Soule, 44 Vt. 265.. 352
Carter v. Central Vt. R. Co., 72
  Vt. 190 446
Carver v. Astor, 4 Pet. 1...... 33
Casey v. La Societe de Credit
  Mobilier, 2 Wood 77...... 126
Central Transp. Co. v. Pull. Car
  Co., 139 U. S. 24........ 308
Chandler v. Spear, 22 Vt. 388. 234

Chapman v. Goodrich, 55 Vt.
354 320
Chapman v. Kellogg, 102 Mass.
246 178
Chasemore v. Richards, 7 H. L.
Cas. 349 245
Chatfield v. Wilson, 31 Vt. 358 252
Chicago Fire Proofing Co. v.
Park Nat. Bank, 145 Ill.
481 125
Chicago, etc. R. Co. v. Rouse,
44 L. R. A. 410........... 272
Child v. Merrill, 66 Vt. 308... 233
Churchill v. Bradley, 58 Vt. 403 220
City of Galesburg v. Hawkinson, 75 Ill. 152........... 375
Clement v. Gould, 61 Vt. 573.. 64
Cobourn v. Graff, 87 Minn. 510 283
Collins v. Adams, 53 Vt. 433.. 220
Com. v. McKibben, 90 Ky. 384. 166
Com. v. Murphy, 165 Mass. 66. 196
Com. v. Trefethen, 157 Mass.
180 434
Concord Nat. Bank v. Hawkins,
174 U. S. 364 308
Cooke v. Cholmondeley, 2 Macn.
& G. 18 239
Corgan v. Frew, 39 Ill. 31.... 294
Covington v. Kentucky, 173 U.
S. 231 168
Cross v. Martin, 46 Vt. 14..... 38
Crowninshield v. Crowninshield, 2 Gray 524........ 240
Cummings v. Holt, 56 Vt. 384. 312
Currier v. Richardson, 63 Vt.
620 233
Cutter v. Folsom, 17 N. H. 139 117
Cutter v. Gillette, 163 Mass. 95 102
Davis v. Hemmenway, 27 Vt.
589 367
Davis v. Weed, 44 Conn. 569.. 125
Day v. Essex Co. Bank, 13 Vt.
97 56
Day v. Lamb, 7 Vt. 426...... 320
Dean v. Bailey, 12 Vt. 142.... 348
Dearborn v. Kelley, 3 Allen 426 231
Dennick v. R. Co., 103 U. S. 11 272
Dickerman v. Ray, 55 Vt. 65.. 425
Dill v. Shahan, 25 Ala. 694.... 220
Dix v. Batchelder, 55 Vt. 562... 352
Dowling v. Banks, 145 U. S.
512 357
Downer v. Chamberlin, 21 Vt.
414 117
Downer v. Smith, 32 Vt. 1.... 112

Drake v. Mooney, 31 Vt. 617.. 234
Driscoll v. Place, 44 Vt. 252.. 231
Dumford v. Trotters, 12 M. &
W. 529 56
Dunshee v. Parmlee, 19 Vt. 172 215
Duval v. Wellman, 124 N. Y.
156 130
Earl v. Pennsylvania, 178 U. S.
449 124
Earnstaff v. Russell, 10 M. &
W. 365 411
Eastman v. Barnes, 58 Vt. 330. 230
Eidenmuller v. Eidenmuller,
37 Cal. 364 266
Elliott v. R. Co., 10 Cush. 191. 252
Ellis v. Cleveland, 55 Vt. 358.. 433
Ellsworth v. Hopkins, 58 Vt.
705 178
Elmondorff v. Carmichael, 3
Littell, 472 37
Emack v. Hughes, 74 Vt. 382. 104
Enright v. Amsden, 70 Vt. 183 215
Essex County v. Salem, 153
Mass. 141 164
Est. of Johnson, 57 Cal. 529.. 240
Ex Parte McKennon, 126 Cal.
429 205
Fairbanks v. Benjamin, 50 Vt.
99 234
Felker v. Emerson, 16 Vt. 653 348
Foote v. R. Co., 32 Vt. 633.... 81
Foster's Exrs. v. Dickerson, 64
Vt. 233 237
Foster v. Stone, 67 Vt. 336.... 14
Fowle v. Common Council, etc.,
11 Wheat. 320 402
Fowler v. Kent, 71 N. H. 388. 65
Freese v. Florida, 23 Fla. 267. 196
Frost v. Kellogg, 23 Vt. 308.. 182
Frothingham v. Shaw, 175 Mass.
59 95
Fulkerson v. Holmes, 117 U. S.
380 39
Gardener v. Thomas, 14 Johns.
134 272
Garwood v. Eldridge, 1 Green's
Chancery, 145 220
Gates v. Gorham, 5 Vt. 317.... 208
Gibson v. Hunter, 2 H. Black.
187 401
Gillis v. Chase, 67 N. H. 161.. 252
Godfry v. Downer, 47 Vt. 653. 389
Goell v. Morse, 126 Mass. 480.. 357
Goodrich v. Burbank, 12 Allen
459 249

Goodwin v. Perkins, 39 Vt. 598. 454
Gould v. Lasbury, 1 C. M. & R.
   254 411
Graham v. City of Greenville,
   67 Tex. 62 378
Griswold v. Rutland, 23 Vt. 324 428
Hadley v. Havens, 24 Vt. 520.. 367
Hadley v. Howe, 46 Vt. 142... 40
Hall v. Collins, 4 Vt. 316...... 33
Hall & Keen v. Potter, 3 Lev-
   inz 412 130
Hambrick v. Wilkins, 65 Miss..
   18 112
Hamilton v. Hamilton, 10 R. I.
   538 240
Hapgood v. Goddard, 26 Vt. 401 260
Harrington v. Hill, 51 Vt. 44.. 348
Harrison v. Bishop, 131 Ind.
   161 240
Hartwell v. Root, 19 John. 345 234
Harwood v. Bennington, etc. R.
   Co., 67 Vt. 664.......... 87
Hastings v. Belden, 55 Vt. 273. 215
Hawkins v. Glenn, 131 U. S.
   319 149
Hedrick v. Hedrick, 128 Ind.
   522 266
Heirs of Porter v. Heydock, 6
   Vt. 374 91
Herrick v. Minneapolis, etc.
   Co., 31 Minn. 11........ 272
Herron v. Dater, 120 U. S. 464. 33
Hersey v. Assurance Co., 75 Vt.
   441 75
Hibbard v. Foster, 24 Vt. 542. 39
Higgins v. R. Co., 155 Mass.
   180 272
Higgins v. Water Co., 36 N. J.
   Eq. 358 252
Hill v. Graham, 11 Colo. 536. 125
Holker v. Porritt, L. R. 8 Ex.
   107 246
Holmes v. Holmes, 29 N. J.
   Eq. 9 266
Holsman v. Boiling Springs
   Bleaching Co., 14 N. J. Eq.
   335 245
Hooker v. Eagle Bank of Roch-
   ester, 30 N. Y. 83........ 140
Hoskinson v. R. Co., 66 Vt. 626 275
Houston v. Howard, 39 Vt. 54. 348
Howard v. Bartlett, 70 Vt. 364 319
Howarth v. Angle, 162 N. Y.
   179 150

Howarth v. Lombard, 175 Mass.
   570 148
Hoy v. Sterrett, 2 Watts. 327. 245
Hunt v. Ronsmanese, 8 Wheat.
   174 220
Hutchins v. Moody, 34 Vt. 433 312
Hylton v. Hylton, 2 Ves. 549.. 391
Indiana v. Ky., 136 U. S. 479. 372
Inhabitants of Fredericktown
   v. Fox, 84 Mo. 59........ 378
Inhabitants of Wayland v.
   Com'rs. of Middlesex, 4
   Gray 500 163
In Re Fenton's Will.......... 240
In Re Gangwere's Est., 14 Pa.
   St. 417 240
In Re Hurlburt's Est., 68 Vt.
   366 41
In Re Mullen, 4 Am. B. R. 224 408
In Re Yell, 107 Mich. 228.... 196
Ins. Co. v. Wright, 60 Vt. 515. 234
Irwin v. Williar, 110 U. S. 499 357
Jackson v. Shafer, 11 John. 517 234
Jewett v. Guyer, 38 Vt. 209... 234
Johnson v. Burnham, 22 Vt. 639 353
Johnson v. Hunt, 81 Ky. 321.. 130
Johnson v. Williams, 48 Vt.
   565 312
Jones v. Spear, 21 Vt. 426.... 259
Kennedy v. Gibson, 8 Wall. 498 124
Kensit v. Great Eastern R. Co.,
   27 Ch. D. 122........... 248
Kemp v. Knickerbocker Ice Co.,
   69 N. Y. 45............. 286
Kerby v. Jackson, 42 Vt. 552.. 320
Kidder v. Baron, 74 Vt. 275.... 434
Kilbourne v. Burt, etc. Co., 55
   L. R. A. 275............ 286
Kimball v. Hammel, 92 Am. St.
   R. 52 294
King v. Cochran, 72 Vt. 107.. 145
Kinkead v. United States, 150
   U. S. 483 37
Kleiman v. Gieselman, 114 Mo.
   437 220
Knight v. Smythe, 57 Vt. 529. 434
Laflam v. Missisquoi Pulp Co.,
   74 Vt. 140 228
Lamoille County Bank v. Hunt,
   72 Vt. 357 71
Langdon v. Castleton, 30 Vt.
   285 440
Latremouille v. R. Co., 63 Vt.
   336 399

LaPoint v. Scott, 36 Vt. 603.. 450
Lawton v. Steele, 152 U. S. 133 202
Leach v. Beatties, 33 Vt. 195. 182
Lewis v. Alcock, 3 M. & W. 188 66
Limerick Bank v. Adams, 70
  Vt. 132 82
Long v. State, 74 Md. 565..... 205
Louis & Co. v. Brown, 7 Ore.
  326 286
Lonsdale Co. v. Mores, 21 Month-
  ly Law Rep. 658........... 250
Lord v. Bigelow, 8 Vt. 445..... 33
Lovejoy v. Churchill, 29 Vt. 151 72
Magoon v. Before, 73 Vt. 231.. 454
Martin v. Hurlburt, 60 Vt. 364. 266
Martin v. Johnson, 11 Texas
  Civil App. 628 196
Martin v. McAdams, 87 Tex. 225 238
Marble v. Hinds, 67 Me. 203.. 320
Maryland v. Dalrymple, 3 L. R.
  372 95
Massasoit Steam Mill Co. v.
  Western Assurance Co., 125
  Mass. 110 ......·....... 153
Matter of Hosford, 27 N. Y.
  App. Div. 427 8
Mayer v. Hillman, 91 U. S. 196. 60
McAuley v. Western Vt. R. R.
  Co., 33 Vt. 311............ 238
McCloskey v. Gleason, 56 Vt.
  264 ....:..... 8
McCormic v. Bank, 165 U. S.
  538 ..,...... 308
McCulloch v. Scott, 13 B. Mon-
  roe 172 112
McDaniels v. Bank of Rutland,
  29 Vt. 230 320
McDaniels v. McDaniels, 40 Vt.
  363 189
McDaniels v. Flower Brook Mfg.
  Co., 22 Vt. 274............ 60
McIntosh v. Aubrey, 185 U. S.
  122 266
McKinnon v. Bliss, 21 N. Y. 206 38
McKinstry v. Collins and Lov-
  ell, 74 Vt. 147............ 227
McLeod v. R. Co., 58 Vt. 727... 272
McNeil v. Bean, 32 Vt. 429.... 349
McNeil v. Boston Chamber of
  Commerce, 154 Mass. 277.. 136
Methodist Epis. Soc. v. Lake,
  51 Vt. 353 343
Mexican, etc. Ry. Co. v. Jack-
  son, 89 Tex. 107.......... 272

Middlebury College v. Cheney,
  1 Vt. 336 164
Middlebury College v. Lawton,
  23 Vt. 688 ....,.. 367
Miller v. Cushman, 38 Vt. 598. 230
Miller v. Lapham, 44 Vt. 416.. 64
Miller v. Wood, 44 Vt. 378.... 40
Moffatt v. Longbridge, 51 Miss.
  211 8
Monkton v. Attorney General,
  2 Russ. & Myl. 147........ 41
Moors v. Parker, 3 Mass. 310.. 231
Morrill v. Palmer, 68 Vt. 1.... 454
Morrisette v. Ry. Co., 74 Vt.
  232 ......,.... 273
Morrison v. Rogers, 115 Cal.
  252 130
Mount Holly v. Peru, 72 Vt. 68 106
Murchie v. Gates, 78 Me. 300.. 246
Murtey v. Allen, 71 Vt. 377... 145
Mut. Life Ins. Co. v. Hillmon,
  145 U. S. 285............ 434
Nat. Bank v. Graham, 100 U.
  S. 699 308
Nat. Bank of St. Johnsbury v.
  Peabody & Co., 55 Vt. 492.. 59
Nelson v. Butterfield, 21 Me.
  220 245
Newport v. Unity, 68 N. H. 587. 171
Nofire v. United States, 164 U.
  S. 657 234
Norton v. Volantine, 14 Vt. 239 245
Nuttall v. Bracewell, L. R. 2
  Ex. 1 248
O'Connor v. Gifford, 117 N. Y.
  275 8
O'Connor v. Witherby, 111 Cal.
  523 125
Olcott v. Tioga R. Co., 27 N. Y.
  546 140
Ormerod v. Todmorton Mill Co.,
  L. R. 11 Q. B. 155 Cf...... 248
Paine & Morris v. Smead, 1 D.
  Chip. 56 30
Patterson v. Winn, 11 Wheat.
  388 32
Peach v. Mills, 13 Vt. 501..... 401
Pennoyer v. Neff, 95 U. S. 714. 283
People v. Assessors of Brook-
  lyn, 111 N. Y. 505......... 171
People v. Gillson, 109 N. Y. 389 205
People, Ex. Rel. Madden v.
  Dycker, 72 N. Y. 308...... 205
People v. Maynard, 15 Mich.
  463 378

People *v.* Town of Nevada, 6
  Cal. 143 375
Perkins *v.* Hollister, 59 Vt. 348.   13
Petty *v.* Fleishal et al., 31 Tex.
  169 294
Pierce *v.* Tennessee, etc. R. Co.,
  173 U. S. 1 102
Pitkins *v.* Burch, 48 Vt. 521... 367
Pitkin *v.* Parks, 54 Vt. 301.... 312
Poland, trustee *v.* The Lamoille
  Valley R. R. Co., 52 Vt. 144   43
Polini *v.* Gray, L. R. 12 Ch. D.
  411 37
Polk's Lessee *v.* Wendell, 9
  Cranch. 99 32
Porter *v.* Smith, 20 Vt. 344.... 401
Poull *v.* Mockley, 33 Wis. 482. 250
Price *v.* Hickok, 39 Vt. 292.... 282
Purple *v.* Whithed, 49 Vt. 187.   91
Quimby & Rogan *v.* B. & M. R.
  R. Co., 71 Vt. 301........ 87
R. *v.* Sutton, 4 Maule & Sel.
  532 37
Randall *v.* Bacon, 49 Vt. 20.... 319
Randolph *v.* Scruggs, 190 U. S.
  533 60
Re Est. of Swift, 18 L. R. A.
  709 95
Re Hodges Est., 66 Vt. 70..... 12
Redfield *v.* Gleason, 61 Vt. 220. 186
Remeler *v.* Hall, 31 Vt. 582.... 101
Reson *v.* Knapp, 4 N. B. R.
  349 408
Rice *v.* Minn. & N. W. R. Co.,
  66 U. S. 358 32
Rich *v.* Sowles, Admr., 64 Vt.
  408 72
Richardson *v.* Cook, 37 Vt. 605. 228
Richardson *v.* R. Co., 98 Mass.
  85 272
Richardson *v.* School Dist., 38
  Vt. 602 263
Richmond *v.* Irons, 121 U. S. 56 124
Ripton *v.* McQuivery, 61 Vt. 76. 220
Robinson *v.* Swift, 3 Vt. 377.. 287
Rood *v.* Johnson, 26 Vt. 64.... 64
Rothmiller *v.* Stein, 143 N. Y.
  581 393
Rowell v. Fuller, 59 Vt. 688.... 336
Royalton *v.* Royalton, etc. Turn-
  pike Co., 14 Vt. 311...... 101
Royce *v.* Maloney, 58 Vt. 437.. 393
Rugg *v.* Brainard, 57 Vt. 364.. 220
Russell *v.* Phelps, 73 Vt. 390.. 175

Sabariego *v.* Maverick, 124 U.
  S. 261 33
Sanborn *v.* Kittredge, 20 Vt. 632 426
Sanderson *v.* Osgood, 52 Vt. 309 336
Sands *v.* Taylor, 5 Johns. 395. 112
Sargeant *v.* Sunderland, 21 Vt.
  284 234
Scott *v.* Armstrong, 146 U. S.
  507 124
Sharpleigh *v.* San Angelo, 167
  U. S. 646 378
Shedd *v.* Leslie, 22 Vt. 498.... 64
Sherman *v.* Champlain Transp.
  Co., 31 Vt. 162............ 408
Shumway *v.* Simons, 1 Vt. 53.. 245
Sleeper *v.* Croker, 48 Vt. 9.... 216
Smith *v.* Barre R. Co., 64 Vt. 21 87
Smith *v.* Smith, 1 R. I. 398.. 294
Somerset *v.* Glastenbury, 61 Vt.
  449 374
Somerville *v.* Waltham, 170
  Mass. 160 171
Southern Express Co. *v.* Walker,
  92 Va. 59 196
Spaulding *v.* Wakefield's Est.,
  53 Vt. 660 12
Spring *v.* Aver. 23 Vt. 516.... 260
St. Anthony's Falls Water Power
  Co. *v.* The City of Minne-
  apolis, 41 Minn. 270...... 249
Stanley *v.* Turner, 68 Vt. 315.. 319
Stanton *v.* Wilkeson, 8 Ben. 357 126
State *v.* Beard, 1 Ind. 460.... 37
State *v.* Carlton, 48 Vt. 636.. 433
State *v.* Conover, 42 Atl. 838.. 167
State *v.* Daley, 53 Vt. 442.... 433
State *v.* Dalton, 22 R. I. 77.... 204
State *v.* Fackler, 91 Wis. 418.. 196
State *v.* Freeman, 27 Vt. 523.. 119
State *v.* Gaffney, 34 N. J. L. 131 164
State *v.* Hayden, 51 Vt. 296... 227
State *v.* Intoxicating Liquor, 55
  Vt. 82 429
State *v.* Johnson, 72 Vt. 118... 312
State *v.* Leatherman, 38 Ark. 81 379
State *v.* Lockwood, 58 Vt. 378. 228
State *v.* Noakes, 70 Vt. 256.... 226
State *v.* One Bottle of Brandy,
  43 Vt. 297 428
State ex rel. Page *v.* Smith, 48
  Vt. 266 81
State *v.* Peterson. 41 Vt. 504.. 429
State *v.* Rodman, 58 Minn. 393. 196
State *v.* Welch, 65 Vt. 55..... 228

Stearns v. Stearns, 66 Vt. 187. 191
Stiles v. Guy, 16 Sim. 230..... 8
Stockport Waterworks Co. v.
  Potter, 3 H. & C. 300...... 245
Storrs v. Barker, 6 John. Ch.
  166 220
Stribblehill v. Brett, 2 Vern.
  Ch. 445 130
Sturges v. Bridgman, 11 Ch. D.
  855 245
Swann v. West, 41 Miss. 104.. 112
Sweat v. Hall, 8 Vt. 187...... 178
Sweetser v. French, 13 Met. 262 294
Taylor v. Gilman, 25 Vt. 411.. 186
Thomas v. Warner, 15 Vt. 110. 425
Thompson v. Schaetzel, 2 S. D.
  395 125
Trask v. Wheeler, 7 Allen, 109. 369
Tully v. Tully, 159 Mass. 91... 266
United States v. Ross, 92 U. S.
  281 86
Vaughn v. Barrett, 5 Vt. 333.. 91
Virginia v. Tenn., 148 U. S. 503 372
Vliet v. Sherwood, 35 Wis. 229. 245
Wade v. Pulsifer, 54 Vt. 45.... 391
Waite v. Mining Co., 37 Vt. 608 81
Wakeman v. Wheeler & Wilson
  Mfg. Co., 101 N. Y. 205.... 102
Walcott v. Mead, 12 Met. 516.. 230
Walker's Admr. v. Walker, 66
  Vt. 285 357
Walton v. Hall, 66 Vt. 455.... 91
Waterman v. Buck, 58 Vt. 519. 102
Webb v. Bird, 13 C. B. N. S.
  814 245
Webb v. Webb, 16 Vt. 636.... 258
Weller v. Burlington, 60 Vt. 28. 166

Wells v. Tucker, 57 Vt. 223.... 220
Welsh v. Village of Rutland,
  56 Vt. 228 166
West Hartford v. Com'rs of
  Hartford, 44 Conn. 360.... 163
Western R. Co. v. Miller, 19
  Mich. 306 272
Whipple v. Fairhaven, 63 Vt.
  226 102
White & Co. v. Allen, 30 Vt. 484 231
White v. Equitable Nuptial Ben-
  efit Union, 76 Ala. 251.... 130
Whiting v. Adams, 66 Vt. 679. 425
Whitlock v. Baker, 13 Ves. 514. 40
Whitney v. Bank, 50 Vt. 389.. 308
Wilbur v. Prior, 67 Vt. 508... 186
Wilkins v. Rutland, 61 Vt. 336. 166
Willard v. Wing, 70 Vt. 123.. 449
Willard v. Pike, 59 Vt. 202.... 173
Willey v. Bank, 47 Vt. 546.... 308
Willey v. Boston & Maine R.
  Co., 72 Vt. 120 447
Williams v. Vance, 30 Am. Rep.
  26 286
Williams v. Williams, 90 Ky.
  28 238
Wilmarth v. Pratt, 56 Vt. 474.. 182
Windham v. Chester, 45 Vt. 459 232
Witherell v. Goss & Delano, 26
  Vt. 748 232
Witters v. Sowles, 61 Vt. 366.. 124
Woodward v. Barnes, 46 Vt.
  332 175
Wright v. Burroughs, 61 Vt.
  390 179
Wright v. Marvin, 59 Vt. 437.. 231

CASES ARGUED AND DETERMINED

IN THE

SUPREME COURT OF VERMONT.

D. P. WALWORTH'S ESTATE *v.* B. W. BARTHOLOMEW'S ESTATE.

January Term, 1903.

Present: TYLER, MUNSON, START, WATSON, STAFFORD, and HASELTON, JJ.

Opinion filed October 13, 1903.

Administrator—Accounting—Due Diligence—Burden of Proof—Interest—Commingling Funds—Services.

An administrator who gives his personal note in payment of a claim against the estate is entitled to a credit in his account for the amount thereof.

Since the commissioner was warranted in assuming that the administrator had given his personal obligation for a distributive share, credit to the administrator for the amount thereof was properly allowed.

When heirs are paid different sums for a partial distribution, it is for the Probate Court on final decree to equalize the difference.

The burden is on the administrator to show that an uncollected note belonging to the estate was uncollectible.

That an administrator took by foreclosure the property securing such note, which was then worth the amount of the note, and disposed of it for the benefit of the estate, is sufficient to rebut the presumption of negligence in allowing the note to outlaw.

When an administrator has wrongfully transferred to himself stock
belonging to the estate, the dividends afterwards received thereon
are chargeable to him, or his estate, as of the time they were received.

It was proper for the commissioner to allow the plaintiff estate to
withdraw certain items of its specification.

An administrator who has used the funds of the estate for his own
profit will be allowed nothing for the care of the funds, and will
be charged with annual interest; and this rule applies when the
account is presented by his administrator.

If the settlement of the estate involves other duties, faithfully and legally performed, such administrator is entitled to compensation
therefor.

When an estate consists of income producing property, and the settlement properly covers a number of years, the Probate Court may,
on final settlement, credit the administrator's services at the end
of each year, though no previous accounts have been rendered.

When the settlement of a deceased administrator's account is delayed
by causes not chargeable to him or his representative, it will be
made as of the date of said administrator's death, and simple interest only will be allowed on the balance then in his hands.

So far as the expense of settlement of a deceased administrator's account is made necessary by his improper conduct, it falls upon his
estate; otherwise, it may be charged in his account.

APPEAL FROM PROBATE COURT. Heard on a commissioner's report and exceptions thereto, at the December Term,
1902, Orange County, *Tyler*, J., presiding. *Pro forma* judgment for the defendant estate for the sum named in the report. The plaintiff estate excepted.

Young & Young for the plaintiff estate.

The commissioner having found that the administrator's
services were worth $150.00 per year, this allowance should be
credited at the end of each year. Otherwise, the adjustment
of interest on the annual balances would be unjust to the administrator.

A balance should be stated at the end of each year and interest computed thereon to the time the report is made, without a rest at the time of Walworth's death. *Landon* v. *Castleton,* 30 Vt. 285; *Spencer* v. *Woodbridge,* 38 Vt. 492; *Davis* v. *Smith,* 48 Vt. 52; *Flannery* v. *Flannery,* 58 Vt. 576; *Yearteau* v. *Bacon's Est.,* 65 Vt. 516.

The Jennie E. Walworth note was given by the administrators to discharge so much of the indebtedness of the Bartholomew estate. The Walworth estate is entitled to credit for the amount of it.

The objections to the allowance for services performed by Walworth were unfounded. The commissioner does not find that the funds of the estate were commingled with those of the administrator, and this fact cannot be presumed. *Darling* v. *Ricker,* 68 Vt. 471; *Wolcott* v. *Hamilton,* 61 Vt. 79.

Simple interest only should be allowed on the funds in Walworth's hands. Such was the agreement between the administrators, and such would be the rule of law under the circumstances. *In re Hall's Est.,* 70 Vt. 458.

The $5,000 paid to the administratrix of George H. Walworth was through an allowance of the commissioners on George's estate. That allowance must have been based upon an agreement to pay that sum.

The commissioner was correct in not adding interest upon the bank dividends received by Walworth. *Landon* v. *Castleton,* 30 Vt. 285; *Newell* v. *Keith's Est.,* 11 Vt. 214; *Evarts* v. *Nason's Est.,* 11 Vt. 122.

The commissioner was also right in not allowing anything on account of the Prescott, Craigie, and Palmer notes. Negligence must be proved. It is never presumed. *McCluskey* v. *Gleason,* 56 Vt. 264.

The Ramsdell notes were paid in full by the decree on the land securing them, though the whole series was not included in the foreclosure.

Cook & Williams and *F. J. Martin* for the defendant estate.

The Jennie E. Walworth note cannot be allowed, because it was never paid. The fact that it was not paid and that Walworth did not charge it in his account indicates that it was a personal obligation, and that it had been discharged.

The Ramsdell note should be charged to Walworth. They were not collected and had outlawed when turned over to the present administrator. The same is true of the Craigie and Palmer, and the Prescott notes. In the absence of a finding that they were not collectible they should be charged, with interest. *McCluskey* v. *Gleason*, 56 Vt. 264; *Holmes* v. *Bridgeman*, 37 Vt. 28; *In re Hall's Est.*, 70 Vt. 458.

The dividends on the bank stock should be charged as of the dates they were received.

Nothing should be allowed for Walworth's services in view of the manner in which the business was conducted, and annual interest should be charged on balances found in his hands.

MUNSON, J. B. W. Bartholomew, of Washington, in the County of Orange, died intestate in February, 1873. His only heirs were Armina P. Braley, and George H. and Jennie E. Walworth, children of deceased sisters. N. W. Braley, of Barre, the husband of one of the heirs, and D. P. Walworth, of Coventry, the father of the other two, were appointed administrators. George H. Walworth died in 1876, leaving a widow and children. Jennie E. Walworth died in 1886, without having married.   N. W. Braley, one of the administrators, died in 1880, and B. W. Braley, his son, and Joel Foster, were appointed his administrators. D. P. Walworth, the other administrator, died in 1887, and administration upon his estate was granted to E. A. Stewart and George D. Walworth. After N. W. Braley's death, D. P. Walworth was sole administrator of the Bartholomew estate, and B. W. Braley acted as his agent in looking after matters in Washington and vicinity.   Neither N. W. Braley and D. P. Walworth jointly, nor D. P. Walworth as surviving administrator, presented any account to the Probate Court. Upon D. P. Walworth's death, B. W. Braley was appointed administrator *de bonis non* of B. W. Bartholomew's estate, and in 1888 he cited the administrators of D. P. Walworth's estate before the Probate Court to settle the account of their intestate as administrator of the Bartholomew estate.   That proceeding is the one now before us.

The inventory showed an estate of some over $3,000, but $150,000 or more came into the hands of the administrators. A few small debts were allowed, which were soon paid, and after this the families of the original administrators were the only persons interested in the estate.   In 1874 the administrators distributed $120,000 of the estate among the heirs.   A further sum of $15,000 was distributed in 1884.

At the time of his death, B. W. Bartholomew was administrator with will annexed on the estate of Charles White, and had most, if not all, the estate in his hands in the shape of securities. The three persons above named as heirs of Bartholomew were among the legatees named in this will, and the interests of most, if not all, the other legatees had been purchased by N. W. Braley.   H. A. White was appointed administrator *de bonis non* of Charles White's estate, and under an arrangement between him and the administrators of Bartholomew, the latter gave their joint notes in payment of the amounts coming from the White estate to said heirs and to Braley. Item 217 of the Walworth specification is a credit claimed for $1,565.21, the amount of the note given to Jennie E. Walworth. The Bartholomew estate objects to its allowance.

There can be no doubt as to the nature of the transaction. The administrator of the White estate, instead of requiring the Bartholomew estate to pay over the funds needed to meet these demands, permitted the administrators of Bartholomew to satisfy them by a direct payment; and the persons entitled to payment were willing to accept the notes of the administrators. In giving their notes, the administrators advanced so much for the benefit of the estate, and became entitled to corresponding credits. This view of the transaction leaves no ground for the objections urged; and, with the administrator's interest account adjusted as it will be, the credit may properly stand as of the date of the note, without inquiring whether the estate then had funds available for the payment. The item was properly allowed.

Item 361 of the Walworth specification is a credit of $15,000 for money distributed to the heirs. The Bartholomew estate claims that the $5,000 included therein as the share of George H. Walworth should be disallowed. The commissioner finds that the shares of Mrs. Braley and Jennie E. Walworth were paid at the time, but says there was no evidence that the George H. Walworth share was then paid. George H. Walworth had been dead about eight years at this time, and his widow was the administratrix of his estate. She presented a claim for this $5,000, and interest, against the estate of D. P. Walworth, and it was allowed and paid. Nothing further appears in regard to this. The claim could be allowed only upon the ground that it was the personal obligation of the deceased, and this commissioner might fairly assume that the administratrix had accepted the obligation of D. P. Walworth, in some form, in satisfaction of the claim of George H. Walworth's estate against the Bartholomew estate for his share in that distribution; and upon this basis the claim would stand like the preceding item. The allowance is sustained.

Item 212½ is a charge under date of March, 1874, for $240 paid to George H. and Jennie E. Walworth. This charge is made to equalize the distribution of 1874. That distribution was by a division of the estate's holding in the stock of the Barre National Bank, then worth $120 a share. George H. and Jennie E. each had 333 shares, and Mrs. Braley 334. No payments corresponding to this item were made. But it appears that the commissioners on D. P. Walworth's estate allowed to George H. Walworth's estate $73.33 as of December 13, 1887, for a one-third share of stock and dividends from July, 1874. The principal of this sum might be allowed as of March, 1874, on the ground indicated in disposing of the preceding item. But if D. P. Walworth adjusted the George H. Walworth share by assuming the amount indicated by the claim afterwards allowed against his estate, that affords no ground for crediting his account with a larger sum. Jennie E. Walworth lived twelve years after the distribution, and there is nothing to indicate that any adjustment of this difference as regards her share was ever attempted. The interest charge of the administrator cannot be reduced by crediting him, as of the date of the distribution, with payments which he did not make or assume. It is for the Probate Court to equalize this difference among the heirs in making its final decree of the balance found in the administrator's hands.

After B. W. Braley's appointment as administrator *de bonis non,* the administrators of D. P. Walworth turned over to him the papers of the Bartholomew estate; but for some reason not appearing certain notes were not included, which became barred by the statute without any attempt having been made to collect them. Items 15½, 16, and 17 of the Bartholomew specification are charges for the amount of these notes. It is evident that the statute ran upon the notes covered by the first two charges before Mr. Walworth's death. As to these the commissioner reports that he is unable to find that they were collectible. This will not justify their disallowance. The burden was upon the administrator to show that they were not collectible. To hold otherwise would be inconsistent with our system of probate accounting, and with our decisions upon questions of like nature. It was held in *McCloskey* v. *Gleason,* 56 Vt. 264. 48 Am. Rep. 770. that, when money of the estate is retained by an agent employed to collect it, the burden is upon the administrator to show that he has exercised due diligence; and in *Blodgett's Est.* v. *Converse's Est.,* 60 Vt. 410, 15 Atl. 109, that a financial agent who holds interest-bearing securities is presumed to receive interest thereon, and that the burden is upon him to show that he has not. It is very generally held that the burden is upon the administrator to account for a failure to collect. 11 Am. & Eng. Enc. Law, (2d ed.) 1002, 1004, 1201, citing *Brazeale* v. *Brazeale,* 9 Ala. 491; *Moffatt* v. *Loughridge,* 51 Miss. 211; *Brooker* v. *Armstrong,* 93 Mo. 49; *O'Connor* v. *Gifford,* 117 N. Y. 275; *Stiles* v. *Guy,* 16 Sim. 230; *Matter of Hosford,* 27 N. Y. App. Div. 427, 50 N. Y. Supp. 550.

The securities covered by Item 17 were three witnessed notes with a good indorser, part of a series of twelve mortgage notes. The three notes had some ten years to run as regards the statute at the time of D. P. Walworth's death, but were barred when delivered to the administrator *de bonis non*. The entire series belonged to the estates of B. W. Bartholomew and N. W. Braley, the first owning seventy-one per cent., and the other twenty-nine. In 1882, D. P. Walworth, administrator of the Bartholomew estate, and B. W. Braley, administrator of the Braley estate, joined in foreclosing the mortgage, each signing the petition personally. These three notes were not embraced in the foreclosure. The commissioner finds that at the time of the decree the property was worth the amount of all the notes, and that it was taken possession of by the two estates, and afterwards disposed of for the benefit of both. The present finding as to the value of the property is certainly enough to indicate that Walworth had reasonable ground for treating the three notes as satisfied by the decree, although not included in the foreclosure, and foregoing suit against the endorser. So the facts reported are sufficient to rebut the presumption of negligence that would otherwise arise from the possession of notes barred by the statute.

There came into the hands of the administrators as a part of Bartholomew's estate twenty shares of the stock of the Lamoille County Bank, and a few months after his appointment Mr. Walworth, with the knowledge of his co-administrator, had the stock transferred to himself individually, and it remained so until his death. His administrators found nothing to indicate that it was not his property, and received and held the dividends for about ten years before transferring it to Bartholomew's estate. The commissioner has charged Walworth's estate with these dividends in bulk as of December,

1892, and Bartholomew's estate claims that they should be entered each year so as to carry interest. We think the account should be so made. But for the administrator's improper transfer, the ownership would have been known, and the stock would have gone into the hands of the administrator *de bonis non* upon his appointment, and the estate would have had the benefit of the dividends from the time of their payment.

Items 350 to 356 of the Walworth specification represent matters growing out of N. W. Braley's share in the settlement of the Bartholomew estate, and the adjustment thereof made between the Bartholomew and Braley estates. These were withdrawn at the hearing with the consent of the commissioner, and no evidence was offered to support them. The Bartholomew estate objected to this, and now asks the Court to disallow the items. We see no reason to question the propriety of the course taken by the commissioner.

The remaining questions relate to allowances for services and interest. The commissioner has allowed Walworth's estate $2,175 for his services, being $150 per year for the whole period, crediting the same in bulk at the date of his death; and has allowed further sums for the services of his administrators in preparing and settling his account, crediting the same annually; and has charged his estate with simple interest on annual balances both before and after his death. It is claimed in behalf of the Bartholomew estate that the handling of its funds was such that nothing should be allowed Walworth or his administrators for their services, and that his estate should be charged the highest rate of interest known to the law. The Walworth estate claims that it should have the benefit of annual credits for the services of its intestate, that simple interest only should be charged, and that no rest should be made at the date of his death in computing interest on the annual balances.

The commissioner says that he fails to find such a commingling of the funds of the estate with the administrator's funds, as, in his opinion, would justify a charge of interest at the highest rate. This involves a conclusion of law, and does not relieve the Court from an examination of the facts reported. The finding that the administrator acted in good faith does not dispose of the matter. Back of this lies the question whether he acted in conformity with the established rules by which the duties and liabilities of administrators are determined. *McCloskey* v. *Gleason,* 56 Vt. 264, 272.

August 15, 1873, about six months after their appointment, D. P. Walworth and N. W. Braley, the two administrators, agreed in writing that whatever funds belonging to the estate had come into the hands of either, except a certain bank deposit, should be accounted for at six per cent. interest. $6,812.33 came into Walworth's hands on that day, but his books do not show what interest he received upon this sum, nor upon the balance thereof, if any, remaining in his hands at the close of the year. He kept accounts in the form of debt and credit and memoranda, from which a statement could be made of the amount of the estate's funds in his hands. These accounts did not show how the funds were invested, but showed receipts and payments. It appears from the account as presented that there was generally a balance of several thousand dollars in his hands belonging to the estate. It did not appear that these moneys were kept in any other name than his own, individually, except that for three years he kept a small bank account as administrator. During the time he held the funds of the estate, he was receiving interest at a rate higher than six per cent. It did not appear from the books, and was not shown otherwise, whether the funds loaned at more than six per cent. belonged to the estate or to himself personally. It did not appear how the balance in his hands at the date of his death has been invested since that time, or whether it has been invested.

We have several cases bearing upon the questions presented by the above statement. In *Farewell* v. *Steen,* 46 Vt. 678, the guardian collected the securities belonging to his ward, mingled the avails with his own money, and gave no account of the exact amount of interest included; and made from the fund so formed investments in which the moneys of the ward could not be traced directly and wholly, and received therefrom more than six per cent. interest; and the guardian was charged with annual interest on the whole trust fund. Here the referee had allowed the guardian for taking care of the fund, and no question was raised in regard to that; but the Court took occasion to say that a guardian should not be allowed compensation for taking care of his ward's money while he was the borrower of it. In *McCloskey* v. *Gleason,* 56 Vt. 264, 272, the administrator had mingled the trust estate with his own, made no separate investment, and kept no separate account of the fund nor of the interest received; and the Court held that he thereby made himself the debtor of the estate, and was chargeable with the highest legal rate of interest on the money so intermingled, and could be allowed nothing for his services in caring for it. Other cases hold the same. *Spaulding* v. *Wakefield's Est.,* 53 Vt. 660, 38 Am. Rep. 709; *Re Hodges' Est.,* 66 Vt. 70, 44 Am. St. Rep. 820. In *Barney* v. *Parsons,* 54 Vt. 623, 41 Am. Rep. 858, the guardian included a sum due to his ward in a note payable to himself, and the promisor became bankrupt, and the money was lost. The Court construed the report as containing an affirmative finding of honesty and diligence, and in view of this, and of the fact that an exact record of the ward's interest in the note was kept, held the guardian discharged. This case, as far as it is in conflict with the rule above indicated, is repudiated in *Re Hodges' Est.* In *Perkins* v. *Hollister,* 59 Vt. 348, 7 Atl. 605, the executor had in good faith mingled and loaned the funds of the estate with his own, but disclosed all the profits; and, having suffered losses without fault, claimed no deduction therefor, and claimed nothing for his services; and was found by the commissioner to have received less than simple interest on the fund; and upon this case the Court charged him with simple interest only.

It is evident that these funds went into the body of Mr. Walworth's estate, and that the balance has remained there; that they have not been and cannot be distinguished or separated from his individual property; and that while the funds were so held he was making loans and receiving more than six per cent. interest. In these circumstances it must be presumed that some of the administrator's extra gains were due to the possession of this fund. There can be no doubt as to what the conclusion would be upon these accounts if the administrator were rendering them in person, and we know of no reason why the result should be different when the settlement is made by his personal representatives. There is nothing better settled, nor more universally held, than that a trustee who has used the fund for his own profit cannot have pay for caring for it; and it is equally well settled in this State that he shall also be charged with annual interest.

But the investment of this cash balance was but a part of the duty which devolved upon the administrator in the management of this estate. There was another branch of administrative duty in which the service of the administrator was not only honest, but in strict accord with legal requirements.   It appears that the investments remaining after the distribution of 1874 consisted largely of farm mortgages and other loans on note.   Much of the property held as security came into the hands of the administrators by foreclosure or otherwise.   Farms were held and rented, awaiting an opportunity to sell; and were finally sold with small payments down, and in some instances were taken back and sold over again in the same way.   Complications arose out of Bartholomew's connection with unsettled trusts, and the estate was involved in a good deal of litigation, some of which was of an important character.   Considerable time and attention was given to the adjustment of controversies and to the trial of cases.   It is evident that a substantial part of the compensation allowed the administrator was earned in the line of service above indicated, and the forfeiture which the law enforces for the improper investment of funds should not be extended to this part.   This is but another application of the principle adopted in *Foster* v. *Stone,* 67 Vt. 336, 31 Atl. 841.

When the estate consists of income-producing property, and the circumstances are such that its settlement properly covers a number of years, it is clearly within the discretion of the Probate Court, even in making a final settlement where no previous accounts have been rendered, to credit the services of the administrator for each year at the end of the year.   We think that in the circumstances of this case that method may properly be adopted.

The course taken by the commissioner in ascertaining the amount of the estate at the date of Walworth's death, and making that the basis of a new computation, accords with the nature of the accounting and the practice as we understand it. The personal representative of a deceased administrator does not take and administer his trust, but proceeds at once to settle his account, ascertain the balance in his hands, and pay it over to his successor. This points to an accounting as of the date of his death. The fact that the settlement of 'this account has occupied years does not take the case out of the rule.

Ordinarily, the account of a deceased administrator will be settled in such time that the question whether the interest allowed after his death shall be simple or annual will not be important. But here sixteen years have elapsed since the death of the administrator, during fifteen of which the account has been in process of settlement. It is obvious that this long delay is at most but remotely chargeable to the administrator's method of handling the estate. For fifteen years the matter has been in the hands of the Courts, and subject to such orders as the administrator of Bartholomew might apply for and show himself entitled to. The facts reported regarding the delay are not such as to charge the Walworth estate with the consequences of it. We think that, when annual interest is allowed, and the charges for Walworth's services in caring for the fund are disallowed, in arriving at the balance in Walworth's hands at the time of his death, the matter will be fairly disposed of by the allowance of simple interest on such balance.

The only question remaining relates to the charges of Walworth's administrators for their services and expenses in settling his account. So far as those services and expenses were made necessary by any improper conduct of the administrator, the loss must fall upon his own estate instead of that of Bartholomew. Otherwise they are a proper subject of charge. The commissioner will make any revision of his allowance that may be required by this holding.

Judgment reversed and cause remanded that the report may be recommitted to the commissioner with instructions to determine the yearly sums earned by the administrator in the management of the estate not including the care of the funds in his hands, and otherwise adjust the account in accordance with this opinion.

MARY A. CHENEY'S EXR., ET AL. *v.* E. C. STAFFORD, ET AL.
MARY A. CHENEY'S EXR., ET AL. *v.* CARRIE A. STAFFORD.

January Term, 1903.

Present: TYLER, MUNSON, START, WATSON, STAFFORD AND HASELTON, JJ.

ɩ   .   Opinion filed October 15, 1903.

Will—Construction—Power—Failure to Exercise—Effect— Invalid Conveyance.

When a will contains two provisions so inconsistent that both cannot be carried into effect, the last will prevail.

A will which makes mandatory provision for the payment of a mortgage out of other property, creates an interest in the final beneficiaries of the mortgaged premises, of which the donee of the power cannot deprive them by failing to execute it.

Equity will secure to such beneficiaries the same benefit that they would have received if such power had been executed.

A power involving no trust fails upon the death of the donee.

Authority given in a will to sell certain "building lots" does not include the right to sell a lot on which a building then stood.

APPEALS IN CHANCERY. The first named case was heard on pleadings and an agreed statement of facts, at the September Term, 1901, Rutland County, *Start,* Chancellor. The last named case was heard on pleadings, a special master's report and exceptions thereto, at the September Term, 1902, Rutland

County, *Stafford,* Chancellor. *Pro forma* decree for the defendants and appeal by the orators in each case.

Edward Dana, G. L. Rice, and *Lawrence & Lawrence* for the orators.

So far as the provisions in the will affect the land standing in the name of Gershom Cheney, the attainment of the object for which the power was created has become impossible, and the power fails. *Sharpsteen* v. *Tillon,* 3 Cow. 651; *Hetzel* v. *Barber,* 69 N. Y. 1; *Jackson* v. *Ellsworth,* 6 Johns. 73.

This power is purely personal, and dies with him for whose benefit it was created and in whom it was reposed.

The power to sell lots to pay the mortgage on the land of the testatrix was likewise purely personal. The will, taken as a whole, indicates that it was the intention to leave the matter to his discretion.

The right to sell "building lots" cannot be construed to include the right to sell the lot on which the tenement house stood.

Joel C. Baker for the defendants.

The conditions of the will are positive and imperative the mortgages are to be paid by sale of building lots. There is no discretion given to the husband, and the whole scheme of the will is defeated, if that is not done.

The power of sale is coupled with a trust, which cannot be defeated. 1 Perry on Trusts, s. 248; *Greenough* v. *Wells,* 10 Cush. 571; *Montpelier* v. *East Montpelier,* 29 Vt. 22; *Ferre* v. *American Board,* 53 Vt. 162; Notes to 53 Am. St. Rep. 69.

The power to sell building lots on Jackson Avenue covered the whole tract of seventeen acres. The will makes no distinction between the lots, and the fact that No. 2 was improved makes no difference.

MUNSON, J. These suits both relate to the will of Mary A. Cheney, and were heard together. The first bill prays for a construction of the will and directions to the executor. The second seeks to avoid a deed given by the husband of the testatrix, upon whom a certain power was conferred by the will. The clauses particularly in question are as follows:

"I give, devise and bequeath to my husband, Gershom Cheney, should he survive me, the use of all my estate, real and personal, of every description, during his natural life, but in case the use of such estate, together with the use of such property as he may own in his own right, shall be insufficient to support him comfortably and according to the requirements of his age, I hereby authorize and empower him to sell and convey such and so many of the building lots on Jackson Avenue in Rutland Village, as he shall from time to time judge and determine to be necessary to provide means for such support, and to use and appropriate so much of the proceeds for such support as he shall require.

"In case there shall exist any mortgage indebtedness at the time of my decease upon any real estate owned either by me or by my said husband, I hereby authorize and direct him to sell such and so many of said building lots as shall be necessary to raise means to pay off such mortgage indebtedness, and I direct my said husband to therewith pay off and discharge such mortgage indebtedness."

The will was executed in September, 1890. The testatrix then owned nineteen vacant lots that were left out of fifty which had been plotted and put on the market in 1873, and another of the fifty lots upon which a double tenement had been built before 1885. This ownership continued until her death.   Both the vacant lots and the tenement property were located on Jackson Avenue.

The testatrix died in September, 1891.   At the time of her death, she owned a house and lot on South Main street, where the family had been living, and her husband also owned a house and lot.   There was a mortgage on each place.   The will provided for a sale of the home place by the executor after the death of the husband, and for the ultimate payment of nearly the entire avails of the sale to the children of Aletta A. Stafford, a daughter of the husband by a former wife.   The residuary legatees are three sisters of the testatrix.

The husband sold three of the vacant lots for his support, but did not exercise the authority conferred upon him as regards either mortgage, and a decree of foreclosure was obtained upon each at the March Term, 1896, with the equity limited to March 1, 1897.   The husband died January 29, 1897, and the decree against his place became absolute.   The executor sold the testatrix' place before the equity expired, and paid the decree out of the avails.

The provision made for the payment of the mortgage indebtedness by Gershom Cheney is mandatory in its terms.   It is suggested, however, that it should be construed to be optional, in view of the authority given him in a previous clause, to sell "such and so many" of the building lots as he might consider necessary to provide means for his support.   But this treatment of the two provisions, whatever may be said as to the degree of their inconsistency, would be at variance with established rules of construction.   In the case of two provisions which are so inconsistent that both cannot be carried into effect, it is held that the last must prevail; and there is certainly no reason here why the positive direction of the last should be

modified to give the largest possible scope to the discretionary
power conferred by the first.   The will was evidently framed
in the belief that the building lots were sufficient to meet both
requirements; and these provisions are to be construed as
directing the sale of enough of them to pay the mortgages,
and authorizing the sale of as many of those remaining as
might be needed to supplement the other means of support.

But in considering the effect of the direction concerning
the mortgages, a distinction must be made between the two
properties.   The purpose of the provision, as regards the testatrix' house and lot, was not limited to the benefit of Gershom, and did not fail upon his death.   The testatrix' scheme
embraced not only the use of the property by Gershom, but
the ultimate payment to his grandchildren of the money derived from a sale of it.   The appropriation for the payment of
this mortgage was one of several provisions by which the testatrix undertook to effect a division of her estate between her
family and that of her husband.   It is evident that in directing a sale of the homestead after her husband's death and the
subsequent disposition of its avails, she had in mind the value
of the premises, and not the uncertain margin that might remain after the mortgage had run for an indefinite period.   This
provision for removing the incumbrance created an interest in
the final beneficiaries, of which the donee of the power could
not deprive them by failing to execute it.   Equity will secure
to them the same benefit that they would have received if the
property had come to the hands of the executor unincumbered.

But this effect cannot be given to the provision in its
application to the other mortgage.   The testatrix could not
by the most positive direction compel her husband to pay off
the mortgage on his own land. The authority given amounted
only to a gift which he could accept or reject at his pleasure.

It conferred no interest upon any other person, for, after relieving the property from incumbrance, he could have disposed of it as he saw fit. This was a mere power—a mandate involving no trust,—and it failed upon the death of the donee. We know of no ground upon which the heirs of the donee can now require Mrs. Cheney's estate to do for the benefit of the donee's descendible property what the donee himself thought best to leave undone.

The pro forma decree dismissing the bill praying for a construction of the will is reversed, and the cause is remanded with instructions that a decree be entered construing the will in accordance with this opinion.

In June, 1893, Mr. Cheney concluded it was necessary for his comfortable support that he have the attendance of his granddaughter, Carrie A. Stafford; and she became an inmate of his family, and gave him through the remainder of his life such care and attention as she could outside of school hours, and was to receive fair compensation therefor. On the 22nd day of July, 1895, he gave her a deed of the tenement property before described, as compensation for the services she had rendered him and such as she might thereafter render, reciting therein his right to make the conveyance under the power given him to sell building lots for his support. This is the deed which the executor asks to have set aside.

The term "building lot" is ordinarily used to designate a parcel of land which is held or offered as a place suitable to be built upon. When the property is put to the intended use, it ceases to be a building lot and becomes a house and lot. It would require a forced construction to bring within this provision a lot upon which a tenement house had stood for years. There is no purpose disclosed in the will that calls for this forced construction. In executing a deed of the tenement property Mr. Cheney was outside the authority given him, and the orators are entitled to have his conveyance decreed to be invalid.

The pro forma decree dismissing the bill which seeks an avoidance of the deed is reversed, and the cause is remanded with instructions that a decree be entered in accordance with the prayer of the bill.

EQUITABLE MANUFACTURING CO. v. H. C. ALLEN.

January Term, 1903.

Present: MUNSON, START, WATSON, STAFFORD, and HASELTON, JJ.

Opinion filed October 15, 1903.

Sale—Duplicate Memoranda—Statute of Frauds—Alteration by Agent—Non-acceptance.

When a buyer, at the time of the sale and with the knowledge of the selling agent, adds a provision to the duplicate memorandum of sale furnished him by such agent, such provision becomes a part of the completed agreement.

That such agent fails to change his copy of the memorandum to correspond with that of the buyer, does not render it insufficient to satisfy the Statute of Frauds.

The alteration of a written instrument by an agent who holds it for transmission to the principal does not render it invalid.

That the terms of payment were not specified in the invoice sent with the goods did not afford sufficient grounds for their non-acceptance.

GENERAL ASSUMPSIT. Plea, the general issue. Heard on the report of a referee at the December Term, 1902, Orange County, *Tyler,* J., presiding. Judgment for the defendant. The plaintiff excepted.

M. M. Wilson for the plaintiff.

The alteration by the plaintiff's agent had no effect on the contract. *Bigelow* v. *Stilphens,* 35 Vt. 521.

Even if the defendant had a right to rescind, a shipment to Providence cannot avail him. *Norton* v. *Gleason,* 61 Vt. 480; *Ricker* v. *Adams,* 59 Vt. 154.

J. D. Denison for the defendant.

The writing required by the Statute of Frauds must state the terms of the contract. This contract fails in this particular. Brown on Frauds, 468; *Dana & Henry* v. *Hancock,* 30 Vt. 616.

On receipt of the goods not billed as agreed, the defendant had a right to refuse to receive them. He returned them to the advertised factory of this manufacturing company.

MUNSON, J. At a personal interview between the plaintiff's salesman and the defendant, negotiations were had for the sale by plaintiff to defendant of an assortment of jewelry for $100. The contract was prepared in duplicate upon order blanks furnished by the salesman, and the two papers were signed by both the salesman and the defendant, and one was retained by each. · When defendant signed the copy kept by him, he wrote upon it, "Date May 1, 1901. Ship April 1, 1901." This was done in the presence of the salesman and with his knowledge. The words, "Date May 1, 1901," were never written upon the plaintiff's duplicate, but the words, "Ship April 1, 1901," were written on it at the time it was signed. The salesman afterwards changed this, without the knowledge of either plaintiff or defendant, making it read, "Ship Feb. 15, 1901." The plaintiff, supposing the duplicate as received by it was the contract as executed, shipped the goods at the earlier date fixed by the alteration. The defendant had no knowledge of the alteration until after the goods were received and reshipped, and his action was not taken because of the premature shipment.

The defendant claims that the minds of the parties never met, and that if they did, no contract in writing was completed. We cannot take this view of the case. The leaving of the defendant's duplicate with him, after he had made the additional entry with the salesman's knowledge, was an assent to the change made, and completed the agreement. It was then the duty of the salesman to alter his duplicate to correspond, but his failure to do so did not do away with the agreement. So there was a completed contract in the minds of the parties, identical in terms with the defendant's duplicate; and it was not necessary that both duplicates should be perfected to satisfy the Statute of Frauds. A written statement of the bargain agreed upon, signed by the party to be charged thereby, was taken by the vendee.

The alteration of the plaintiff's duplicate was made by the salesman after the contract was completed, and before the duplicate was forwarded. It is now well settled that the alteration of a written instrument by a stranger will not render it invalid. One who procures a writing as an agent, and holds it temporarily for transmission to his principal, is held to be a stranger, within the meaning of the rule. *Bigelow* v. *Stilphen,* 35 Vt. 521. The salesman was the plaintiff's agent to negotiate a contract of sale and procure and transmit the evidence of it, and there his authority ceased. The alteration was a wrongful act, for which his employer was in no way responsible. Nor has anything been done to ratify the act. The suit was not brought until after the expiration of the time of credit as determined by the defendant's entry, and nothing is claimed at variance with the duplicate held by the defendant.

In shipping the goods, the plaintiff placed upon the box an invoice, at the top of which was a statement that all claims must be made upon receipt thereof, and on which was the word "Terms," followed by a blank not filled. The referee finds that the only reason why the defendant refused to accept the goods was because the terms of the sale were not upon the invoice. This was not a sufficient ground for non-acceptance. The defendant held a duly executed written contract as evidence of the terms of the sale.

Judgment reversed, and judgment for plaintiff.

GEORGE H. DAVIS ET AL. *v.* WILLIAM J. MOYLES.

October Term, 1902.

Present: TYLER, MUNSON, START, WATSON, STAFFORD, and HASELTON, JJ.

Opinion filed October 27, 1903.

Land Titles—New York Grant—Validity—Evidence—Recitals—Private Acts—Ancient Documents—Proof of Heirship—Declarations.

The preamble to the Constitution of 1777 refers only to lands held under original charter from New Hampshire, and does not invalidate the title to lands originally granted by the Governor of New York after that government was given jurisdiction by royal decree.

A grant from the State conveys only such title as the State then had.

A petition to the General Assembly, with the report of a legislative committee and the indorsements of legislative officers thereon, and private Acts passed and official doings thereunder, are not evidence of a fact therein recited.

Private Acts are evidence only against the persons procuring them and, in certain cases, the State.

What is said as to the effect of recitals in *Cross* v. *Martin*, 46 Vt. 14 is *obiter dictum*.

When the recitals in an ancient document are mere narrations of past transactions of which they form no part, they are inadmissible.

A tenant in common of real estate can maintain an action of trespass in his own name and recover the whole damage for the benefit of himself and his co-tenant.

In laying the foundation for the receipt of declarations in the matters of pedigree, the relationship of the declarant must be shown by evidence independent of the declarations themselves.

Such declarations are inadmissible when made after a controversy has arisen which is capable of being litigated and is of a nature likely to bias the mind of the declarant.

TRESPASS under V. S. 5020. Plea, the general issue. Trial by Court at the March Term, 1902, Windham County, *Rowell*, C. J., presiding. Judgment for the plaintiff. The defendant excepted.

A. E. Cudworth and *J. L. Martin* for the plaintiff.

The grant of February 13, 1770, shows title in James Rogers and his associates. The deed from his associates to him was signed, sealed and witnessed, and it must be presumed to be in accordance with the legal requirements then existing. *Middlebury College* v. *Cheney*, 1 Vt. 336; *Brown* v. *Edson*, 23 Vt. 435.

This instrument existed before any statute required an acknowledgment; it was long acquiesced in, and was recognized by the Legislature in the proceedings relative to Rogers' estate. It was therefore admissible, and its weight was for the triers of fact to determine. *Stevens* v. *Griffith*, 3 Vt. 448.

There is no pretence that this territory, Kent, was ever in any part covered by any grant under New Hampshire authority. If it were held that all New York title was abrogated or repudiated, it rested in the power of the new State to grant the land upon its own terms and conditions. The grant to Aiken, Fletcher and Tyler in 1780 was not to them in their own right, but they were made the hand of the State to hold the property and convey it to purchasers. In 1795 the *locus* remained in their hands, held by them for the State.

If the State did not have such control of it, it was the property of James Rogers, the elder, and descended to James Rogers, the younger. It is to be presumed that James Rogers, Jr., was the son of James Rogers named in the grant of 1770. *Cross* v. *Martin,* 46 Vt. 14. At least the younger Rogers was a tenant in common with the other heirs of his father.

This title had the recognition and warrant of the State, and all the facts stated in the preamble to the Act of 1797 are established by the recitals therein. *Lord* v. *Bigelow,* 8 Vt. 445; *Cross* v. *Martin, supra.*

All the facts stated in the petition of James Rogers in 1799 were found to be true by the committee, and this finding was confirmed by the General Assembly.

From the younger Rogers, the plaintiff's chain of title is complete.

The copy of the record of the Cobb will from the town clerk's office was properly admitted. R. S. Chap. 53, sec. 13; V. S. 3008. Unless such will and the proceedings in probate thereof were so recorded, it would not be admissible. *Royce* v. *Hurd,* 24 Vt. 620.

The plaintiff may recover though other co-tenants may exist. *Bigelow* v. *Rising,* 42 Vt. 678.

Clarke C. Fitts for the defendant.

The preamble to the Constitution of 1777 destroys the validity of the New York grant which forms the basis of the plaintiff's title. If the grant of Kent is recognized, the charter of Londonderry is void for it is subsequent to the Constitution of 1777 and in violation of Article 9 of the Constitution.

The petition of James Rogers, wherein he is described as one of the heirs of James Rogers, one of the grantees of Kent, is not evidence of such heirship. Nor is the recital in such petition of certain proceedings of confiscation evidence of that fact.

The Act of 1795 contains several conditions precedent. Nothing in the case tends to show that they were fulfilled.

The conveyance from Aiken and his associates is inoperative. It is not sealed. Nobody in the plaintiff's chain of title was ever in possession, so no presumption of the deed's validity arises. The record must show plainly that the original instrument was sealed. *Williams* v. *Bass*, 22 Vt. 352; *McCarley* v. *County*, 58 Miss. 749; Tiedman on Real Prop. § 808.

The copy of the probate proceedings under the Cobb will was inadmissible. Due notice must appear. *Stone* v. *Peaseley*, 28 Vt. 716. The warrant to the appraisers and commissioners should be set forth and it should appear that the warrant had been returned. *Robinson* v. *Gilman*, 3 Vt. 165. The proof should be by certified copy from the office of the Register of Probate. *Abbott* v. *Pratt*, 16 Vt. 626; V. S. 2333.

WATSON, J. This action is trespass *quare clausum fregit* for treble damages, under Vermont Statutes Sec. 5020, for

cutting timber standing and growing on land in the town
of Londonderry. The trial was by the Court. The plaintiff
claimed title by deed to the *locus in quo,* and in order to show
it, introduced in evidence, subject to the defendant's objections and exceptions, certified copies of divers instruments
and records. Hereupon the principal questions before us
arise.

The plaintiffs introduced without objection a certified
copy of the New York Charter of the township of Kent, now
Londonderry and Windham, dated February 13, 1770,
whereby the township was granted to James Rogers and
twenty-two others, his associates. This charter is relied
upon by the plaintiffs as the basis of their title. It is said
by the defendant that the preamble to the Constitution of
1777 of Vermont so destroys the validity of the New York
grants that whatever part of the plaintiffs' title is based in
any way upon the grant of 1770 must fall.

A careful examination of this preamble shows that, so
far as it has any bearing upon the question here, it has reference to the actions of the authorities of New York touching
lands held by the inhabitants under charters granted by the
Governor of New Hampshire while the territory which is
now the State of Vermont was a part of the Province of
New Hampshire. Indeed the preamble says that the late
Lieut.-Governor of New York with others "did in violation
of the tenth Command, covet those very lands." No griev-
ances are set forth therein regarding the treatment of the
inhabitants by the government of New York respecting lands
originally granted by the governor of that province. And
so is the history of the Grants before they became an independent State.

The lands covered by the charter in question had never
been granted by the Governor of New Hampshire. The title

thereto had always been in the Crown, and a grant by the
Governor of New York after that government was given
jurisdiction by royal decree was good to pass title. Consequently the plaintiffs' title may legally be based upon the
grant received in evidence. *Paine and Morris* v. *Smead,* 1 D.
Chip. 56.

On February 20, 1770, James Rogers became the sole
owner of the land thus granted by a deed of conveyance to
him of that date from all of the other grantees named in said
charter.

To make out their claim of title from the said James
Rogers, the plaintiffs introduced as evidence subject to defendant's objection and exception in each instance among other
things the following:

1. A certified copy of the charter of Londonderry,
granted by the Governor, Council and General Assembly of
the Representatives of the Freemen of Vermont, unto Edward Aiken, Samuel Fletcher and Joseph Tyler, a committee
appointed for the purpose, dated April 20, 1780.

2. A certified copy of a petition of another James
Rogers to the General Assembly of the State of Vermont,
dated October 14, 1795, of the indorsements thereon by the
officers of the General Assembly, and of the report thereon
of the committee to which it was referred, dated Oct. 20, 1795,
which said petition alleged that the petitioner's father, Col.
James Rogers, was at the commencement of the then late war
possessed in fee of the township of Kent, then Londonderry,
and prayed that for the reasons therein stated, said committee
be authorized and required to convey to the petitioner all the
land in Londonderry that remained unsold and unappropriated, upon such conditions as the General Assembly should
deem meet.

3. A certified copy of an act of the General Assembly, passed October 23, 1795, entitled "An Act directing certain trustees to deed the land therein mentioned," and which authorized and directed Edward Aiken, Samuel Fletcher, and Joseph Tyler, trustees, etc., "to convey by deed of quit-claim to James Rogers, for the use of himself and the other heirs of Col. James Rogers, their respective heirs and assigns forever, all the lands in the township of Londonderry, public rights excepted, which are now unconveyed by said trustees," upon certain conditions therein named.

4. A certified copy of an act of the General Assembly, passed November 6, 1797, entitled "An Act directing certain trustees to make the conveyances and transfers therein mentioned" and which recited that in 1778 the then township of Kent was confiscated as the property of James Rogers, late of Upper Canada, deceased, and was on the 20th April, 1780, granted by the name of Londonderry to Edward Aiken, Samuel Fletcher and Joseph Tyler, as trustees, to dispose of the same for the use of the State, part of which township remained in the care of said trustees, and that James Rogers, son and heir of James Rogers above mentioned, had petitioned that said land and the avails thereof be granted to him; therefore the said Aiken, Fletcher and Tyler were authorized and required to convey to James Rogers by deed of quit-claim all right and title to lands in Londonderry and Windham that said trustees then held in right and behalf of the State, and also all right and property that said trustees had as such in lands in said towns by virtue of mortgage, etc., on certain conditions therein named.

5. A certified copy of a petition of the second named James Rogers to the General Assembly, dated October 16, 1799, of the report thereon of the committee to which it was referred, dated October 21, 1799, and of the indorsements

thereon by the officers of the General Assembly, and of an Act of the General Assembly entitled "An Act directing the treasurer of this State to give up a certain bond" passed October 23, 1799.

6. A certified copy of the record of a quit-claim deed from Edward Aiken, Samuel Fletcher and Joseph Tyler, trustees as aforesaid, to James Rogers, dated October 27, 1795, of "all and singular the land, tracts and parcels of land in the township which was formerly called Kent, late London-derry, now Londonderry and Windham, which are not deeded or conveyed by us."

The *locus in quo* is a part of the "Hartford Tract," so called. But there was no evidence that either the plaintiffs or any of those under whom they claim title were ever in actual possession of the "Hartford Tract" or any part thereof. The defendant stands as a stranger to the title.

The grant from the State to Edward Aiken, Samuel Fletcher, and Joseph Tyler, committee, of Londonderry, could convey to the grantees only such title in the thing granted as the State had, and if it had no title thereto, the grant is abso-lutely void. *Polk's Lessee* v. *Wendell*, 9 Cranch, 99, 3 L. Ed. 665; *Patterson* v. *Winn*, 11 Wheat. 388, 6 L. Ed. 500; *Rice* v. *Minn. & N. W. R. R. Co.*, 66 U. S. 358, 17 L. Ed. 147.

Since the title of the first named James Rogers under the New York charter was good and valid, no evidence was intro-duced tending to show subsequent title in the State, unless the certified copies of the petitions of the second named James Rogers to the General Assembly, together with the Acts of the General Assembly and of its committees, and under its authority, based thereon, and the recitals contained in said petitions and in the Acts passed by the General Assembly in consequence thereof, to the effect that the township of Kent was confiscated in 1778, as the property of the first named

James Rogers, constitute evidence of such a tendency. Were they legitimate evidence that the property was so confiscated? If they were, then the evidence tended to show the title in the State; if they were not, the case was without such evidence. Whatever force these documents have as evidence of that nature is given by the recitals therein and by the presumptions of law and fact arising thereon by reason of the acts shown to have been performed by public officers within the apparent scope of their authority. Neither the State nor its grantees were shown to have any connection with the earlier title of the first named James Rogers under the grant from the Crown in any other manner than by the recitals in these petitions and in the acts of the General Assembly, themselves. The general rule is that recitals in a deed are binding, by way of estoppel, upon the parties and those who claim under them, but they do not bind mere strangers or those who claim by title paramount the deed. Mr. Starkie, in stating this rule, says that such recitals operate by way of admission, and therefore they are not evidence against a stranger to the second deed. 1 Stark. Ev. 369. See, also, *Hall* v. *Collins*, 4 Vt. 316; *Lord* v. *Bigelow*, 8 Vt. 445; *Paine and Morris* v. *Smead*, before cited; *Carver* v. *Astor*, 4 Pet. 1, 7 L. Ed. 761; *Herron* v. *Dater*, 120 U. S. 464, 30 L. Ed. 748; *Sabariego* v. *Maverick*, 124 U. S. 261, 31 L. Ed. 430.

As illustrations of the rule, these cases are much in point. In *Paine and Morris* v. *Smead*, the action was ejectment for lands in Windsor. The township of Windsor was originally a royal grant through the Governor of New Hampshire. Evidence was introduced that after holding this grant for some years, the proprietors caused it to be surrendered into the hands of the Governor of New York for the Crown, in consequence of which that governor issued letters patent in confirmation of rights under the New Hampshire charter. The Act by

which surrender of the last named charter was made, was not
produced in evidence, but the New York charter recited that
the other charter was surrendered. The plaintiffs claimed
under the New York grant, and the defendant stood in the
place of his father who was a proprietor of several rights
under the New Hampshire grant. The evidence showed that
the father was one of the proprietors who caused that grant
to be surrendered for the New York grant, and that he accepted lands under the latter in full for his claim under the
former. It was held that the New York grant issued after
the New Hampshire grant had been surrendered was valid,
and that the recital therein was *prima facie* evidence of such
surrender. In *Lord* v. *Bigelow,* the action was ejectment for
certain lands in the township of Wheelock. The plaintiff was
President of Dartmouth College and he brought suit as President of Moor's Charity School and successor of John Wheelock, as a corporation sole. The Legislature of this State, in
1808, passed a declaratory and confirming statute, in which
they recognize and declare that on the 14th June, 1785, a
grant was made under the authority of the State, and a charter
issued to John Wheelock, President of Moor's Charity School,
and to the trustees of Dartmouth College, of a township of
land, one moiety thereof to the said president and his successors in office. The defendant claimed under title through
several mesne conveyances from John Wheelock, President,
etc. The original grant was not produced. It was insisted
that the statute should not have been admitted in evidence
without producing the charter. The Court, holding the evidence admissible, said that as the preamble or recital respects
those parties, it was evidence of the grant or charter mentioned therein; and that no principle was better established
than that the recital of a deed in a subsequent deed is evidence
of the former against a party to the latter, though it may not

be against a stranger or against one who derives title from
the grantor before the deed which contains the recital. In
Herron v. *Dater*, both parties claimed under the Commonwealth of Pennsylvania. The defendant in error stood upon
the legal title of one Thomas Ruston established by a warrant
and survey perfected February 23, 1795. One assignment
of error was based upon the refusal of the trial court to
admit in evidence the certified copy of a patent from the Commonwealth to one Peter Grahl, dated April 12, 1797, with a
recital therein of the fact that Lewis Walker, by deed dated
November 27, 1793, had conveyed the tract of land in question to Peter Grahl. The Court, speaking through Mr. Justice MATTHEWS, said that the patentee was not connected with
the title under the warrant and survey, otherwise than by the
recital contained in the patent itself, that the tract had been
previously conveyed to him by Lewis Walker. Clearly, that
recital was not evidence against the plaintiffs, for if the patent
could not take effect against them without it, it could not give
any effect to that recital. In *Sabariego* v. *Maverick*, the court
below excluded evidence offered by the plaintiffs by way of
documents and recitals therein upon which they relied with
the aid of presumptions supplied by law, to establish the truth
of the fact recited and on the basis of which alone the proceedings to which they related could be lawful, including the
principal fact of a lawful confiscation of an estate of one
Miguel Losoya to the tract of land under consideration, by
a grant from the King of Spain. After reviewing authorities,
the Court speaking again by Mr. Justice MATTHEWS, said:
"By all these cases the question was whether the documents,
with the recitals therein, and the presumption of law and fact
arising thereon, shown to have been executed by officers of
the government, within the apparent scope of their authority,
were sufficient in the first instance to show that the title of

the government assumed by them to exist passed by the conveyance which undertook to transfer it.   In no case, however, have they been held sufficient, when the fact in issue was whether the government at that time had any title to convey, to establish the fact in dispute, as against parties claiming a pre-existing, adverse and paramount title in themselves.   All that can be reasonably or lawfully claimed as the effect of such documents of title, is that they passed such estate, and such estate only, as the government itself, in whose name and on whose behalf the official acts appear to have been done, had at the time,· but not to conclude the fact that the estate conveyed was lawfully vested in the grantor at the time of the grant."   The Court further said, "notwithstanding all these recitals, and the inferences and implications that are sought to be drawn from them, it still remains that the alleged confiscation of the property of Miguel Losoya, if it ever took place, could have been lawfully effected only by means of a formal judicial proceeding, which must be primarily proved by the official record of the transaction or a duly certified copy thereof; and, secondarily, in case of its loss, by proof of its previous existence and of its contents.   The certificates of other officers referring to it only incidentally and collaterally, although as the basis of their own official action, are not legal proof of the fact itself."

In *United States* v. *Ross*, 92 U. S. 281, 23 L. Ed. 707, the Court by Mr. Justice STRONG, in speaking of the maxim that all acts are presumed to have been rightly and regularly done, said: "The presumption that public officers have done their duty, like the presumption of innocence, is undoubtedly a legal presumption; but it does not supply proof of a substantive fact.   Best, in his Treatise on Ev., sec. 300, says: 'The true principle intended to be asserted by the rule seems to be, that there is a general disposition in courts of justice to uphold judicial and other acts rather than to render them inoperative; and with this view, where there is general evidence of acts having been legally and regularly done, to dispense with proof of circumstances, strictly speaking, essential to the validity of those acts, and by which they were probably accompanied in most instances, although in others the assumption may rest on grounds of public policy.' Nowhere is the presumption held to be a substitute for proof of an independent and material fact."

But there is another reason why the recitals under consideration are not evidence of the fact recited. The petitions containing such recital were the actions of the second named James Rogers and, the Acts of the General Assembly based thereon were private acts procured by him and for his benefit. The recitals of public acts are regarded as evidence of the facts recited, for every subject is, in contemplation of law, privy to the making of such acts. 1 Stark. Ev. 164; *R.* v. *Sutton*, 4 Maule & Sel. 532. The converse of the reason for this rule is the maxim, applicable to the law of evidence, that a transaction between two parties ought not to operate to the disadvantage of a third. From this it follows that recitals in a private act are not evidence except against the persons who procured the enactment, or perhaps in certain cases, the State. Endlich Interpretation of Statutes, sec. 375; *Branson* v. *Wirth,* 17 Wall. 32, 21 L. Ed. 566; *Kinkead* v. *United States,* 150 U. S. 483, 3-7 L. Ed. 1152; *Elmondorff* v. *Carmichael,* 3 Littell, 472; *Polini* v. *Gray,* L. R. 12 Ch. D. 411; *State* v. *Beard,* 1 Ind. 460. Nor is this rule affected in the case before us by the fact that the petitions for such enactments were referred to a committee by the General Assembly, and that such committee made its reports thereon affirming the truth of the allegations in the petitions, for by the same maxim a person cannot be affected by any evidence, decree or judgment to which he was not actually, or in consideration of law, privy. Broom's Leg. Max. 954; *McKinnon* v. *Bliss,* 21 N. Y. 206.

The plaintiffs rely on *Lord* v. *Bigelow,* and on *Cross* v. *Martin,* 46 Vt. 14, as sustaining their contention that the facts stated in the preamble to the Act of November 6, 1797, are established by the recitals therein.   Reference has already been made to *Lord* v. *Bigelow,* and, as seen, it in effect states the general rule as it is here stated, and that case was within it. In *Cross* v. *Martin,* to show title in himself, the plaintiff introduced without objection a certified copy of the charter of Harris Gore, dated October 30, 1801, which recited that the same territory was granted by an Act of the General Assembly, passed February 25, 1782, to Elijah Gore and associates. The plaintiff introduced other evidence both oral and documentary in making out his case, some of which was received without objection and some under exception by defendant. The Court found from the evidence title to the lots in question in the plaintiff, to which defendant excepted.   Immediately following this exception and as a part of the same paragraph, the original bill of exceptions,—which we have examined,— states: "The same questions were raised, and same objections were made by defendant's counsel to the sufficiency of proof to show title in plaintiff after the evidence was closed, as was raised and made on the introduction of the evidence, and no others."   This shows that the question of the force of the recitals in the charter of 1801, as evidence, was not raised, and that what is said thereon in the opinion is *obiter dictum.*

Nor does the fact that the recitals in question are contained in ancient documents make them evidence of the facts recited; for they are mere narrations of a past transaction of which they formed no part.   Under the rules governing

the admissibility of ancient documents as such it is requisite·
that they be a part of the transaction to which they relate.
1 Greenl. Ev., sec. 144.

It is urged by the plaintiffs, however, that if the State
had no title to the property to pass by its grant, the first
named James Rogers continued to be the owner, and at his
death the property descended to his heirs, of whom it is contended the second named James Rogers was one. If the latter was such heir, and together with his co-heirs thus inher-
ited the property, then the plaintiffs as grantees of his
undivided part of the land can maintain an action in
their own names against a stranger to the title for trespass
thereon and recover the whole damage to the property for
the benefit of themselves and co-tenants. *Bigelow* v. *Rising,*
42 Vt. 678; *Hibbard* v. *Foster,* 24 Vt. 542.

The question then arises whether the recitals in the petitions to the effect that the first named James Rogers was the
petitioner's father are evidence tending so to show, for if they
are not, there is no evidence of the heirship contended for, in
the case. The declarations, oral or written, of deceased persons who were related to the family in question by blood or
marriage may be given in evidence in matters of pedigree
when a proper foundation is laid therefor. In laying the
foundation, the relationship of the declarant with the family
must be shown by evidence independent of the declarations
themselves. No evidence of this fact was introduced, hence
the declarations contained in the recitals were not proper evidence. *Fulkerson* v. *Holmes,* 117 U. S. 380, 29 L. Ed. 915.
The cases where declarations of deceased persons in relation
to boundary lines and monuments are received in evidence are
analogous in principle. There before such evidence can be
received, the declarant's knowledge at the time he spoke must

be proved by evidence *dehors* the declarations. *Hadley* v. *Howe*, 46 Vt. 142; *Miller* v. *Wood*, 44 Vt. 378.

In addition to this, it must appear that the declarations were *ante litem motam;* for they are admitted "upon the principle," said Lord ELDON, "that they are the natural effusions of a party, who must know the truth, and who speaks upon an occasion when his mind stands in an even position, without any temptation to exceed or fall short of the truth." *Whitlock* v. *Baker*, 13 Ves. 514, 11 Eng. Rul. Cas. 309. In the case before us, the declarations were made by the second named James Rogers in petitions to the General Assembly for the purpose of having it act thereon in passing an Act directing that the lands before owned by the alleged ancestor but then claimed by the State, be conveyed to the petitioner for the benefit of himself and "other heirs," not named. His petition of October 14, 1795, alleges "that the estate of your petitioner's father not being confiscated by law of this State, the Commissioners of American Claims, appointed by the Court of Great Britain 'to inquire into the losses and services of all persons who suffered in the rights, properties and possessions during the late war in America in consequence of their loyalty to the Crown and Government of Great Britain,' would not allow compensation for the lands in Londonderry, except such parts thereof as were actually sold previous to the treaty of peace betwixt his Britannic Majesty and the United States of America, the said Commissioners alleging that agreeable to said treaty all property belonging to loyalists' estates ought to be restored which had not been legally confiscated or absolutely sold." To constitute *lis mota* it is not necessary that a suit be pending. It is sufficient to render the declarations inadmissible on the ground of *lis mota* if at the time they were made a controversy had arisen capable of being litigated, which was of a nature likely to bias the mind of the declarant. It appears from the above allegations that a controversy had been had upon the matter of the legal status of the lands in question before this petition was preferred to the General Assembly, and that failing to get an allowance by the Commissioners of American Claims as compensation for them, the declarant petitioned the General Assembly for the lands themselves which remained unsold and unappropriated. The property rights he was thus seeking were large and his interest was great. Under the rules of law, when such a controversy has arisen, it is supposed to create a bias in the mind of the declarant and his declarations are inadmissible. *Butler* v. *Viscount Mountgarret,* 7 H. L. Cas. 633, 11 Eng. Rul. Cas. 335; *Monkton* v. *Attorney General,* 2 Russ. & Myl. 147; *In Re Hurlburt's Estate,* 68 Vt. 366.

We hold, therefore, that the certified copies of the petitions to the General Assembly and the acts of the General Assembly thereon, and the doings of the public officers under the authority of the General Assembly in consequence thereof, had no tendency to show that the lands of the first named James Rogers had been confiscated by the State. Also that the recitals in the petitions were not proper evidence that the second named James Rogers was heir at law of the James Rogers first named. It follows that these copies were not proper evidence for any purpose, and that they together with the Vermont Charter should have been excluded. This being so, the plaintiffs' record title fails, and they had no constructive possession of the *locus in quo* at the time of the alleged trespass.

The other exceptions are not considered.

Judgment reversed and cause remanded.

JAMES D. BELL, ET AL. *v.* ST. JOHNSBURY & LAKE CHAM-
PLAIN R. R. CO.

October Term, 1902.

Present: ROWELL, C. J., TYLER, MUNSON, START, and WATSON, JJ.

Opinion filed October 28, 1903.

*Railroads—Mandate—Construction—Notice—Sufficiency—
V. S. 3803—Net Earnings.*

The right to maintain this bill to reach the net earnings is determined by the mandate heretofore sent down in this cause.

That mandate limits this right to such orators as had no notice of
the pendency of certain chancery proceedings; and this means
notice according to the practice and usage of the court of chancery in such cases.

A notice published by the solicitors for the orators in those proceedings
of their own motion, and without an order of court or the master,
has no legal efficacy.

A claim for stationery and printing is not within the provisions of
V. S. 3803.

In computing net earnings, only such expenditures as are actually
made can be deducted from the gross earnings.

Amounts paid for interest and extraordinary repairs on locomotives
should be deducted from the gross earnings in such computation.

The expenses of litigation which arose in matters anterior to the
appointment of receivers and with which they had nothing to do
as such, should not be deducted from gross earnings to determine
the net earnings of the receivership.

APPEAL IN CHANCERY. Heard on the pleadings, mandate, report and supplemental report of special masters and
exceptions thereto, and the records and files in the Poland
case, referred to in the opinion, at the June Term, 1902, Caledonia County, *Start,* Chancellor. *Pro forma* decree for the
defendant. The orators appealed.

George W. Wing for the orators.

Young & Young for the defendant.

ROWELL, C. J.   The orators are preferred creditors. under V. S. 3803 for services rendered and materials furnished to keep the railroad now owned by the defendant in repair, and to run the same, before and at the time it went into the hands of receivers on October 18, 1877.   By their bill they seek to enforce payment of their several demands out of the fund derived from a judicial sale of personal property on which creditors under said statute had a first lien, which sale was ordered and made under the cross-bill of Howe and others, creditors under said statute, filed in the case of *Poland, trustee,* v. *The Lamoille Valley R. R. Co. and others,* reported in 52 Vt. 144, to which reference is had; and failing this, they seek payment out of the net earnings of the road while in the hands of the receivers.

The original bill, with amendments, was entered in the Caledonia County Court of Chancery at the June Term, 1880, when the orators asked to intervene in the Poland case, then pending in said court on remand from the Supreme Court, and to share in said fund with the orators in the Howe cross-bill, and in the personal property and net earnings of the road, on such terms and conditions as to the court should seem just and equitable.   Such leave was denied, but the orators were permitted to file their bill as an original bill, which they did, and the court proceeded with the Poland case in due course.   Subsequently the orators filed their supplemental bill, to meet the changed condition of things since the original bill was filed; and as the St. Johnsbury & Lake Champlain Railroad Company had come to be the only necessary party defendant, the bill was dismissed as to all the other defendants, either by agreement or order of court.

The decree in the Poland case on the Howe cross-bill, made pursuant to mandate, established the claim of divers of the orators in said bill, and fixed the amount thereof; ordered that the receivers and the mortgagees under the preference mortgage and the first mortgage, which were being foreclosed in said case, should pay said claims in full, with interest and costs, on or before June 1, 1880; adjudged that until such payment, said claims should be and continue a first lien on all the personal property of the railroad companies that went into the hands of the receivers at the time of their appointment, and also on all property of like kind acquired by them after their appointment; that in default of such payment, all of said property, or so much thereof as was necessary for the purpose, should be sold by order of court, and the avails thereof applied *pro rata* in extinguishment of said claims, interest and costs; that if on such sale and application, any portion of said claims remained unpaid, the same should be a first and paramount lien on the net earnings and income of said roads and property, and that the receivers, and all other persons succeeding to the possession, management, and control of said roads and property, should pay over to the clerk of the court from time to time, said net earnings for *pro rata* distribution to said claimants; that the lien on said earnings should continue until full payment should be made, and said cause be kept on the docket until said claims were paid or secured as therein provided, with liberty to the claimants to apply.

And it was further ordered and decreed that said mortgagees should have no right to take possession of said roads and property under the decree of foreclosure, nor to receive the earnings thereof, until said claims were fully paid, unless they should secure the payment thereof as therein provided, in which case they could take possession.

The bill in the case at bar alleges the sale of said property by order of court for about $58,000; payment of all the claims established and allowed in the Howe cross-bill; a settlement and discharge of the receivers; and the taking of possession of the roads by the defendant, organized in the interest of said mortgagees; and prays, among other things, that an account be taken of the value of the personal property at the time it went into the hands of the receivers, and of the earnings of the roads during the receivership, and payment thereout of the orators' claims.

The answer states the substance of the decree in favor of the orators in the Howe cross-bill, and alleges the non-payment of their claims and the failure to secure the same within the time limited; the consequent sale of the property by order of court for $57,450, the defendant being the purchaser; the confirmation of said sale; and that upon such confirmation the court ordered that if the defendant should within thirty days, file discharges of all the claims allowed' under said cross-bill, the same should be received as full payment for said property; but on failure to procure and file such discharges, said sale should be vacated, and the possession of said property restored to the receivers; that the defendant did procure and file discharges of all of said claims, which amounted to about $106,000, and also paid a considerable sum in costs.

The answer denies the allegations of the bill concerning net earnings of the roads and property while in the hands of the receivers, and that such earnings were expended in building new road and in permanent improvements on the line, and alleges that all of the earnings during that time were very little if any more than enough to pay running expenses and such repairs of the road as were necessary to keep it in safe condition to operate, and that the sums expended by the receivers in the purchase of new personal property and in repairing the old, all of which was sold for the benefit of the lien creditors, very largely exceeded all the net earnings of the road and property while operated by the receivers, so that the lien creditors have had the full benefit of all net earnings by the receivers.

The answer admits that the receivers made some improvements on the roads of a permanent character, but alleges that whatever they expended in that behalf was mainly for repairs that were necessary to enable the roads to be safely run and the receivers to perform their duty to the public; that at the expiration of the receivership, the receivers were indebted to divers persons to about the sum of $100,000, which the defendant had to pay or secure before it took possession of the roads, in addition to what it had to pay the lien creditors; that said debts of the receivers were more than all the expenditures made by them upon the roads that could be called permanent; and so the defendant says that no net earnings made by the receivers ever came into its hands in any form; but that whatever there might have been, have already been paid to the lien creditors in the sale of said personal property.

The answer was traversed and testimony taken, and the case heard on the pleadings and the testimony, and the bill dismissed, with costs, and the orators appealed. The case was heard in the Supreme Court at the General Term, 1884, and again at the General Term, 1885, when a mandate was sent down, that as the personal property in the bill mentioned that came into the hands of the receivers, to which the creditors had a right to resort, had been sold by order of court, and the avails thereof distributed and paid to the creditors who came in and proved their claims in said cross cause of

Howe and others, who are not parties hereto,—the orators herein have no equitable right to any portion of said avails; but that the net earnings, if any, of the road while in the hands of the receivers should go to pay debts incurred for operating the road, instead of paying bondholders or expenses for permanent improvements on the road, and that such of the orators as had no notice of the pendency of the Poland case and of the cross cause of Howe and others, have a right to have this bill maintained, to reach the net earnings, if any, of the road while in the hands of the receivers; and that the court of chancery refer the cause to a master, to ascertain and report the net earnings of the road while in the hands of the receivers, and the names of the orators who had no notice of the pendency of the Poland case and the cross cause of Howe and others, and what notice, if any, the several orators had thereof, and to find and report the amount due the several orators; and upon the coming in of the report, to make decree according to mandate.

Pursuant to said mandate, the case was referred to masters, who find and report that the net earnings of the road while in the hands of the receivers, namely, from October 18, 1877, to July 1, 1880, when the defendant took possession, were $39,496.78, subject, however, to such reduction as the court thinks ought to be made on the facts found; and it is out of these earnings that the orators ask to be paid.

It appears that the amount of the claims allowed in the Howe cross cause, with costs, was $103,081.30, and that the defendant paid the same in full before taking possession of the road, thereby paying $45,631.30 more than the price at which it bid off the personal property. Therefore the defendant says, that as it was decreed that if the avails of that sale were not enough to pay said claims, the unpaid balance should be a first and paramount lien on the net earnings, which should be paid over to the clerk from time to time for *pro rata* distribution to said claimants; and as said sale was confirmed, thereby fixing the avails of it at $57,450,—it should be taken that for the purpose of relieving the net earnings of the lien thereon, and to enable the defendant to take possession of the road at once, it was willing to assume, and did assume, without an accounting, that the net earnings were sufficient to pay the balance of said claims, and therefore paid the same, thereby paying more than the net earnings are now ascertained to be. The defendant contends that it stands the same as it would had it stood back and compelled an accounting of net earnings, and then paid, which would have discharged it from paying now; that the mandate in this case should be construed to mean net earnings, if any, in excess of what the defendant had already paid to Howe and others; that the orators' remedy, if any they have, is against Howe and others for contribution in respect of the net earnings they have received; and that the order alleged in the answer, made on confirmation of the sale,—that if the defendant should within thirty days, file discharges of all the claims allowed under the Howe cross-bill, the same should be received as full payment and satisfaction of the purchase of said property, otherwise the sale should be vacated, and the possession of the property restored to the receivers,—should not be taken to have made the price of the property $103,081.30 to the defendant, but as intended to enable the receivers to operate the road till said sum was paid or secured to the extent of the property and the net earnings, thereby satisfying the lien on both.

But it is to be noticed that the answer does not present the case in that way. It denies that there were any net earnings of any amount, if indeed there were any at all, which

it does not admit; alleges that "whatever there might have
been," the lien creditors had the benefit of in the sale of the
personal property, because the amount expended by the receivers in the purchase of new personal property and in repairs
of the old, very largely exceeded all the net earnings; and
denies that any net earnings ever came into the hands of the
defendant by way of permanent improvements of the road,
which it admits were made to some extent, because the indebtedness of the receivers, which the defendant had to pay, was
more than all their expenditures for such improvements. And
Judge Poland took the same ground in his arguments for the
defendant when the case was here before. He said that there
was not only an entire failure to show that the bondholders
received in any form any earnings of the road that belonged
to another class of creditors, but that it was conclusively
demonstrated they did not—that there were no net earnings;
that they were quite ready to account on the basis of the doctrine announced in the Poland case, namely, that the net
earnings should go to pay debts incurred for operating the
road instead of going to the bondholders; and that if the road
was improved as claimed, the bondholders had been compelled
to restore, and had restored, at least double the amount.

   In view of all this, the mandate is not fairly capable of
the construction contended for by the defendant. If the court
meant, "net earnings, if any, in excess of what the defendant
had already paid to Howe and others," it is reasonable to suppose it would have said so. But it did not. That idea is
not gatherable from the mandate read by itself, nor when read
in the light of the case. On the contrary it would seem that
the court regarded the amount paid to Howe and others as
paid for the property rather than to have the sale of it set
aside, and it go back into the hands of the receivers. And

this view finds support in the wording of the order that discharges filed in accordance therewith "should be received as full payment for said property." These discharges were to be of all the claims allowed under the Howe cross-bill. Nothing is said about the excess above the price at which the property was bid off being treated as a payment on net earnings, and said earnings relieved from the lien of creditors to that extent, which one would suppose would have been said had such been the intention.

We hold, therefore, that the right of the orators in the mandate mentioned to maintain this bill to reach the net earnings, is adjudged and determined by the mandate, and that the case as now presented is merely one of accounting under the mandate.

According to the mandate, only the orators who had no notice of the pendency of the Poland case and the cross cause of Howe and others, are entitled to maintain this bill. The defendant contends that this does not necessarily mean notice by order of court, either by the service of process or publication, but that knowledge as distinguished from such notice is sufficient, and refers to 2 Pom. Eq. 8th ed. § 592, and Story's Eq. § 396, in support of the claim. But we cannot adopt this construction in the absence of laches on the part of the orators. These authors are speaking of what notice will make one a *mala-fide* purchaser, and of cases of contest for precedence among holders of different interests in, or claims upon, the same subject-matter, and not of what is sufficient notice to bar a creditor in cases of this kind. We think the court did not intend to take this case out of the general rule, and that the mandate means, notice according to the practice and usage of the court of chancery in such cases, which is this: When a bill is brought by a part of the creditors, not only for themselves but for others standing in like situation who may come in and share in the expense, as the Howe crossbill was, the decree for an inquiry who the creditors are and what the amount of their claims, declares that all the creditors are entitled to the benefit of the decree, and directs the master to cause notice to be given as therein specified for all the creditors to come in before him and prove their debts, and to fix a peremptory day for that purpose, and declares that such of the creditors as do not come in by that day, are to be excluded the benefit of the decree. 2 Smith's Ch. Pr. 2d ed. 261; 2 Daniell's Ch. Pl. & Pr. 3d ed. 1198; Story's Eq. Pl. 7th ed. § 99; *Hallett* v. *Hallett*, 2 Paige, [*15]. All parties beneficially interested are entitled to attend before the master in all proceedings that may affect their interest. 2 Daniell's Ch. Pl. & Pr. 2d ed. *1355; and this rule applies not only to the parties of record, but also to those who are *quasi* parties by having come in under the decree, who are entitled to notice of all proceedings that may affect their interest. Ib. *1358; and the party conducting the cause before the master must take care that all parties entitled to attend have had notice as directed. Ib. *1355.

Although a master was appointed to take an account of the debts due to Howe and others, orators in said cross cause, and to all other creditors whose debts were like theirs, yet no debts were proved before the master except those of the orators in that cause. The order of reference is not before us, but we infer that it contained no direction for notice to creditors to come in, and no declaration of exclusion if they did not come in, for the master gave no such notice, as sufficiently appears, though more by implication than by direct finding. The solicitors for the orators in the cross cause, of their own motion, and without an order of court or of the master, caused an advertisement to be printed three weeks successively in a St. Johnsbury paper, asking all creditors to bring in their claims to them and have them paid. But this notice, of course, had no legal efficacy. Thus it appears that none of the orators in this case had legal notice of the proceedings before the master in that case, and therefore none of them are barred thereby. "The principle is as old as the law, and of universal justice, that no one shall be personally bound until he has had his day in court, which means, until citation is issued to him, and an opportunity to be heard is afforded." Field, J., in *Mason* v. *Eldred*, 6 Wall., at page 237.

The claim of M. B. Warren for stationery and printing, allowed at $856.82, cannot be recovered here, as it is not within the statute. It makes no difference that it was allowed without objection, especially as the masters allowed it subject to the opinion of the court on the facts found. With this claim out, the aggregate amount of the claims allowed is $19,001.13, which amount is recoverable here if the net earnings are sufficient, with interest on the principal thereof from June 7, 1892, the date to which the masters computed interest.

The net earnings reported are the excess of gross earnings are sufficient, with interest on the principal thereof from accounts were kept by the receivers. There are sixteen items, aggregating $111,805.78, that were not treated by the receivers as operating expenses, but were classed by them as "expenses in addition to operating expenses." The defendant claims that $4,551.08 of No. 4 of these items, which is $5,864.23 for "new fences built during the receivership," and all of items 5, 9, and 16, amounting in the whole to $14,-797.75, should be deducted from gross earnings, thereby making the net earnings $24,699.75.

As to item 4 the masters find that when the receivers took possession of the road, seventy miles of it had no fence; that upon fifty miles of it there was a fence that had been built from four to seven years; that the receivers expended the amount of said item for new fences built; and that the average life of a railroad fence of the quality of the fence built on this road, is fifteen years. They were unable to find whether anything was expended by the receivers in repairing fences, but find that the full amount of this item was an expense for permanent improvements, and not an operating expense that should be deducted from income to find net earnings, but say that if the court holds that the net earnings reported should be reduced by a sum expended in new fences sufficient to keep the old fences good, they find that the expense of keeping in repair the fences already built when the receivers took the road, would have been $4,551.08 during the receivership.

But we cannot hold this, for no actual expenditure was made for such repairs, and only such expenditures as are actually made can with any propriety be deducted from gross earnings.   *United States* v. *Kansas Pacific Railway Co.,* 99 U. S. 455, 459.

Item 5, $2,433.28 for interest, and item 9, $1,500 for extraordinary repairs on locomotives, must, on the findings, be deducted from net earnings.

As to item 19, $6,313.39 for litigation, the masters find in their supplemental report that the litigation arose in matters anterior to the appointment of the receivers, and with which they had nothing to do as such, and that the expenditure did not accrue in any manner in their operation of the road, except as to matters stated in their original report. But those matters do not militate against this finding, under which this item cannot be deducted. Thus, by deducting $3,933.28, the amount of items 5 and 9, the net earnings are reduced to $35,563.50, at which sum they are adjudged and established.

Decree reversed and cause remanded with mandate that the bill be dismissed as to the orator Warren, with costs in this court, but that a proper decree be entered for all the other orators in accordance with this opinion, with costs in this court. Let the question of costs below be there determined.

ROSWELL W. BELKNAP *v.* ALBERT BILLINGS.

May Term, 1903.

Present: TYLER, MUNSON, START, WATSON, and STAFFORD, JJ.

Opinion filed November 7, 1903.

Replication—Special Traverse—Duplicity.

A replication to a plea of accord and satisfaction which denies that the note set up in the plea was accepted in satisfaction, and alleges that such note was accepted in satisfaction only on condition that it be paid at maturity, and concludes with a verification, is not double and is sufficient as a special traverse.

A special demurrer reaches only such defects of form as are therein pointed out.

TRESPASS FOR ASSAULT. The pleadings are stated in the opinion. Heard on special demurrer to the replication to the fourth plea, at the June Term, 1902, Windsor County, *Haselton*, J., presiding. Demurrer overruled and replication adjudged sufficient. The defendant excepted.

Gilbert A. Davis for the defendant.

The replication is double since it denies that the note was received in satisfaction, and then sets up new matter— that the note was accepted in satisfaction only on a condition which had not been fulfilled. *Durkee* v. *Goodnough*, 65 Vt. 257; *Downer* v. *Powell*, 26 Vt. 397; Ch. Pl. (13th Am. Ed.) 649, 594, 611; *Russell* v. *Rogers*, 15 Wend. 351; *Luce* v. *Hoisington*, 55 Vt. 341; Stephen Pl. § 259.

J. C. Enright and *Edw. R. Buck* for the plaintiff.

The replication is not double. It only alleges such facts as are necessary to avoid the effect of the plea. *Vaughn* v. *Evarts*, 40 Vt. 530; *Matt* v. *Hazen*, 27 Vt. 208.

TYLER, J. This action is trespass for an assault and battery; pleas, first, the general issue; second, that the plaintiff was in the defendant's dwelling-house making disturbance, and that the defendant, after requesting him to cease making disturbance and depart, which the plaintiff refused to do, gently removed him from said dwelling-house in defense of his possession thereof; third, that in attempting to remove the plaintiff for the cause aforesaid the plaintiff assaulted him; that he defended himself, and that whatever injury he did to the plaintiff he did in necessary self-defense; fourth, that he gave the plaintiff a certain promissory note, with a surety, in full satisfaction and discharge of the alleged cause of action, and that the plaintiff accepted the same in satisfaction thereof.

The second and third pleas are traversed; to the fourth there is a replication. The only question before us is in respect to the sufficiency, on special demurrer, of the amended replication to the fourth plea.

After the introductory part the replication avers that the plaintiff ought not to be barred of his action because, "the note in the defendant's fourth plea mentioned was not accepted by the plaintiff nor by any one in his behalf as payment and satisfaction of the trespasses and injuries in the plaintiff's declaration alleged, but that the note was accepted as satisfaction only on condition that it be paid when it became due. And the plaintiff avers that the note was long overdue before the commencement of this suit, and that neither the defendant, nor the surety, * * * named in the note, though requested, has ever paid the note or any part thereof, * * * and that it remains unpaid, and this he is ready to verify; wherefore he prays judgment," etc.

We think that this replication amounts to a special traverse. It contains a direct denial of the acceptance of the note in satisfaction, etc., as alleged in the defendant's fourth plea, followed by an inducement of new matter indirectly denying that allegation; and it amounts in substance to an answer to the plea and concludes with a verification. 1 Chit. Pl. 620; Perry's Pl. 259-263; *Day* v. *Essex Co. Bank,* 13 Vt. 97.

The only contention is that the replication is double because it contains a traverse and also allegations of new matter. But since the new matter is pleaded as a necessary inducement to the allegation containing the direct denial, it does not operate to make the pleading double. Steph. Pl. (Heard's Ed.) 262.

The replication is informal in that the inducement follows the direct denial instead of preceding it; but if this is a defect, it is in form only and not in substance. Such defect is not reached by the general demurrer and is not pointed out by the special demurrer. *Dunford* v. *Trotters,* 12 M. & W. 529; *Lewis* v. *Alcock,* 3 M. & W. 188; 1 Chit. Pl. 620.

Demurrer overruled; replication to fourth plea adjudged sufficient; cause remanded.

RUFUS E. HILLIARD v. THE BURLINGTON SHOE CO., ET AL.

October Term, 1903.

Present: ROWELL, C. J., MUNSON, START, WATSON, and STAFFORD, JJ.

Opinion filed November 18, 1903.

Judgment—Effect—Assignment—Validity—Interest of Assignee—Preference—Deed of Corporation.

A judgment in favor of a garnishee, in a suit in which the defendant is not served with notice and does not appear, is not binding upon such defendant; hence it does not estop the plaintiff therein from controverting, in a subsequent suit against such defendant, facts therein litigated.

An assignee is not so interested in the provisions of an assignment as to invalidate it against creditors, simply because as attorney he had caused attachments to be placed upon the property, subject to which the assignment is made.

A statutory assignment is not invalid on the ground of a preference when the real estate is conveyed subject to attachments.

Such an assignment is valid unless impeached in bankruptcy within four months from its execution.

It is not essential to the validity of the deed of a corporation that it show on its face the authority for its execution.

APPEAL IN CHANCERY. Heard on pleadings, master's report, and exceptions thereto, at the September Term, 1902, Chittenden County, *Tyler,* Chancellor. Decree for the defendants. The orators appealed.

Edward H. Deavitt for the orator.

The assignee, being the attorney of the attaching creditors, was interested in the assignment and it is not valid against creditors. V. S. 2171. The assignment created a preference in favor of the attaching creditors, and is therefore void under the same section of the statute. See *Fair* v. *Brackett,* 30 Vt. 346; *Bank* v. *Strong,* 42 Vt. 295.

The assignment is void under the Bankruptcy Act of 1898. *Insurance Co.* v. *Insurance Co.*, 14 N. B. R. 316; *Barnes* v. *Ritten,* 8 Phila. 141; *In re Smith,* 3 N. B. R. 18; *In re Railroad Co.*, 10 N. B. R. 178; *Platt* v. *Preston,* 10 N. B. R. 241; Burrill Assigns. §§ 27-30.

The deed of the corporation, which in the granting part thereof does not show that any person is authorized to execute it, is of no force to convey title to the assignee. *Dietrich* v. *Hutchinson,* 73 Vt. 134; *McDaniels* v. *Manufacturing Co.*, 22 Vt. 274; *Isham* v. *Iron Co.*, 19 Vt. 230.

When an assignment is void, a creditor who has obtained a lien may have it perfected in equity. *Bank* v. *Strong,* 42 Vt. 295; *Kimball* v. *Evans,* 58 Vt. 655.

The orator is not estopped. *Bank* v. *Peabody,* 55 Vt. 492; 1 Herman Estop., §§ 258, 259.

Powell & Powell and *W. L. Burnap* for the defendants.

ROWELL, C. J. The validity of a statutory assignment by The Burlington Shoe Co. for the benefit of its creditors, is here called in question. The defendants say that the orator is estopped from denying its validity, because of a judgment against him in Philadelphia, where he brought a garnishment suit on the same day, but after the assignment papers were filed in the clerk's office of Chittenden County, to collect his debt out of a claim of The Burlington Co. or of The Champlain Shoe Co., the *alter ego* of the Burlington Co., as it was formed for the purpose of enabling the Burlington Co. to do indirectly what it had contracted not to do at all.

Neither of said companies was served with process in said suit, and neither appeared therein. The Court submitted two questions to the jury; (1) whether the garnishee was indebted to the Burlington Co. or to the Champlain Co. as

another separate and distinct corporation, and (2) whether
this assignment was perfected by filing all the papers in Vermont before service of the garnishment papers in Philadelphia. The jury returned a general verdict for the garnishee
without special findings, and judgment was rendered thereon,
which was affirmed in the Supreme Court. But as that judgment does not bind said companies nor either of them,—
National Bank of St. Johnsbury v. Peabody & Co., 55 Vt.
492,—it does not estop the orator from denying the validity
of the assignment, for estoppels must be mutual.

The orator claims that the assignee was so interested in
the provisions of the assignment as to invalidate it against
the creditors of the assignor. The assignee was at the time
in question, and now is, a lawyer, and as such had in his
hands for collection certain claims against the assignor, and
a few days before the assignment was made, caused suits
to be brought thereon, and the real estate in question to be
attached as the property of the assignor, and had control of
the suits until they were settled by payment of the claims
in full before judgment, out of money raised for that and
other purposes on the joint note of several persons who were
stockholders and directors of the assignor company.

The assignee's relation to those suits as attorney gave
him no lien for his fees on the land attached—22 Vt. 598—
but at most, only an inchoate lien on the judgments when recovered, and possibly on the causes of action before judgment.
But this was no interest in the provisions of the assignment,
within the meaning of the statute.

The claim cannot be sustained that here was an invalidating preference because the assignment purports to be for the
benefit of all the creditors of the assignor in proportion to
their respective claims, whereas the assignor's real estate was
conveyed to the assignee subject to said attachments. Those

attachments were prior liens on the land, not created by the assignor, but by the law, and the attaching creditors never assented to the assignment by coming in under it nor otherwise, but stood upon their attachments, which were hostile to the assignment, until they were paid in full.

It is claimed that the Bankruptcy Act of 1898 suspends the operation of our assignment act, as that act is in the nature of an insolvency law. But such is not the case. It was not so under the Bankruptcy Act of 1867, but such assignments were good notwithstanding that Act, if not impeached by proceedings in bankruptcy within four months from their execution. *Mayer* v. *Hellman,* 91 U. S. 496. The same is true under the present Bankruptcy Act, although it expressly provides that such an assignment is an act of bankruptcy. *Randolph* v. *Scruggs,* 190 U. S. 533.

It is objected to the validity of said deed that the granting part does not show that any person was authorized by the corporation to execute it. But that is not necessary. *McDaniels* v. *Flower Brook Manufacturing Co.,* 22 Vt. 274.

It is further objected that the deed does not show that there was any vote of the directors to execute it, and that it nowhere appears that Wm. W. Walker was authorized to make the conveyance as agent; that the acknowledgment that Walker acknowledged the deed to be his free act and deed and the free act and deed of the corporation, does not disclose any authority in Walker to execute the deed for the corporation, and that the signature, "Burlington Shoe Company, by Wm. W. Walker, Pres., duly authorized by the Board of Directors," is not a statement that Walker was authorized, and cannot cure the lack of statement in the granting part of the deed. This objection is to the same effect as the other, namely, that the deed must in the granting part, or at all events somewhere on its face, show the authority for its execution. But this, as we have in substance said, is not necessary. No other objection is made to the deed for lack of authority to execute it, nor to the manner of its execution, and therefore no other is considered.

Decree affirmed and cause remanded.

HARTFORD WOOLEN CO. *v.* CHARLES L. BUGBEE, ET AL.

October Term, 1902.

Present: ROWELL, C. J., TYLER, MUNSON, START, WATSON, and HASELTON, JJ.

Opinion filed November 25, 1903.

Water Right—Grant—Construction.

In the grant or reservation of a water right, a reference to an existing use will be considered as a measure of quantity merely, unless the contrary intention appears from the language used or the surrounding circumstances.

A grant of "sufficient water to carry" certain machines named is of the right to draw a certain quantity of water, without regard to the use or place.

When a water right is "not to be used for any purpose to the injury of any machinery now in use" by a certain owner, it is subject to the water right then used to operate the machinery referred to.

APPEAL IN CHANCERY. Heard on pleadings and master's report at the December Term, 1902, Windsor County, *Stafford,* Chancellor. Decree for the orator. Defendant Bugbee appealed.

George W. Wing for the defendant.

Pingree & Pingree and *William E. Johnson* for the orator.

HASELTON, J.   There is, and for more than 90 years has been, a dam across White River in Hartford village; and the parties hereto are the owners of the power stored thereby. Generally there is sufficient power for the uses of all, but in dry times there is not enough.   This case is here on appeal from a decretal order fixing the relative rights of the parties in the water power.   There are questions in the case which remain to be determined by the Court of Chancery after the cause is remanded.   There is no dispute as to one-half of the power.   That half is utilized on the south side of the stream, and is owned in equal shares by the orator and the defendant Pease.   Prior to the conveyance hereinafter mentioned, one James Fuller owned the other half of the power and with it operated a saw mill, a grist mill, and an oil mill, which was afterwards a plaster mill, situated on the north side of the river.

In 1846, Fuller conveyed to Sylvester Morris the oil mill, with certain water rights, and in 1847 he conveyed to said Morris the grist mill, together with a water right defined as follows: "Sufficient water to carry the grist mill when in proper repair, as it now is, to wit, to carry four run of stones, corn cracker, smut mill and two bolts."   Thereafter, one Moses French acquired an interest in said water rights, and in March, 1849, he and said Sylvester Morris conveyed to George P. Bugbee, by their separate deeds, real estate on the north bank of the stream and a 100 inch water right thus defined: "A privilege to draw water when it is not wanted to carry the grist mill, and the right to draw 10 inches of water. * * * It is meant that said Bugbee has a right to draw water at a 10 inch gate."   The water right so conveyed to

George P. Bugbee is now owned by the defendant, Charles L. Bugbee, and is called Bugbee's First Right.

After the conveyance to Bugbee, above referred to, but in the same year, S. & E. Morris, who were owners of the grist mill right, and the said James Fuller from whom it had been derived, submitted to arbitration the extent of that right. The arbitrators made an award May 26, 1849, which determined as follows: "That sd. S. & E. Morris shall have the right to draw two hundred square inches of water over and above what they now draw, which is 1868 square inches on his grist mill, for water saved by a different arrangement of his mill,—not to be used for any purpose to the injury of any machinery now in use by sd. Fuller on sd. dam." August 4, 1852, Sylvester Morris conveyed to George P. Bugbee 50 inches of water, in addition to that conveyed in March, 1849, and this grant is now owned by the defendant, Charles L. Bugbee, and is called Bugbee's Second Right. The conveyance defines this right as follows: "The privilege of drawing fifty inches of water in addition to the amount of water heretofore deeded said Bugbee by Moses French on the 22nd day of March, 1849; said water is to be taken from the flume as said Bugbee now draws it, under the plaster mill in lieu of the place mentioned in said French's deed. It is understood that the said Bugbee is not to have the privilege of drawing said water when it is wanted for the grist or plaster mill."

From the recitals in the conveyances referred to it would appear that Bugbee's right to draw the 50 inches of water was made subject to a plaster mill right to which his right to draw the 100 inches was not servient. However, no such claim is made against Bugbee and in view of the pleadings and all the facts reported by the master, Bugbee's First Right and his Second, are treated as standing alike in their relation to other rights in question.

The grist mill itself was destroyed by fire in 1886 and has never been rebuilt. Later in the same year the orator acquired title to the grist mill site, mill privilege, and water power. Since then the grist mill site has been left unoccupied. The orator uses the grist mill right on the south side of the river in connection with its rights hereinbefore referred to.

With respect to Bugbee's right to draw 150 inches of water, the question is whether it is subordinate to a right on the part of the orator to draw, on the south side of the river, a quantity of water sufficient for the purposes of the grist mill as used when George P. Bugbee acquired his First and Second Rights. We think that the grist mill right in question was a right to draw a certain quantity of water, and not simply a right to draw a quantity of water for a particular use or at a particular place. In a grant or reservation of a water right reference to an existing use will be considered as a measure of quantity merely, unless a contrary intention is apparent from the language used or from the surrounding circumstances. *Adams* v. *Warner*, 23 Vt. 395; *Rood* v. *Johnson*, 26 Vt. 64; *Miller* v. *Lapham*, 44 Vt. 416; *Albee* v. *Huntly*, 56 Vt. 454. In *Shedd* v. *Leslie*, 22 Vt. 498, and *Clement* v. *Gould*, 61 Vt. 573, the contrary intention referred to was apparent and governed, and these cases show the limitation of the rule. In the Shedd case a right was granted to use water so long as the grantee should carry on the business of a clothier at or near a designated place. The grant recited that the conveyance was for the purpose of having the business of a clothier carried on. In *Clement* v. *Gould*, the conveyance of water rights was for certain enumerated purposes "and for these purposes only."

The rule of construction which governs our cases is that which, speaking generally, prevails in this country. In a recent New Hampshire case, *Fowler* v. *Kent,* 52 Atl. 554, 71 N. H. 388, construction was put upon the conveyance of a water right attached to a grist mill. The language of the conveyance was as follows: "The privilege of drawing the water in the same manner it has been accustomed to run, meaning the first right to draw water for the use of the mill as it now is." The Court says: "This language was used to describe the quantity of water that went with the privilege, rather than to limit the manner in which, the purpose for which, or the place at which the water was to be used."

The passage above quoted from the opinion aptly illustrates the application to this case of the true rule of construction. It is reason enough for the rule that reference to a use is a natural and convenient method of designating the extent of a water right. The method does not call for scientific calculations and computations, yet the result is exact because capable of being made so. Other cogent reasons for the rule are stated in the cases referred to.

In 1894 the orator conveyed to the defendant, Bugbee, the grist mill site and water power, reserving the right to draw the 1868 inches of water named in the award as the measure of the original grist mill right. The said Bugbee accepted the conveyance; and the extent in inches of the original grist mill water right is not questioned. By this last conveyance the defendant, Bugbee, acquired the 200 inches of water named in the before mentioned award. This 200 inches is called Bugbee's Third Right. Meanwhile the water right of the said James Fuller, not disposed of as hereinbefore mentioned, had passed to the defendant Gates.

By the terms of the award defining Bugbee's Third Right the quantity of water to which it relates was not to be used for any purpose to the injury of any machinery then in use by said Fuller on said dam. The language used seems in an inartificial way to impose such a limitation as to make the 200 inch right subject to the water privilege used at the date of the award in operating the machinery referred to. At any rate, the bill alleges and the answer of the defendant, Bugbee, admits that the right of Bugbee to draw the 200 inches of water is subject to the right of Gates. Bugbee's Third Right is treated as the pleadings treat it, and that right is held to be subject to the right of Gates to the use of the water "needed to operate the machinery, or the equivalent of the machinery, used by Fuller at the date of the award.".

These holdings sustain the action of the Court of Chancery and make it unnecessary to decide other questions discussed in argument.

The decretal order of the Court of Chancery is affirmed, and the cause is remanded to be further proceeded with.

CITY OF MONTPELIER ET AL. *v.* BARRE AND MONTPELIER

TRACTION & POWER CO.

May Term, 1903.

Present: TYLER, MUNSON, START, WATSON, STAFFORD, and HASELTON, JJ.

Opinion filed November 25, 1903.

Street Railway—Franchise—Condition—Consolidation— Transfers.

A traction company operating a street railway in a city under a franchise fixing the fare in such city and providing that the company should give transfers to all of its own lines, which acquires the right of another company, operating a street railway in another city under a franchise fixing the fare in that city and providing that such company should give transfers to all of its own lines, and which thereafterwards operates a consolidated line in and between said cities, cannot be compelled to issue to its patrons in one city transfers to its line in the other city.

PETITION FOR MANDAMUS. Heard on petition, answer, and evidence filed, at the May Term, 1903.

Frederick P. Carleton for the petitioner.

The powers in the charter of the Consolidated Lighting Company, so far as they were purchased by the respondent, merged into that company. Beach on Corp. § 360; *Town* v. *Whitworth,* 117 U. S. 139.

The franchise must be construed most favorably to the public. *Wabash R. R. Co.* v. *Depianer,* 52 Oh. St. 262; *Railway Co.* v. *Railway Co.,* 127 Ind. 369; *Railway Co.* v. *James,* 34 Fed. 579; *R. R. Co.* v. *Chicago,* 121 Ill. 176; *Stein* v. *Water Co.,* 141 U. S. 67.

Richard A. Hoar and *Rufus E. Brown* for the respondent.

HASELTON, J. This is a petition for a writ of mandamus. The petitioners are the City of Montpelier and Frank M. Corry, its mayor, who petitions on his own behalf and on behalf of all the citizens and inhabitants of the city of Montpelier. The defendant is a corporation operating lines of street railway within the cities of Barre and Montpelier and the town of Berlin. Its lines or systems have been so connected that it now operates a continuous line from the city of Montpelier through the town of Berlin to the city of Barre; and the petition is for a writ of mandamus directing the defendant to issue to its Montpelier patrons transfers to the lines of the defendant in Berlin and Barre. The testimony, however, establishes that the defendant carries a pas-

senger over its lines in the city of Montpelier and the town of
Berlin to the Barre line on payment of a single five cent fare.

The defendant was incorporated by an act of the Legislature in 1892. February 10, 1896, the city council of the
city of Barre granted it the right to construct and operate a
street railway over various streets of said city, and made it a
condition of the grant that the fare for riding upon the lines
of the company, within the city limits, should be five cents,
and that the company should give transfer tickets to all of
its own lines. At this time the defendant had no authority
under its charter to construct or operate a street railway
within the limits of Montpelier.

July 8, 1896, the City Council of the city of Montpelier
granted to the Consolidated Lighting Company, a corporation,
the right to construct and operate an electric railway over
various streets in Montpelier. It was a condition of this grant
that the fare for riding upon the lines of the grantee within
the limits of Montpelier should be five cents, and that the
grantee should give transfer tickets to all of its own lines.
June 16, 1896, the selectmen of the town of Berlin granted
to the Consolidated Lighting Company the right to construct
and operate a street railway over certain streets in that town.
It was provided that the fare within the town limits should
be five cents, and that the grantee should give transfers to
all of its own lines. The Consolidated Lighting Company,
to which the Montpelier and Berlin grants were made as recited, had no authority to construct or operate a street railway in Barre.

Afterwards, under legislative authority, and in accordance with a previous agreement, the defendant company took
an assignment of the rights, privileges, and franchises of the
Consolidated Lighting Company in respect to the construction

and operation of lines of street railway in Montpelier and Berlin, and so succeeded by operation of law to all the obligations of the latter company in respect to fares and transfers. But these obligations were neither diminished nor augmented by the assignment.

Later, the city of Montpelier granted to the defendant the right to construct and operate a line of street railway which would connect the lines hereinbefore referred to; and at and before the date of the bringing of this petition the defendant had in operation a line of street railway from within the city of Montpelier through the town of Berlin into the city of Barre and also a branch line in the city of Montpelier and a branch line in the city of Barre. This last named grant or franchise contained nothing such that by accepting and acting under it the defendant obligated itself to issue to its Montpelier patrons transfer tickets to its lines in the city of Barre; nor can we find from the evidence taken that the defendant has in any other way become so obligated.

None of the rights or obligations of the defendant with respect to its road within the limits of Barre were either directly or indirectly derived from or imposed by the city of Montpelier. Neither the city of Montpelier nor its mayor nor the Montpelier patrons of the defendant's road can complain because the defendant requires of a person riding on its road within the limits of the city of Barre payment of the fare which that city permits it to charge.

No consideration is given to questions not arising upon facts found or conceded, nor to questions unnecessary to a decision of the case.

The petition is dismissed with costs.

WILLIAM L. SOWLES' ADMR. *v.* ALEXANDER SARTWELL.

October Term, 1903.

Present: ROWELL, C. J., MUNSON, START, WATSON, and STAFFORD, JJ.

Opinion filed November 30, 1903.

Case Presented—Sufficiency—Verdict—Conclusiveness—Motion to Recommit—Decree against Administrator.

It is for the appellant in chancery to furnish this Court a case that affords a foundation for the legal question sought to be raised.

A special verdict is conclusive in a subsequent chancery suit between the same parties.

An orator is bound to show the amount of a payment properly chargeable to the defendant.

A motion to recommit a master's report is addressed to the discretion of the chancellor.

One who brings a bill as administrator cannot complain because a decree is made against him in his representative capacity.

APPEAL IN CHANCERY. Heard on pleadings, master's report, and orator's exceptions thereto, at the March Term, 1903, Franklin County, *Tyler,* Chancellor. Decree overruling the exceptions and for the defendant to recover the balance found due. The orator appealed.

E. A. Sowles and *R. O. Sturtevant* for the orator.

C. G. Austin & Sons and *E. A. Ayres* for the defendant.

STAFFORD, J. The orator, in his brief, claims that the master erred in receiving and rejecting various pieces of evidence, but, save in one instance only, the report and the case as presented here afford no basis for raising the question. It is necessary that the report, either in itself or by reference to exhibits or testimony, which the advancing party spreads before us, should furnish the foundation for the legal question sought to be raised. It is not enough that the party, in his brief, or even in his exceptions filed to the report, states such supposed matters of fact.

The bill seeks an accounting for the proceeds of a farm carried on by the defendant at the halves. The orator claims that the lease was for one year only. The defendant claims it was for five. In a previous action at law, wherein the defendant was plaintiff and the orator and one acting under his orders were defendants, the same question had been involved, and the verdict of the jury had been taken with a special finding, which was that the lease was for five years. The master, finding that the real parties were the same in both cases, treated the verdict as conclusive, refused to receive evidence offered by the orator to show that the lease was for one year only, and found the fact that the lease was for five years solely upon the basis of the verdict. Whether he was correct in so doing he submits to the Court, and that question is thus saved to the orator. It cannot avail him, however, for "such findings are a part of the verdict and effective as such." *Lamoille County Bank* v. *Hunt,* 72 Vt. 357, 361.

The defendant was bound to pay one-half the taxes; but the orator, as the advancing party, was bound to show what such half was. Instead of doing so, he deliberately and against warning left the evidence in such a state that the master was unable to ascertain the fact,—apparently proceeding upon the theory that the duty was upon the defendant to furnish the proof. After the report was drawn and exhibited, but before it was filed, he requested the master to open the case and receive further testimony upon this point, which request, instead of granting, the master referred to the Court of Chancery. In that Court the orator moved to recommit the report for the same purpose and the motion was denied. Whether the report should have been recommitted was, in the circumstances, a question of discretion and, no abuse thereof appearing, is not revisable here. *Lovejoy* v. *Churchill,* 29 Vt. 151.

The bill is in the name of the orator as administrator, and the decree, being for a balance in the defendant's favor growing out of his deal with the orator in that capacity, was made against him in his representative character. It is urged that this was error, and reliance is placed upon *Rich* v. *Sowles, Admr.* 64 Vt. 408, wherein it was held that an administrator could not contract a debt against the estate; that a writ at law against him as administrator ran against him personally, the title being words of description merely; and that a judgment following the writ in this respect was not a judgment against the estate, but only against the individual. We see no ground for the orator to complain when a decree is rendered against him in the very name and capacity in which he prays for a decree in his favor. Whether he will have it to pay himself or will be reimbursed from the estate, is another question, and one that is not determined by the form of the decree.

Decree affirmed and cause remanded.

CHARLES C. MILLER *v.* LESTER WILBUR.

October Term, 1903.

Present: ROWELL, C. J., MUNSON, START, WATSON, and STAFFORD, JJ.

Opinion filed November 30, 1903.

Common Counts—Special Promise.

One who buys property subject to a chattel mortgage, assuming the
debt as a part of the purchase price, and afterwards expressly
promises the mortgagee to pay it, is not liable to an action of
general assumpsit by the mortgagee.

GENERAL ASSUMPSIT.   Plea, the general issue. Trial by
jury at the September Term, 1902, Windham County, *Tyler,*
J., presiding.   Judgment for the plaintiff on verdict ordered.
The defendant excepted.

F. D. E. Stowe for the defendant.

None of the common counts is adapted to the case. The
executed special agreement which is maintainable under the
common counts is confined to goods sold, work done or money
passed. *Way* v. *Wakefield,* 7 Vt. 228; *Royalton* v. *Turnpike
Co.,* 14 Vt. 321.

Defendant's promise was *collateral* to that of the maker
of the notes; so the count must be special.   7 Pet. 113; *Arbuckle* v. *Templeton,* 65 Vt. 205.

Herbert G. Barber for the plaintiff.

The common counts are sufficient where defendant has
received the plaintiff's money or its *equivalent. Burnap* v.
Partridge, 3 Vt. 144; *Kinney* v. *Pearsons,* 41 Vt. 386.

The contract is completely executed, and so the common counts will lie. *Royalton* v. *Turnpike Co.*, 14 Vt. 311; Groot v. *Story*, 41 Vt. 533; *Bradley* v. *Phillips*, 52 Vt. 517.

STAFFORD, J. Miller, the plaintiff, sold certain goods to Luther Wilbur, taking a mortgage back to secure a part of the price. Luther Wilbur in turn sold the goods to Lester Wilbur, the defendant, subject to the mortgage, and Lester assumed the mortgage debt as a part of the price, and also promised the plaintiff directly that he would pay. In consideration of which the plaintiff, who might lawfully have taken possession, there being no stipulation to the contrary in the mortgage, forebore to do so for a time; but afterwards, the defendant failing to keep his promise, foreclosed, applied the proceeds, and brought this action for the balance. The declaration is the common counts in assumpsit accompanied by a specification of the amount of the mortgage notes less the proceeds of the foreclosure sale. The plea is the general issue. The defendant excepted to all evidence of the foregoing facts upon the ground that it was not admissible under the pleadings, and that is the question here.

The only one of the common counts which could possibly be appropriate is that which declares upon a promise in consideration of goods sold and delivered by the plaintiff to the defendant, and we think it would be a stretch of language and of reason to say that the plaintiff's forbearance to take the goods into his possession constituted a sale and delivery. The plaintiff did sell and deliver to the original mortgagor, and he in turn sold and delivered to the defendant. There was never a novation; the original purchaser was not released by the plaintiff; and the only consideration moving from the plaintiff to the defendant was the temporary forbearance.

We think, therefore, that the exception must be sustained.

It was suggested that the case falls within the principle that when a special contract has been fully executed by the plaintiff leaving nothing to be done except for the defendant to pay money, general assumpsit may be maintained. But that is true only in cases where the service performed under the special contract would raise an implied promise if there were no special promise,—not in cases like the present, where there would be no contract liability whatever, except for the special promise. *Hersey* v. *Assurance Co.,* 75 Vt. 441.

Judgment reversed and cause remanded.

ADELAIDE E. BUCK *v.* TROY AQUEDUCT CO.

January Term, 1903.

Present: TYLER, MUNSON, START, WATSON, and STAFFORD, JJ.

Opinion filed November 30, 1903.

Corporations—By-laws—Modification—Directors—Number—
V. S. 3717—Corporate Action—Course of Business—
Signature of Note—Informality—Husband and Wife—
Action by Wife—V. S. 2644—Transfer of Note—Evi-
dence—Relevancy.

Though the by-laws of a corporation provide it shall have five directors, yet, if with the consent of all the stockholders, a board of only three directors conduct the business of the corporation for a long series of years, such by-laws are changed accordingly, the charter being silent as to the number of directors, and V. S. 3717 requiring only three.

Two of its board of three directors can bind a corporation in the transaction of its ordinary business, without the consent, or even knowledge, of the third.

The borrowing money to use in repairing its property and giving the corporation's note therefor, is an act in the transaction of its ordinary business.

That one of the three directors acts in the double capacity of agent for both borrower and lender, does not invalidate such note when the corporation suffers no detriment thereby.

A note to which a director signs the corporate name only is valid, the corporation having only three stockholders, who are also its only directors, and having no other officers, and two of said directors being present when the note is signed and taking part in the transaction.

When a husband transferred to his wife, without indorsement, a note which he then owned, payable to a third person, or bearer, as collateral security for money borrowed from her by him, which he still owes and which is more than the amount of the note, she is the lawful owner of the note and may maintain an action thereon against the maker.

A husband who, without indorsement, transfers to his wife, as collateral security for a debt which he owes her, a note owned by him and payable to a third person, or bearer, does not become bound to her in any way thereby.

An offer in the alternative must be taken in the view less favorable to the offerer.

Evidence that while one held a note as agent of the payees, he misappropriated money which during that time he had received as the agent of the maker, does not tend to show payment of the note.

GENERAL ASSUMPSIT, with specification relying on a promissory note. Pleas, the general issue with notice denying the execution of said note; payment, and Statute of Limitations. Heard on the report of a referee and exceptions thereto, at the September Term, 1902, Orleans County, *Haselton*, J., presiding. Judgment for the defendant. The plaintiff excepted.

Said note was payable to "Jesse Buck estate, or bearer," and was signed "Troy Aqueduct Company," and not otherwise.

The other facts sufficiently appear in the opinion.

Young & Young for the plaintiff.

The defendant can not raise the question of its corporate existence, not having denied same in its pleadings. *Boston Type Foundry* v. *Spooner*, 5 Vt. 93; *Lord* v. *Bigelow*, 8 Vt. 445; *Aetna Ins. Co.* v. *Wires*, 28 Vt. 93.

The note was so executed as to bind the defendant. *Bank of Middlebury* v. *R. Co.*, 30 Vt. 159; *Foote* v. *R. Co.*, 32 Vt. 633; *State ex. rel. Page* v. *Smith*, 48 Vt. 66; *Waite* v. *Mining Co.*, 37 Vt. 608.

The fact that the corporation took and used the money procured on this note ratified the same. *Windham Prov. Inst.* v. *Sprague*, 43 Vt. 502; *Bank* v. *Fassett*, 42 Vt. 432.

The note has a sufficiently definite payee.   *Shaw* v. *Smith*, 150 Mass. 166; *Petier* v. *Babillion*, 45 Mich, 384; *McKinney* v. *Harter*, 43 Am. Dec. 96; *Cox* v. *Beltzhoover*, 47 Am. Dec. 145; *Robertson* v. *Seward*, 1 M. & G. 511, 39 Eng. C. L. 882; *U. S.* v. *White*, 37 Am. Dec. 374; *Grant* v. *Vaughn*, 3 Burr. 1516.

A note payable to A. B., or bearer, is equivalent to a note payable to bearer.   4 Am. & Eng. Enc. of Law, 134; *Eddy* v. *Bond*, 19 Me. 61; *Doyle* v. *Weeks*, 4 Mass. 451; *Truesdale* v. *Thompson*, 12 Met. 565; *Hutchins* v. *Low*, 13 N. J. L. 246.

The plaintiff is the bearer of the note and can recover thereon. *Bank* v. *Adams*, 70 Vt. 132; *Blaney* v. *Pelton*, 60 Vt. 275; *Fletcher* v. *Fletcher*, 29 Vt. 98; *Boardman* v. *Rogers*, 17 Vt. 589; *Ellis* v. *Watkins' Est.*, 73 Vt. 371.

Plaintiff had a valid equitable claim against her husband. *Ballard* v. *Goodno*, 73 Vt. 88; *Hackett* v. *Moxley*, 65 Vt. 71; *Atkins* v. *Atkins' Est.*, 69 Vt. 270; *Purdy* v. *Purdy's Est.*, 67 Vt. 50.

Cook & Williams for the defendant.

Neither husband nor wife can contract with the other, so the note could not be transferred by the plaintiff to her husband. 6 L. R. A. 559; 12 L. R. A. 600; V. S. 2644.

The note was not executed by defendant. The charter provided for by-laws, and the by-laws provided for five directors. There were only three directors of the defendant, and only two took part in the transaction, or even knew about it. Morawetz on Priv. Corp. (2nd Ed.) §§ 474, 475, 476, 503, 512, 517, 531, 532.

D. H. Buck could not act as the agent of both the payee and the maker of the note. Morawetz on Priv. Corp. §§ 520 and 528.

STAFFORD, J. The defendant is sued as a corporation. In the earlier stages of the case some question seems to have been made in regard to its legal existence, but that is not urged in this court, and upon the findings, the defendant is to be treated as having been organized under the statute creating it, No. 101, Acts 1861. Its by-laws provided that it should have five directors, a secretary, treasurer, collector and superintendent,—all to be elected annually. Every year from 1864 to 1881, it chose a full board, but from 1882 to 1892, it chose only three, although no change appears to have been made in the by-laws. In June 1893, the time which becomes important here, the three directors were Aiken, Buck and Hammond, who were likewise the only stockholders. Hammond owned but one share; Buck owned seven and Aiken the remaining twenty-three. No officers except directors had been chosen in many years. When such were last chosen, Buck had been collector and treasurer and Aiken secretary and superintendent, and each had continued to act in those respective capacities, and was acting as such and as director at the time in question. Hammond took no part in the management of the business. The corporation was now in need of money to repair its aqueduct. Buck, as agent of his father's heirs, had in his hands $500 belonging to that estate, and this, he, as such agent, loaned to the corporation, writing and receiving therefor a note which Aiken signed with the corporation's name, "Troy Aqueduct Co.," only, and the money was used in making the repairs. The note is dated June 23, 1893, and runs "to Jesse Buck estate or bearer." Hammond knew nothing about it. The action is brought by a subsequent holder as bearer, and thus is based solely upon the instrument itself, and the question is whether the note is binding upon the corporation. In order to determine this point it may be necessary to consider whether Aiken, Buck and Hammond constituted a legal board of directors. In dealing with the question alluded to at the outset, whether the defendant is a legal corporation or merely a voluntary association, the referee has reported facts which may aid in the decision of the present inquiry. After finding that the defendant was legally organized, provided the evidence is held to warrant him in so doing, (and about that no question is now made), he goes on to say that, if the evidence does not justify him in finding the due organization and legal existence of the corporation, he still finds "that said stockholders have transacted all business of the Troy Aqueduct Co. since March 29, 1862, as a corporation and not as an association, and have held themselves out to the world, and are now acting and holding themselves out to the world, as such, and that, from that time down to the giving of the note in suit, said corporation has controlled and managed all property and rights of said association the same as if such property and rights had been the property and rights of said corporation," and, in another connection,—"that the stockholders, who were all members of said association, after said meeting of March 29, 1862, held themselves out to the world and transacted business as a corporation,"—"that the present stockholders, who have succeeded to the ownership of the stock of said association, are now transacting business as a corporation and holding the Troy Aqueduct Co. out to the world as such."

Thus the findings appear to be clear and satisfactory that Aiken, Buck and Hammond, who were all the stockholders of the company and consequently the only persons eligible as directors under our statute (V. S. 3677), were carrying on the business of the corporation through a board of three directors, for if the corporation was acting at all it was acting through that board. Although Hammond himself did not act as director, yet these findings compel us to say that as a stockholder he did act through this board by consenting that the corporation should continue its business through and by means of it. The stockholders for a long series of years had been doing the same. In such circumstances it must be held that the by-law requiring a board of five was changed by the unanimous consent of the stockholders, and that the board of three was a legal board,—the act of incorporation being silent as to the number of directors and the statute, if it applies at all to corporations by special act, being satisfied with a board of that number. V. S. 3717.

That a by-law may be modified by unanimous consent of the stockholders, to a regular course of corporate action inconsistent therewith, is well settled. Thomp. Corp., sec. 945; Taylor Private Corp. (5th ed.), sec. 197; Clark & Marshall Private Corp., vol. 3, 1952, and the numerous cases cited by those authors.

Buck and Aiken, being a majority, had the power to bind the defendant in the transaction of its ordinary business without the concurrence of Hammond and even without notice to him. *Bank of Middlebury* v. *R. Co.*, 30 Vt. 169; *Foote* v. *R. Co.*, 32 Vt. 633; *Waite* v. *Mining Co.*, 37 Vt. 608; *State ex. rel. Page* v. *Smith*, 48 Vt. 266.

The borrowing of money for its use, and, in the circumstances stated, the giving of the corporation's note therefor, was an act "in the transaction of its ordinary business." Such is the well established American rule. Thomp. Corp., secs. 3988, 3989.

That Buck acted in a double capacity, as agent for borrower and lender alike, does not invalidate the note. The corporation has not been imposed upon, and has undertaken only to pay back with interest the money it has received and used in its business, which is no more than the law would have required it to do without a note. It has no offset against the Buck estate and so is put in no worse plight by being required to pay to bearer. The rule invoked was intended to protect principals from the wrong of their agents, not to enable principals to wrong others through their agents. If wrong would otherwise be presumed from the existence of the double relation, it is rebutted by the findings.

Neither do we think that there is any such informality in the signature as makes the note invalid in the circumstances of the case.

The next question is whether the plaintiff, who is the wife of Buck, can recover upon the note. Her husband became the owner of it when the estate was, without administration divided among the heirs; and being already indebted to his wife and about to borrow of her a further sum, he delivered to her this note as collateral security for the whole, which was more than the amount of the note. She has never been paid any part of her debt and has held the note in her exclusive possession and control ever since she received it.

That the plaintiff is a married woman is no reason why she may not recover upon a contract between herself and the defendant. V. S. 2644. Presenting, as she does, a note payable to bearer, she is *prima facie* entitled to recover thereon. V. S. 2307. *Limerick Bank* v. *Adams*, 70 Vt. 132, 40 Atl. 166.

Then the only question is whether the facts above stated rebut the presumption and show that she is not the lawful holder of the note. Her husband is not a party to the note, as it reads; he has not endorsed it, nor become bound to her in any way by delivering it to her. He has simply put it in her hands as security. His debt to her is one the law recognizes and will enforce if appealed to by a bill in equity. The only difference between such a debt and one not between husband and wife is that it cannot be enforced by the ordinary action at law. How then can it be said that she is not the lawful holder? The facts instead of showing that she is not, show that she is.

One question of evidence arises. When the note was delivered to the wife it was overdue. We quote from the report:

"The defendant offered to show that Buck from the date of the note in suit to the time of its alleged transfer, collected and received moneys as collector of said corporation to the amount of more than $600; that he did not pay out said money for any purpose other than for his own private matters or to pay the note in suit; that at the time of said alleged transfer to his wife, said Buck was very short of money and wanted it for immediate use, as tending to prove that said Buck did 'take of the funds of said corporation between said two dates for his own private use and that the same is and was a payment on said note between said dates. To this offer the plaintiff objected, and the evidence was excluded subject to the defendant's exception."

The note was given June 23, 1893. Buck held it as agent for the estate until September, 1894, when it became his and was thereafter held by him as his own until he delivered it to his wife in December, 1896. Suppose that while holding the note as agent for the heirs he did collect and keep or pay out for his private use moneys of the defendant sufficient in amount to pay it; that does not show, nor tend to show, that the note was paid. The offer was not limited to the time when he held the note as owner and all the money may have been received while he held it as agent. The offer is in the alternative, to show that he either applied the money on this note or to his private use, and must be taken in the view less favorable to the one making the offer, which is that he used the money for himself and did not apply it on the note he was holding for others. An agent, whose principal has entrusted him with a note against A, is also, as it happens, agent for A, and, as such, receives and misappropriates A's money. Can that be said to constitute payment of the note, or even to tend to show it? Yet that is the case made by the offer.

Judgment reversed, and judgment for the plaintiff for the amount of the note.

ARTHUR DELPHIA v. RUTLAND RAILROAD CO.

October Term, 1903.

Present: ROWELL, C. J., TYLER, MUNSON, START, and STAFFORD, JJ.

Opinion filed November 30, 1903.

Railroads—Duty to Fence—V. S. 3874-3877.

The duty to fence the sides of its road imposed upon a railroad company by V. S. 3874-3877, is owed, at any given point, to the immediate abutter only.

When the side of a railroad opposite land of two adjoining abutters is unfenced, and a horse lawfully on the land of one, wrongfully goes onto the land of the other, and thence onto the track, and is there killed by a locomotive, the company is not liable to the owner of the horse for not maintaining a fence.

CASE for killing plaintiff's horse which escaped from private land onto defendant's track. Heard on an agreed statement, at the June Term, 1903, Addison County, *Watson*, J., presiding. Judgment for the defendant. The plaintiff excepted. The facts sufficiently appear in the opinion.

Cushman & Russell for the plaintiff.

V. S. 3877, as construed by *Quimby & Rogan* v. *B. & M. R. Co.*, 71 Vt. 301, fixes the liability of the defendant. See also *Hardwood's Admr'x* v. *R. Co.*, 67 Vt. 664.

Statutes upon this subject rest upon the police power. *Thorpe* v. *R. Co.*, 27 Vt. 140; Elliott on R., Vol. 3, § 1182.

If defendant is liable for injuries to animals coming onto the track from a highway, whether because of a defective fence or a defective cattle guard, but is not so liable when the animal comes from private land unless they are lawfully on such land, then the owners of animals injured because of defective cattle guards at *farm crossings* can not recover unless their animals were lawfully on the premises whence they came upon the track.

The law in respect to maintaining fences and cattle guards is the same. *Trow* v. *R. Co.*, 24 Vt. 487.

P. M. Meldon and *H. H. Powers* for the defendant.

The duty of fencing its tracks imposed upon a railroad company by V. S. 3874, is to afford protection to adjoining owners alone. The Legislature in a separate section (V. S. 3871) also imposes the duty upon railroads to maintain cattle guards at crossings. And while a right of action is given in a single section (V. S. 3877), for the violation of either provision, the principles upon which the right is based in each case are different.

The horse was unlawfully upon the land whence it went upon the track, and the duty was to the individual owner, or rightful occupier at that point, and not to the plaintiff. Redfield on Railways, p. 375; Sher. & Red. on Neg., p. 368; Field on Corp., p. 691; Pierce on Railroads, 412; *Rust* v. *Low*, 6 Mass. 90; *Eames* v. *R. Co.*, 98 Mass. 560; *Trow* v. *R. Co.*, 24 Vt. 488; *Jackson* v. *R. Co.*, 25 Vt. 150; *Hurd* v. *R. Co.*, 25 Vt. 123; *Bemis* v. *R. Co.*, 42 Vt. 375; *Congdon* v. *R. Co.*, 56 Vt. 390; *McDonnell* v. *R. Co.*, 115 Mass. 564.

STAFFORD, J. The Vermont Statutes require a railroad to construct and maintain on the sides of its road a good and sufficient fence (3874), and provides that if it fails to do so any person aggrieved may construct it, in which case the selectmen of the town may appraise the value and the railroad shall pay (3875); but declare that the provisions requiring the construction and maintenance of fences shall not apply to a case where the railroad has settled with and paid the land

owner for building and maintaining them (3876); and if
the person so paid for keeping up the fence neglects to do so
the railroad may do it and recover the expense of such person
or his grantee (3876); and that until such fences, as well as
sufficient cattle guards at farm and highway crossings, are
duly made, the railroad shall be liable for the damage done
by agents or engines to cattle, horses, or other animals thereon, if occasioned by want of such fences and guards (3877).

The plaintiff occupied a lot abutting to the west upon
the defendant's right of way. There was no fence between
this lot and the railroad. Next south of the plaintiff's lay
the lot of another owner also abutting to the west upon the
defendant's right of way, and likewise unfenced. The plaintiff's horse, which was tethered to a stone upon the plaintiff's
land, becoming frightened by a passing train, ran with the
weight into the lot of this adjoining owner and from that lot
to the track, in front of the locomotive, and was killed. The
question is whether the plaintiff can recover the value of the
horse; and this depends upon whether the defendant's duty
to maintain a fence at the place where the horse passed from
private land to the defendant's right of way was a duty from
the defendant to the plaintiff as one of the general public
or only from the defendant to the abutting owner at that
point,—for the horse was not rightfully upon the land of the
abutting owner directly from which he escaped to the track.

The plaintiff contends that the duty was one which the
defendant owed to the general public; but this cannot be held
without disregarding that section of the statute which declares that there shall be no liability for want of a fence in
case the land owner has been paid or settled with for building it; for that clearly recognizes the right of the abutting
owner to waive the building of the fence against his own

land, a thing he could not do if it was a duty from the railroad to others than himself and those rightfully in possession under him. In this respect the statute distinguishes between fences and cattle guards. Whether a distinction is made between cattle guards at public or highway crossings and those at private or farm crossings, we are not called upon to decide; nor are we bound to find the statute wise or even logical and consistent throughout. It is enough that the two sections, having stood side by side for more than fifty years, must be read together, and each, if possible, be given some force.

We do not understand that our decision is in conflict with any previous holding of this court. In *Quimby & Rogan* v. *B. & M. R. Co.*, 71 Vt. 301, 45 Atl. 223, the horse escaped through a defective cattle guard at a highway crossing. Such was the fact in *Harwood* v. *Bennington & Rutland R. Co.*, 67 Vt. 664, 32 Atl. 721. And those are the only cases claimed to be inconsistent with the view we are now adopting. On the other hand, in *Smith* v. *Barre R. Co.*, 64 Vt. 21, 23 Atl. 632, the principle of the present decision was distinctly recognized and applied. There the plaintiff's horse was being pastured by one whose pasture itself did not abut upon the railroad, but whose meadow, adjoining the pasture, did. The horse escaped from the pasture to the meadow and thence, for want of a sufficient fence, to the track. The case turned upon the question whether the horse was rightfully in the meadow; and it was considered that he was, because, it being the duty of the owner of the pasture to confine him, he was in the meadow either by consent or fault of the abutting owner, and so the owner of the horse stood in the right of the owner of the meadow. "The statute requiring a railroad to fence its track," said the court in that case, "is for the protection of the land owners through whose land it runs."

Judgment affirmed.

IN RE JOYSLIN'S ESTATE.

October Term, 1902.

Present: ROWELL, C. J., TYLER, MUNSON, START, STAFFORD, and
HASELTON, JJ.

Opinion filed November 30, 1903.

Inheritance Tax—Nature of—Subject of—Decedent's Credits
—Situs of—No. 46, Acts 1896.

Debts due a deceased person from nonresidents of Vermont should not
be included in fixing the amount of estate subject to the collateral inheritance tax imposed by No. 46, Acts 1896.

The collateral inheritance tax imposed by No. 46, Acts 1896, is a tax
upon the right to succeed to estate left vacant by death.

Debts due resident decedents from nonresident debtors have their
situs in the place where the debtor resides, pass by the law of
that place, and are not subject to our law.

APPEAL from a decree of the Probate Court adjudging
the entire estate of Clara E. Joyslin subject to the collateral
inheritance tax imposed by No. 46, Acts 1896. Heard on an
agreed statement, at the December Term, 1901, Windsor
County, *Stafford, J.,* presiding. Judgment *pro forma* that
the entire estate is subject to said tax, and that said estate
should pay to the State of Vermont, as such tax, the sum of
four hundred thirty-nine dollars and thirty-nine cents. The
estate excepted.

Said Clara E. Joyslin, at the time of her death, lived at Rochester, Vt. She died testate about March 23, 1901. Her will was duly established before the Probate Court within and for the district of Hartford in this State, and an administrator with the will annexed appointed by said court. The will was never proved, nor letters of administration granted thereon, in any other state.

The following is quoted from said agreed statement: "At the decease of the testatrix she owned in her own name two notes for four hundred dollars each, signed by James and Nancy McNeil, residents of the State of Illinois, and secured by mortgages on real property in that state. Also a note for four hundred and fifty dollars signed by one George W. West, a resident of Illinois, and secured by a mortgage of real property situated in that state. This last named note and mortgage were taken in the name of George W. Benedict of Geneseo, in the State of Illinois, but for her sole use and benefit. At her decease the testatrix had a deposit amounting to forty-four dollars and seventy-five cents in the Farmer's National Bank of said Geneseo, for which a certificate of deposit had been issued. The proceeds of said notes and certificate of deposit have been remitted to the administrator in this state; and out of such proceeds he has already paid legacies under said will to Carrie A. Hayward and Julia S. Duffer, both residents of Illinois, of five hundred dollars each, less fifty dollars retained by him to pay the tax in question upon said legacies, should the court so determine. By the terms of said will these legacies were not required to be paid out of any specified fund."

It further appears from said agreed statement that at the time of her death the testatrix also owned the following property: One-half of a bond for two thousand dollars, signed by residents of Iowa and secured by a mortgage on real property in that state; the sum of five hundred thirty-seven dollars and twelve cents on deposit in the German's Savings Bank of Davenport, Iowa. All of said notes, bonds, and deposits were "physically absent from the State of Vermont" at the death of the testatrix.

The estate, after the payment of debts and expenses of administration, amounted to the sum of eight thousand seven hundred eighty dollars and thirty-six cents, and was all "devised and bequeathed to persons not related to the testatrix and to persons only collaterally related to her."

Marvelle C. Webber for the estate.

The right of the state to impose a succession tax is based upon its dominion over the property within its bounds. *Matter of James*, 144 N. Y. 6; *Frothingham* v. *Shaw*, 175 Mass. 59; *Callahan* v. *Woodbridge*, 171 Mass. 595.

The debts in question were not "within the jurisdiction of this state." *Abbott* v. *Coburn*, 28 Vt. 664; *Bullock* v. *Rogers*, 16 Vt. 294; *Vaughn* v. *Barrett*, 5 Vt. 333; *Purple* v. *Whitehead*, 49 Vt. 187.

J. E. Cushman, Commissioner of State Taxes, for the State.

No. 46, Acts 1896, is copied from the law of Massachusetts. The courts of that state hold that personal property for the purpose of this tax has its situs at the domicile of the deceased. *Frothingham* v. *Shaw*, 175 Mass. 59. To the same effect is the case of State Tax on Foreign-Held Bonds, 15 Wall, 300, 324; *In Re Dingman*, 66 App. Div. 228; *Bonapart* v. *Tax Court*, 104 U. S. 592; *McKeen* v. *County*, 49 Penn. St. 519; *In Re Henry Bronson*, 150 N. Y. 1; *Kirtland* v. *Hotchkiss*, 100 U. S. 491; *State* v. *Bank*, 74 Vt. 246.

The tax in question is not a tax on property, but is a succession tax. *Minot* v. *Winthrop,* 162 Mass. 113; *Maryland* v. *Dalrymple,* 3 L. R. A. 373; *Walker* v. *People,* 192 Ill. 106; *Plummer* v. *Coler,* 178 U. S. 115.

STAFFORD, J. The case calls for a construction of No. 46, Acts of 1896, providing for a tax upon collateral inheritances.

The decedent died domiciled in this state and leaving a will, which has been duly established, by the provisions of which the whole estate passes collaterally. The question is, whether debts that were due to her from non-residents of Vermont are to be included in fixing the amount of the estate subject to the tax.

The act applies in terms to "all property within the jurisdiction of this state . . .whether tangible or intangible, which shall pass by will or by the intestate laws of this state." What is meant by the phrase, "within the jurisdiction of this state?" Must it not mean within its probate jurisdiction? If so, these debts were not within the jurisdiction, for immediately upon the death of the creditor they became *bona notabilia,* or assets in the jurisdiction where the debtor resided. Nothing is better settled in this state. *Vaughn* v. *Barrett,* 5 Vt. 333; *Heirs of Porter* v. *Heydock,* 6 Vt. 374; *Bullock's Admr.* v. *Rogers,* 16 Vt. 294; *Abbott* v. *Coburn,* 28 Vt. 664; *Purple* v. *Whithed,* 49 Vt. 187; *Walton* v. *Hall,* 66 Vt. 455, 29 Atl. 803.

That the act applies to estates both real and personal of non residents is apparent from the first section, which declares that it shall apply to all property "whether tangible or intangible," and "whether belonging to inhabitants of this state or not" provided it be within the jurisdiction of the state and passing by will or the intestate laws thereof. The same thing also appears from section 10, which provides that the court of probate having *either principal or ancilliary* jurisdiction of the settlement of the estate of the decedent shall have jurisdiction to hear and determine all questions in relation to said tax that may arise affecting any *devise, legacy or inheritance* under this act." Suppose, then, a non-resident die leaving debts due to him from residents of this state. Such have always been held subject to our probate jurisdiction and are evidently within the purview of the act. How, then, can we refuse to say that debts due to resident decedents from non-resident debtors are beyond our jurisdiction?

And what is meant by the phrase, "pass by will or by the intestate laws of this state?" Does it not mean, pass by virtue and force of the law of this state governing testate or intestate succession? If so, this portion of the estate did not pass by force of our law at all, for that law had no force in the domicile of the debtors. It passed by force and virtue of the law of those jurisdictions. If they recognized our law as the rule to be followed in distributing the personal estate, just as they would have recognized the law of the place where a contract was made as the law of the contract, that did not make it that the property passed by force of the law of this state, but only that it passed in the same manner as it would have passed by our law. It so happens that the states where these debtors resided do recognize the law of the decedent's domicile as the rule governing the descent of personal estate; but if they had resided elsewhere the rule might have been different. In Mississippi, for example, even personal estate, there situate, descends according to the statutes of Mississippi although the power was domiciled elsewhere. Hence it would be necessary to inquire in each instance whether the law of the *situs* permitted the estate to pass according to the law of the domicile, which is enough to show that it really passes by force and virtue of the law of the *situs*. If we should refuse to inquire whether the law of the *situs* did permit it, and should insist upon holding that the law of the domicile governs, we should be giving our law force beyond its territory and should be exacting a tax upon estate supposed to be passing to collaterals, when perhaps by force of the law of the *situs* it was prevented from passing to collaterals at all. Moreover, by our decisions, a foreign administrator has no authority. He cannot release and discharge a debt here so as to bind the resident administrator. *Vaughn* v. *Barret*, 5 Vt. 333. His authority depends upon the law of the state where the property to be administered is located, which may or may not be liberal enough to recognize it, which may require him to be appointed there, and may even forbid the appointment of a non-resident. If we should hold an administrator appointed here responsible for the tax upon personal property situated abroad, we should be treating him as clothed with authority which he might not possess, and which, if he did possess it, he would possess by virtue of the law of the other jurisdiction,—not by virtue of our law.

All agree that this is a tax upon the right to succeed to estate left vacant by death and is imposed by the sovereignty bestowing and regulating that right, in virtue of its authority to enforce contribution from those who become invested with property by its grace and power. The hand that passes the estate from one generation to another retains a portion as a sort of toll for the service. Which sovereignty is that? Clearly the one which has the right to say who shall succeed. And that, by the decisions of this court, is the sovereignty in which the assets are located, which in the case of debts is the place where the debtor resides. We have maintained the right

.of the ancillary jurisdiction, not merely to administer for the
protection of creditors, but even to proceed to final decree and
.distribution, although as matter of convenience and comity,
the proceeds may be remitted to the domicile; and we have
·explicitly held that the law governing the distribution is the
law of the place of administration, even when it proceeds, as
it does almost universally as to personal estate, in accordance
with the law of the domicile. *Heirs of Porter* v. *Heydock,*
.6 Vt. 374.

Equally pronounced is *Walton* v. *Hall,* 66 Vt. 455. John
Walton died domiciled in Vermont, leaving a will made in
Illinois while he was domiciled there, and leaving property
both real and personal in each state. The will was probated
in Illinois, but not in Vermont. A legatee, with the approval
·of the Illinois executor, made a settlement with the widow
in Vermont, by the terms of which, portions of the estate in
both jurisdictions were attempted to be disposed of. Later,
an administrator was appointed in Vermont, no notice being
taken of the will, and the validity of the settlement as to the
·different portions of the estate came in question. It was held
that the settlement was effective as to the estate situated in
Illinois, and of no effect as to the estate situated here. A part
·of the estate so held to have its *situs* in Illinois consisted of
debts due to the decedent from residents of Illinois; and a
·part so held to have its *situs* in Vermont consisted of debts
·due to the decedent from residents of this state. Thus was
the line sharply and positively drawn between the jurisdic-
·tions, and the right of the foreign probate court unequivocally
recognized. We quote briefly from the opinion by ROWELL,
J.: "The *situs* of the debts due evidenced by those notes was
in Illinois where. the debtors resided. The notes therefore
were assets in that jurisdiction and passed by the will and so

it was competent for the parties to deal with them as they
did." (P. 462.). "Inasmuch as there was property in Illinois
on which the will was to be operative, the proper probate
court of that state obviously had jurisdiction to probate it,
notwithstanding the testator was domiciled here at the time
of his death. This necessarily results from the independent
character of our state governments. Resort must be had to
the laws of the state to protect and to secure property within
it. Therefore, states take jurisdiction of the estates of deceased persons situate and found therein for the benefit of
those entitled thereto; and by comity they will sometimes
execute the law of the domicile of the decedent, instead of
their own law, as far as the descent and distribution of personal property are concerned. But this is a mere matter of
comity, and is done or not according to the will of the sov-
ereign."

We are aware that the courts of some other states have
reached an opposite conclusion. *Frothingham* v. *Shaw*, 175
Mass. 59; *Maryland* v. *Dalrymple*, 3 L. R. 372, 17 Atl. 82;
Re Est. of Swift, 18 L. R. A. 709, and note. But they have
also held otherwise touching the authority of the foreign administrator and the relation of the ancillary administration to
that of the domicile. We feel bound to follow our own decisions.

There is no occasion to question *Bullock* v. *Guilford*, 59
Vt. 517, 9 Atl. 360, for while the creditor lives there is no
doubt that debts owing to him attend his person and are taxable against him where he resides.

*The pro forma judgment of the county court is reversed
and judgment is entered that the estate pay to the State of
Vermont as the amount of the tax two hundred and sixteen*

dollars and eleven cents; this judgment to be certified to the probate court.

J. H. PARKER *v.* McKANNON BROS. & CO.

October Term, 1903.

Present: ROWELL, C. J., TYLER, MUNSON, WATSON, and STAFFORD, JJ.

Opinion filed December 2, 1903.

Contract—Breach during term of—Damages—Prospective —Evidence.

When parties, who have agreed that for a definite time, which has not yet expired, they will take and sell instruments made for them by another, refuse to take any more instruments, and the other is ready and offers to deliver, the latter may treat the contract as absolutely and finally broken.

In an action for breach of such a contract, both past and prospective damages may be recovered.

Immediately upon breach of such a contract a right of action accrues to the plaintiff, although he has then suffered no damage.

As bearing upon the value of such a contract to the plaintiff, evidence is admissible showing the cost of the instruments made under the contract, what portion of the cost was labor, how many instruments plaintiff could make per week, his business since the breach, and whether he could furnish instruments till the contract expired.

Questions, which the exceptions do not show were raised in the court below, will not be considered in the Supreme Court.

SPECIAL ASSUMPSIT upon a written contract. Plea, the general issue, with notice of special matter. Said notice has not been furnished the reporter. Trial by jury at the March Term, 1903, Chittenden County, *Start,* J., presid-

ing. General and special verdicts for plaintiff. Defendants'
motion to set aside verdicts overruled. Judgment *pro forma*
on verdicts. The defendant excepted.

The contract declared upon was executed by both plaintiff and defendants, was dated October 30, 1899, and provided, among other things, that the plaintiff should make and
furnish to the defendants, exclusively, at their store in Burlington, a certain musical instrument known as the Parker
Bandola, of which plaintiff was the patentee; that the defendants were to pay the plaintiff for such instruments, as
they were delivered, the actual cost of manufacturing the
same, which was fixed at four dollars and twenty-five cents
and upwards for each instrument, according to finish; that
plaintiff was to furnish these instruments as fast and in such
quantities as the trade should demand, but the defendants
were to take at least three instruments each week, if plaintiff
should so desire; that defendants were to take these instruments so furnished, and sell them on the market in the same
way as they sold other musical instruments in which they
were dealing, for which they were to have the actual reasonable expense incurred in so selling, and the remainder of the
proceeds of such sales was to be equally divided between the
plaintiff and the defendants. This contract was to continue
in force for five years, with the option on the part of the defendants, for another five years after the expiration of the
first five years.

The evidence of the plaintiff tended to show a subsequent modification of this written contract, by which the
material for the manufacture of these instruments was to be
furnished by the defendants, and the price to be paid the
plaintiff by the defendants was to be reduced, on account of

the cost of this material, to three dollars per instrument, which represented the cost of manufacture, exclusive of material.

The plaintiff's evidence tended to show that in June, 1900, after he had made and delivered sixty-six instruments, the defendants refused to take any more instruments made by him under said patent, though the plaintiff was ready to deliver and in fact tendered more instruments.

The plaintiff's evidence also tended to show the market price of, and the profits on, the instruments sold, and that the defendants never divided the profits.

The defendants' evidence tended to show that the plaintiff represented to them that his instrument was a new and valuable invention, and that no instrument embodying his claimed improvement had ever before been made or patented; that they soon discovered that the plaintiff's instrument was an infringement of a certain patent held by one Pollman, and that the plaintiff's claimed improvement had been known and used by others for more than two years prior to his application for his said patent; that they notified plaintiff of these facts and told him that they should not go on under the contract, having been notified by said Pollman to desist, and that plaintiff acquiesced in the abandonment of the contract.

The defendants objected to the testimony of the plaintiff as to the cost of making the instruments, as to what portion of such cost was labor, and as how many he could make per week, and excepted to the ruling of the court admitting such testimony.

The plaintiff testified as follows, subject to the objection and exception of the defendant:

Q. You may state whether, considering the amount of teaching and instruction which you have to do, you could furnish the defendants now, and until the time the contract expires, three instruments each week?

A. At present I could, and for some time I could do that. Of course, that depends entirely on how much teaching I would have.

Q. You may state whether you could furnish three each week until the expiration of the five year period, if things remain as they are now? A. Yes, sir. Q. You may state whether or not you are ready to do so? A. Yes, sir.

There was no other testimony upon this point, except as plaintiff's testimony as to the number of instruments he had been able to furnish up to the time of trial, tended to show his ability to furnish to the end of the contract period.

To the ruling of the court permitting the plaintiff to demonstrate by sounding, the difference between the tone of his instrument and that of the Pollman instrument, and also permitting the plaintiff to testify that such difference in tone was due to the difference in the shape of the instruments, the defendant excepted, but the exceptions do not show that the question of whether plaintiff was an expert was raised.

The court instructed the jury that if they found for the plaintiff, they should include in their general verdict damages from the time the contract was terminated by its breach to the time of trial, March 15, 1903. To this defendants excepted, claiming that no damage could be recovered which plaintiff suffered since suit was brought.

The jury returned a general verdict for the plaintiff for the sum of $740.50, and also the two following special verdicts:

(1) "Q. What sum have you included in your verdict for damages sustained by the refusal of the defendants to re-

ceive and pay for instruments between August 2, 1900 (date of writ), and March 5, 1903, (time of trial)?

A. We have included $740.50, as damage for refusal to receive any more instruments."

(2) "Q. What damages do you find the plaintiff will sustain between the fifth day of March, 1903, and the thirtieth day of October, 1904, by reason of the refusal of the defendants to receive and pay for any more instruments?

A. $387.00."

The defendants moved to set aside the verdicts for the reasons given in the opinion. The court overruled this motion, and rendered judgment *pro forma* for the plaintiff to recover the amount of the general verdict and the amount of the special finding, and costs, to which defendant excepted.

V. A. Bullard and *W. L. Burnap* for the defendants.

It was error to direct the jury to include in their verdict damages accruing after suit brought, or to give judgment for damages found to have thus accrued, or for prospective damages. This is an instalment contract,—no instalment being in any way dependent or related to the other,—running through a period of five years. Damages should have been limited to the time suit was brought. Future damages are the subject of future investigation and determination, when all the factors are available for estimating same. The record shows that there was no definite evidence upon which such assessment could be made. Whether plaintiff could meet the terms of the contract, is uncertain, remote, and speculative, as the record shows. 5 Vt. 181; *Spear* v. *Stacy,* 26 Vt. 61; *Whipple* v. *Fair Haven,* 63 Vt. 226; 4 Pick. 107.

The verdict finds that all damage accrued after suit brought; this is equivalent to finding that the suit was brought upon a claim which at that time had no foundation.

R. W. Taft and *E. C. Mower* for the plaintiff.

Upon breach of this contract the plaintiff might treat it as rescinded, and at once bring an action for damages; or he might treat the contract as continuing, and sue for breach thereof; or he might defer suit until the end of the term and sue for the actual damage he had sustained. No matter which of these he elected, his action would have been one for damages. *McMullan* v. *Dickson Co.*, 51 Am. St. Rep. 511; *Hamilton* v. *Love*, 152 Ind. 641; 71 Am. St. Rep. 384.

Prospective damages may be recovered in such suit. *Cutter* v. *Gillette*, 163 Mass. 95; 8 Am. & Eng. Enc. (2 Ed.) 651; *Wakeman* v. *Wheeler, etc. Co.*, 54 Am. Rep. 676; *Remelee* v. *Hall*, 31 Vt. 582.

WATSON, J. The contract between the plaintiff and the defendants was dated October 30, 1899, and was for a term of five years.

The verdict has established that in June, 1900, the defendants refused to take any more instruments made by the plaintiff under his patent, though the plaintiff was ready to deliver and in fact tendered more to them. This was such a breach of the contract by the defendants as gave the plaintiff the right to treat the contract as absolutely and finally broken. The plaintiff elected so to treat it and brought this action for damages.

That upon such a breach of a contract damages may be recovered for a non-performance of the whole contract, that is, prospective as well as what had already been sustained at the time of the commencement of the suit, was laid down by this court in *Royalton* v. *Royalton and Woodstock Turnpike Co.*, 14 Vt. 311, and again in *Remelee* v. *Hall*, 31 Vt. 582. Hence the question must be considered as settled in this State. See also *Pierce* v. *Tennessee Coal, Iron & Railroad Co.*, 173 U. S. 1, 43 L. Ed. 591; *Cutter* v. *Gillette*, 163 Mass. 95, and *Wakeman* v. *Wheeler & Wilson Mfg, Co.*, 101 N. Y. 205, 54 Am. Rep. 676.

Nor are the cases of *Waterman* v. *Buck*, 58 Vt. 519, 3 Atl. 505, and *Whipple* v. *Fairhaven*, 63 Vt. 226, 21 Atl. 533, relied upon by the defendants, in conflict therewith. In *Waterman* v. *Buck*, the orator brought his bill for an injunction to restrain the defendants from depositing sawdust and waste in a certain stream, whereby the orator's meadow was damaged, and for damages. It was held that damages accruing subsequent to the bringing of the bill could not be considered because not brought upon the record by supplemental bill.

In *Whipple* v. *Fairhaven*, the orator sought an injunction restraining the defendant from maintaining a certain culvert, and for damages already suffered by the orator by reason of the discharge of water through the culvert upon his premises. The report of the case does not show that the pleadings stood differently from those in *Waterman* v. *Buck*, and it was held, upon the authority of that case, from which it was said not to be distinguishable in principle, that nothing could be recovered for damages done after suit brought.

The value of the contract to the plaintiff at the time of the breach was shown by assessing the entire damages. As bearing upon that question, evidence showing the cost of the instruments under the contract, what portion of the cost was labor, how many instruments the plaintiff could make per week, the work or business in which the plaintiff was engaged during the time between the bringing of the suit and the trial, and whether he could furnish instruments according to the contract thenceforth to the expiration of its term, was properly received; for it was legitimate to show the nature of the contract, the circumstances surrounding and following its breach, and the consequences naturally and plainly traceable to it. *Wakeman* v. *Wheeler & Wilson Co.* before cited.

The defendants introduced expert testimony in defense tending to show that there was no patentable difference between the plaintiff's instrument and the Pollman instrument. To meet this evidence, the plaintiff, in rebuttal and subject to defendants' exception, was permitted to testify and "demonstrate" by sounding, the difference between the tone of his instrument and that of the Pollman instrument upon which defendants' evidence tended to show the plaintiff's instrument was an infringement, and was also permitted to testify that the difference in tone was due to the difference in the shape of the instruments. It is argued that this was permitting the plaintiff to testify as an expert, to do which he was not competent. But the exceptions do not show that the question of his competency was raised in the trial court, hence it is not for consideration here.

In submitting the question of damages to the jury, in case their verdict should be for the plaintiff, the jury were instructed to return a general verdict for the amount of damages found covering the period up to the time of the trial. Also to state as a special finding what sum they had included in the general verdict, for damages sustained by the refusal of the defendants to receive and pay for instruments between the time of the commencement of the suit and the time of the trial. The amount of damages specified in the general verdict and in the special finding so made were the same.

The jury also found specially the amount of damages for the period between the time of the trial and the expiration of the term of the contract.

The defendants moved to set aside the verdict and award a new trial on the ground that the verdict was so uncertain, inadequate, irregular, ambiguous, defective and illegal that no judgment could be legally rendered thereon. This motion was overruled and judgment rendered *pro forma* for the plaintiff to recover the full amount of damages named in the general verdict and in the special finding, to which the defendants excepted.

It is urged that by one of the special findings it appears that the plaintiff had suffered no damages by reason of the breach of the contract before the commencement of this suit, which, it is contended, is equivalent to a finding that the suit was brought upon a claim at that time without foundation. But this position is untenable, for upon the breach of the contract the plaintiff's right of action accrued. *Emack* v. *Hughes,* 74 Vt. 382, 52 Atl. 1061.

Judgment affirmed.

TOWN OF ESSEX *v.* TOWN OF JERICHO.

October Term, 1903.

Present: ROWELL, C. J., TYLER, MUNSON, START, WATSON, and STAFFORD, JJ.

Opinion filed December 2, 1903.

V. S. 3171-3172—Paupers—Action for Support—Notice— Requisites—Wife—Residence.

It is a condition precedent to a right of action by one town against another for the support of a pauper, under V. S. 3171, 3172, that the overseer of the plaintiff give notice to the overseer of the defendant "of the condition of such person."

Our pauper law will not allow a wife to gain a residence different from that of her husband, though she leaves him with the declared purpose never to return, and agrees with him never to call upon him for support.

ASSUMPSIT to recover for the support of an alleged pauper. Heard on an agreed statement at the March Term, 1903, Chittenden County, *Start*, J., presiding. Judgment *pro forma* for the plaintiff. The defendant excepted. The opinion states the facts.

I.. F. Wilbur for the defendant.

The alleged pauper had gained a residence in Underhill. This case differs from *Mount Holly* v. *Peru*, 72 Vt. 68, in this, that here the wife left the husband with the declared intention not to return, and with the agreement with him that she should never call upon him for support.

The notice is defective in not stating the condition of the alleged pauper.

Allen Martin for the plaintiff.

Under our pauper law a wife can, under no circumstance, gain a residence different from that of her husband. *Mount Holly* v. *Peru*, 72 Vt. 68, Jacobs' Law of Domicile, §§ 209, 215, 216; *Marshfield* v. *Tunbridge*, 62 Vt. 455.

The notice is sufficient. *Mount Holly* v. *Peru*, *supra*.

TYLER, J. This suit was brought upon the claim that Maggie M. Howe had become poor and in need of assistance in the plaintiff town, which had expended money for her support; that the defendant was the town of her legal residence and therefore liable to the plaintiff for the money so expended.

1. It is a prerequisite to a right of action by one town against another town to recover for assistance furnished to a

person under V. S. 3171, that the overseer of the town thus seeking to recover give notice "of the condition of such person" to the overseer of the poor of the town where the person last resided for the space of three years, supporting himself and family, and that sixty days elapse after giving the notice before suit is brought.   In the present case the notice was as follows:

"Essex, Vt., May 8th, 1902.

James Hutchinson, Esq.,
> *Overseer of Poor, Jericho, Vt.*

DEAR SIR:—

Mrs. Maggie M. Howe (wife of Martin Howe) has applied to me for assistance from this town and I understand she is a legal resident of Jericho, therefore I hereby notify you accordingly, and from this date all necessary expense for her maintenance and support must be paid by the town of Jericho.

GEORGE BEECHER."

It is clear that the notice is not in compliance with V. S. 3172, in that it contains no statement of the "condition" of the person who had applied for assistance.   It was held in *Randolph* v. *Roxbury,* 70 Vt. 175, Atl. 49, that it is not essential that the town giving the notice had furnished assistance to the person in question, nor that such person had applied to that town for assistance, but that it is essential that the notice should state facts showing that the person was in such a condiion as to require assistance, so that the town sought to be charged might have the time and the data for ascertaining whether the person required assistance, and if so, whether that town was liable for the person's support.   *Mount Holly* v. *Peru,* 72 Vt. 68, 40 Atl. 103.

2.   It appears by the agreed statement that this woman was married in October, 1890, to Martin Howe, who then was, and continued to be a resident of Jericho until his death in May, 1897; that the parties lived together in that town until September, 1895, when they voluntarily separated, the wife conveying to her husband her interest in the homestead upon which they had resided and receiving from him five hundred dollars in money.   Mrs. Howe then went to Underhill where she continuously lived and supported herself until December, 1899, when she moved to Essex.

When Mrs. Howe left her husband she declared her purpose never to return, and agreed with him that she would never call upon him for support.   But this separation did not change her residence, for the purpose of support, from the town of her husband's legal residence while he lived.   The Act of 1886, does not enable a married woman to gain a residence separate from that of her husband.   *Mount Holly* v. *Peru* is full authority upon this point.

By reason of the defect in the notice this action cannot be maintained.

Pro forma judgment reversed, and judgment for the defendant.

HERBERT BARRETT v. W. W. TYLER AND C. A. CHADWICK.

October Term, 1903.

Present: ROWELL, C. J., TYLER, START, WATSON, STAFFORD, and
HASELTON, JJ.

Opinion filed December 2, 1903.

Fraud—Recission of Contract—Election—Determination of.

To rescind a contract of sale, voidable on account of the vendor's
fraud, a manual tender of the property sold is not necessary,
when the vendor expressly refuses to take it back.

When a contract of sale is voidable on account of the vendor's fraud,
and he refuses to take back the property, the vendee may still
elect whether he will stand upon the contract, or upon the recission.

But if, after such refusal, and without prior notice to the vendor of
his intention to do so, the vendee sells part of said property and
receives other property in part payment, this determines his
election to stand upon the contract.

ASSUMPSIT by an indorsee of a promissory note against
the makers.   Plea, the general issue with notice.   Said
notice has not been furnished the reporter.   Trial by jury
at the June Term, 1903, Orange County, *Munson,* J., presiding.   Verdict ordered for the plaintiff for the amount of the
note, and judgment thereon.   The defendants excepted.

The case was disposed of on the defendants' evidence and
offers, the offers being treated as proved for the purposes of
the trial.   It did not appear what the plaintiff actually gave
for the note.   The execution of the note and of the indorsement was conceded.   Also conceded that the indorsement was
after maturity.   It appeared that before and at the time of the
sale, said Holman represented to both defendants, in substance,
that the horses were sound, good workers, and had no defects,

save what could be seen. It appeared that these representations were relied upon by the defendants, and induced them
to make the contract. The defendants' evidence tended to
show that these representations were false, and that Holman
knew they were false. No claim was made that either of the
defendants knew of the defects in the horses before the trade.
The other facts appear from the opinion.

N. L. Boyden and *Darling & Darling* for the defendants.

The note having been procured by fraud, and transferred
to the plaintiff after maturity, is subject to all equities existing *at the time of transfer. Britton* v. *Bishop,* 11 Vt. 70;
Baxter v. *Little,* 6 Met. 7; *Robinson* v. *Lyman,* 10 Conn. 30,
25 Am. Dec. 52.

The defense of fraud is available against this plaintiff,
and may be shown under the general issue. *Foot* v. *Ketchum,*
15 Vt. 258; *Limerick Nat. Bank* v. *Adams,* 70 Vt. 132. Defendants' explanation of the sale of the horse after suit was
that they sold it because it was dangerous. The defendants
were entitled to have this evidence weighed. *Stearns* v.
Gosselin, 58 Vt. 38; *Hulett* v. *Hulett,* 37 Vt. 581; *Lindsay* v.
Lindsay, 11 Vt. 621.

The defendants had elected to disaffirm the contract on
account of fraud. It is a legal presumption that this intention
continued. *Chilson* v. *Buttolph,* 12 Vt. 231; *Austin* v. *Bingham,* 31 Vt. 577; *Farr* v. *Payne,* 40 Vt. 615; *Childs* v. *Merrill,*
63 Vt. 463.

Upon the refusal of the vendor to take back the property,
the vendee holds it as bailee of the vendor and must account
to *him* for it. *Hambrick* v. *Williams,* 65 Miss. 18, 7 Am. St.
Rep. 631; *Smith's Admr.* v. *Smith,* 30 Vt. 139. The plaintiff

can not take advantage of the sale of this horse. It does not concern him.

If the plaintiff were a *bona fide* holder of the note, he could not recover on the facts as they stand; for proof of fraudulent inception of the note throws on the plaintiff the burden of showing that he gave value therefor, which he has not done. *Collins* v. *Gilbert*, 94 U. S. 753; *Sistermans* v. *Field*, 9 Gray 331; *Vallett* v. *Parker*, 6 Wend. 613.

M. M. Wilson and *R. M. Harvey* for the plaintiff.

The sale of part of the property, as his own, was a waiver of all rights to rescind, and of previous offers to rescind. *Downer* v. *Smith*, 32 Vt. 1; *McCullough* v. *Scott*, 56 Am. Dec. 560; *Buffington* v. *Quantin*, 17 Pa. St. 310.

WATSON, J. The note upon which the plaintiff seeks to recover was given by the defendants to one Holman for the purchase price of two horses and two harnesses bought of him by the defendants and was endorsed to the plaintiff after maturity. The defense was put solely upon the ground that the note was invalid at its inception by reason of fraud. The defendants' evidence and offers of evidence tended to show that before and at the time of the making of the contract, false representations were made by Holman to the defendants of and concerning the horses, which representations were relied upon by the defendants and induced the making of the contract.

It appeared that as soon as practicable after discovering that the horses were not as represented, and while Holman was the holder of the note, one of the defendants saw Holman and demanded that he take all the property back and give up the note; but Holman refused to do so on the ground that the horses were all right. Later and before a transfer of the note, other like demands were made by the defendants upon Holman and refused by him. Defendants also offered to show that before this suit was brought on receipt of notice from plaintiff's attorney that he held the note, the defendants made an offer to said attorney to return the property for the note. On none of these occasions was the property itself brought and manually tendered by the defendants or either of them, although at the time of each demand and refusal, and at the time this suit was brought, all the property was in defendant Tyler's hands so that it could have been returned.

A short time after the suit was commenced and before trial, Tyler sold one of the horses for five dollars and a wagon worth five or six dollars. Defendants offered to show that the reason why Tyler sold the horse was because he considered it a dangerous and unsafe animal to keep in his barn or on his premises, and of no use. It did not appear whether or not the plaintiff was notified of the intended sale of the horse before it was made, nor what disposition was made of the money and wagon received therefor. Nothing had been paid on the note. The court directed a verdict for the plaintiff for the amount of the note, to which defendants excepted.

In order to rescind the contract, it devolved on the defendants within a reasonable time after discovering the fraud, to put Holman in *statu quo* by returning or offering to return to him the property purchased. But whether a manual tender of the property was necessary to effect a rescission we need not inquire for, if it was, the refusal by Holman to take the property back rendered such tender unnecessary. The recission was complete without it.

The property being in the defendants' possession after the rescission because of the sellers' refusal to receive it back, the

defendants had the right then to elect whether they would
stand upon the rescission, or acquiescing in the refusal by the
other party, treat the property as their own under the purchase, and claim damages for the fraud.

But they could not do both. The contract was not void.
It was only voidable. And if after the discovery of the fraud
the defendants acquiesced in the contract either by express
words or by any unequivocal act, it was an election on their
part to stand upon the purchase and they could not later reject
the property. We think the subsequent sale of one of the
horses by the defendants for five dollars in money and for a
wagon worth five or six dollars more was such an act as determined their election, and they could not thereafter go back
to their rescission in avoidance of the sale. Benj. on Sales,
Sec. 675; *Downer* v. *Smith*, 32 Vt. 1; *McCulloch* v. *Scott*, 13
B. Monroe, 172, 56 Am. Dec. 561.

It is said that after the rescission and the refusal of the
seller to take back the property the defendants held the property as bailee and that they were not obliged to hold it awaiting the end of the controversy between the parties. The law
to this effect seems to be well settled. But it is equally well
settled as a part of the same law that if the purchaser would
thus hold the property as bailee, he must no longer interfere
with it more than may be necessary for its preservation or protection; and if he would relieve himself by sale of the property,
it must be in good faith after notice of his intention to the
owner. *Sands* v. *Taylor*, 5 Johns. 395; *Swann* v. *West*, 41
Miss. 104; *Hambrick* v. *Wilkins*, 65 Miss. 18, 7 Am. St. Rep.
631.

The defendants cannot stand upon the right to sell as
bailee without showing a compliance with the law in this regard, which they have not done. Failing to offer or introduce

any evidence tending so to show, it must be taken that the sale was made by them not as bailee, but as of their own property; and so it particularly appears from the fact that a wagon was taken in part payment. The right to sell as such bailee on account of the owner does not include the right to exchange for other property. And when no notice is given to the owner by the bailee of his intention to sell, and by the contract of sale other property is taken in full or part payment, without any knowledge or consent of the owner of the property sold, the sale is such an unequivocal act on the part of the party selling, as in law shows him to be acting under his right as purchaser, and not as bailee after recission.

Judgment affirmed.

WILLIAM T. FOSS v. CLARENCE SMITH.

October Term, 1903.

Present: ROWELL, C. J., TYLER, MUNSON, START, STAFFORD, and HASELTON, JJ.

Opinion filed December 3, 1903.

Assault and Battery—Self Defense.

When one is assaulted he may immediately repel the assault, using no more force than in the circumstances reasonably appears to him to be necessary.

TRESPASS FOR ASSAULT AND BATTERY. Pleas, the general issue, and *son assault demesne*. Trial by jury at the December Term, 1902, Caledonia County, *Watson*, J., presiding.

Plaintiff's motion to direct a verdict overruled. Verdict and judgment for the defendant. The plaintiff excepted. This is all the reporter knows about the case except what appears in the opinion.

Harland B. Howe and *Porter & Thompson* for the plaintiff.

Dunnett & Slack for the defendant.

STAFFORD, J. Trespass for assault and battery. Plea that plaintiff committed the first assault and that defendant used no more force than was necessary in self defense.

The only exception relied upon is to the refusal to direct a verdict. The plaintiff claims that the defendant's own testimony showed that, after he had completely passed the plaintiff in the highway, and when he might have driven on without danger of receiving further injury, he came back to where the plaintiff was and committed the assault for which the action is brought. Upon reading the testimony we are not satisfied that the claim is well founded, but think, rather, that the view of it most favorable to the defendant is that although his horses had passed the plaintiff's sled before stopping, he himself was practically opposite the plaintiff, and on being assaulted by the latter immediately repelled the assault, using no more force than in the circumstances reasonably appeared to him to be necessary.

Judgment affirmed.

J. WARREN BAILEY'S ADMX. *v.* H. CLAY GLEASON.

May Term, 1902.

Present: ROWELL, C. J., TYLER, MUNSON, WATSON, STAFFORD, and
HASELTON, JJ.

Opinion filed December 8, 1903.

Discharge in Bankruptcy—Plea of—Necessary Allegations.

In pleading a discharge in bankruptcy granted under the U. S. Bankruptcy Act 1898, it is not necessary to allege the facts which gave
the United States District Court jurisdiction of the subject matter,
or of the parties.

When the declaration counts upon a debt *prima facie* provable under
the U. S. Bankruptcy Act 1898, a plea of a discharge under said
Act need not state that such debt is provable.

When a declaration counts upon a debt *prima facie* provable under
the U. S. Bankruptcy Act 1898, which excepts from the operation
of the discharge certain classes of provable debts, a plea of a
discharge under said Act need not negative such exceptions.
That is matter of replication.

Though the declaration counts upon a debt *prima facie* provable under
the U. S. Bankruptcy Act 1898, a plea of a discharge under said
Act must state that such debt was duly scheduled, or that the
creditor had notice of the bankruptcy proceedings.

SPECIAL ASSUMPSIT against the defendant as surviving
partner of Ambro Hildreth, deceased, upon a promissory note
signed with the firm name of H. C. Gleason & Co. Heard on
general demurrer to the defendant's second plea, at the March
Term, 1902, Washington County, *Start*, J., presiding. Demurrer sustained *pro forma*, and plea adjudged insufficient.
The defendant excepted.

The plea demurred to is as follows: "And for a further
plea in this behalf, etc., the defendant says that the plaintiff
ought not to have or maintain, etc., because the defendant

says, that after the said several supposed debts and causes of
action in said declaration mentioned 'were contracted and accrued, and before the commencement of this suit by the plaintiff in this behalf, to wit, on the eighteenth day of October,
1898, the said defendant became and was adjudged a bankrupt, in accordance with an Act of Congress entitled 'An act
to establish a uniform system of bankruptcy throughout the
United States,' at, to wit, Burlington aforesaid, and that the
said defendant received his discharge as such bankrupt on, to
wit, the first day of May, 1899, from the United States District Court for the district of Vermont, and that the debts were
contracted, and the said causes of action,—if any there be—
in said declaration mentioned, and each of them, did accrue to
the said plaintiff before the said defendant so became a bankrupt as aforesaid, to wit, at Richmond in the county of Chittenden on the eleventh day of June, 1888, and of this the said
defendant puts himself on the country."

Cushman & Sherman for the defendant.

The plea of bankruptcy is sufficient, at least against a
general demurrer.   3 Chitty Pleading, 10 Am. Ed. *956; The
Bankruptcy Act 1898, § 21, f; *Downer* v. *Chamberlin,* 21 Vt.
414; *Belnap* v. *Davis,* 21 Vt. 409.

In the reported cases when a discharge in bankruptcy
has been pleaded, and the plaintiff claimed that his case was
not affected by such discharge, the plaintiff has replied specially.   *Batchelor* v. *Low,* 43 Vt. 662; *Barron* v. *Benedict,* 44 Vt.
518; *Hayes* v. *Nash,* 129 Mass. 62; *Burnside* v. *Brigham,* 8
Met. 75; *Tyrrel* v. *Hammerstein,* 6 Am. B. Rep. 430; *Collins*
v. *McWalters,* ibid. 593; Collier on Bankruptcy, 3rd Ed. 212.

T. J. Deavitt for the plaintiff.

To constitute a good plea of a discharge in bankruptcy it is necessary to aver that the claim sued on was one *provable* under the Bankruptcy Act, and to have been duly scheduled in time for proof and allowance, or that the creditor had notice, or actual knowledge of the bankruptcy proceedings. *Tyrrel* v. *Hammerstein,* 6 Am. B. Rep. 430; *Collins* v. *McWalters,* ibid. 593; *Clay* v. *Severance,* 55 Vt. 300; *Sackett* v. *Andross,* 5 Hill 327; *Hayes* v. *Flowers,* 25 Miss. 169; Bump on Bankruptcy, 725.

The plea ought to have shown that the Court of Bankruptcy had jurisdiction. *Cutter* v. *Folsom,* 17 N. H. 139; *Wiggins* v. *Shaplugh,* 20 N. H. 444; *Wyman* v. *Mitchell,* 1 Cowens 316; In Re Stokes, 1 Am. B. Rep. 35; *Roosevelt* v. *Kellogg,* 20 Johns. 208.

MUNSON, J. In pleading the judgment of a superior court of general jurisdiction it is not necessary to allege the facts that gave the court jurisdiction of the subject matter or the parties. The judgments of a district court of the United States in bankruptcy proceedings are held by our court to be within this rule. *Downer* v. *Chamberlin,* 21 Vt. 414.

The declaration counts upon a promissory note and money loaned. Such claims are *prima facie* provable. It is not necessary that the defendant allege this fact when it thus appears from the declaration, whatever the rule may be in other cases. "The plea need not allege that the debt was provable where the debt alleged in the declaration is *prima facie* provable." Bump on Bankruptcy, 11 Ed. 724, citing *Cutter* v. *Folsom,* 17 N. H. 139.

The statute excepts from the operation of the discharge certain classes of provable debts. It is not necessary for the defendant to show by his plea that the debt was not within any of these excepted classes. It is for the plaintiff to bring the debt within some exception by his replication. We are aware that some courts hold otherwise, but we adopt this rule as more consistent with the established principles of pleading.

The exception relating to debts not scheduled in time for proof and allowance, although included in the list referred to, is a provision of a different character. This relates to matters essential to the operation of the discharge upon claims of every nature. To give the discharge effect as to the claim in suit, it must appear, not only that the debt was provable, but that it was duly scheduled by the debtor or that the creditor had knowledge of the proceedings. It is this which gives the court jurisdiction of the particular creditor, and makes its discharge a discharge from his claim. The ordinary presumptions of regularity do not touch him, for unless named in the schedule he is unknown to the proceedings. Unless connected with the proceedings by the schedule or by knowledge of them, there is no discharge as to him. So in pleading the discharge in bar of his claim there must be an allegation of that which makes the discharge effective against him.

Judgment affirmed, and cause remanded.

STATE v. PATRICK TAGUE.

October Term, 1903.

Present: MUNSON, START, WATSON, STAFFORD, and HASELTON, JJ.

Opinion filed December 10, 1903.

Criminal Law—No. 90, Acts 1902—Intoxicating Liquor— Giving is Furnishing.

Giving away intoxicating liquor is "furnishing" it, within the pro- hibition of No. 90, Acts 1902.

COMPLAINT for furnishing liquor without first procuring a license, in violation of No. 90, Acts 1902. Plea, not guilty. Trial by court in the City Court of the city of Montpelier, *Woodward*, Judge.   Judgment, guilty of one offense, and sentence thereon.   The respondent excepted.

The trial court found that the respondent had not at the time of the alleged offense any license for the sale of intoxicating liquor; that upon the occasion named in the complaint the respondent *gave away* a drink of reduced alcohol; that there was no evidence that the respondent had violated the law in any other respect.

H. C. Shurtleff for the respondent.

Frank A. Bailey, State's Attorney, for the State.

STAFFORD, J.   The question is whether the giving away of intoxicating liquor is forbidden by our present statute, Acts 1902, No. 90.   Furnishing is forbidden, and to give away is to furnish.   *State* v. *Freeman*, 27 Vt. 523.   The argument is that the repealed statute did in terms forbid giving away, while the present does not.   But it was evidently intended that furnishing should include giving away.   For example, in the exception allowing private hospitality in one's dwelling, the word is furnish (Sec. 21).   The construction contended for would lead to such absurdities as that minors and habitual drunkards, although they could not be sold to nor otherwise furnished, might be given liquor, and that treating, though forbidden at the bar, could be practiced on the sidewalk.

The respondent takes nothing by his exception.

FRANK L. FISH, RECEIVER, v. HULDA OLIN.

January Term, 1902.

Present: ROWELL, C. J., TYLER, MUNSON, START, and STAFFORD, JJ.

Opinion filed December 18, 1903.

National Bank—Receiver—Title to Assets—Action by in State Court.

A receiver of a national bank, appointed under the provisions of §5234 of the Revised Statutes of the United States, has the legal title to the assets of such bank, and may maintain an action at law in his own name in the state courts.

DEBT on the statutory liability of a stockholder of a national bank. Heard on a general demurrer to the declaration, at the December Term, 1901, Addison County, *Watson,* J., presiding. Demurrer sustained, and declaration adjudged insufficient. The plaintiff excepted.

The declaration alleged, among other things, the organization of the Farmers' National Bank of Vergennes; the defendant's ownership of stock therein; the insolvency of said bank; the appointment of the plaintiff as its receiver by the Comptroller of the Currency of the United States under the provisions of §5234 of the Revised Laws of the United States; that in order to pay the obligations of said bank it was necessary to enforce the individual liability of the stockholders thereof as prescribed by the said Revised Statutes, to the extent of one hundred dollars upon each and every share of the capital stock of said bank held or owned by them at the time of its failure, that said Comptroller had made an assessment and requisition upon said stockholders for such amount; that by virtue of his appointment as such receiver it was the duty of the plaintiff to take all necessary proceedings, by suit or otherwise, to enforce said liability; that the capital stock of said bank is $60,000, and that the defendant owns one thousand dollars of said stock, and did own it at the time of the said failure of said bank; that she refused to pay said assessment, though requested to do so.

Frank L. Fish, Receiver, *pro se.*

The receiver of a national bank must be a party to all suits relating to the choses in action of the bank, because the same belong to him. *Scott* v. *Armstrong,* 146 U. S. 499; National Bank Act & Its Meaning (by Bolles) § 428; Gluck & Becker on Receivers, 239.

The receiver may sue for demands due the bank, either in his own name as receiver, or in the name of the bank. *Bank* v. *Kennedy,* 17 Wall. 19; *Kennedy* v. *Gibson,* 8 Wall. 198; *Stanton* v. *Wilkeson,* 8 Bened. 357; *Bank of Bethel* v. *Pahquioque Bank,* 14 Wall. 383; *Case* v. *Bovine,* 22 La. An. 321; High on Receivers § 360. He is expressly empowered by U. S. Statutes to bring a suit in his own name. U. S. Statutes § 5234; Beach on Receivers, § 484; *Stanton* v. *Wilkeson,* 8 Bened. 357.

The contention is that there is no such title in the receiver that he can mantain an action in his own name. Not one case can be found that even hints that a receiver of a national bank can not maintain a suit in his own name. It has been the custom in Vermont, as well as elsewhere in common law states, to bring suit in the federal courts in the name of receivers of insolvent national banks. These suits have been brought for the collection of notes as well as for stock assessments. There is no statute which authorizes bringing suits in the name of the receiver except for stock assessments, therefore all other suits must have stood on common law grounds. If the title is not in the receiver he could no more sue in his own name for the collection of a note in the federal courts than in the state courts.   ·

Joel C. Baker for the defendant.

Title LXII, of the Revised Statutes of the United States, constitutes statute law under which the national banks of this country are organized, perform their functions, and when insolvent, are wound up.   When a national bank is insolvent the Comptroller takes charge.   He appoints a receiver.   Under his direction the receiver does all that the receiver is authorized to do, and must make his report to the Comptroller.   The powers of a receiver of a national bank are much more limited than those of an ordinary receiver.   His duties are confined to converting the property into cash, and the collection of the assets and placing them in the United States Treasury.

It is well settled that in the case of a receiver appointed by a court of equity, the possession is the possession of the court.   *In Re Higgins,* 17 Fed. Rep. 443; *Bruce* v. *R. Co.,* 29 Fed. Rep. 345; *Hewitt* v. *Adams,* 50 Me. 280; *Ellis* v. *R. Co.,* 107 Mass. 28; *Railroad* v. *Railroad,* 47 Vt. 789.   The appointment of a receiver does not change the title to the property.   *Bank* v. *Bank,* 136 U. S. 236.

The receiver of a national bank has not title to the assets, but holds them in trust for creditors under the direction of the Comptroller.   *Lease* v. *Barschal,* 106 Fed. Rep. 763; *Scott* v. *Armstrong,* 146 U. S. 507; *Booth* v. *Clark,* 17 How. 527.

The settlement of the affairs of an insolvent bank is one proceeding from beginning to end, and as was said by *Wheeler,* J., *In Re Slack,* 3 Fed. Rep. 525, in reference to the bankruptcy act, the assets are in the custody of the law, and the bankrupt is seized in his own right, until the property has gone out of the estate by sale by the trustee.

It is a fundamental rule of the common law that an action at law can only be maintained on a legal title. *Lansing* v. *Manton*, 14 Fed. Cas. No. 8077; *Heald* v. *Warren*, 22 Vt. 413; Kerr on Receivers, 206, note 1.

Congress has no power over the remedy in the state courts. Congress can give a right of action, but when suit is brought in a state court, the state law governs as to the remedy.

MUNSON, J. It is claimed in support of the demurrer that the receiver of a national bank cannot maintain an action at law in his own name in the courts of this state; and *Murtey* v. *Allen*, 71 Vt. 377, 45 Atl. 752, is one of the authorities cited. It was held in that case that the only remedies at law available in this state to a foreign receiver are those given him by the common law, and that his appointment does not confer the legal title essential to the maintenance of a suit at law. Without considering whether any other or different question can arise in this case because of federal supremacy, we pass at once to the inquiry whether the federal law gives to a receiver of this class the legal title to the property covered by his appointment.

The arguments drawn by defendant's counsel from the general provisions relating to the receiver's duties are not very conclusive. The legal title may rest in the receiver, whatever the restrictions placed upon his independent action. The fact that he holds the property merely to work out the purposes of a certain trust does not indicate that the legal title is elsewhere. The duties of an ordinary trustee relate wholly to the rights of his beneficiaries, but he holds the legal

title for the benefit of his trust. It is not claimed that this
question is disposed of by any definite provision of the statute,
and we must look to the decisions of the United States Supreme Court for whatever may have been said by way of
construction.

The general relation which the receiver sustains to the
scheme of the statute is set forth in *Kennedy* v. *Gibson*, 8
Wall. 498, where it is said that the receiver is the instrument
of the comptroller; that it is for the comptroller to decide
when it is necessary to enforce the personal liability of the
stockholders; that when the whole amount is sought to be recovered the proceeding must be at law; that the receiver is
the statutory assignee of the association, and the proper party
to institute all suits; that they may be brought both at law and
in equity, in his name or in that of the association. The following cases may also be referred to as bearing upon some
or all of these propositions. *Bank of Metropolis* v. *Kennedy*,
84 U. S. 19; *Richmond* v. *Irons*, 121 U. S. 56; *Witters* v.
Sowles, 61 Vt. 366, 18 Atl. 191.

It is said in *Earl* v. *Pennsylvania*, 178 U. S. 449, that
the statute contemplates that all the assets of the suspended
bank shall pass in the first instance to the receiver; but the connection is not such as to give the expression any special significance upon the question of title.

It was considered in *Scott* v. *Armstrong*, 146 U. S. 507,
that, the charter having been forfeited and the bank dissolved
by decree of the Circuit Court, the title to the assets was necessarily thereby transferred to the receiver. This would seem
to imply that no transfer of the title had been effected by the
previous appointment of the receiver. In *Bank of Selma* v.
Colby, 88 U. S. 609, a case cited in the above opinion, there
had also been a decree forfeiting the charter and dissolving

the bank. Reference should be had in this connection to *Bank of Bethel* v. *Pahquioque Bank,* 81 U. S. 383, where it is said that the appointment of a receiver does not work a dissolution of the bank, but that it continues to exist as a legal entity, and may sue and be sued in all cases where it is necessary that the corporate name be used for the purpose of closing up its affairs. But whatever the expression in *Scott* v. *Armstrong* may be thought to indicate, it is to be noted that in *Bushnell* v. *Leland,* 164 U. S. 683, decided in 1897, the case of *Kennedy* v. *Gibson* is referred to with the fullest approval.

Suits by national bank receivers to enforce the statutory liability of stockholders have been maintained without question in the state courts for many years. Some of these suits were in states where the procedure is in accordance with the rules of the common law, and the views expressed in the decisions of other states, afford support to the claim that the receiver is vested with the legal title. *Davis* v. *Weed,* 44 Conn. 569; *Chicago Fire Proofing Co.* v. *Park National Bank,* 145 Ill. 481; *Brinckerhoff* v. *Bostwick,* 88 N. Y. 52; *O'Connor* v. *Witherby,* 111 Cal. 523; *Hill* v. *Graham,* 11 Col. 536; *Thompson* v. *Schaetzel,* 2 S. D. 395.

We have not found in our examination of the United States cases any direct statement that the receiver has the legal title by virtue of his appointment. The plaintiff does not cite us to any case which he claims to be in terms conclusive upon this matter; but he insists that when the language of the statute, the judicial comments upon it, and the course of procedure are considered, there is no escape from the conclusion that the receiver is regarded by the federal courts as possessed of the legal title.

We are disposed to consider the statement in *Kennedy* v. *Gibson,* that the receiver is the statutory assignee of the

association, a sufficient indication that he has the title required
by our courts, notwithstanding the further statement that he
has power to sue at law in the name of the association. Indeed, the designation of the receiver as a "statutory assignee,"
if the term is to be given its full significance, definitely classes .
him with those receivers who have the legal title. The circuit
courts of the United States have apparently taken this view
of the case. *Stanton* v. *Wilkeson*, 8 Ben. 357; *Casey* v. *La
Societe de Credit Mobilier*, 2 Wood 77. It is said in the case
last cited that the receiver's title is the same as that of an assignee in bankruptcy. Substantially the same is said, but
without citation of cases, in Beach on Receivers § 481, and
in High on Receivers § 359.

If it be true that the United States Supreme Court, as
matter of construction, treats the assignee as having the legal
title, we cannot treat him differently. It is our duty to follow
the construction adopted by that court, whether it be a definite
construction given to the particular provision, or a construction
apparent from its treatment of the statutory system of which
that provision is a part. We think it is clear that the United
States Court treats the receiver as having the legal title to
the right in question.

*Judgment reversed, demurrer overruled, declaration ad-
judged sufficient, and cause remanded.*

Oughtney Jangraw v. Joseph Perkins.

October Term, 1903.

Present: Rowell, C. J., Munson, Start, Watson, Stafford, and
Haselton, JJ.

Opinion filed December 19, 1903.

Mortgage—Marriage Brokerage Contract—Assumptions in Aid of—Hastening Intended Marriage.

A contract to hasten an intended marriage is a marriage brokerage contract, and void.

A mortgage, conditioned that a third party who is about to marry the daughter of the mortgagee shall do so immediately, is a marriage brokerage contract and void, when neither the mortgage, nor the facts alleged, disclose any reason why such third person should marry the daughter, nor why the mortgagor should concern himself in the matter.

No facts will be assumed in aid of a contract which on its face, and on the facts alleged, is a marriage brokerage contract.

Appeal in Chancery. Heard on demurrer to the bill of complaint at the March Term, 1903, Washington County, *Stafford,* Chancellor, presiding. Decree, *pro forma,* overruling the demurrer, and adjudging the bill sufficient. The defendant appealed. The opinion states the facts.

Heaton & Thomas and *Frank S. Williams* for the defendant.

To cause the marriage to happen was the thing that the defendant was to undertake. A mortgagor always undertakes to perform the condition of the mortgage. *Tuttle* v. *Armstead,* 53 Conn. 175; *Mitchell* v. *Burnham,* 44 Me. 299; *Cook* v. *Bartholomew,* 60 Conn. 24. This is a marriage brokerage contract, and so void. *Crawford* v. *Bussell,* 62 Barb. 92; *Johnson*

Admr., v. *Hunt*, 81 Ky. 321; Albany Law Journal, Vol. 48, p. 508; Parsons on Contracts, 5, Ed. Vol. 2, p. 74; Addison on Contracts (Morgan's Ed.) Vol. 3, 441; *Stribble* v. *Brett*, 2 Vernon's Chan. 445; *White* v. *Equitable, etc. Union*, 52 Am. Rep. 325; *Morrison* v. *Rogers*, 56 Am. St. Rep. 95.

Nor does it matter that defendant undertook to carry into effect an existing agreement to marry. *Morrison* v. *Rogers, supra.*

This contract is also void because it is in the nature of a wager contract. *Danforth* v. *Evans*, 16 Vt. 538; *West* v. *Holmes*, 26 Vt. 530; *Chalfant* v. *Payton*, 91 Ind. 202.

R. M. Harvey and *E. M. Harvey* for the orator.

This is not a wagering contract any more than if defendant had given orator a bond against the fraud and dishonesty of the man who was going to marry his daughter. This contract does not tend to induce future separation. Greenhood on Public Polity, 483; *Farnum* v. *Bartlett*, 52 Me. 570; *Wyant* v. *Lesher*, 23 Pa. St. 338; *Wright* v. *Wright*, 55 L. R. A. 261; *O'Connell* v. *Noonan*, 1 App. Cas. 332; *Hann* v. *Crickler*, 43 Atl. 1063; *Squires* v. *Squires*, 53 Vt. 208; *Clark* v. *Fosdick*, 6 L. R. A. 132; *Born* v. *Hortsman*, 5 L. R. A. 577; *Richardson* v. *Mellish*, 2 Bing. 229; *Barrett* v. *Carden*, 65 Vt. 431.

STAFFORD, J.   A bill in chancery, which is demurred to. The allegations are these:

The defendant being indebted to the complainant in the sum of five hundred dollars, in consideration thereof and to secure the payment of the same, gave him a mortgage on his land with a condition that it should be void if Revett, who was about to marry the complainant's daughter should do so immediately and should for six years support her to the best of his ability and otherwise perform the marriage contract. In the event of Revett's failure in any respect, and three months' notice thereof to the defendant, the latter was to pay five hundred dollars to the complainant in trust for the daughter and any children of her body then living. Revett married the daughter, but in all other respects the condition has been broken. Prayer that the defendant pay the five hundred dollars or be foreclosed. In the Court of Chancery there was a *pro forma* decree adjudging the bill sufficient. The defendant appealed, and insists that there is no equity in the bill because the mortgage is against public policy and void, in that it placed the defendant under the obligation, or at least the financial inducement, to bring about or hasten a marriage between Revett and the complainant's daughter. Neither the mortgage nor the bill discloses any reason why Revett should have married the person proposed, nor any reason why the defendant should have concerned himself in the marital relations of either.

By the contract, what the complainant said to the defendant was in effect this: "You owe me five hundred dollars, give me a deed of your land to secure the debt and if Revett shall marry my daughter at once, and be for six years her faithful husband, the debt shall be satisfied, otherwise you shall pay me the five hundred dollars to be held in trust for her."

On the other part, what the defendant said to the complainant was this: "I owe you five hundred dollars, and I deed you this land to secure the debt; but if Revett shall marry your daughter at once and be for six years her faithful husband the debt shall be satisfied, otherwise I must pay you the five hundred dollars to be held by you in trust for her."

This was a marriage brokerage contract, under which the defendant by procuring the immediate marriage of Revett and the complainant's daughter and the faithful performance of the marriage contract on Revett's part for six years, could be relieved of a mortgage debt of five hundred dollars. As such it is void. *Hall and Keen* v. *Potter,* 3 Levinz, 412; *Stribble-hill* v. *Brett,* 2 Vern. Ch. 445; *Duval* v. *Wellman,* 124 N. Y. 156; *Johnson* v. *Hunt,* 81 Ky. 321; *White* v. *Equitable Nuptial Benefit Union,* 76 Ala. 251, 52 Am. Rep. 325; 15 Am. & Eng. Encl. 954.

That Revett was about to marry the daughter makes no difference for a contract to hasten an intended marriage is as obnoxious to the objection as a contract to bring about a marriage between strangers. *Morrison* v. *Rogers,* 115 Cal. 252, 56 Am. St. 95.

If the contract does not mean that the debt itself is to be extinguished in case Revett marries and fulfils his marriage contract, but only that the mortgage shall be extinguished leaving the debt in force, then there was no consideration for the mortgage. The privilege of getting the mortgage alone released would be no inducement to the giving of the mortgage. There is no allegation that the daughter married Revett relying upon the defendant's contract.

The complainant's argument is that if the contract could be supported upon any supposable state of facts we should assume such facts to exist; and suggests that probably the daughter was with child by Revett. But we cannot assume that, nor any other fact not appearing. The contract being on its face and on the facts alleged open to the objection urged, it was the duty of the complainant to bring upon the record,

in traversable form, any claimed facts which might relieve it
of the objection.

*The pro forma decree of the Court of Chancery is re-
versed and the cause remanded with a mandate that the demurrer be sustained and the bill adjudged insufficient and dismissed unless the complainant shall there obtain leave to
amend.*

JOHN A. ROEBLING'S SONS CO. v. BARRE & MONTPELIER
TRACTION & POWER CO.

October Term, 1903.

Present: ROWELL, C. J., MUNSON, START, WATSON, STAFFORD, and
HASELTON, JJ.

Opinion filed December 21, 1903.

*Corporations—Directors—Delegated Authority—Executive
Committee—Exceptions—Transcript Controlling.*

When the executive committee of three from its board of directors
orders wire for a corporation, and another of said committee,
without objection, sees the bills charging the corporation therefor, and sees the wire made part of its plant, and the third member is ignorant of the transaction, the corporation is bound, if
said committee itself can bind it.

A by-law of a corporation providing for an executive committee, and
requiring the assent of the directors to be had before the acts of
such committee shall be binding, does not require that transactions in the ordinary course of business should be specially
authorized.

The purchase of necessary material for a corporation is a transaction
in the ordinary course of business, and as such, may be delegated
by the directors to an executive committee, without violation of
the rule that discretionary powers can not be delegated.

The authority to purchase necessary material for a corporation is conferred by the board of directors upon its executive committee, by unanimous acquiescence in the conducting of the ordinary business of the corporation by such committee.

When the transcript of the evidence is made controlling by the bill of exceptions, the construction put thereon by the Supreme Court will govern as to the tendency of the evidence, even in contradiction of an allegation as to such tendency in the bill of exceptions.

GENERAL ASSUMPSIT to recover for certain copper wire. Pleas, the general issue, and declaration in offset to recover eight hundred dollars which defendant claimed was paid plaintiff without consideration and without authority. The general issue was pleaded to the declaration in offset. Trial by jury at the March Term, 1900, Washington County, *Tyler*, Judge, presiding. At the close of all the evidence the plaintiff moved the court to direct a verdict for the plaintiff. This motion was overruled, to which the plaintiff excepted. Verdict for the defendant to recover his costs, and to recover eight hundred dollars on its declaration in offset. Judgment on verdict. The plaintiff excepted.

The reporter has not been furnished with the transcript of the evidence. The following is quoted from the bill of exceptions.

"The defendant claimed, and its evidence tended to show, that the purchase in question was not made upon the credit of the defendant company and that said Ferguson had no authority, either general or special, to make such purchase, and that there had been no subsequent ratification of the purchase by the defendant, nor had the defendant any knowledge or reason to suspect that the purchase had been made upon its credit. The plaintiff's evidence tended to show the contrary, and in this connection the defendant introduced evidence tending to show that the firm of Ferguson & Richardson, of which said Ferguson was a member, had taken the contract for the construction and equipment of its road from Barre to Montpelier, and had undertaken to furnish all the material and supplies necessary to make the road safe, complete and capable of operation as an electric road, including the purchase of all necessary feed wire requisite for its completion."

"Said Ferguson testified that he made said purchase as a director and executive committee of the defendant company, having full authority in that behalf. The plaintiff's evidence tended to show that Kennedy and Ferguson agreed upon the necessity for the purchase of said feed wire in order to complete the road, and that it should be bought without delay, the conversation occurring in the month of August, 1898, and that said Kennedy, who besides his office of executive committee, was president of the defendant company at the time, instructed him to make the purchase for the defendant. This conversation was denied by said Kennedy, who was introduced as a witness by the defendant. There was no question but that all negotiations in relation to the purchase of said feed wire were between the plaintiff's agent and said Ferguson."

"The evidence of the plaintiff tended to show the road in operation from July, 1898, and during the months of July, August, and September, and subsequently, and that the wire in controversy was received and put up during the month of September, by workmen employed and working under the direction of Thomas E. Smith, the defendant's superintendent, and who was at that time superintending the construction and operation of the defendant's road, and against the objection and exception of the defendant, introduced evidence of approval by said Smith of the bills in question. To meet this the defendant, against the objection and exception of the plaintiff, was allowed to introduce the evidence of said Smith,

to the effect that he was employed as superintendent of the
construction of said road by direction of Mr. Murch, the agent
of the Worcester Construction Company, and that at the time
of placing the wire in question, he was acting under the instructions of Mr. Ferguson and Mr. Barnes, the agent of
Messrs. Ferguson & Richardson, the contractors; and the defendant also further, against the objection and exception of
the plaintiff, introduced evidence of witnesses to the effect that
during the months of July, August and September, and including the time when the wire was put in place as part of the
defendant's electric system, Messrs. Ferguson & Richardson,
the contractors, operated the road exclusively."

The other facts appear in the opinion.

J. P. Lamson and *Herbert Noble* for the plaintiff.

Authority was by implication conferred upon Ferguson
to order this wire. *Scofield* v. *Parlin, etc. Co.* 61 Fed. Rep.
804; *Merchants Bank* v. *State Bank*, 77 U. S. (10 Wall.)
604; *Case* v. *Bank*, 100 U. S. 446; *Greggs* v. *Selden*, 58 Vt.
561; *Commercial, etc. Ins. Co.* v. *Union Mutual Ins. Co.*, 19
How. 322; *R. R. Co.* v. *Coleman*, 18 Ill. 298; *Oil Co.* v. *Gil-
son*, 63 Pa. St. 150; *Bank* v. *R. R. Co.*, 30 Vt. 170.

The defendant is chargeable with notice of the transac-
tion with the plaintiff. *Fulton Bank* v. *Bank*, 4 Paige 127;
Bridgeport Bank v. *R. R. Co.*, 30 Conn. 231, 270; *N. Y. etc.
R. Co.* v. *Schuyler*, 34 N. Y. 30, 84; *New Hope, etc. Co.* v.
Bank, 3 N. Y. 156; *Railway Co's.* v. *Keokuk Bridge Co.*, 131
U. S. 371; *Bank* v. *Davis*, 2 Hill 445; *Union Bank* v. *Camp-
bell*, 4 Humph. (Tenn.) 394; *Kennedy* v. *Green*, 3 Mylne &
K. 699; *Fishkill Sav. Inst.* v. *Bank*, 80 N. Y. 162; *Martin* v.
Webb, 110 U. S. 7.

The act of Ferguson in ordering the wire was ratified by the defendant, hence it is bound. *Taylor* v. *A. & M. Assn. etc.,* 68 Ala. 229; *Begou* v. *Tihe,* 23 La. Ann. 788; *Medomak Bank* v. *Curtis,* 24 Me. 36; *Grape Sugar Co.* v. *Small,* 40 Md. 395; *Wood Co.* v. *King,* 45 Ga. 34; *Bucher* v. *R. Co.,* 43 Vt. 133; *State* v. *Smith,* 48 Vt. 266; *Hooker* v. *Bank,* 30 N. Y. 83; *People's Bank* v. *Bank,* 101 U. S. 181; *Scott* v. *Ry. Co.,* 86 N. Y. 200; *Wyndham* v. *Sprague,* 43 Vt. 502.

Defendant ratified purchase by failure to disaffirm within a reasonable time. *Fitzgerald Cons. Co.* v. *Fitzgerald,* 137 U. S. 98; *Indianapolis Rolling Mill* v. *St. Louis, etc. R. Co.,* 120 U. S. 356; *Olcutt* v. *R. Co.,* 27 N. Y. 546.

The purchase was ratified by failure of defendant to place plaintiff *statu quo,* or to offer to do so. *Yeoman* v. *Bell,* 151 N. Y. 234; *Nichols* v. *Palmer,* 18 N. Y. 312; *Neal* v. *Reynolds,* 38 Kan. 432.

The court should have directed a verdict for plaintiff. *Bank* v. *Fassett,* 42 Vt. 432.

The $800.00 was a voluntary payment and can not be recovered. *Stevens* v. *Head,* 9 Vt. 174; *Wheatley* v. *Waldo,* 36 Vt. 237; *Taggart* v. *Rice,* 37 Vt. 47; *Williams* v. *Colby,* 44 Vt. 40; *Sowles* v. *Soule,* 59 Vt. 131.

Hunton & Stickney for the defendant.

The evidence of the defendant tended to show that Ferguson was never authorized to pledge its credit; that the wire was material which the contractors were bound to furnish. Plaintiff's motion for a verdict ignores defendant's evidence and was properly overruled. The evidence was conflicting and the jury found for the defendant. *Lyndon Mill Co.* v. *Lyndon Inst.,* 63 Vt. 581; *Saville, Somes & Co.* v. *Welch,* 58 Vt. 683; *Boynton* v. *Braley,* 54 Vt. 92.

STAFFORD, J. The defendant is a Vermont corporation running an electric railroad between Barre and Montpelier, and is sued for six miles of copper feed wire which the plaintiff, a corporation of another state, claims to have sold and delivered to it in August, 1898. The defense is that the wire, although received by the defendant and made a part of its plant, was purchased by Ferguson & Richardson, a firm of contractors, who, it is claimed, were bound to and did furnish it, as a part of the equipment, under their contract with the road. Ferguson, of the firm of contractors, was likewise a director of the defendant and a member of its executive committee. It was he who ordered the wire of the plaintiff. In doing so he claimed to be acting for the corporation as director and committee-man, and so far as the plaintiff's understanding and intention are concerned the wire was furnished upon the credit of the defendant. Kennedy, the president of the defendant and at the same time a member of the executive committee, saw the bills of the wire soon after it came and noticed that it had been procured on the credit of the defendant. He also knew that it was being made a part of the plant. Yet he took no steps to notify the plaintiff that it must not look to the defendant for its pay. Thus a majority of the executive committee acted in a way to bind the defendant if the committee itself could have bound it. *McNeil* v. *Boston Chamber of Commerce*, 154 Mass. 277. The third member knew nothing of the transaction and took no active part in the management. There were nine directors, indeed, but the whole business of the corporation was managed by the officers of the board, and the officers took their instructions from Ferguson who was allowed to control everything. This appears from the testimony of the directors themselves. Kennedy, Ferguson and Flynn, three of the number, were themselves the executive committee whose conduct and attitude have been described. Bush testified that the general business of the company was left to the committee. Howland said the same. Miles declared that he let it run itself. Humphrey, the nominal treasurer, left all the duties of his office to Butman, the assistant treasurer, and knew no more of the money business of the concern than as if he had not been treasurer. Butman himself repeatedly dealt with the plaintiff on the basis of the company owing for the wire and sent it a check for $800 on account. Pierson, the only other director, died before the wire was ordered. We find no evidence to the contrary.

A claim was advanced that the road, from the time the cars began to run until after the wire had been put up, was being operated by Ferguson as contractor for the purpose of testing it, and not by him as an officer of the corporation. An offer was made to show this and a ruling obtained that it might be shown; but the testimony produced had no tendency to support the offer. A few answers, if taken alone, might be thought to do so, but read in connection with other answers of the same witness and with the unquestioned facts, they cannot be considered to have the effect claimed.

It was June 28th when the cars began to run. It was the last of August when the wire was ordered. It was the first of September when the wire was received, and the end of September when the last of it was installed. From July 3d the superintendent of the road was Smith. The assistant, and only acting, treasurer was Butman. The man who controlled the corporation was Ferguson. During these three months the road was in active operation in the name of the defendant. There is no pretense that anything was left to be done towards its construction unless it was the supplying of the wire in question. The daily receipts were collected by the superintendent and deposited to the credit of the defendant and disbursed by the assistant treasurer for the expenses of the company, including the wages of the employees and the salary of the superintendent. Books of account were kept by the assistant treasurer showing receipts and disbursements. The wire was put up by the superintendent under direction of Ferguson and the work paid for in the first instance by the defendant and sometime later, perhaps after this controversy arose, charged over to the builders. Smith testified that he kept the account of this work separate because he did not regard it as "any part of our work,"— that is, any part of the work of the corporation which he, as superintendent, was carrying on, which could only mean the operating of the road. The wire was necessary for the safe and regular conduct of the business of transportation and was especially desired and called for by the superintendent and president in anticipation of an unusual amount of traffic which would attend the opening of a fair at Barre on the 7th of September. During these three months, as afterwards, the bills against the company were approved by the superintendent and by him sent to and paid by the assistant treasurer. The contract for the construction of the road gave the contractors no right to operate it after it was constructed. The defendant had been fully organized and was doing business before the contract for constructing the road was entered into. All the directors understood how the business was being done. We shall now notice the answers alluded to above. Humphrey, the nominal treasurer, referred to already, who does not testify to any means of knowledge except that he was frequently over the road, says that the orders for running it were given by Ferguson & Richardson, and that "as far as he knew" the corporation was not running the road; that "there

was somebody else running the road: We hadn't accepted
it." But later he says the road was never accepted, although
he admits that it has long been operated by the defendant. It
is evident that he is giving merely his opinion of the situation and not testifying to any matter of fact in conflict with
those above recited. An attempt was made to show by Kennedy, the president, that the road was not being operated for
the corporation, but he declines to make that statement, saying only that Ferguson was the man in control. Smith says
he received instructions from Ferguson and from Barnes, an
agent of Ferguson & Richardson. To say that these answers
taken in connection with the uncontroverted facts have any
tendency to show that the road was not being operated by
the defendant, is hardly possible. We are aware that the bill
of exceptions affirms that there was evidence tending to show
that the road was being operated by the contractors as such,
but the bill makes the transcript of the testimony controlling
and a careful examination of the whole has led us to the
conclusion we have just stated.

So we must add to the facts summed up in the beginning
the further fact that the wire was purchased and appropriated
at a time when the road was being operated by the defendant.

The question then is whether the corporation is bound
by the action of the committee.

A by-law provided for "an executive committee of three
to perform the general duties of directors, the assent of the
directors to be had before the acts of such committee shall be
binding upon them." But we do not regard that as altering
the rule of law touching the power of directors to act through
a committee. It can not mean that ordinary every-day matters must be specifically authorized one by one, for that would
make the committee useless, and on the other hand matters

requiring the exercise of discretionary powers could not be delegated even if the by-law had been silent upon the subject.

The principle that a board of directors is the depositary of discretionary powers to be exercised by the board itself and not to be delegated by it to any smaller body even of its own members is entirely consistent with the other principle that it may delegate authority to perform such duties as are required in the usual and ordinary course of its business. The act here questioned was the procuring of material or supplies necessary for the prompt and orderly conduct of its daily business and for the safety of human life, and in our opinion falls within the second principle. The authority to perform such an act must be held to have been conferred by the unanimous acquiescence of the directors in the course of business which had been pursued.

The directors were all consenting to the operating of the road by the committee. By so consenting they did exercise their judgment and discretion, and impliedly authorized those who were actually operating to do the things and procure the supplies needful therefor. The latter, as agents of the board, were therefore acting within the scope of their authority in procuring them. *Hooker* v. *Eagle Bank of Rochester*, 30 N. Y. 83, 86 Am. Dec. 351; *Olcott* v. *Tioga R. Co.*, 27 N. Y. 546, 84 Am. Dec. 298, 303; *McNeil* v. *Boston Chamber of Commerce*, 154 Mass. 277.

If the officer who purchased the material on the credit of the corporation was under contract with the latter to furnish it himself that may afford a subject for adjustment or litigation between the officer and the corporation, but is not enough to defeat a plaintiff otherwise entitled to recover.

There being no dispute as to the amount due the plaintiff, if entitled to recover, it moved the court for a verdict,. and we think its motion ought to have been granted.

Judgment reversed, and cause remanded.

GEORGE H. KING, RECEIVER, *v.* ALEX. COCHRAN.

January Term, 1901.

Present: ROWELL, C. J., TYLER, MUNSON, START, WATSON, and STAFFORD, JJ.

Opinion filed January 4, 1904.

Foreign Corporations—Stockholders—Statutory Liability— Determination of:—In Foreign Jurisdiction—Action on in this State—Receiver—Title to Assets—Declaration— Sufficiency.

In an action at law by a foreign receiver against a stockholder to recover on the latter's statutory liability, an allegation in the declaration that under the laws of the state of his appointment, the plaintiff, as such receiver, acquired the legal title to all the assets of the corporation, and the right to enforce the liability of the stockholders, is a sufficient allegation of title in the plaintiff.

A declaration counting on the liability of a stockholder under a foreign statute, setting forth such statute, and alleging that under said statute, as interpreted by the Supreme Court of the state, "the liability of the defendant as a stockholder is a contractual liability, and arises upon the contract of subscription to the capital stock made by the defendant in becoming a stockholder, and that, in subscribing to said stock and becoming a stockholder, he thereby guaranteed payment to the creditors of an amount equal to the par value of the stock held and owned by

him, which should be payable to the receiver of the corporation,
and that such receiver is the only person who can enforce said
liability," sufficiently shows that the liability of the stockholders
is a secondary asset of the corporation, available for the payment
of its debts.

A stockholder of a foreign corporation, even without notice thereof,
is bound by proceedings had in the foreign jurisdiction, in pursuance of the statute which controls the settlement of the affairs
of the corporation, to ascertain the deficiency for which he is
holden upon his statutory liability; and this liability, so determined, may be enforced in the courts of the stockholder's residence.

DEBT on the statutory liability of a stockholder in a foreign bank. Heard on a general demurrer to the declaration,
at the June Term, 1900, Caledonia County, *Taft,* J., presiding. Demurrer sustained, *pro forma,* and declaration adjudged insufficient. The plaintiff excepted.

This demurrer is to the amended declaration filed after
the case had been once to the Supreme Court. The amended
declaration, among other things, alleged the incorporation of
the Washington Savings Bank of Seattle, under the laws of
the Territory of Washington, for the purpose of conducting
a banking business; that under and by virtue of the laws of
the State of Washington it is provided as follows: "Each
and every stockholder shall be personally liable to the creditors of the company, to the amount of what remains unpaid
upon his subscription to the capital stock, and not otherwise;
provided, that the stockholders of every bank incorporated
under this act, or the Territory of Washington, shall be held
individually responsible, equally and ratably, and not one
for another, for all contracts, debts, and engagements of such
association accruing while they remain such stockholders, to
the extent of the amount of their stock therein at the par
value thereof, in addition to the amount invested in such

shares"; that the same provision existed by virtue of the laws of the Territory of Washington at the time the bank was incorporated, and has continued in force continuously, under the laws of the Territory of Washington and under the laws of the State of Washington, during all the time since the bank was incorporated; that under the aforesaid statute, as interpreted by the Supreme Court of Washington, the liability of the defendant as a stockholder, is a contractual liability, and arises upon the contract of subscription to the capital stock made by the defendant in becoming a stockholder, and that in subscribing to said stock and becoming a stockholder he thereby guaranteed payment to the creditors of an amount equal to the par value of the stock held and owned by him, which should be payable to the receiver of said corporation duly appointed by the Superior Court of the State of Washington, in and for King County, whenever said Court should order an accounting of the assets and liabilities of said corporation, and should decree that said amount so guaranteed, or any part thereof, should be necessary to pay the debts of said corporation; that under the aforesaid statute, as interpreted by said Court, the receiver is the only person who can enforce said liability of stockholders, and the only person who can lawfully demand payment of said assessment from the defendant, as a stockholder.

Said amended declaration further alleged that the bank is insolvent; that the defendant is now, and at the time of said insolvency was, a stockholder in said bank, and the owner of ten shares of its stock of the par value of one hundred dollars each; that the plaintiff was appointed receiver under said statute by the Court of Washington; that an accounting of the assets and liabilities of said bank has been had by said Court; that said Court has made an order directing the plaintiff, as receiver, to levy an assessment against the stockholders of said bank of seventy per cent of the par value of the stock owned by them for the purpose of liquidating the debts owed by said bank, and that said order was made after said Court, upon hearing, had determined the necessity thereof; that the plaintiff, as such receiver, had demanded of the defendant the amount of said assessment on his stock, and defendant refused to pay the same.

The amended declaration also alleged that under the above quoted statute, as interpreted by the Supreme Court of Washington, the plaintiff, as such receiver, acquired the legal title to all the assets of said corporation, including choses in action; and more particularly acquired the right to enforce the liability of stockholders of said corporation, and especially the liability of the defendant as a stockholder to the creditors of said corporation, arising from his contract of subscription to the capital stock made by the defendant in becoming a stockholder.

T. J. Deavitt and *Edward H. Deavitt* for the plaintiff.

The liability is alleged to be contractual. It was so held in *Barton Nat. Bank et al.* v. *Atkins et al.*, 72 Vt. 33, 38. The receiver has the legal title to the assets, and no other person has the right to enforce this liability. *Wilson* v. *Book,* 13 Wash. 676, 682, 683, 684; *Waterson* v. *Masterson,* 15 Wash. 511, 514, 515; *Birch* v. *Taylor,* 1 Wash. 245, 247, 248; *Cole* v. *R. R. Co.,* 9 Wash. 487; *Hardin* v. *Sweeney,* 14 Wash. 129.

The receiver is really bringing debt on the decree of the Court in Washington. The stockholder is bound by the proceedings leading up to the assessment. This decree can not be collaterally attacked. *Hawkins* v. *Glenn,* 131 U. S. 319;

Hancock Nat. Bank v. *Farnum,* 176 U. S. 640; *Glenn* v. *Liggett,* 135 U. S. 533; *Great Western Tel. Co.* v. *Purdy,* 162 U. S. 329, 337; *Howarth* v. *Lombard,* 175 Mass. 570; *Casey* v. *Galli,* 94 U. S. 673; *U. S.* v. *Knox,* 102 U. S. 422; *Richmond* v. *Irons,* 121 U. S. 27, 55; *Howarth* v. *Angle,* 162 N. Y. 179; *Howarth* v. *Eliwanger,* 86 Fed. Rep. 54; *Sheaf* v. *Larimer,* 79 Fed. Rep. 921.

Dunnett & Slack for the defendant.

The statutory liability of stockholders is a liability to the creditors, it is not a corporate asset, and does not go to the receiver as such, hence he has no right to enforce it. Smith on Receivers § 78; *In Re People's, etc. Co.* 56 Minn. 180; Cook on Stocks and Stockholders, § 218; *Olson* v. *Cook,* 57 Minn. 552; *Minn. etc. Co.* v. *City Bank,* 66 Minn. at p. 455; *Jacobson* v. *Allen,* 20 Blatch. 525; *Bristol* v. *Sanford,* 12 Blatch. 341; High on Receivers, § 317a; *King* v. *Cochran,* 72 Vt. 107; *Murtey* v. *Allen,* 71 Vt. 377; *Newell* v. *Fisher,* 24 Miss. 392; *Yearver* v. *Wallace,* 44 Pa. St. 294; *Relph* v. *Rundell,* 103 U. S. 222; *Glen* v. *Marbury,* 145 U. S. 499; *Boothe* v. *Clarke,* 21 How. 535. Each stockholder is liable only for the proportion of his debt. This proportion can only be ascertained upon an account of the debts and stock, and a pro rata distribution of the indebtedness among the several stockholders. This can only be done by a suit in equity. *Bank* v. *Atkins,* 72 Vt. 33.

Munson, J. The original declaration in this case was examined in *King* v. *Cochran,* 72 Vt. 107, 47 Atl. 394, and was adjudged insufficient upon the authority of *Murtey* v. *Allen,* 71 Vt. 377, 45 Atl. 752. It was held in the case cited that in this State a receiver has no remedy at law other than those given him by the common law; that he cannot sue at law in his own name without having the legal title to the thing in controversy; that he does not acquire by virtue of his appointment the title to the property received; and that the declaration in question did not show that the plaintiff had such a title as would enable him to maintain an action at law in his own name.

The case is now before us·upon an amended declaration demurred to generally. No question is made as to the form of action. The sufficiency of the count, as against any objections that are urged against it, depends upon whether it alleges a legal title to the cause of action declared upon, and whether that cause of action is one enforceable at law.

The count alleges that under the statute of Washington, as interpreted by the Supreme Court of that state, the receiver, by virtue of his appointment, "acquired the legal title to all of the assets of said corporation including choses in action and more particularly the right to enforce the liability of stockholders of said corporation and especially the liability of the defendant as a stockholder to the creditors of said corporation arising from his contract of subscription to the capital stock made by the defendant in becoming a stockholder." The defendant contends that this is merely an allegation of a right to enforce the liability, and not of a title to the liability.

But we think the sentence quoted, properly construed, is an allegation of title. Its fair meaning is that the receiver acquired the legal title to all the assets of the corporation including choses in action, and of these choses in action more particularly the right to enforce the liability of stockholders, and of these liabilities more particularly that of the defendant.

It is said, however, that this is not an asset of the corporation, but a liability to the creditors of the corporation, and therefore not within the allegation. But the count sets up the statute of Washington, and alleges that under that statute, as interpreted by the Supreme Court of the State, "the liability of the defendant as a stockholder is a contractual liability, and arises upon the contract of subscription to the capital stock made by the defendant in becoming a stockholder, and that in subscribing to said stock and becoming a stockholder he thereby guaranteed payment to the creditors of an amount equal to the par value of the stock held and owned by him, which should be payable to the receiver of said corporation * * ", and further alleges that under that statute as so interpreted, "such receiver is the only person who can enforce said liability." It sufficiently appears from this that the liability of the stockholders is a secondary asset of the corporation available for the payment of its debts.

The nature of this liability was considered in *Barton National Bank* v. *Atkins,* 72 Vt. 33, 47 Atl. 176, where it was said: "Such a provision is entirely for the benefit of creditors, and is in effect a requirement that the stockholders, by availing themselves of the advantages to be derived from such an organization, shall impliedly agree to be responsible for the debts of the corporation to the extent by law provided. * * * This provision, with the capital of the corporation, was the basis of its credit. The creditors contracted with reference to it. It became a part of the law of their contracts, and constituted security for any debt contracted by the company. * * * The creditors had a right to understand that, although the debts contracted were the debts of the corporation and that, in their enforcement, the remedy against it and its primary assets must first be exhausted, if such assets proved insufficient, they had, as security for the deficiency, this liability of the stockholders. The stockholders knew the law and voluntarily assumed that responsibility, and while it was not enforceable by the corporation, it is a secondary asset for that purpose, and constitutes a trust fund to be resorted to by the receiver in the marshalling of assets, if necessary for the full satisfaction of the indebtedness for which it is holden."

The manner of enforcing this obligation was considered in *Howarth* v. *Lombard,* 175 Mass. 570, and the Court saw nothing in the nature of the liability to prevent a holding that the legal title was in the receiver. The opinion says: "The receiver is called by the Washington court a *quasi* assignee for creditors. He is charged with the administration of a trust fund which does not take form or come into actual existence until after his appointment, and he is the only person who can collect it. By virtue of his official relation to the corporation and its creditors he is the owner of the legal title to this fund as a trustee for the creditors. A suit could not have been brought in the name of the corporation, and he is the only person who can now, or who ever could, legally demand and collect the money. We are of the opinion that the action is rightly brought in his name."

It is clear that the liability is not to the creditors in any sense which prevents its being an asset of the corporation and therefore a chose in action of which the receiver has the legal title. The statement that the stockholder guaranteed payment to the creditors and the recital of this guaranty as a liability to the creditors must be construed in connection with the various allegations which disclose the nature of the liability, and especially in connection with the allegations that the amount was to be payable to the receiver, that the title is in him, and that a recovery can be had by no one else. When the allegations are read together there is no room for doubt as to the meaning of the words in question.

But it is said that if the receiver has the legal title, he has no case upon which a suit at law can be maintained. It is argued that the defendant is not bound by the proceedings in which the individual liability of the stockholders was determined in the State of Washington because not a party to those proceedings, and that he can be made liable here only in a Court where an accounting of the assets and indebtedness of the bank can be had. This calls for an inquiry as to the effect to be given to the account taken and assessment made by the Washington Court having jurisdiction of that matter. If these proceedings are an adjudication conclusive upon the defendant, the amount of his liability is ascertained, and a suit at law is the appropriate remedy.

In *Hawkins* v. *Glenn*, 131 U. S. 319, an assessment ordered by a Court which had jurisdiction of the corporation was held binding upon stockholders residing in another state, although not made parties as individuals. It is said in the opinion that a stockholder is so far an integral part of the corporation that in the view of the law he is privy to the proceedings touching the body of which he is a member; that a decree against the corporation in respect to corporate matters, such as the making of an assessment in the discharge of a duty resting on the corporation, necessarily binds its members in the absence of fraud, and that this is involved in the contract created in becoming a stockholder. It is true that the assessment sued upon in the case cited was on a subscription for stock, but we see no ground upon which the two liabilities can be distinguished as regards the question under consideration; and other courts have held the same.

Howarth v. *Lombard,* 175 Mass. 570; *Howarth* v. *Angle,* 162 N. Y. 179.

The ground upon which foreign stockholders are held concluded by the proceedings taken to ascertain the deficiency for which they are holden upon their secondary liability is fully and clearly stated in *Howarth* v. *Lombard.* The liability is contractual as well as statutory. The law provides that each stockholder shall be liable equally and ratably for the obligations of the corporation to an amount equal to the amount of his stock in addition to the stock itself, and that if the corporation becomes insolvent and a receiver is appointed he shall pay to the receiver the amount of such liability when the same shall be ascertained and decreed by the Court having jurisdiction of the case. The stockholder contracts with reference to these requirements when he takes his stock, and is as much bound by them as if they were incorporated in a written agreement bearing his signature. His agreement covers not only the liability, but the manner in which the extent of the liability shall be determined; and when required to contribute in accordance with his undertaking he cannot be permitted to question the conclusiveness of the proceeding.

The defendant, as a stockholder of the Washington Savings Bank, is bound by all valid proceedings had in pursuance of the statute which controls the settlement of its affairs. In becoming a member of the corporation he submitted himself to the laws of Washington in matters touching his relations to the bank and its creditors. As represented by the corporation, he had notice of and was present at the hearing when the account was taken and the assessment made. If the suit were in equity, he could not cast that proceeding aside and demand a fresh accounting. He could impeach the record only for fraud, and that he can do in a court of law.

Judgment reversed, demurrer overruled, declaration adjudged sufficient, and cause remanded.

CATHERINE McCLOSKEY, MARGARET BROOKS, AND MARY LARKIN *v.* SPRINGFIELD FIRE AND MARINE INS. CO.

October Term, 1903.

Present: ROWELL, C. J., TYLER, MUNSON, START, and WATSON, JJ.

Opinion filed January 4, 1904.

Fire Insurance Policy—Surrender—Mental Capacity of Insured—Question for Jury.

In an action on a fire insurance policy, to the defense that the policy had been surrendered and cancelled in accordance with its terms, it is a good reply that the insured, by reason of mental disease, was incapable of understanding the nature and consequence of the act of surrender; and this question is properly submitted to the jury.

ASSUMPSIT on a fire insurance policy. Plea, the general issue, with notice of the surrender and cancellation of the policy. Trial by jury at the September Term, 1902, Rutland County, *Stafford*, J., presiding. Defendant's motion for a verdict overruled, to which the defendant excepted. Verdict and judgment for the plaintiff. The defendant excepted.

The defendant's motion for a verdict was made at the close of all the evidence, and was upon the ground: "First, because the surrender and cancellation of said policy was not the making of a contract, but the exercise of a right, and it mattered not whether the plaintiff was sane or insane at the time. Second, because if the plaintiff was without sufficient mental capacity, as the evidence tended to show, that this condition had existed from a time considerably before the issuing of the policy until after its surrender, and the plaintiffs can not take advantage of the issuing of the policy, and avoid the cancellation; and Third, because there was no evidence tending to show that the defendant knew, or in the exercise of reasonable prudence, ought to have known, of the want of mental capacity on the part of the plaintiff."

Charles L. Howe for the defendant.

The surrender and cancellation of the policy is not a contract, but the exercise of a right, and the plaintiff, whether sane or insane, could exercise this right. Ostrander on Fire Ins. 2 Ed. § 17; *Massasoit, etc. Co.* v. *Western, etc. Co.,* 125 Mass. 110; *Lincoln* v. *Buckmaster,* 32 Vt. 653.

Butler & Moloney for the plaintiffs.

The cancellation or discharge of a contract requires the same capacity in the parties that it requires for making. Clark on Contracts § 256; *Wheeler* v. *R. Co.,* 115 U. S. 29.

The question is did the insured have the mental capacity to understand what she did. *Stewart* v. *Flint,* 59 Vt. 152; *Davis* v. *Cummings,* 60 Vt. 282; *Day* v. *Seeley,* 17 Vt. 542; *Falch* v. *Goltschalk,* 71 Am. St. Rep. 418.

Defendant can not avoid its contract by reason of the insanity of the other party. *Atwell* v. *Jenkins,* 47 Am. St. Rep. 463.

TYLER, J. Action to recover the amount of loss under an insurance policy, issued by the defendant to the plaintiffs June 20, 1900, and insuring them for five years against loss by fire on their dwelling house. The plea and notice raise the question of a surrender and cancellation of the policy. The property was destroyed by fire July 8, 1901.

It was provided in the policy that it might be cancelled at any time at the request of the insured, or by the company by giving the insured five days' notice, and that if it should be cancelled, or become void, the premium having been actually paid, the unearned portion should be returned on surrender of the policy, the company retaining the customary short rate, except that, if the policy was cancelled by the company by giving notice, it should retain only the pro rata premium.

February 20, 1901, Mary Larkin, one of the plaintiffs, surrendered the policy to the defendant's agent and was paid $5.40 as return premium, and the policy was cancelled. The plaintiffs claim that this act was void by reason, as they allege, of the plaintiff's want of mental capacity to understand the nature and consequences of her acts, and that the policy was therefore in force when the fire occurred.

The policy was by its terms to continue in force until the expiration of the risk unless sooner terminated by the exercise of the option of one of the parties, as provided, or by the agreement of both. There is a manifest distinction, as claimed by the defendant and as laid down by the authorities cited, between the abrogation of an insurance contract by agreement of the parties and its cancellation by one party in the exercise of a right reserved in the contract. Ostrander on Fire Ins., 2nd Ed. s. 17; *Massasoit Steam Mill Co.* v. *Western Assurance Co.*, 125 Mass. 110. But these authorities do not support the defendant's position, that the plaintiff, though insane but having no guardian, could and did exercise the right of option, and that the defendant was bound to respect it and return the premium. It may not have required as much mental capacity to perform this voluntary act as it did to make the insurance contract, but some capacity was required to exercise the right reserved in the policy; therefore the court properly submitted to the jury to decide—not whether the plaintiff was sane or insane—but whether, by reason of mental disease, she was incapable of understanding the nature and consequences of her act. As the jury found her incapable, the surrender was not her act.

The exceptions state that the defendant made no other question during the trial than that of Mrs. Larkin's mental capacity with reference to the exercise of this right.

Judgment affirmed.

JOHN STILES, COLLECTOR OF TAXES, *v.* VILLAGE OF NEWPORT.

October Term, 1901.

Present: ROWELL, C. J., MUNSON, START, and WATSON, JJ.

Opinion filed January 7, 1904.

Taxation—Municipal Corporations—Water System—Public Use—Exemption—Pipe Line—Real Property.

A municipal corporation is, by implication, exempt from taxation; but this exemption extends only to property devoted to a public use.

There is a distinction in the meaning of the term "public use," as employed in the law of eminent domain, and in that of taxation.

When a municipal corporation has constructed, and has since maintained, a water system for fire protection and other municipal purposes, and also for the purpose of furnishing its inhabitants with water for domestic use for a certain compensation; the latter use of the water is not a mere incident of the former.

The furnishing water by a municipality to its inhabitants for domestic purposes, in consideration of a compensation which even yields an incidental profit to the municipality, is a "public use," within the meaning of that term as used with reference to exemptions from taxation.

A water system owned by a municipality, and used for fire protection and other municipal purposes, and also to supply water to its inhabitants for domestic purposes in consideration of a compensation which yields an incidental profit to the municipality, even though part of the system is within the territory of another municipality, is property devoted to a public use, and is exempt from taxation, both by implication, and by the seventh subdivision of V. S. 362.

A branch from its main water system, built by a municipality outside of its corporate limits, and devoted wholly to the needs of another village, and which can never be made available for its own municipal service, is not property devoted to a public use, and is not exempt from taxation.

The pipes and hydrants of a water system are real property.

Assumpsit for the collection of taxes, commenced by trustee process under V. S. 506. Plea, the general issue. Trial by jury at the March Term, 1901, Orleans County, *Tyler,* J., presiding. At the close of all the evidence, on motion of the defendant, a verdict was ordered, *pro forma,* for the defendant to recover its costs. Judgment on verdict. The plaintiff excepted.

Defendant's motion for a verdict was mainly upon the ground that the property in question is by implication exempt from taxation, and is expressly exempt under the seventh subdivision of V. S. 362, as being property sequestered for public uses.

The taxes for which this suit was brought were assessed against the defendant in the years 1899, and 1900. On the first day of April in each of those years, the defendant owned a water system, a part of which, consisting of about five miles of main pipe, besides branch lines, all buried in the ground, and several hydrants, and land used for a reservoir, was situated in the town of Derby. It is upon this part of its system, situated in the town of Derby, that the taxes in question were assessed against the defendant.

Under the provisions of its charter, and in the exercise of the power of eminent domain, the defendant took water for this system from Derby Pond in the town of Derby, and constructed an aqueduct from said pond to the village of Newport. About five miles of the main line of this aqueduct was in the town of Derby. Very near the end of this five miles, the defendant, in the exercise of the power of eminent domain, condemned between one and two acres of land in the town of Derby, and thereon constructed a reservoir which it used as part of said system for storage purposes, and fenced the whole about with a tight board fence. At very near the end of this five miles of main line in the town of Derby is situate the village of West Derby, a village of about nine hundred inhabitants. At this point the defendant installed a branch system from its main line, all in the town of Derby; and from this branch system sold water to the inhabitants of West Derby for domestic use. The defendant also installed in this branch system sixteen hydrants for the use of which for fire protection the defendant received from the corporation, the village of West Derby, two hundred and forty dollars annually. There were also six hydrants in this branch system in the International mill yard in Derby, used for fire protection only, for which defendant received one hundred dollars annually. The total receipts of the defendant for all water furnished in the town of Derby from its system was about one thousand six hundred seventy-nine dollars annually.

That part of defendant's water system situated in the town of Derby was constructed as an extension of a system

which it already owned, which was inadequate, and no part
of which was situate in the town of Derby. That part of this
extension situated in the town of Derby, cost the defendant
about fifty thousand dollars. The defendant had an outstanding bonded debt on account of this extension, of about
forty thousand dollars.

The defendant also sold the water from this system to
the inhabitants of the village of Newport for domestic purposes; and used the water for fire protection, for sprinkling
the streets, for flushing the sewers, for supplying a public
water trough, and for supplying the school house, in said
village.

The defendant was also selling to one customer in the
village of Newport water from said system sufficient to run
a water motor of three or four horse power, which was used
to operate the machinery in a printing office. The defendant
also furnished water from said system to two churches in
said village, without charge. One of these churches used a
small water motor to pump its organ. No other water was
furnished from said system for mechanical purposes, except
that for five years previous to the year 1900, the defendant
had furnished water from said system to the Boston & Maine
Railroad Company for its engines and for fire protection and
for drinking purposes, at its stations and buildings in the
villages of Newport and West Derby, for three hundred dollars
per year. In November, 1900, this arrangement was aban-
doned, on account of shortage in the water supply.

J. W. Redmond, Seneca Haselton, and *Josiah Grout* for
the plaintiff.

All provisions of exemption from taxation are to be
strictly construed. Cooley on Tax. p. 146; *Mayor* v. *Baltimore, etc. R. Co.,* 48 Am. Dec. 531. Municipal corporations

are not expressly exempt by V. S. 362, and such exemption cannot be implied because of V. S. 360. *Nimblet* v. *Chaffee,* 24 Vt. 628; *In Re Varnum,* 70 Vt. 147; *State* v. *Hartford,* 47 Am. Rep. 622; *State* v. *Collins,* 37 Atl. 623.

The property is not devoted to a public use within the meaning of exemptions from taxation. The use is a private one, for the immediate corporate benefit of the defendant. *Welsh* v. *Village of Rutland,* 56 Vt. 228; *Weller* v. *Burlington,* 60 Vt. 28; *Wilkins* v. *Rutland,* 61 Vt. 336; *Bates* v. *Rutland,* 62 Vt. 178; Tiedeman on Munic. Corp. §§ 9 & 10; *Mount Hope Cemetery* v. *Boston,* 158 Mass. 509; Cooley on Taxation, p. 172. The village of Newport could just as well start a bakery in the village of Derby to supply good bread, and claim this devoted to a public use.

There is a distinction in the meaning of the term "public use" as employed in the law of taxation and in that of eminent domain. Cooley on Taxation, (1 Ed.) p. 80; Desty on Taxation, p. 25.

This property is therefore taxable. *Newport* v. *Unity,* 44 Atl. 704; *Negley* v. *City,* 4 Munic. Corp. Cases, 704; *Commonwealth* v. *Makebben,* 29 Am. St. Rep. 382; *Sanitary Dist. etc.* v. *Martin,* 64 Am. St. Rep. 110; *Louisville* v. *Commonwealth,* 85 Am. Dec. 624; *Essex County* v. *Salem,* 153 Mass. 141; *County of Erie* v. *City of Erie,* 6 Atl. 138; *University* v. *People,* 22 Am. Rep. 187; *Worcester* v. *Worcester,* 116 Mass. 193; *Newark* v. *Clinton,* 8 Atl. 296; *Camden* v. *Village,* 1 Atl. 689; *Toledo* v. *Hosler,* 10 Ohio Cir't Ct. 257; *People* v. *Amsterdam,* 157 N. Y. 42.

If this property is exempt, then towns can take all the real property from another town and force it to raise its taxes on personal property. An exemption is virtually an additional tax upon other property. The exemption of this property in Derby for the benefit of Newport, is a tax upon the people of Derby for the benefit of the people of Newport, and is unconstitutional. Cooley on Taxation p. 105.

The branch used to supply the village of West Derby is certainly not devoted to a public use. This is a purely private business enterprise. *Tyler* v. *Beacher,* 44 Vt. 548, *In Re Barre Water Co.* 72 Vt. 413.

The pipe line and hydrants are real property. *Willard* v. *Pike,* 59 Vt. 223; *Inhabitants of Paris* v. *Norway, etc. Co.,* 35 Am. St. Rep. 371; *State* v. *Berry,* 52 N. J. L. 308; *People* v. *Martin,* 48 Hun. 193.

Young & Young for the defendant.

Municipalities cannot tax each other. Each is independent of the other. In this respect they are like nations. Vattel's Law of Nations, p. 494; *Coe* v. *Erroll,* 116 U. S. 517; *Van Brocklin* v. *Anderson,* 117 U. S. 151-180.

Property of a municipality is by implication exempt from taxation. *Buckley* v. *Osburn,* 8 Ohio 180; *Piper* v. *Singer,* 4 Serg. & R. 354; *Directors, etc.* v. *School Directors,* 42 Pa. 21; *People* v. *Doe,* 36 Cal. 220; *Worcester Co.* v. *Worcester,* 116 Mass. 193; *Trustees, etc.* v. *Taylor,* 30 N. J. Eq. 618; *Trustees, etc.* v. *Trenton,* Ibid. 667; *Rochester* v. *Rush,* 80 N. Y. 302; *State* v. *Hartford,* 50 Conn. 89; *Fagan* v. *Chicago,* 84 Ill. 227; *Inhabitants, etc.* v. *County Com'rs.* 4 Gray 500; *Doyle* v. *Austin,* 47 Cal. 353; *Summerville* v. *Waltham,* 170 Mass. 160; *People* v. *Solomon,* 51 Ill. 37, 52; *People* v. *Brooklyn Assessors,* 111 N. Y. 505; *Galveston, etc. Co.* v. *Galveston,* 63 Tex. 14; *West Hartford* v. *Hartford,* 44 Conn. 360; *Rex* v. *Inhabitants of Liverpool,* 14 E. C. L. 37; *King* v. *Trustee, etc.,* 14 E. C. L. 41; *King* v. *Commissioners, etc.,* 33 E. C. L. 239; *Queen* v. *Mayor, etc.,* 40 E. C. L. 12; *Queen*

v. *Shee*, 45 E. C. L. 1; *State* v. *Collins*, 37 Atl. 1097; *U. S. B. & O. R.*, 17 Wall. 322; *Merriweather* v. *Garrett*, 102 U. S. 472; *Smith* v. *Mayor, etc.*, 88 Tenn. 464, 7 L. R. A. 469; *People* v. *U. S.*, 34 Am. Rep. 155; *Kleien* v. *New Orleans*, 99 U. S. 150; *Sherwin* v. *Wigglesworth*, 129 Mass. 64.

This aqueduct is devoted to a public use. History shows that aqueducts have always been regarded as public institutions. 2 Enc. Brit., 222; 2 Curtis Hist. Greece, 388, (Scribner Ed.) 2 Mommsen's Hist. Rome, 85; 4 Ibid. 168, 169, 173.

The defendant acquired this property by the legitimate exercise of the right of eminent domain. But this right can be legitimately exercised only for a public use. Hence this property is devoted to a public use. *Snow* v. *Sandgate*, 66 Vt. 451; *In Re Barre Water Co.*, 62 Vt. 27; *Foster* v. *Bank*, 57 Vt. 128.

This property is equally exempt as devoted to a public use, whether situate within or without the corporate limits of the defendant. See cases above cited.

MUNSON, J. The defendant village is authorized to provide a supply of water for fire, domestic and other purposes, and to sell and furnish water for domestic and other purposes to persons or corporations within or without said village. No. 201, Acts 1878; No. 283, Acts 1894; No. 196, Acts 1898. A part of the defendant's water system, including its reservoir and aqueduct, lies in the town of Derby. The land for the reservoir was acquired under the right of eminent domain. The defendant uses the water for fire protection and other municipal purposes, supplies it to its inhabitants for domestic purposes at a certain compensation, and sells to one inhabitant enough to run a small motor for manufacturing purposes. The defendant also supplies the village of West Derby, a manufacturing establishment located in that village, and two properties in the town of Derby outside the village limits, with water for fire protection, and the inhabitants of West Derby with water for domestic purposes; receiving compensation from all these sources. Defendant also supplied the Boston & Maine R. R. Co., at its yard in Derby, with water for its engines, for an agreed compensation, until November first, 1900. In 1899 and 1900 that part of the system located in the town of Derby was set to the defendant in the Derby grand list, and this suit is brought to recover the taxes assessed thereon. The defendant claims that the property is not taxable.

The only general provisions exempting property from taxation are those contained in V. S. 362. The first, seventh and ninth subdivisions of this section contain the only provisions that exempt property solely on the basis of ownership. The owners named in these provisions are the State, the United States, colleges, academies and other public schools, and cemetery associations. Other provisions exempt property because of the use to which it is put, and among these is the first clause of subdivision seven, which exempts property "granted, sequestered or used for public, pious or charitable uses." The defendant's claim of exemption is based upon two grounds; first, that the property of a municipal corporation is exempt by implication; second, that this property is devoted to a public use, and is therefore expressly exempted.

It will be noticed that as to some of the owners mentioned in section 362 the statute does not create the exemption, but merely declares it. The United States is exempt because of Federal supremacy. The State is exempt because of its sovereignty. Municipal corporations are not mentioned; but these are instrumentalities of the State, and the defendant contends that they are exempt, although not mentioned, the same as the State would have been.

But the plaintiff contends that any implication of this character that might otherwise have existed is cut off by the provision of section 360, that all real and personal estate shall, except as otherwise provided, be set in the list. It is argued further, that inasmuch as owners necessarily and impliedly exempt are included in the list named, the omission of municipal corporations is equivalent to a legislative declaration that the property of such corporations is taxable unless otherwise specially exempted. It is said that if the Legislature had intended that the property of municipal corporations should be exempt because of their relation to the State, it would have mentioned them in connection with the State.

These considerations alone will not suffice to deprive municipalities of any implied exemption to which they may otherwise be entitled. General statutory provisions like those referred to are treated as having reference only to such property as the law considers the subject of taxation. For instance, if the State had not been mentioned as exempt, the sweeping provision cited would certainly not have been held to require the taxation of its property. The most express language would be needed to overcome the presumption that the State does not tax itself. It is certain that there is also an implied exemption in favor of municipal corporations, but the extent of that exemption is open to inquiry.

It is doubtless true that the implied exemption in favor of the State is absolute and unlimited, but it by no means follows that the exemption in favor of municipal corporations is of equal scope. The municipality is an agent of the State, but it is often something more. It is frequently permitted to hold property for purposes which are not within the scope of its governmental duties, but which are nevertheless recognized as conducive to the public welfare. This leaves room for the question whether the property of a municipal corporation is exempt from taxation because of such ownership and regardless of the use to which it is put.

It has been repeatedly said in general discussions that property owned by a municipal corporation cannot be taxed without express statutory authority; that the nature and purpose of taxation are such as preclude the idea of its being made a burden upon public property; and that tax laws will not be held applicable to municipal holdings unless the language positively requires it. These statements are doubtless made with reference to the general rule that a municipal corporation does not and cannot hold property except for public use. They certainly have failed to control when the courts have met with exceptional cases where the ownership was municipal and the use distinctly private. It will be well to refer to some of these cases, that we may guard against giving general statements of this character an undue effect in the further discussion.

In *West Hartford* v. *Com'rs. of Hartford,* 44 Conn. 360, one of the cases most relied upon by the defendant in support of its main contention, the city bought a larger tract than was needed for its reservoirs because it could trade most advantageously upon that basis, and the part not used for the reservoirs was held taxable. In *Inhabitants of Wayland* v. *Com'rs. of Middlesex,* 4 Gray 500, another case specially relied upon by the defendant, the municipality acquired the fee of the land needed for its aqueduct, and it was said with reference to this, that "if the land was valuable for and used for purposes other and distinct from those of the aqueduct, the property so used, to the extent it was so used, would be

liable to taxation." In *Essex County* v. *Salem,* 153 Mass.
141, it was held that land purchased by the county for the
purpose of enlarging its jail and jail grounds, was subject to
taxation while leased for private purposes and a source of income to the county. In *State* v. *Gaffney,* 34 N. J. L. 131,
where land bought and property held for a city reservoir but
not yet put to use was declared exempt, the court recognized
the limitation of the right of exemption by distinguishing this
from previous decisions, saying that in the case before it the
land was being held for a necessary purpose, and without being used for any other purpose.

It is doubtless in recognition of this class of cases that
most writers treat the rule as requiring not only municipal
ownership but appropriation to a public use. We are satisfied
that under the doctrine of implied exemption as applied to
municipalities, the ultimate test is not municipal ownership
but public use; so that this doctrine gives the defendant no
greater right than it has by our statute, and the question
whether the use is public will be controlling under either
branch of its claim.

We have seen that the defendant's plant is designed and
used to supply its inhabitants with water for domestic purposes; and our next inquiry is, whether this is a public use
within the meaning of the laws relating to taxation. We
have no cases bearing directly upon this question, and not
many that will be specially helpful in its determination.

In *Middlebury College* v. *Cheney,* 1 Vt. 336, and in
Willard v. *Pike,* 59 Vt. 202, 9 Atl. 907, there is some discussion of the question of public use as related to colleges
and academies. The first case was ejectment for land in
Albany which the defendant claimed under a tax title. The
plaintiff contested this title upon two grounds: first, that the

college was authorized to hold lands of the yearly value of two thousand dollars free from taxation; second, that the land was non-taxable because sequestered for public, pious and charitable uses. The court sustained both contentions, saying with reference to the second that a conveyance for the use of the college was to a public use. In the second case cited, the validity of a list was contested because of the omission of certain buildings owned by the St. Johnsbury Academy, which were partly occupied by teachers and students and partly rented. The Court rejected certain authorities from other states on the ground that our statute differed from theirs in placing the exemption on the ground of ownership alone without mention of use; but considered that the building in question was held to a public and charitable use; and left undecided the question whether buildings acquired and held solely as an investment would be exempt.

Here the defendant is a municipal corporation, and its use of property is public in a different sense. Its functions are ordinarily such as justify the condemnation of whatever property may be necessary for their exercise. It is undoubtedly true that the furnishing of water to the inhabitants of a village for domestic purposes is a public use within the meaning of the law of eminent domain; and the defendant contends that this determines the character of the use as regards the right of taxation. This view is supported by *Inhabitants of Wayland* v. *Com'rs. of Middlesex*, above cited, but the weight of authority is against it; and Mr. Cooley considers it settled that the meaning of the term in the two uses is not the same. So this test will not be accepted as determinative.

On the other hand, the plaintiff says that the property would have been taxable in the hands of a private company which had acquired the right and was distributing the water in the same way, and that this determines that it is taxable in the hands of the defendant. He insists that as regards undertakings which are not imposed upon the municipality but are voluntarily assumed and carried on for compensation, the municipality is to be treated the same as a private company, and that to hold otherwise would be inconsistent with the position we have taken in negligence cases.

It is true that in considering the liability of municipal corporations for their negligent acts, a distinction is made between acts done in the performance of their governmental duty as agents of the State and those voluntarily undertaken for corporate gain as well as for the public good. *Welsh* v. *Village of Rutland*, 56 Vt. 228; *Weller* v. *Burlington*, 60 Vt. 28, 12 Atl. 215; *Wilkins* v. *Rutland*, 61 Vt. 336, 17 Atl. 735; *Bates* v. *Rutland*, 62 Vt. 178, 20 Atl. 278; *Buchanan* v. *Barre*, 66 Vt. 129, 28 Atl. 878. These cases certainly determine that the use is private as distinguished from municipal, but they cannot be taken as a conclusive determination that the use is private within the meaning of the laws relating to taxation.

In supplying water for domestic purposes, the municipality is acting both for the public good and for corporate gain. Serving this double purpose, the property may be subjected to liability as private, or protected from liability as public, according to the nature of the demand. The individual suffering from negligence, and the municipality seeking revenue, approach the question upon different lines. When the municipal owner disputes the right of its sister municipality to tax the system, it is no answer to say that the use is so far private as to permit a recovery of compensatory damages. In *Com.* v. *McKibben*, 90 Ky. 384, 29 Am. St. 382, the reasoning of the New York court in the negligence case of *Bailey* v. *The Mayor of New York*, 3 Hill, 531, 38 Am. Dec. 669, was relied upon as applicable and controlling upon the question of taxation. But this cannot be the prevailing view, for generally the courts permit a recovery of damages upon the dual theory, and yet deny the right of taxation. We conclude, therefore, that the question before us is not disposed of by the position taken in our cases above cited.

In this case, as in cases generally, the water is supplied for domestic purposes in connection with a provision for fire and other municipal purposes; and the defendant contends that, whatever the holding might be in the case of a system devoted wholly to domestic use, this additional use of a system required for the performance of a municipal duty will not subject the property to taxation. It is said that the main purpose of the system is to meet the needs of the municipality, and that its use for domestic purposes is only incidental to the municipal use. It is true that the work of distribution is done in connection with the performance of strictly municipal duties, and in part by way of a more complete utilization of a strictly municipal expenditure. · But it is clear that the use is not incidental in the sense in which the term is applied to the supplying of water for manufacturing purposes from a surplus properly taken but not needed for present use. The authorization combines the two uses, and the works are designed and constructed, and the supply secured, with reference to both. There is no contemplation of a time when the supplying of domestic needs shall cease because of the increased demand for other purposes. The use for domestic purposes is treated as incidental in *State* v. *Conover*, 42 Atl. 838, (N. J. L.), but we are not content to rest the decision upon this ground.

So the question recurs, whether the supplying of water for domestic purposes to the inhabitants of the municipality is in itself a public use within the meaning of the term as used with reference to taxation. It is said by Mr. Cooley that in the case of property held to supply such needs as are commonly supplied by a private corporation, such as water or gas works, the presumption of an intention to exempt from taxation would be very slight and perhaps would not arise at all. Cases from Kentucky are referred to in this connection. The constitution of Kentucky exempts "public property used for public purposes." In that state "public purposes" is held to mean the same as "governmental purposes," and municipal water works used in part for the supply of the inhabitants have always been regarded as taxable. *Covington* v. *Kentucky,* 173 U. S. 231, is referred to by plaintiff as sustaining this view, but it cannot be given that effect, for the Court was careful to say that it was bound by the construction given by the Supreme Court of Kentucky to the constitution of that state, however much it might doubt the soundness of any interpretation which implied that lands and buildings owned and used by a municipal corporation under legislative authority for the purpose of supplying that corporation and its people with water, were not public property used for public purposes. In several states, municipal water-works, devoted to the usual purposes, have been held exempt by implication, on the ground of public use, without any distinction being made between the different purposes. The case most exactly in point, and freest from other matters that might be supposed to have influenced the decision, is *West Hartford* v. *Com'rs. of Hartford,* already referred to.

The acts under which water-works have been provided by municipal corporations have almost invariably authorized a provision for fire, sanitary and domestic purposes. This grouping of uses is evidently in recognition of general needs which cannot be fully met by individual effort. The first two have always been regarded as public uses, while the last has often been denominated private. But this last is not without some of the elements of public use that pertain to the other two. Both the provision for subduing fire and that for household use are designed to promote the municipal good through the benefit conferred upon private interests. The municipality itself seldom owns many buildings to be protected from fire or supplied with water. In these two purposes we are dealing with public use in a different sense from that applicable to public property as necessary to the exercise of governmental functions. The municipality has no other material basis than the property and health of its inhabitants, and in taking measures for the protection of either it is serving a municipal interest. The provision for sanitary purposes is ordinarily treated as having reference to the cleansing of streets and the flushing of sewers. This use is public in a closer signification than either of the others, for the streets are in a sense municipal property and their maintenance an imperative governmental duty. But even this use, viewed as it is designated, looks rather to the preservation of health than to the care of property. Sanitary measures are those designed to promote and preserve health. The supply for domestic purposes comes partly within this provision, for the household use is in part sanitary. It would be idle to distinguish in classification between the water used in the closet and the same water after it reaches the sewer. But this does not exhaust the sanitary aspect of the supply for domestic purposes. The requirement for fire protection and street and closet use is that there be an abundant supply. The requirement for drinking and culinary purposes is that the supply be pure and wholesome. This element of purity also serves a sanitary purpose of the highest order. Without a supply of this character the public health would be in constant danger. These various uses are so interwoven in their relations to the municipality that it is difficult to say that one is public and the other private; and when all are served through the same system it is difficult to say that one is incidental to the other in any other sense than that the common supply is available for either use according as the demand is made. But we think no violence is done to reason in holding that the furnishing of water by a municipality to its inhabitants for domestic purposes is a public use within the meaning of the term as used with reference to exemptions.

The question of public use may be tested in another way. Taxes can be levied only for public purposes. We take it that a tax levied to establish and operate this system would not be made invalid by the fact that the plant was designed to meet both domestic and municipal needs. Then the supply of domestic needs is a public use within the meaning of the laws relating to the imposition of taxes, and if so, it may properly be regarded a public use within the rules relating to exemptions.

The use being public in its nature, the taking of compensation does not require that it be otherwise treated. The manner of distribution and the difference in individual requirements are such as make the imposition of rates advisable, and the fact that the expense is thus apportioned according to the use, instead of being provided for by taxes levied equally upon all, does not make it any the less a public use. The charge is in the nature of a special assessment graduated to the benefit received.

The fact that an incidental profit may accrue to the municipality and that this may in time become available for the payment of general corporate expenses, will not subject the system to taxation as serving a private use. The use will remain public notwithstanding this incidental result of the scheme of compensation, and if the working of that scheme is not what it should be, the regulation of municipal affairs is always in the hands of the Legislature.

But the plaintiff contends that this implied exemption of municipal property appropriated to public uses, does not apply to property located without the territorial limits of the municipality. It is said that an application of the rule that would lessen the taxable property of one municipality for the benefit of another cannot have been intended; and *Newport* v. *Unity,* 68 N. H., 587, 44 Atl. 704, is cited in support of this view. The facts of that case were such as would make the decision applicable here, but the conclusion of the Court seems to have resulted somewhat from a consideration of various statutory provisions. But whatever effect this case may be entitled to, it is certain that there are well considered decisions to the contrary. It has been distinctly held in several states, and we think upon sufficient grounds, that municipal property put to public use, even though located in another municipality, is not taxable, unless the Legislature so enacts. Among the cases so holding are *People* v. *Assessors of Brooklyn,* 111 N. Y. 505; *Somerville* v. *Waltham,* 170 Mass. 160.

It remains to consider whether the conclusions previously reached regarding the use of the system in the defendant village are applicable to the action of the defendant in furnishing water to the village of West Derby and its inhabitants. The municipal duty of the village of Newport as regards the maintenance of mains and hydrants is confined to its territorial limits. The municipal relation which enters into the question of domestic supply is confined to its own inhabitants. The furnishing of water to the inhabitants of the defendant village is held to be a public use upon the ground that the making of such a provision, while not strictly a municipal duty, is protective of the public health, and therefore a public use within the meaning of the laws relating to taxation. But this reasoning fails when the furnishing of water to the village of West Derby is in question. We see no ground upon which the West Derby branch of this system can be held to be devoted to a public use, either as regards fire protection or domestic needs. The village of Newport owes no municipal duty to the village of West Derby or its inhabitants, and has no municipal interest there. Its sale of water to that village and its inhabitants is for the revenue obtainable thereby, independent of any connection with municipal duty or interest. Although disposed of for the same purposes, the sale cannot be regarded as a public use, because of this want of municipal relation.

It appears, then, that the defendant is the owner of property in the town of Derby, a part of which is devoted to private uses; and we have already seen that municipal property may be subjected to taxation by being put to a private use. It is not necessary to determine here what the rights of taxation may be as regards property put to both public and private uses. We cannot say upon the case before us that the reservoir and aqueduct are larger than might properly be provided for the village of Newport, having reference to its prospective needs; and any further benefit that might properly be derived from them would be treated as incidental. So these could not be listed for taxation upon any basis.

This may suggest the further question, whether the defendant's supplying of water to the village of West Derby for municipal and domestic purposes, although in itself a private use, should not be treated as an incidental use of a surplus properly provided, and so be classed as a public use. The question is not the same that would have been presented if the West Derby system had been in existence, and the action of Newport village had been confined to a sale of its surplus water. Here, the village of Newport has built and installed a branch outside its corporate limits, which is devoted wholly to the needs of another village, and can never be made available for its own municipal service; and the question is whether the property so created and circumstanced shall be treated as serving an incidental and therefore a public use. It might not be easy to frame a safe and acceptable definition of an incidental use, but we think it may safely be said that the supplying of the municipal and domestic needs of another municipality through a complete system of distributing pipes and hydrants created for that purpose, is not such a use. The plaintiff has assessed the hydrants located in Derby, and we hold that they are taxable.

The property is listed as real estate, and the defendant claims that it is personal property. It was held in *Willard* v. *Pike,* 59 Vt. 202, 9 Atl. 907, that the iron pipe in which water was brought from the springs to the reservoir, partly in the highway and partly in fields of various owners, was real estate. Following this case, we hold that the hydrants were properly classed. The decision referred to was made without discussion, but was in accord with a number of well reasoned cases.

NOTE. This case was heard by all the Judges qualified to sit. The above opinion was made public at the October Term, 1902, but without entry of judgment, the Court being unable to agree upon a minor point touching the validity of the list. No agreement upon that point having been reached at the October Term, 1903, a reargument of it was ordered for the January Term, 1904. Counsel thereupon waived a reargument, and agreed upon an entry disposing of the case.

OCTAVE B. BRUNNELL ET UX *v.* EUGENE W. CARR ET UX.

October Term, 1903.

Present: ROWELL, C. J., MUNSON, START, WATSON, STAFFORD, and
HASELTON, JJ.

Opinion filed January 7, 1904.

*Husband and Wife—Joint Deed—Deceit—Liability—Interest
—Date of Computation.*

It not appearing that the land conveyed by the joint deed of husband
and wife was hers, she is not liable for deceit which consists of
a false statement contained in the deed as to the amount of incumbrance on the land conveyed.

In such case the husband is liable for his tort, and should pay the
grantees the amount the latter had to pay by reason thereof, with
interest from the commencement of the suit, it not appearing
when such payment was made.

CASE FOR DECEIT in the sale of land. Plea, the general
issue. Trial by court in the city court of the city of Montpelier, *Laird,* Acting Judge. Judgment for the defendants to
recover their costs. The plaintiffs excepted.

The deed from the defendants to the plaintiffs was a warranty deed in the usual form, and warranted the premises free
from incumbrance "except a mortgage in favor of L. C.
Parker of Calais in the County of Washington, on which there
is now due six hundred and forty dollars, which said mortgage the said Brunnells hereby assume to pay as part consideration of this deed."

The court found, from oral evidence received without
objection, that the six hundred dollars named in the deed as
the amount of the mortgage, was the full purchase price of
the land; that the amount of said mortgage, at the time said
deed was executed by the defendants, was in fact eight hun-

dred dollars; that the plaintiffs have paid the mortgagee eight hundred dollars with the interest thereon since the deed was made.

The court held, as matter of law, that by the terms of said deed the plaintiffs assumed and agreed to pay the mortgage which said Parker held upon the real estate, and rendered judgment for the defendants to recover their costs.

H. C. Shurtleff for the plaintiff.

Sargent for the defendant.

Rowell, C. J.   This is case for deceit in the sale of land conveyed to the plaintiffs by the joint deed of the defendants. The deceit consisted in a statement in the deed that the premises were free from incumbrance, except a certain mortgage whereon was then due $640, which the grantees assumed and agreed to pay as a part of the price, whereas there was more then due thereon, to the knowledge of the defendants, which the plaintiffs had to pay.

It not appearing that the land was Mrs. Carr's, the case does not come within the Married Women's Act, but must stand upon the common law, and at the common law a married woman is not liable for torts based upon her contracts, but only for her torts *simpliciter*. *Woodward* v. *Barnes*, 46 Vt. 332; *Russell* v. *Phelps*, 73 Vt. 390, 50 Atl. 1101.

But Mr. Carr is liable for his tort in the matter, and should pay to the plaintiffs $167.70, the amount they had to pay by reason thereof, with interest thereon by way of damages from the commencement of the suit, the record not showing when the payment was made.

Judgment affirmed as to Mrs. Carr, but reversed as to Mr. Carr, and judgment against him for said last-mentioned sum, with interest thereon as aforesaid, and costs. Certified exccution granted.

ARTHUR C. SPENCER *v.* THOMAS E. STOCKWELL.

October Term, 1903.

Present: ROWELL, C. J., TYLER, START, WATSON, and STAFFORD, JJ.

Opinion filed January 14, 1904.

Husband and Wife—Promissory Note—Intermarriage of Maker and Payee—V. S. 2644-2647.

Under V. S. 2644-2647, if a woman, who is the payee and owner of a valid promissory note, marries the maker, she retains all her rights in respect of the note, except the right to sue her husband thereon in her own name.

Under V. S. 2644-2647, if a woman, who is the payee and owner of a valid promissory note, marries the maker, and subsequently indorses the note to a third person for collection only, such person may maintain an action thereon in his own name against the husband for the benefit of the wife.

ASSUMPSIT upon a promissory note. Heard on an agreed statement, at the April Term, 1903, Windham County, *Munson,* J., presiding. Judgment for the plaintiff. The defendant excepted.

The note in question is payable to "Rosa B. Richardson, or order." The opinion states the other facts.

E. L. Waterman, J. L. Martin, and E. W. Gibson for the defendant.

V. S. 2644, does not give the wife the right to sue her husband. This is really the case of a wife suing her husband.

A note from husband to wife is void. *Sweat* v. *Hall,* 8 Vt. 187; *Ellsworth* v. *Hopkins,* 58 Vt. 705.

The right of action which the wife had was destroyed by the marriage. *Miller* v. *Miller,* 44 Pa. 170; *Burleigh* v. *Coffin,* 22 N. H. 124; *Flenner* v. *Flenner,* 29 Ind. 468; *Power* v. *Lester,* 23 N. Y. 527; *Patterson* v. *Patterson,* 45 N. H. 164; *Farley* v. *Farley,* 91 Ky. 497; *Smiley* v. *Smiley,* 186 Ohio St. 543; *Bank* v. *Mitchell,* 84 Fed. Rep. 90; *Abbott* v. *Winchester,* 105 Mass. 115.

If there is any right in the wife it must be enforced in Chancery. *Wallingford* v. *Allen,* 10 Pet. 583.

Clarke C. Fitts for the plaintiff.

The husband acquired no interest in this note by marriage. V. S. 2647; *Wright* v. *Burroughs,* 61 Vt. 390; *Butler* v. *Ives,* 139 Mass. 202; *Bemis* v. *Call,* 10 Allen 512; *Tucker* v. *Fenno,* 110 Mass. 311; *Ellis* v. *Watkins' Est.,* 73 Vt. 371.

TYLER, J.   It appears by the agreed statement of facts, that the defendant being indebted to Rosa B. Shepardson for money that she had loaned him, gave her his promissory note for the amount; that a few months afterwards the parties intermarried, and that the marriage relation has ever since existed between them; that the note belongs to the wife and was overdue when this suit was brought; that she indorsed it to the plaintiff for the purpose of collection only, and that suit was brought after demand of payment.

I.   Under the Married Women's Act, No. 84, laws of 1884, which is incorporated into V. S. 2644 to 2647, inclusive, the note continued to be the property of the wife after the marriage. It is true, as the defendant contends, that this statute, which gives married women the right to hold all personal property and rights of action acquired by them before marriage to their sole and separate use, only enables them to make contracts with all persons *other* than their husbands, and to sue and be sued upon such contracts. But the contention cannot be maintained that the note in this case became null and void and the debt extinguished by the intermarriage, for this is contrary to the express provisions of the statute. It is immaterial that the wife acquired the property in this note from the defendant while the parties were sole. It was the payee's property until the marriage, and the statute is broad enough to include it within its terms. It says, "All personal property * * * acquired by a woman before coverture," * * *. It makes no exception.

Sweat v. *Hall*, 8 Vt. 187, and *Ellsworth* v. *Hopkins*, 58 Vt. 705, 5 Atl. 405, are not authorities for the defendant. They only hold that a promissory note given by a husband to his wife during coverture is void because of the legal incapacity of the parties to contract with each other. But both these cases recognize the doctrine that where the note represents a separate statutory or equitable property in the wife, a Court of Equity will protect it.

The defendant cites *Abbott* v. *Winchester*, 105 Mass. 115, where it was indeed held that a note given by a man to a woman whom he afterwards married became a nullity upon the marriage and was not revived by the husband's death. But the doctrine held in that case and in *Chapman* v. *Kellogg*, 102 Mass. 246, was repudiated in *Butler* v. *Ives*, 139 Mass. 202. In the latter case a husband advanced money to his wife for the benefit of her separate estate, and she gave her promissory note therefor, secured by mortgage, to a third person who assigned the note and mortgage to the husband. The husband assigned the note and mortgage to a fourth person who foreclosed the mortgage and brought a writ of entry against the person who was claiming under the wife; held, that the writ could be maintained.

But it is unnecessary to consider the decisions of courts of other states. The doctrine of the common law by which all the personal property of the wife became her husband's upon marriage has been abrogated by our statutes. *Wright* v. *Burroughs,* 61 Vt. 390, 18 Atl. 311, is authority that, under existing laws, the note in this case was the sole property of the wife when she transferred it to the plaintiff. It was held in that case that the husband was improperly joined as a party plaintiff with his wife in a suit upon her note against a third person.

II. It is further contended that, as the wife could not sue her husband upon the note, she could not give the plaintiff authority for that purpose. It is a sufficient answer to this claim that the wife retained every right in respect to the note after her marriage that she possessed before, except the right to sue her husband upon it. She could sell the note absolutely, or transfer it for collection as well after as before her marriage. The statute places no inhibition upon this act; on the contrary, it gives her the same authority to deal with the note as if she were unmarried. She did not confer authority upon the plaintiff to sue the defendant; that authority was incident to the plaintiff's legal title to the note, although the equitable interest remained in the wife.

Judgment affirmed.

SUSAN B. SOWLES v. EUGENE MARTIN, E. P. ADAMS, AND
ALBERT SOWLES.

May Term, 1902.

Present: MUNSON, START, WATSON, STAFFORD, and HASELTON, JJ.

Opinion filed January 18, 1904.

Landlord and Tenant—Letting on Shares—Products—Tenants in Common—Sale—Accounting—Parties.

In the ordinary case of letting a farm on shares, though the owner is
to have a "lien and ownership" on the entire products of the
farm as security for her share, she and the tenant are tenants in
common of such products.

If, in the ordinary case of letting a farm on shares, it is agreed that
the owner is to have "a lien and ownership" on the entire products of the farm as security for her share, she may sell, upon
the tenant's default, but she must account to the tenant as to
the owner of an equal share.

In the ordinary case of letting a farm on shares, though it be agreed
that the owner is to have "a lien and ownership" on the entire
products of the farm as security for her share; if the tenant has
misappropriated some of the products, and the owner has done
nothing inconsistent with the relation established by the contract, she may maintain a bill in equity for an accounting.

It is proper to make a party defendant to such suit, a person to whom
the owner of the farm sold certain hay, under the agreement that
the buyer should retain the tenant's share of the proceeds till
the account between the owner of the farm and the tenant should
be adjusted, and who paid over the tenant's share in violation of
the agreement.

APPEAL IN CHANCERY, Franklin County. Heard at
Chambers, on demurrer to the bill, *Rowell*, Chancellor. Demurrer sustained. The oratrix appealed.

The bill stated the ordinary case of letting a farm at the
halves by the oratrix to the defendant, Martin, and alleged

that "your oratrix furnished much more than one half, her share, of the seeds and materials to carry on said farm, for which she was to have a lien and ownership on the entire products and profits of said farm and crops, until her full share of the profits and income and advancements were paid;" that Martin had not fulfilled his part of the contract, but had misappropriated certain of the income and products of the farm. The bill prayed for a discovery and an accounting.

It is alleged in the bill that Albert Sowles is a creditor of Martin, and as such, had brought suit against Martin, and attached certain products of said farm, which suit was still pending. The opinion states the other facts.

E. A. Sowles for the oratrix.

The bill shows oratrix and Martin to be tenants in common, and alleges fraud on the part of Martin, and that he has misappropriated the common property. This gives equity jurisdiction. *Glastonbury* v. *McDonald,* 44 Vt. 450; *Bacon* v. *Bronson,* 7 John. Ch. R. 201; *Frost* v. *Kellogg,* 23 Vt. 308; *Leach* v. *Beaters,* 33 Vt. 195; *Lyon* v. *McLaughlin,* 32 Vt. 428.

C. G. Austin for the defendants.

The oratrix has a full remedy at law. The bill alleges that she was to have "a lien and ownership" of the products. She was the absolute owner. This is not a case of tenants in common. *Willmarth* v. *Pratt,* 56 Vt. 474.

MUNSON, J.   The bill sets up a contract with defendant Martin for carrying on the oratrix's farm on shares, and alleges that the oratrix was to have "a lien and ownership" on the entire products of the farm for whatever she might ad-

vance and for her share of the products until the same were
fully paid, and that she furnished more than her share of the
seeds and materials, but that Martin has not delivered to her
her share of the products.

The owner of a farm and a tenant on shares are tenants
in common of the products, in the absence of any special provision modifying their relations. *Frost* v. *Kellogg,* 23 Vt.
308; *Leach* v. *Beatties,* 33 Vt. 195. But in *Willmarth* v.
Pratt, 56 Vt. 474, a stipulation like the one above set forth,
was held to entitle the lessor to maintain trespass against the
tenant for products sold. This was upon the ground that the
general ownership was in the lessor, and that the tenant's
right of possession was terminated by his unauthorized sale.
But that decision is not an authority against the lessor's right
to maintain a bill in equity upon a lease so framed under the
circumstances now presented.

In this case the tenant was in default, and there are general allegations of the misappropriation and clandestine sale
of some of the products; but it does not appear that the oratrix
had, by suit or otherwise, treated the tenant as having done
anything inconsistent with the relation established by the contract. The hay taken by defendant Adams was sold him by
the oratrix, but upon terms which recognized the tenant's interest. The sale was upon condition that Adams should pay
one-half of the consideration to the oratrix, and hold the tenant's half until the account between the oratrix and the tenant
was adjusted, and then pay the same as the adjustment might
determine.

We think that the oratrix and defendant Martin are to
be treated as tenants in common of the products. The title to
the tenant's share was in the oratrix for purposes of security
merely, and while this gave her the right to sell upon the ten-

ant's default, she was to account to the tenant as the owner of an equal share. The tenant had done nothing that was treated as terminating the existing relation, and remained rightfully in possession of this hay until the sale. But the oratrix's sale passed the entire title to Adams, and her bill touches only the disposition of the avails. These, however, are the avails of property held by the parties as tenants in common, and the accounting in that behalf is within the jurisdiction of equity. So the bill can be maintained against defendant Martin.

It remains to inquire whether the bill can be maintained against Adams. It appears that Adams finally paid Martin for his half of the hay in disregard of the above agreement; and the oratrix seeks an accounting with Martin to determine the extent of her lien, and a decree charging Adams with the amount so paid over. It is alleged, obscurely but we think sufficiently, that Martin agreed with the oratrix and Adams regarding the holding of his share of the avails as above set forth. So Adams was dealing with both the oratrix and Martin in this particular, and became a trustee of the fund for the purposes agreed upon. He is therefore a proper party to the proceedings in which the rights of the oratrix and Martin in the fund are to be determined.

Decree reversed, demurrer overruled, bill adjudged sufficient, and cause remanded.

F. H. C. REYNOLDS v. BURTON S. HOOKER.

October Term, 1903.

Present: ROWELL, C. J., TYLER, START, WATSON, STAFFORD, and
HASELTON, JJ.

Opinion filed January 26, 1904.

*Specific Performance—Mutually Dependent Contracts—Parol
Evidence.*

When two written options are executed and delivered at the same
time, one for the purchase of real estate and the other for the
purchase of stock, in a suit for specific performance of the latter
option, parol evidence is admissible to show that neither option
was to have effect, unless both were accepted.

When two separate written options are executed and delivered at the
same time, one for the purchase of real estate and the other for
the purchase of stock, with the verbal understanding that neither
option was to have effect unless both were accepted, specific performance of one option will not be decreed, if the orator, on his
part, has not tendered performance of the other.

APPEAL IN CHANCERY. Heard on the bill, answer, master's report and exceptions thereto, at the December Term,
1903, Orange County, *Munson*, Chancellor. Decree dismissing the bill with costs. The orator appealed. The opinion
states the facts.

David S. Conant, R. M. Harvey and *Senter & Senter* for
the orator.

In the absence of fraud, accident, or mistake, parol evidence was not admissible to show that neither option was to
take effect unless both were accepted. *Abbott* v. *Choate*, 47
Vt. 53; *Morse* v. *Low*, 44 Vt. 561; *Perkins* v. *Young*, 16
Gray 389; *Ripley* v. *Page*, 12 Vt. 353; *Dixon* v. *Blondin*, 58

Vt. 689; *Isaacs* v. *Elkins*, 11 Vt. 679; *Allen* v. *Furbish*, 4 Gray
504; Parsons on Contracts, Vol. 2, p. 553.

John B. Peckett and *Smith & Smith* for the defendant.

Specific performance is matter of discretion. Ency. Pl.
& Pr. Vol. 20, p. 390, and note 1.

The two options were executed at same time, were one
transaction, and are to be construed together. 17 Wall. 96;
Reed v. *Field*, 15 Vt. 672; *Rutland etc. R. Co.* v. *Crocker*, 29
Vt. 540.

Contracts relating to personalty will not, as a rule, be
specifically enforced. *Gage* v. *Fisher*, 31 L. R. A. 557; *Welty*
v. *Jacobs*, 40 L. R. A. 98.

START, J. The defendant, being the owner of twenty-
three shares of the capital stock of the Bradford Electric
Company, and of a grist-mill and water privileges which furnished the power for the Bradford Electric Company's lighting plant, was asked by the orator if he would sell his stock
in the Bradford Electric Company. The defendant replied,
that, if he sold his stock, he should want to sell his grist-mill
with its water power. The orator said he wished to purchase
the water power, and asked the defendant if he would give
an option on the stock and real estate. The defendant replied that he would. Thereupon, the orator presented to the
defendant written options for the purchase of the stock and
real estate; the defendant read over both options and said he
thought they were all right, with the understanding, that, if
the option for the sale of the stock was accepted, the option
for the sale of the real estate should also be accepted, as he
did not wish to sell his stock unless he sold his real estate.
The orator replied that he so understood it, that he wanted
both, and, with this express understanding and agreement,

the defendant signed and delivered both options. The defendant has relied upon this agreement, and has at all times been ready and willing, and has offered, to carry out on his part both options. The orator asks the Court to decree specific performance, by the defendant, of the contract for the sale of the stock, without tendering performance, on his part, of the contract for the sale of the real estate.

The master found, from parol evidence, that the parties agreed that the option to purchase the stock should not be enforceable if the orator did not elect, and purchase, the real estate, which was received subject to the orator's exception. This exception is not sustained. The orator having resorted to a court of equity for relief, and prayed for the specific performance of the option for the purchase of the stock, without tendering performance, on his part, of the option for the purchase of the real estate, parol evidence was admissible to show, that, at the time of the execution of the option, it was agreed by the parties that this option should not be enforced against the defendant if the orator did not elect to, and carry out, the option for the purchase of the real estate. *Redfield* v. *Gleason,* 61 Vt. 220, 17 Atl. 1075; *Adams* v. *Smilie,* 50 Vt. 1; *Wilbur* v. *Prior,* 67 Vt. 508, 32 Atl. 474; Brown on Parol Evidence, §§ 37, 50; Pomeroy's Equity Jurisprudence, Vol. 2, 2 Ed., § 866. It appearing that the stock option was not to be enforceable unless the orator purchased the defendant's real estate, specific performance of the option will not be decreed. To do so, would be to aid the orator in the consummation of a fraud upon the defendant. The orator's attempt to enforce the stock option, according to its legal import, when it is shown that he agreed that it should not be enforceable unless he purchased the real estate, is a violation of his agreement and a fraud upon the defendant. *Taylor* v. *Gilman,* 25

Vt. 411; *Adams* v. *Smilie,* 50 Vt. 1; Pomeroy's Equity Jurisprudence, Vol. 2, 2 Ed. §§ 860, 866.

Decree affirmed and cause remanded.

GRAND TRUNK RAILWAY CO. *v.* MARSH H. DAVIS.

October Term, 1903.

Present: ROWELL, C. J., TYLER, MUNSON, START, WATSON, and
STAFFORD, JJ.

Opinion filed January 26, 1904.

New Trial—Party's Statements in Presence of Jury—His Intent—Presumption.

The verdict of a jury will be set aside and a new trial granted, when
during a recess, after the opening argument, in the trial of a suit
for personal injuries, the plaintiff made statements, in the presence and hearing of some of the jurors who were trying the case,
which would naturally prejudice the jury against the defendant
and induce a verdict for the plaintiff, although it does not appear
that such statements did have that effect.

When statements are made by a party to a suit or trial, in the presence and hearing of some of the jurors who are trying the case,
which would naturally prejudice the jury in his favor, he will be
presumed to have intended such statements to have that effect.

PETITION FOR A NEW TRIAL, brought under V. S. 1662,
to the Supreme Court for Essex County at its May Term,
1903, and heard at the October Term, 1903, on testimony
taken and filed.

Dale & Amey and *R. N. Chamberlin* for the petitioner.

Petitioner need not prove that the verdict was affected
by the conduct complained of. *Johnson* v. *Root,* 2 Cliff. 108,

128; Thompson on Trials § 2617; *Hix* v. *Drury*, 5 Pick. 296; *McDaniels* v. *McDaniels*, 40 Vt. 363.

J. W. Redmond and *E. A. Cook* for the petitionee.

START, J. This is a petition for a new trial. It is alleged, that the petitionee obtained a verdict in his favor at the March Term, 1903, of the Essex County Court; that, during the trial, some of the jurors who were empanelled to try the cause were talked with upon the subject matter of the cause, in a manner favorable to the petitionee; and that the petitionee himself talked to, and in the presence and hearing of, the jurors in a manner calculated to influence them to return a verdict in his favor. It is found, that, after the opening argument of the petitionee's counsel, a recess was taken, and the petitionee, some of the jurors and others went upon the steps of the court house; that the petitionee, there, and in the presence and hearing of the jurors, commented upon the petitioner's conduct in making him unnecessary expense, and stated that he had subpoenaed about twenty witnesses to show that he was a man of his word; and that it would cost him about twenty dollars, and explained why he was lamer at some times than at others. He also engaged in conversation with one Cote, whom the petitioner had procured to attend the trial as a witness but had not called as a witness, and charged in that connection that the petitioner's counsel did not dare to put him upon the stand, and stated that he, the petitionee, got hurt, and that Cote knew it.

These remarks may have influenced the jury to return a verdict for the petitionee to recover a larger sum than they would have if the remarks had not been made in their presence and hearing. The statements were calculated to prejudice the jury against the petitioner, and to thereby disqualify them for the proper and unbiased discharge of their duties; and the fact that the prejudicial statements were made in the course of a conversation provoked or induced by an outside party does not excuse the petitionee, nor render the statements harmless. The fact that the remarks were made by a party to the cause, and that they were calculated to prejudice the jury against the petitioner and to induce a verdict favorable to the petitionee, is a sufficient reason for setting aside the verdict. Such deliberate statements by a party, claiming to have been injured by reason of the neglect of the other party, in the presence and hearing of the jury, would naturally, and probably did, create in the minds of the jury a prejudice against the petitioner, and affect the verdict returned by them; and the petitionee is presumed to have intended his statements to have such effect. This being the natural and probable consequence of the petitionee's misconduct, and he, presumably, having intended such results, a new trial will be granted, notwithstanding it does not appear that the verdict was in fact affected thereby. The verdict of a jury may be properly set aside and a new trial granted, where, during the trial, conversations were had by a party to the cause, in the presence and hearing of the jury, which were calculated and intended to influence them to return the verdict they did, though it is not shown that the verdict was in fact influenced thereby. *McDaniels* v. *McDaniels,* 40 Vt. 363.

Verdict set aside, and new trial granted.

ELLEN R. CARTER *v.* SAMUEL W. CARTER.

October Term, 1903.

Present: ROWELL, C. J., TYLER, MUNSON, START, WATSON, and
STAFFORD, JJ.

Opinion filed January 26, 1904.

Divorce—Alimony—Antenuptial Contract.

A promissory note executed and delivered by a man to the woman
whom he subsequently marries, which is expressed to be in consideration of the intended marriage, and to be in full payment
of all that she, or her heirs or assigns, will ever claim against
his estate, and which he has paid according to its terms, does
not contemplate a divorce through the fault of the husband, nor,
in the event of such divorce, prevent the court from awarding her
alimony.

PETITION FOR DIVORCE. Heard at the June Term, 1903,
Lamoille County, *Haselton,* J., presiding. Divorce and permanent alimony granted. The petitionee excepted. The opinion states the facts.

George M. Powers for the petitioner.

This contract does not bar alimony. *Logan* v. *Logan,* 2
B. Mon. 149; 2 Bishop on Marr. & Div. § 369, n; *Stearns* v.
Stearns, 66 Vt. 187.

If this agreement was made to bar alimony it is against
public policy. 1 Bishop on Marr. & Div. § 635; note to *Clark*
v. *Fosdick,* 6 L. R. A. 132.

H. N. Deavitt for petitionee.

Petitioner is barred from claiming alimony by the contract. *Chaffee* v. *Chaffee,* 70 Vt. 231.

START, J. This is a petition for a divorce, with a prayer
for alimony. The petitionee, in bar of the petitioner's claim
for alimony, offered to prove, that, prior to the marriage of
the parties, they entered into an antenuptial contract of the
following tenor: "For value received, I promise to pay to
the order of Ellen R. Wilson three thousand dollars on demand with interest; said note is in consideration of a marriage this day to be solemnized and is in full payment for all
sums said Ellen R. Wilson or her heirs or assigns will ever
claim against me or my estate in law or in equity; said sum
to be subject to her order and control, and is in full payment
for all she will ever claim of me or against my estate." The
petitionee also offered to show that he had complied with the
terms of the contract. The evidence was excluded. A divorce
was granted for the adultery of the petitionee, and certain
real and personal estate belonging to him was decreed to the
petitioner as alimony.

It has been held by this Court, that contracts like the
one in the case at bar do not contemplate a divorce, through
the fault of the husband; that they do not relate to, nor touch
upon, the subject of the husband's duty, under the marital
contract, to support his wife, nor upon her right to be supported until the contract of marriage comes to an end by the
removal of one of the parties by death; and that they are not
intended to control the rights of the parties, when the husband
so conducts himself that the wife is deprived of the support
which she was entitled to upon the consummation of the
marriage, and do not bar the wife from permanent alimony.
Stearns v. *Stearns,* 66 Vt. 187, 28 Atl. 875. In the case before cited, the petitioner, before the consummation of the
marriage, agreed to relinquish all rights to the property which
the petitionee then had or might acquire, and that she should

be forever barred and estopped from having, or claiming
to have, any right, title or interest therein; and it was held
that the agreement did not bar the petitioner from permanent
alimony. For the purpose of decreeing permanent alimony
out of property belonging to a husband, at the time a divorce
is granted for his adultery, the agreement in this case cannot
be distinguished from the petitioner's agreement in the case
at bar, that she would make no claim against the petitionee
or his estate. It is, therefore, held, in accordance with the
former holding of this Court, that the Court below had authority, under V. S. 2691, to decree specific property, belonging to the petitionee, to the petitioner as permanent alimony,
and that the antenuptial contract, and evidence to show that
it had been complied with, were rightfully excluded.

Judgment affirmed.

STATE v. G. CONSTANTINO.

October Term, 1903.

Present: ROWELL, C. J., TYLER, MUNSON, START, WATSON, STAFFORD, and
HASELTON, JJ.

Opinion filed January 26, 1904.

*Intoxicating Liquor—No. 90, Acts 1902—Selling and Keep-
ing for Sale, Without a License—Penalty—Constitutional—Complaint—Sufficiency—Construction.*

The minimum fine of $300, imposed by No. 90, § 68, Acts 1902, for
selling, or keeping for sale, intoxicating liquor, without a license,
is not so disproportionate to the offense as to justify the Court in
questioning the action of the Legislature in prescribing it.

Section 68, No. 90, Acts 1902, is not unconstitutional because it fixes
   no maximum fine.
In a complaint, charging the respondent with furnishing, selling, and
   exposing for sale, intoxicating liquor, without authority, and
   without having a license therefor in force, the negation of a
   license covers all the acts complained of.
Such complaint is not founded upon the theory that two licenses are
   necessary. And though it be inferred that respondent had a
   license at some time, which had expired leaving him with the
   liquor on hand, it can not be further inferred that he was keeping liquor for sale when his license should again come into force.

COMPLAINT for selling, and keeping for sale, intoxicating liquor, without a license. Heard on general demurrer to
the complaint, at the June Term, 1903, Caledonia County,
Stafford, J., presiding. Demurrer overruled, and complaint
adjudged sufficient. The respondent excepted.

The complaint contains twenty-four counts. Twenty-
three of the counts are the same, except the date of the offense charged. Each of said twenty-three counts charges
that the respondent "at Hardwick in the County of Caledonia,
did sell, furnish and expose for sale, intoxicating liquor, without authority, and without having a license therefor in force,
contrary to the form and effect of the statute," etc.

The other count charges that the respondent, "at Hardwick in the County of Caledonia, did expose and keep for sale
intoxicating liquors, without authority, and without having
a license therefor, contrary to the form," etc.

Taylor & Dutton for the respondent.

Chapter II, § 32, of the Constitution of Vermont, provides "All fines shall be proportioned to the offenses." In
order to accomplish this the Legislature must fix a maximum
and a minimum penalty, and give the judicial department

discretion between these limits. *State* v. *O'Neil*, 58 Vt. 140; *Gregory* v. *State*, 94 Ind. 384; Ency. Law, Vol. 5, p. 90.

This discretion is a judicial function. It is for the Legislature to make the laws, but it is for the judiciary to interpret and *apply* them. Cooley on Const. Lim. p. 109, 110; *Merrill* v. *Sherburn*, 1 N. H. 199, 8 Am. Dec. 52.

M. G. Morse, State's Attorney, for the State.

The prohibition in the U. S. Constitution, against excessive fines, does not apply to the states. Am. & Eng. Ency. of Law, Vol. 13, p. 60 (2 Ed.); Cent. Dig. Vol. 15; *State* v. *Hodgson,* 66 Vt. 134. The statute is not unconstitutional because it does not prescribe a maximum limit to the fine. Cent. Dig. Vol. 15, Column 1088, § 3305; Am. & Eng. Ency. Law, (2 Ed.) Vol. 13, p. 62; *Freese* v. *State*, 23 Fla. 267; *In Re Yell,* 107 Mich. 228; *Martin* v. *Johnson,* 11 Tex. App. 628; *Southern Ex. Co.* v. *Com.* 92 Va. 59; *State* v. *Fackler,* 91 Wis. 418; *Com.* v. *Murphy,* 165 Mass. 66.

No specific defect in the complaint having been pointed out in county court, that question is not here. *State* v. *Preston,* 48 Vt. 12.

The offense is set out in the words of the statute. This is sufficient. *State* v. *Daley,* 41 Vt. 564; *State* v. *Cook,* 38 Vt. 437; *State* v. *Jones,* 33 Vt. 443; *State* v. *Mathews,* 42 Vt. 542; *State* v. *Clark,* 44 Vt. 636; *State* v. *Benjamin,* 49 Vt. 101; *State* v. *Higgins,* 53 Vt. 198; *State* v. *Miller,* 60 Vt. 90; *State* v. *Campbell* and note, 94 Am. Dec. 251; *Com.* v. *Smith,* 116 Mass. 140; *People* v. *Clements,* 26 N. Y. 193.

It is not necessary to name the person to whom the sale was made, or to state the kind of liquor sold. *Com.* v. *Conant,* 6 Gray 482; *State* v. *Blaisdell,* 33 N. H. 388; *Plunkett* v. *State,* 69 Ind. 69; *State* v. *Munger,* 15 Vt. 290; *People* v. *Adams,* 17 Wend. 475; *Green* v. *People,* 21 Ill. 125.

As to negation of license, see *State* v. *Munger*, 15 Vt. 290, and note in Annot. Ed.

ROWELL, C. J.   This is the complaint founded on sec. 68, No. 90, Acts of 1902, for furnishing, selling, and exposing for sale, intoxicating liquor without authority, and without having a license therefor in force; and for exposing and keeping for sale intoxicating liquor without authority, and without having a license therefor in force. The sanction of the section is a fine of not less than three hundred dollars, or imprisonment for not less than three nor more than twelve months, or both.   .

The respondent demurs, and objects that said section is unconstitutional, for that the Legislature attempts therein to exercise judicial power, and for that it provides for a fine not proportioned to the offense, fixes no maximum fine, prescribes an excessive minimum fine, and thereby virtually compels the court to require excessive bail.

The claim that it is an attempt on the part of the Legislature to exercise judicial power, is based upon the idea that it is for the courts, under the Constitution, to proportion fines to the offenses, and consequently that the Legislature cannot fix a definite and certain sum as a fine, leaving no discretion in the courts to reduce that sum to meet the circumstances of the concrete case. Counsel go so far as to claim that the minimum fine must in all cases be fixed by the Legislature at a nominal sum, otherwise the judicial power is trenched upon.

But the constitutional provision that fines shall be proportioned to the offenses is addressed to the Legislature as well as to the courts. The Legislature has the right to prescribe fines, and especially for the punishment of offenses that it creates, and to its judgment and discretion in this behalf

a wide latitude must necessarily be accorded. Fines are to
be fixed with reference to the object they are designed to accomplish. The degree of criminality of the offense, the illegal-
ity or impolicy of the act intended to be punished or prevented, are elements that must be considered. The peace of
the State and the welfare of community often require the
Legislature to create new offenses and to prescribe fines for
their punishment, and to alter fines already prescribed. In
performing this duty the Legislature has no guide but its
judgment and discretion and the wisdom of experience, and
the courts cannot properly question its action, unless the
minimum fine is so large as to be clearly out of all just proportion to the offense. 13 Am. & Eng. Ency. Law, 2d Ed.
60; *Southern Express Co.* v. *Walker,* 92 Va. 59; *State v.
Rodman,* 58 Minn. 393, 402; *Commonwealth* v. *Murphy,*
165 Mass. 66.

Considering the character of the business, and the ease
with which the unlawful traffic in intoxicating liquor can be
carried on, we think the minimum fine here objected to is not
so disproportionate to the offense as to justify the court in
questioning the action of the Legislature in prescribing it.

In *Freese* v. *Florida,* 23 Fla. 267, a fine of not less than
$600 for selling liquor without a license, with no maximum,
was held not to be excessive. So in Ex parte *Swann,* 96
Mo. 44, a minimum of $300 for a similar offense was held
not to be excessive.

Nor is the section unconstitutional because it fixes no
maximum fine. This has been often ruled in other jurisdictions.   13 Am. & Eng. Ency. Law, 2d Ed. 62; *Southern Express Co.* v. *Walker,* 92 Va. 59; *Frese* v. *Florida,* 23 Fla.
267; *In re Yell,* 107 Mich. 228; *State* v. *Fackler,* 91 Wis-
418; *Martin* v. *Johnson,* 11 Texas Civil App. 628.

Whether a fine beyond the minimum can be imposed by the court, we express no opinion, as the question is not raised.

It is further objected that the respondent is not charged with not having a license in force for selling, but only with not having one in force for keeping for sale. But the negation of a license clearly covers all the acts complained of.

Nor does the complaint proceed upon the theory that two licenses are necessary; one for selling and one for keeping for sale. And suppose the fair inference from the complaint is, as claimed, that the respondent had a license in force at some time, which, for some reason, lost its force, and left him with the liquor in question on hand, it cannot be further inferred, as claimed, that he was keeping the liquor for sale when his license should again come in force, for the allegation is that he did the things complained when he had no license in force.

Affirmed and remanded.

STATE *v.* WALTER B. DODGE.

October Term, 1903.

Present: ROWELL, C. J., TYLER, MUNSON, START, WATSON, and STAFFORD, JJ.

Opinion filed January 26, 1904.

No. 123, Acts 1898—Trading Stamp Law—Unconstitutional.

No. 123, Acts 1898, prohibiting the giving of any stamp, coupon, or other device, in consideration of, or in connection with, the sale of property, as therein provided, violates the Fourteenth Amendment of the Constitution of the United States, and is void.

COMPLAINT for the violation of No. 123, Acts 1898, by delivering to the purchaser certain stamps, or coupons, in consideration of the sale of goods. Plea, not guilty, and trial by Court upon an agreed statement, in the City Court for the city of Burlington, *Hawkins*, Judge. Judgment, guilty. The respondent moved to quash the complaint on the ground that the law under which the complaint is drawn is unconstitutional, in that it is in violation of the Constitution of the State of Vermont, and of the Fourteenth Amendment of the Constitution of the United States. Motion overruled, *pro forma.* The respondent excepted.   ·

The agreed statement shows that the respondent was a drug clerk, and in that capacity sold to the person named in the complaint a tooth brush, and at the same time, and as part of the transaction, delivered to that person three stamps, or coupons, which entitled the purchaser to demand of Sperry & Hutchinson Company any one of a number of articles on exhibition at the store of that company. It did not appear where this store was situated, nor by what arrangement with Sperry & Hutchinson Company said stamps were procured. Sperry & Hutchinson Company is a corporation organized under the laws of the state of New Jersey. The opinion states the other facts.

Frank W. Tillinghast, John S. Murdock and *Joseph T. Stearns* for the respondent.   ·

The legislative determination as to what is a proper exercise of the police power is not final, but subject to the supervision of the courts. *Yick Wo* v. *Hopkins,* 118 U. S. 356: *People* v. *Marx,* 99 N. Y. 377.

The police power, in its primary and proper sense, means the power of the Legislature to make such regulations of personal and property rights as look to health, safety, morals, and peace of the community. The regulation of property affected with a public interest does not rest upon the police power, but upon general governmental powers. Guthrié on the Fourteenth Amend., pp. 73-76; Thayer's Cases on Const. Law, Vol. 1, p. 693; *Munn* v. *Ill.* 94 U. S. 113.

The statute in question is unconstitutional in that it deprives the respondent of liberty and property without due process of law. *Powell* v. *Penn.*, 127 U. S. 678; *Allgeyer* v. *La.*, 165 U. S. 578.

The word "liberty" in the Fourteenth Amendment, means liberty to make contracts. *People* v. *Marx*, 99 N. Y. 377; Matter of Jacobs, 98 N. Y. 98; *Easton* v. *R. Co.*, 51 N. H. 501; *People* v. *Gillson*, 109 N. Y. 389.

This sort of legislation has been held unconstitutional in other states. *People ex rel Madden* v. *Dycker*, 72 Ap. Div. Rep. (N. Y.), 308; *State* v. *Dalton*, 22 R. I. 77; *Comm.* v. *Emerson*, 165 Mass. 146; *Comm.* v. *Sisson*, 178 Mass. 578; *Long* v. *State*, 74 Md. 565; Ex parte McKenna, 126 Cal. 429; *State* v. *Walker*, 105 La. 492.

There is nothing in the nature of a lottery in the trading stamp business. A lottery has in it an appeal to chance. Bishop, Stat. Crimes, § 952; Bouv. Law Dic. 281; *Hull* v. *Ruggle*, 56 N. Y. 424; *Wilkinson* v. *Gill*, 74 N. Y. 66; *People* v. *Noelke*, 94 N. Y. 137; *People* v. *Gillson*, 109 N. Y. 389, 402.

M. G. Leary, State's Attorney, for the State.

A Court will not declare an act void unless it is clear beyond a doubt that it is in violation of the Constitution. *Fletcher* v. *Peck*, 6 Cranch, 87, 128; 7 Harv. Rev. 129; Funding Cases, 99 U. S. 700, 718; *Atchison, etc. R.* v. *Mathews*, 174 U. S., 96; *Taylor* v. *Place*, 4 R. I. 324.

The U. S. Constitution does not limit the State in the exercise of its police power. *Barbier* v. *Connolly,* 113 U. S. 27; *Comm.* v. *Alger,* 7 Cush. 53; *Gibbons* v. *Ogden,* 9 Wheat. 1; *Lawton* v. *Steel,* 14 S. C. Rep. 499; Slaughter House Cases, 16 Wall. 36; *Powell* v. *Pa.,* 127 U. S. 678; *R. R. Co.* v. *Beckwith,* 129 U. S. 26; *Giozza* v. *Tiernan,* 148 U. S. 657; *Hooper* v. *Cal.,* 155 U. S. 648; *Holden* v. *Hardy,* 169 U. S. 366.

The question here is, did the Legislature enact this measure in the exercise of a reasonable discretion? *Petterson* v. *Ky.,* 97 U. S. 501; *Mugler* v. *Kan.* 123 U. S. 623; *Powell* v. *Pa.* 127 U. S. 678; *Plumley* v. *Mass.* 155 U. S. 461. This act is a valid exercise of the police power to prevent a lottery. *Dunn* v. *People,* 40 Ill. 465; *Taylor* v. *Smetten,* 11 Q. B. P. 207; *Reg.* v. *Harris,* 10 Cox C. C. 352; *Davenport* v. *City,* Pec. Ref. 708; *State* v. *Lumsden,* 89 N. C. 573; *Lansburgh* v. *Dist. of C.,* 11 D. C. App. 512; *Humes* v. *Fort Smith,* 93 Fed. Rep. 857; *Stone* v. *Miss.* 101 U. S. 814; *Phalen* v. *Vir.* 8 How. 163; *Patapsco Guano Co.* v. *N. C. Board of Agr.,* 171 U. S. 345; *Steiner* v. *Ray,* 84 Ala. 93; *State* v. *Corbett,* 57 Minn. 345; *State* v. *Browne, etc. Mfg. Co.,* 18 R. I. 16; *People* v. *Cannon,* 139 N. Y. 32; *Comm.* v. *Roswell,* 53 Atl. 132; *Singer* v. *Md.* 79 Md. 464; *Comm.* v. *Gardner,* 183 Pa. St. 284; *Shelton* v. *Mayor, etc.* 30 Ala. 540.

This statute is not subject to the objection that it is class legislation. *Soon Hing* v. *Crawley,* 113 U. S. 703; *Wick Wo* v. *Hopkins,* 118 U.S. 118, 356; *Ky. R.R. Tax Cases,* 115 U.S. 321; *Missouri, etc. R. Co.* v. *Mackay,* 127 U. S. 205; *Minn. R. R. Co.* v. *Beckwith,* 129 U. S. 26; *State* v. *Broadbelt,* 45 L. R. A. 433; *Orient Ins. Co.* v. *Daggs,* 172 U. S. 557.

Start, J. The respondent is charged with the offense of selling to one Claude Graton certain property for a certain sum of money, and with giving and delivering to Graton in connection with, and in consideration of, the sale three stamps or coupons, which entitled Graton to receive of The Sperry & Hutchinson Company certain property other than the property sold as aforesaid, to wit, a certain watch chain, on presentation of the stamps or coupons to The Sperry & Hutchinson Company, contrary to No. 123 of the Acts of 1898, which is as follows:

"Section 1. No person or company shall in the sale, exchange or disposition of any property, give or deliver in connection therewith or in consideration of said sale, exchange or disposition, any stamp, coupon or other device, which entitles the purchaser or receiver of said property or any other person to demand or receive from any person or company, other than the person making said sale, exchange or disposition, any other property than that actually sold or exchanged; and no person or company other than the person so selling or disposing of property shall deliver any goods, wares or merchandise upon the presentation of such stamp, coupon or other device.

Section 2. Any person or company who violates any provision of the foregoing section shall for each offense be punished by fine of not less than twenty nor more than five hundred dollars."

The respondent insists that this statute is unconstitutional, in that it deprives him of liberty and property without due process of law, which is guaranteed to him by the Fourteenth Amendment to the Constitution of the United States.

A person living under the Federal Constitution is at liberty to adopt and follow such lawful industrial pursuits as he sees fit, and has a right to the full exercise and enjoyment of his faculties in a lawful pursuit or calling, in a proper manner, subject only to such restraints as are necessary for the common welfare. When it is claimed that an act of the Legislature infringes upon such liberty or right, and the consideration of the act is properly before the Court, it is the duty of the Court to declare the act invalid, if it infringes upon such liberty or right; and this is so whether the act purports to be an exercise of the police power of the Legislature, or of its general governmental power to regulate business affected with a public interest. *Lawton* v. *Steele,* 152 U. S. 133; *Allgeyer* v. *Louisiana,* 165 U. S. 578. The business which the act prohibits is not of a public nature. Property, the transfer of which is prohibited, is not affected with a public interest. The merchant who, by the act, is subject to a penalty if he delivers stamps or coupons contrary to its provisions, is under no duty to serve the public, nor to sell his wares to any one; and it cannot be said that the enactment is a proper exercise of the general governmental power of the Legislature to regulate business that is affected with a public interest, nor is it claimed by the counsel for the State that the prohibited business in any way affects the public health or safety. Therefore, the cases where statutes regulating such business have been considered are not controlling upon the question in the case at bar.

But the counsel for the State contend that the act is a valid exercise of the police power of the Legislature, for the reason that it prohibits schemes which are in the nature of a lottery. This contention cannot be sustained. There is no element of chance, nor anything in the nature of gaming, in the business shown by the complaint to have been conducted by the respondent; on the contrary, it is alleged that the three stamps delivered by the respondent entitled the purchaser to receive from The Sperry & Hutchinson Company certain property, to wit, one watch chain. The agreed case shows, that these stamps are given to the purchaser of goods

from the merchant and are taken to the store of the Company,
where they are exchanged for any one of a large number of
articles that the purchaser may select; that these articles are
on exhibition at all times, are of sound value, and the number
of stamps necessary to obtain the article is indicated thereon;
that merchants that give stamps for cash trade display signs
in their windows to that effect; that every purchaser can
select at the store of the company, before he purchases from
the merchant who gives stamps, the article that he wants in
exchange for the stamps that are given with the article purchased; that the value of the article given in exchange for
stamps varies according to the number of stamps offered; and
that, in this case, a leather watch fob was given in exchange
for the three stamps. The act itself does not show that the
purpose of its enactment was to prohibit transactions having
an element of chance; on the contrary, it fairly appears that
it was intended to prohibit dealings with reference to some
particular article of property, or some one of a given class of
articles, for it only prohibits the seller of property from giving
a stamp or coupon which entitles the purchaser to demand
and receive property from a third party, and the delivery of
goods, wares or merchandise upon such stamps or coupons.
The seller is still at liberty to give stamps or coupons redeemable by himself in property and, if payable in cash, by a third
party. In principle, there is no substantial difference in
the two methods. They both accomplish the same results,
and in neither method is there an element of chance. The
act, in effect, makes it lawful for a merchant to give a trade
stamp redeemable by himself in cash or merchandise, and by
a third party, in cash, and makes it unlawful for him, under
like circumstances and conditions, to give the purchaser a
trade stamp which is redeemable in some well defined article
by another merchant. This is equivalent to declaring that a

man shall not give an article as an inducement to a buyer to
purchase another article, for it can make no possible difference
that the article given with the sale is delivered to the purchaser by a third person instead of the seller himself. If the
purpose of this act was to prohibit transactions having an
element of chance, there was no occasion for its enactment,
for transactions having such elements were already prohibited by V. S. 5125, 5126, 5127. If the giving and redeeming
of stamps, coupons or other devices is so conducted as to be
in fact a lottery, or chance scheme, the offense is punishable
under this statute; but, as we have seen, the complaint does
not show that the respondent conducted a business having
elements of chance, and, therefore, does not charge an offense
under this statute.

It is further insisted by the counsel for the State that the
scheme aimed at is one which is demoralizing to legitimate
business; but we see nothing in the prohibited business that
can be thus characterized. It does not differ from the ordinary business, except in the method of advertising, and in lawful trade inducements. It is true that this method of doing
business may enable a trader to do more business than he
otherwise would, and more than his competitor across the
street, who does not choose to incur the expense incident to
this method of advertising and increasing his business; but
this furnishes no reason for prohibiting the business. There
must be something in the methods employed which renders it
injurious to the public. It is not enough, to bring a given
business within the prohibitory power of the Legislature, that
it is so conducted as to seriously interfere with, or even
destroy, the business of others. *State* v. *Dalton,* 22 R. I. 77,
46 Atl. 234.

It is also said that this method of doing business is a
device whereby dishonest traders are able to defraud ignorant

and confiding purchasers, but this may be said of many methods of doing business, and may furnish a reason for regulating the business in a manner that will give greater protection to the purchaser; but it furnishes no reason for prohibiting the business. It is not attempted by the act to regulate the giving of stamps or coupons redeemable in goods, wares and merchandise by a person other than the giver of the stamp or coupon, but it absolutely prohibits such transactions. It prohibits the carrying on of a branch of business or trade that is not affected with a public interest, and has no relation to the public health, morals or safety, and imposes an arbitrary and unnecessary restraint upon lawful business transactions, and, within the meaning of the Fourteenth Amendment to the Constitution of the United States, is an unlawful restraint upon the liberty of a person to make such contracts, not inconsistent with the lawful rights of others, as he judges for his best interest, and upon the use of his business capacities for a lawful purpose, and falls within the constitutional prohibition, and is not a lawful exercise of the police power of the Legislature.

The view of the fact we have thus taken is supported by the reasoning and holdings in *State* v. *Dalton*, 22 R. I. 77, 46 Atl. 234; *People* v. *Gillson*, 109 N. Y. 389; *Ex Parte McKennon*, 126 Cal. 429; *Long* v. *State*, 74 Md. 565, 22 Atl. 4; *People, Ex. Rel. Madden* v. *Dycker*, 72 N.Y. (Ap. Div. Rep.) 308; where similar statutes have been held unconstitutional.

Judgment reversed; motion sustained; complaint adjudged insufficient and quashed; respondent discharged and let go without day.

Ida E. Richardson v. George E. Fletcher.

October Term, 1903.

Present: Rowell, C. J., Munson, Start, Watson, and Stafford, JJ.

Opinion filed January 26, 1904.

*Abatement—Another Suit Pending—Custodian of Will—
Executor—V. S. 2357-2359.*

The cause of action given by V. S. 2359 against the custodian of a
will for unexcused neglect to comply with the requirement of
V. S. 2357, after he knows of the testator's death, is different
from the cause of action given by the same section against an
executor for unexcused neglect to comply with the requirements
of V. S. 2358, after he knows of the testator's death. Therefore,
separate suits, for these distinct causes of action, may be maintained at the same time against a person who is both the executor
and the custodian of the will.

ACTION ON THE CASE, under V. S. 2359, to recover the
penalty therein provided. Heard on a replication traversing
defendant's plea in abatement, and tendering an issue to be
tried by the record, at the June Term, 1903, Windsor County,
Tyler, J., presiding. Judgment that the writ abate. The
plaintiff excepted.

The opinion states the case. The pleadings considered
in this case, commence with new declarations, filed after this
case and *Fletcher* v. *Fletcher* had been once to the Supreme
Court. See 74 Vt. 417, and 430.

George A. Weston and *Gilbert A. Davis* for the plaintiff.

The two suits are not for the same cause of action.
V. S. 2359 gives a penalty for the unexcused neglect of any
one of the three duties required in the two preceding sections.
One suit claims this penalty for the neglect of one of these

duties. The other suit claims the penalty for the neglect of still another duty. The pendency of one suit abates another only when the parties and the cause of action are identical. *Ballou* v. *Ballou*, 26 Vt. 673; *Smith* v. *Blatchford*, 2 Ind. 184.

This matter should have been pleaded in bar. *Barnes* v. *Blackbourne*, Sayer 216 (Eng. K. B. 1755); *Combes* v. *Pitt*, 3 Burr. 1423; *Jackson* v. *Gessing*, 2 Strange 1169; *Payne* v. *People*, 6 Johns. 103.

Hunton and *Stickney* for the defendant.

The sufficiency of the plea is conceded by the replication. The plea sets up a valid defense. *Combe* v. *Pitt*, 3 Burr. 1423. That both actions are the same has been settled by this Court. *Richardson* v. *Fletcher*, 74 Vt. 417; *Fletcher* v. *Fletcher*, 74 Vt. 430. Only one penalty can be recovered. *Forbes* v. *Davison*, 11 Vt. 660, 672; *Suydam* v. *Smith*, 52 N. Y. 383; *Sturgis* v. *Spofford*, 45 N. Y. 447; *Fisher* v. *N. Y. etc.*, 46 N. Y. 659.

WATSON, J. The defendant pleaded in abatement that at the time of the purchase of the writ in this case, another writ was simultaneously purchased in favor of one William W. Fletcher against this defendant returnable to the same Court; that the two writs were simultaneously exhibited to the clerk of the Court; that the suit in favor of said William W. is still depending and undetermined in said Court; and that the causes of action severally declared for in said two writs are one and the same. The plaintiff replied by traversing the allegation in the plea that the causes of action thus severally declared for were the same, concluding with a verification by the record of the two writs and declarations, and prayer that the record may be seen and inspected by the Court. Thus the issue of whether

the two suits were for the same cause of action was tendered
to be tried by the record. The trial Court rendered judgment
that the writ abate, thereby adjudging that the causes of
action were the same. Was* this error, is the question now
for consideration.

When these cases were before this Court, as reported in
74 Vt. 417 and 430, 52 Atl. 1064, it was held in effect that
the cause of action in *Fletcher* v. *Fletcher* was the unexcused
neglect of the defendant to present the will to the Probate
Court, having jurisdiction, within the time specified by law
after he knew of the death of the testatrix; and that in the
other case the cause of action was his unexcused neglect
within the same time to signify to the Court his acceptance
of the trust, or to make known in writing his refusal to accept
it. See V. S. 2358, 2359.

Notwithstanding these duties were closely connected and
in the circumstances shown by the pleadings were required to
be performed within the same period of time, they were different in nature, and the acts necessary for the due performance of either were unlike those to be done in the performance of the other. Consequently the evidence essential to the
support of one action would, to a large extent, be irrelevant
and immaterial to the plaintiff's right of recovery in the other.

To constitute the same cause of action, the offenses
charged must be in point of fact and in contemplation of law
the same; and the test is whether the same evidence will support both of the actions although they may happen to be
grounded on different writs. *Gates* v. *Gorham*, 5 Vt. 317.

Judgment reversed, and cause remanded.

In Re Marietta G. Mather's Will.

October Term, 1903.

Present: Rowell, C. J., Tyler, Munson, Start, and Stafford, JJ.

Opinion filed January 26, 1904.

Wills—Execution—Testatrix's Knowledge of Nature and Contents—Evidence.

Uncontradicted testimony that, with the exception of date and change of executors, the will in question is a duplicate of one executed a few days before, ,which the testatrix had heard read and discussed, and which she destroyed soon after the execution of the will in question, which she made merely to change executors, and which, when the witnesses thereto went into the room occupied by the testatrix, she got up and signed as it lay there upon a desk, and within a few days placed in a bank, where it remained about two years, tends to show that she knew its contents and nature at the time of its execution.

APPEAL FROM A DECREE OF THE PROBATE COURT establishing an instrument as the will of Marietta G. Mather. Ida E. Cook, proponent. Mary A. Wallace, contestant. Trial by Court, Addison County, June Term, 1903, *Watson*, J., presiding. Judgment for the proponent. The contestant excepted.

The Court below found that the testatrix executed the instrument in question, as and for her last will, at the home of her granddaughter, Mary A. Wallace, the wife of William E. Wallace, in Port Henry, N. Y., while the testatrix was there on a visit; that the home of the testatrix at this time was in Orwell, Vt.

The Court further found as follows: "The witnesses were, respectively, invited into the house of Mr. Wallace, and where he so invited them, he asked each of them, in substance, to come into the house to witness a signature; but in neither instance did he, when so inviting them, state whose signature they were to witness, nor the kind of instrument the signature was to be placed upon. After the witnesses went into the house for that purpose they were each introduced to the testatrix, and Mr. Wallace, referring to the testatrix, then and there stated to the witnesses: 'This is Mrs. Mather, whose signature we wish you to witness.' Thereupon the will in question was executed by the testatrix, and witnessed by the witnesses. No one then and there stated in express terms that the instrument then being executed, was the will of the testatrix; but we are satisfied and find, from the circumstances connected with the execution of the instrument, that the witnesses knew it was the will of the testatrix which they were then witnessing. But, if there was any doubt regarding this fact, they certainly knew that they were witnessing some instrument which the testatrix was then and there executing, and that by affixing their names to it, they were attesting its execution as such instrument by the testatrix. At the time of the execution of this instrument, the testatrix, although advanced in age and feeble in health, was of sound mind, and able to transact her own business."

Upon these facts found, the Court adjudged that the instrument was the last will and testament of said Marietta G. Mather.

W. H. Davis for the contestant.

The Supreme Court may review the findings of fact by a trial court when such facts are reported in writing. *Okley* v. *Aspinwall,* 2 Sandf. 7; *Stearns* v. *Fiske,* 18 Pick. 24.

It is the duty of the proponent to prove all the facts essential to the due execution of the will. *Williams* v. *Robinson,* 42 Vt. 658; *Roberts* v. *Welsh,* 46 Vt. 164.

It is essential that the testatrix should know the nature of the instrument and its contents. *Swett* v. *Boardman*, 1 Mass. 259; *White* v. *British Museum*, 6 Bing. 310; *Hastilow* v. *Stobie*, L. R. 1 P. & D. 64. The finding of the Court that the testatrix executed the instrument as and for her last will is not equivalent to finding that she understood the nature and contents thereof. The mere execution of the will by the testatrix has no tendency to show this except in those cases where she herself wrote the will, which is not this case.

E. J. Ormsbee and *Joel C. Baker* for the proponent.

The Supreme Court will not revise the finding of facts of the court below. *Noble* v. *Jewett*, 2 D. Chip. 36; *Nash* v. *Harrington*, 1 Aik. 41; *Kirby* v. *Mayo*, 13 Vt. 103; *Card* v. *Sargent*, 15 Vt. 393; *Stevens* v. *Hewett*, 30 Vt. 262; *Bank* v. *Gale*, 42 Vt. 27; *Foster* v. *Burton*, 62 Vt. 239; *Lumber Co.* v. *Shepardson*, 72 Vt. 188.

START, J. This is an appeal from a decree of the Probate Court allowing an instrument as the last will and testament of Marietta G. Mather. The trial in the Court below was by the Court. To the findings of the Court as to matters of fact and to the judgment thereon, the contestant excepted, because there is no evidence in the case to show that Marietta G. Mather, at the time of the execution of the instrument, knew its nature and contents.

It appears from testimony that was not contradicted, that the instrument was executed on the 29th day of July, 1899, and is a duplicate of a former will executed by the testatrix a few days before the execution of the one in question, except the date and change of executors; that the testatrix had heard the former will read and had discussed its provisions; that the only reason for making another will was for the purpose of changing the executors; that, when the witnesses to the instrument in question went into the room occupied by the testatrix, the draft of the instrument lay upon a desk, and the testatrix got up and went and signed it; and that, within a short time, and on the same day, she destroyed the former will, and within a few days placed the will in question in a bank for safe keeping, where it remained for about two years. These facts tended to show that the testatrix knew the contents and nature of the instrument at the time of its execution.

Judgment affirmed.

EMILY K. WEED *v.* BERTON A. HUNT.

October Term, 1903.

Present: ROWELL, C. J., MUNSON, START, WATSON, and HASELTON, JJ.

Opinion filed January 26, 1904.

Foreign Judgment—Accident—Mistake—Bill in Equity—Demurrer—Frivolousness—Remedy at Law—Negation of Binding—Objection First Taken on Appeal—Available.

When, in a bill in equity, the amount involved is written out in full, and also indicated by figures with the dollar sign, the objection, on demurrer, that the dollar sign is not in the English language is frivolous. But such pleading is very inartificial and should be avoided.

When, in the answer, the whole bill is demurred to for that the oratrix has an ample remedy at law; and the defendant also demurs orally for want of equity, though it does not appear whether this oral objection was made below, it is available in the Supreme Court, when it supports the decree below, and could not have been obviated if made there.

The Court is bound by the allegation that the oratrix has no remedy
at law, which is made in a bill in equity to restrain the enforcement of a foreign judgment, when the defendant, in his answer,
demurs to the bill for that the oratrix has an ample remedy at
law, although the answer sets forth a statute of the foreign jurisdiction giving the oratrix such remedy.

The defendant sues the oratrix in Connecticut and trusteed an insurance company there which owed her; whereupon, the oratrix
sued the insurance company in Vermont; thereupon said company brought a bill of interpleader in Vermont, and obtained an
injunction restraining both suits; oratrix's attorney, who had a
standing arrangement with the clerk to notify him of all orders
filed in his cases, not being informed of the dissolution of said
injunction, and supposing it still in force, was not negligent in
allowing defendant to take judgment by default against the oratrix in the Connecticut suit.

Such case is one both of accident and mistake; accident, in that
the clerk did not notify the attorney; mistake, in that the attorney
supposed the injunction was not dissolved.

APPEAL IN CHANCERY. Heard on demurrer to the bill
at the March Term, 1902, Washington County, *Stafford,*
Chancellor. Decree sustaining the demurrer, and dismissing
the bill. The oratrix appealed. The opinion fully states the
case.

T. J. Deavitt and *Edward H. Deavitt* for the oratrix.

Equity will restrain proceedings at law, even after judgment, whenever, through fraud, mistake, accident, or want of
discovery, one party in a suit obtains an unfair advantage
over another. Bispham's Eq. § 407; *Norton* v. *Woods,* 5
Paige Ch. 249, 251; *Lord Faulconberg* v. *Peirce,* 1 Ambler,
210; *Lansing* v. *Eddy,* 1 Johns. Ch. 49; *Viele* v. *Hoag,* 24
Vt. 46.

Oratrix's attorney was not negligent. *Cobb* v. *Dyer,* 69
Me. 494, 497.

Berton A. Hunt, pro se.

ROWELL, C. J.   The defendant sued the oratrix in Connecticut, and garnisheed an insurance company there that owed her.   Then the oratrix sued the insurance company here. Then the company brought a bill of interpleader here against both of them, and obtained an injunction against their prosecuting their suits against the company till further order. Hunt moved to dissolve that injunction, and the company's solicitor, who was also attorney for the oratrix in her suit here and in the Connecticut suit, was present at the hearing. The chancellor held the matter a few days, and then sent in an order dissolving the injunction, which left Hunt at liberty further to prosecute his suit in Connecticut, which he soon did by bringing the case forward for trial, whereof the attorney of said company in Connecticut notified the oratrix's attorney here, who had the charge and management of her side of the case, and he replied, to let Hunt take judgment there if he dare, supposing that the injunction had not been dissolved, as he had received no notice of it from the clerk, with whom he had a standing agreement that he was to be notified of all orders and entries in cases in which he was counsel.   The result was, Hunt took judgment in Connecticut against the oratrix by default, with damages assessed at $1,246.30, and sued out *scire facias* against the garnishee, to recover what it owed the oratrix.   It was not till after all this that the oratrix's attorney found out that the injunction had been dissolved.

The bill is brought for discovery and an accounting in respect of the matters that went into the judgment, and to enjoin the defendant from further prosecuting his suit in Connecticut, and from taking any action on said judgment in any court, the oratrix offering to pay to the defendant all sums that may be found due him from her in respect of said matters, but denying any liability thereon.

The bill is demurred to in the answer, for that the dollar sign used therein is no part of the English language, and for that the oratrix has an ample remedy at law. The defendant also demurs orally for want of equity, in that the situation complained of is the result of negligence on the part of the oratrix's counsel. It does not appear whether this objection was made below or not; but as it is one that apparently could not have been obviated if made there, as the oratrix seems to have made the most of her case, and is supportive and not subversive of the decree, and there is a cause of demurrer on the record that goes to the whole bill, it can be made here. *Dunshee* v. *Parmelee*, 19 Vt. 172; *Enright* v. *Amsden*, 70 Vt. 183, 40 Atl. 37; *Hastings* v. *Belden*, 55 Vt. 273.

The objection as to the dollar sign is frivolous, for it, and the figures that follow it, may be rejected as surplusage, as the dollars and cents are written out in full. But such pleading is very inartificial, and should be avoided.

The objection that the oratrix has ample remedy at law cannot be sustained, for the bill alleges directly and positively that she has no remedy at law, and we are bound by the allegations, as we cannot take notice of the Connecticut statute recited in the answer, from which it would seem that she had ample remedy at law, though she may have lost it by lapse of time. If the defendant had brought this statute forward by plea, it might have been better.

We think that the oratrix's attorney was not negligent in relying upon the agreement with the clerk to notify him of orders filed in his cases. The case, therefore, is one both of accident and mistake; of accident, in that the clerk did not notify the attorney; of mistake, in that the attorney supposed the injunction was not dissolved when it was. But it is proper to remark what is said in *Sleeper* v. *Croker,* 48 Vt. 9, that a case must be very extraordinary to justify a court of chancery in interfering to correct an irregularity of this character in a judgment at law, and draw the case into chancery, especially if a court of law can grant appropriate relief.

Decree reversed, demurrer overruled, bill adjudged sufficient, and cause remanded.

EDWARD H. DEAVITT *v.* WALTER L. RING, ADMR., ET AL.

October Term, 1903.

Present: ROWELL, C. J., MUNSON, START, WATSON, STAFFORD, and HASELTON, JJ.

Opinion filed February 10, 1904.

Mortgages—Foreclosure—Redemption—Mistake of Law—Relief—Subrogation.

The grantee of that undivided half of premises which has become chargeable with the payment of a mortgage covering the whole premises, as shown by the records in the town clerk's office, is not entitled to be subrogated to the rights of the mortgagee, upon redemption of the mortgage by his grantor with funds furnished by him, although he purchased believing he should be so subrogated, and after consulting two solicitors, who so advised him, and although the owners of the other half of said premises were not parties to said purchase, and are in no way prejudiced thereby, and he disclaims all interest in the premises except the interest of said mortgage.

APPEAL IN CHANCERY. Heard on demurrer to supplemental bill at the March Term, 1903, Washington County,

Stafford, Chancellor. Decree, *pro forma,* sustaining the demurrer, and dismissing the bill. The orator appealed.

All the facts in this case are fully stated in the opinion
of the Court in *Deavitt* v. *Ring, Admr., et al.,* 74 Vt. 431,
supplemented by the statement in the opinion in this case.

Edward H. Deavitt, pro se.

Cancellation under a mistake is no cancellation, and the
doctrine that a mistake, whether of law or fact, annuls a cancellation of a will or a deed is now firmly established. *Perrott* v. *Perrott,* 14 East 423; *Doe* v. *Thomas,* 9 B. & C. 228;
Onions v. *Tyrer,* 1 P. Wms. 345; *Eggleston* v. *Speke,* 3 Mod.
258; *Cocking* v. *Pratt,* 1 Ves. Sr. 400; *Bingham* v. *Bingham,* 1 Ves. Sr. 126; *Smithby* v. *Hinton,* 1 Vern, 32.

Equity will protect from the consequences of a discharge
of a mortgage when done by mistake, and when such relief
will not harm third persons. *Gerdine* v. *Menage,* 41 Minn.
417, 420; *Cobb* v. *Dyer,* 69 Me. 494, 497; *Geib* v. *Reynolds,*
35 Minn. 331, 336; *Bruce* v. *Bronney,* 12 Gray, 107; *Matzen*
v. *Shaeffer,* 65 Cal. 81.

The orator in taking the deed from his grantor did not
become the principal debtor to the insurance company, the
original mortgagee. 2 Pomeroy's Eq. Jur. §§ 797, 788, 798,
1212; *Webb* v. *Williams,* Walker's Mich. Ch. 544; *Muir* v.
Berkshire, 52 Ind. 149.

Equity relieves against agreements made, or acts done by
a party under a mistake by him of his legal rights, when the
party seeking relief has acted in good faith and has not been
negligent himself, and this whether the mistake is one of law
or fact.

Kerr on Fraud and Mistake (Bumps Ed.) 398; *Pusey* v.
Desbouvrie, 3 P. Wms. 315, 320; *Sturge* v. *Sturge,* 12 Beav.

229; *Reynell* v. *Sprye,* 8 Hare, 222, 255; *Coward* v. *Hughes,* 1 Kay & J. 443; *Morgan* v. *Dod,* 3 Col. 551; *Blakeman* v. *Blakeman,* 39 Conn. 320; *Baldwin* v. *Baldwin,* 14 Ore. 543; *Whalen's Appeal,* 70 Pa. St. 410; *Griswold* v. *Hazard,* 141 U. S. 260, 284, 286; *McKenzie* v. *McKenzie,* 52 Vt. 271; *Daniel* v. *Sinclair,* 6 App. Cas. 181.

J. H. Macomber for the defendants.

The orator's mistake is one purely of law, and is not ground for relief. 74 Vt. 431; *Ripton* v. *McQuivey,* 61 Vt. 76; *Churchill* v. *Bradley,* 58 Vt. 403; *McDaniels* v. *Bank,* 29 Vt. 230; *Burton* v. *Willey,* 26 Vt. 430; *Mellish* v. *Robertson,* 25 Vt. 604; *Howard* v. *Puffer,* 23 Vt. 366.

START, J. When this case was before this Court, as reported in 74 Vt. 431, it was held, on the facts as there reported, that the grantee of that undivided half of the premises which has become chargeable with the payment of a mortgage covering the whole premises, as shown by the record in the town clerk's office, is not entitled to subrogation to the rights of the mortgagee, upon redemption of the mortgage by his grantor with funds furnished by him. The material facts since brought upon the record by way of supplemental bill, which is demurred to, are to the effect, that the orator believed that a redemption by his grantor, Elizabeth Ring, after the time of redemption allowed to the administrator of Jane Ring's estate had expired, would enure solely to the benefit of Elizabeth Ring and her grantees; that, after consulting two solicitors whose opinion was the same as his own, he purchased in reliance upon such opinion and belief; that the estate of Jane Ring was not a party to the transaction between himself and Elizabeth Ring, in which the mistake occurred; that Jane Ring's estate has been in no way prejudiced by his mistake; and that he disclaims any interest in the premises, except the mortgage interest of the original mortgagee.

The orator asks for a decree that will, in effect, compel the heirs of Jane Ring to restore to him the money he paid to Elizabeth Ring in consideration of a conveyance by her of the premises in question, or forfeit to him their estate in one undivided half of the premises which they are entitled to hold as against Elizabeth Ring and her grantees, free and clear of the mortgage incumbrance. This he is not entitled to. He did not redeem the premises. He purchased of Elizabeth Ring, believing that he was acquiring title to the whole premises, when, in fact, his grantor owned only one undivided half of the premises; and this, as between his grantor and the heirs of Jane Ring, was chargeable with the mortgage then resting upon the entire premises. He paid the purchase price, and the same was used by his grantor in payment of the mortgage indebtedness, which had so far become an indebtedness of hers, that, in paying it, as between herself and the heirs of Jane Ring, she was paying her own debt. The belief under which the orator took the conveyance and paid therefor was not due to an absence of the means of knowing all the facts respecting his grantor's title, as was held when the case was before us upon the master's report. As the case now stands, it must be taken that the belief under which he acted was induced solely by his ignorance of the legal effect of the redemption of the premises by his grantor; but this was a mistake of law on his part which was in no way induced by the heirs of Jane Ring. They are strangers to the transaction in which the mistake occurred and are not affected by it. The remedy for such a mistake, if any there is, is not against a stranger to the transaction in which the mistake occurred and for whose benefit the money has been used by discharging a binding obligation. A purchaser of property, who, through a mistake of law on his part, does not acquire title to the extent he believed he was doing, cannot pursue and reclaim the purchase money from a stranger to the transaction in which the mistake occurred, who has received it from the vendor in extinguishment of an existing indebtedness. *Ripton* v. *McQuivery*, 61 Vt. 76, 17 Atl. 44; *Churchill* v. *Bradley*, 58 Vt. 403, 5 Atl. 189; *McDaniels* v. *Bank of Rutland*, 29 Vt. 230; *Rugg* v. *Brainard*, 57 Vt. 364; *Wells* v. *Tucker*, 57 Vt. 223; *Collins* v. *Adams*, 53 Vt. 433; *Hunt* v. *Ronsmamese*, 8 Wheat. 174; Am. & Eng. Ency. Law, 816, 817; *Dill* v. *Shahan*, 25 Ala. 694, 60 Am. Dec. 540; *Garwood* v. *Eldridge*, 1 Green's Chancery 145, 34 Am. Dec. 195; *Storrs* v. *Barker*, 6 Johns. Ch. 166, 10 Am. Dec. 316.

In *Ripton* v. *McQuivery*, before cited, McQuivery and wife took a conveyance of a piece of land and agreed to pay a debt then owing to the orator from their grantor, who was then responsible for all his debts. The orator, acting under a mistake as to the legal effect of the deed to the husband and wife, took the husband's note for the debt assumed by him and his wife and his sole mortgage upon a part of the premises to secure the same. After the death of the husband, the orator sought to have the premises charged with an equitable lien thereon to secure the payment of the debt; and the relief asked for was denied. In *Kleimann* v. *Gieselmann*, 114 Mo. 437, 35 Am. St. Rep. 761, it is held that, when the mortgagor and mortgagee of a homestead, mortgaged to raise money with which to pay off a prior mortgage, acted under a mutual mistake in supposing that the homestead belonged to the mortgagor in fee, to the exclusion of her minor children, equity will not grant relief by subrogating such mortgagee to the rights of the prior mortgagee.

The pro forma decree dismissing the bill affirmed, and cause remanded.

MORRIS McKINSTRY *v.* O. R. COLLINS and B. H. LOVELL.

October Term, 1903.

Present: ROWELL, C. J., MUNSON, START, WATSON, and HASELTON, JJ.

Opinion filed February 10, 1904.

Assault—Officer—Justification   Under   Process—Replevin— Bond—When Should   be   Taken—Return—Evidence— Impeachment — Foundation — Presumptions —Instructions.

An amended bill of exceptions, which is properly substituted for the one first filed, need not require the excepting party to furnish a transcript of the record referred to in the original bill.

To reserve an available exception to the exclusion of the testimony of a witness, an offer must be made stating the testimony the witness will give, if permitted to testify, and an exception taken to its exclusion.

Testimony tending to impeach a witness, who is not a party, is properly excluded, when no foundation for its introduction is laid by inquiries of the witness sought to be impeached.

In an action by a husband for an assault upon his pregnant wife, which caused her death, he may show her physical condition before the injury, by her acts and appearance, together with her condition subsequent thereto.

It is proper to allow a duly qualified expert to answer a hypothetical question, which assumes no fact not supported by the evidence.

When, in an action against an officer for an assault upon the plaintiff's wife in his presence, the plaintiff, on cross-examination, testified that after the alleged assault he had pleaded guilty to an assault upon the defendant upon the occasion in question, and that he had testified in a former trial, that, when he did so he understood he was pleading to a charge of resisting an officer, he may, on re-direct examination, testify to the circumstances under which he entered said plea, and what he then understood the plea of guilty referred to.

There is no vested right in a rule of evidence, and it is within the constitutional power of the Legislature to modify, or limit, its effect, and to make such modification, or limitation, apply to pending suits.

In the trial of a case by jury, the Court may, besides the general verdict, submit to the jury a special question, so that it may appear whether certain instructions in respect of the general verdict, if wrong, are also harmful.

An officer may commence the service of a writ of replevin by taking the property into his possession, so that it can be appraised, or its value agreed upon; but he has no right to deliver the property to the plaintiff in the replevin suit, without first taking the bond which is required by V. S. 1472, and if he does so, he cannot justify under his process.

When, in an action against an officer for an assault upon the plaintiff's wife, the defendant attempts to justify under a writ of replevin against the plaintiff, the return thereon is *prima facie* evidence in favor of the defendant, but it is open to contradiction by the plaintiff upon the question whether the officer delivered the property to the plaintiff in the replevin suit before taking the bond required by V. S. 1472.

In an action for an assault upon the plaintiff's wife, the law presumes that the defendant did not commit the assault, and this presumption stands till it is overcome by evidence, and it is error for the Court to refuse to instruct the jury so.

When, in an action against an officer for an assault upon the plaintiff's wife, in his presence, the defendant justifies under a writ of replevin against the plaintiff, and it is claimed by the plaintiff that the officer delivered the property to the plaintiff in the replevin suit before taking the bond required by V. S. 1472, the law presumes the contrary, and it is error for the Court to refuse to instruct the jury so.

CASE FOR AN ASSAULT UPON THE PLAINTIFF'S WIFE. Plea, the general issue, with notice of special matter in justification. Trial by jury at the March Term, 1903, Washington County, *Stafford*, J., presiding. Verdict and judgment for plaintiff. The defendants excepted.

It appeared that some time in the fall of 1896 defendant Collins, in company with Lovell, came to the plaintiff's home. Collins was an officer and had a writ of replevin wherein he was commanded to replevy a certain colt then in the possession of the plaintiff.

The plaintiff's evidence tended to show that Collins did not reveal to him the fact that he was an officer and had said writ of replevin; that plaintiff attempted to lock his barn, and thereupon Collins attempted to prevent the plaintiff from doing so, and they clinched, whereupon plaintiff told his wife and sister, who were present, to take the lock and fasten the door; that thereupon Collins called upon Lovell to assist him; that thereupon Lovell seized plaintiff's wife, who was seven months pregnant, threw her against the carriage wheel, and severely injured her, so that she was taken sick immediately, and continued sick till the 17th day of January following, when she gave birth to a dead child, partly decomposed and covered with red marks; that she continued sick till the 3rd day of February, when she died; that said sickness and death were caused by said assault, by causing the death of the child and resulting blood poisoning in the mother.

Subject to the objection and exception of the defendants, the plaintiff was allowed to ask long hypothetical questions of a duly qualified medical expert. The exceptions state that there was evidence tending to show all the facts assumed by these questions. The following is quoted from the bill of exceptions:

"As tending to show that the plaintiff's wife died of septicæmia the plaintiff called one N. A. Ross, then a clergyman at Woodbury, who saw the plaintiff's wife the night that she died and who testified to the condition of the plaintiff's wife when he saw her and subject to the defendants' objection and exception was allowed to testify that she breathed hard, was struggling hard for breath, was short of breath, and as she would speak there would be a pause before she would speak again."

"The plaintiff had used the plaintiff's mother as a witness who had stated the condition of the plaintiff's wife after December 5th, that she could not go up stairs and could sit up only a part of the time. On cross-examination she stated that plaintiff's wife went to the barn with her occasionally during this time to feed the cattle. On re-examination she was permitted to testify, subject to defendants' objection and exception, that after plaintiff's wife was injured she would sometimes go out with plaintiff's mother, but that the hay was on the barn floor so that they could slip it through to the cattle."

"The plaintiff's sister, who was with his wife a large portion of the time during the claimed sickness which followed her alleged injury, was permitted to testify on behalf of the plaintiff, that during the time that the witness was with her she complained of being in pain through the bowels and back; that she was unable to go up or down stairs because it hurt her back, and that she complained of a bearing down pain after she had been up stairs. Plaintiff's counsel asked this witness the following question:

'Q.—What kind of a woman was Mrs. McKinstry in respect to her disposition, whether lively or melancholy?

Subject to defendants' objection and exception, the witness answered:

A.—She was lively.' "

J. P. Lamson and *George W. Wing* for the defendants.

It was error to allow the plaintiff to explain the circumstances under which he entered the plea of guilty, and what he then understood said plea referred to. *Porter* v. *Gile,* 47 Vt. 623; *Mussey* v. *White,* 58 Vt. 45; *Kimball* v. *Newport,* 47 Vt. 38, 42; *Holt* v. *Thatcher,* 52 Vt. 592.

The officer's return is conclusive upon the question of whether he had bond when he turned over the property. *Bennet, White & Co.* v. *Allen,* 30 Vt. 684; *Thurber & Co.* v. *Town,* 46 Vt. 395; *Bent* v. *Bent,* 43 Vt. 42; *Tripp* v. *Howe,* 45 Vt. 523; *Brown* v. *Clark,* 27 Vt. 575; *Wilder* v. *Stafford, et al.,* 30 Vt. 399; *Wheelock* v. *Sears,* 19 Vt. 559; *Miller* v. *Cushman,* 38 Vt. 593.

The Court should have complied with the defendants' requests as to the presumption of innocence, and the presumption that an officer acts regularly. *Child* v. *Merrill,* 66 Vt. 308; *Greensboro* v. *Underhill,* 12 Vt. 604; *Bradish* v. *Bliss,* 35 Vt. 326; *Weston* v. *Gravlin,* 49 Vt. 507; *Fire Ass'n* v. *Bank,* 54 Vt. 657; *Currier* v. *Richardson,* 63 Vt. 617; *Stevenson* v. *Gunning's Est.,* 64 Vt. 601; *Fairbanks* v. *Benjamin,* 50 Vt. 99; *Drake* v. *Mooney,* 31 Vt. 617; *Wood* v. *Doane,* 20 Vt. 612.

H. C. Shurtleff and *W. A. Lord* for the plaintiff.

Plaintiff was properly allowed to explain the circumstances under which he entered the plea of guilty. *State* v. *Carpenter,* 54 Vt. 551.

A party has no vested right in a statutory mode of proof. *Richardson, Admr.* v. *Cook,* 37 Vt. 603; *Montpelier* v. *Senter,* 72 Vt. 112; *Pratt* v. *Jones,* 25 Vt. 303; Cooley's Const. Lim., Vol. 1, 452, 457, 469.

Declarations of plaintiff's wife, as to her then existing pain were admissible. *State* v. *Howard,* 32 Vt. 404; *Earl and wife* v. *Tupper,* 45 Vt. 284.

The burden was on the defendants to prove their plea of justification.   No presumption is a substitute for such proof. *Bosworth* v. *Bancroft,* 74 Vt. 451; *Davis* v. *Bowers Granite Co.,* 75 Vt. 286; *U. S.* v. *Carr,* 132 U. S. 644; *U. S.* v. *Ross,* 92 U. S. 281.

START, J. The action is for the recovery of damages for an alleged assault upon the plaintiff's wife, which it is claimed caused her death. The defendants, among other things, justified under a replevin writ. The amended bill of exceptions, which was properly substituted for the one first filed, did not require the defendants to furnish a transcript of the record referred to the original bill of exceptions, and there was no occasion for their doing so.

The defendants asked a witness who was present at the time the child was born, what was said when Mr. McKinstry was in the room, in relation to the child's breathing or gasping when it was born. The Court excluded this question, and the defendants excepted. The question was not accompanied by an offer to show any fact, nor does it appear what the answer would have been if taken; therefore, error does not appear. *State* v. *Noakes,* 70 Vt. 256, 40 Atl. 249. Mrs. Widber was called by the defendants. On cross-examination, it appeared that she was present at the former trials and was not called as a witness. The defendants then offered to show by her that the plaintiff's counsel knew, at the time of the former trial, that she was at the plaintiff's house during Mrs. McKinstry's illness. It appeared from her testimony that this fact was known to the plaintiff, and the question of whether his counsel knew was immaterial. A witness, called by the plaintiff, testified, that, on the evening of the day the defendants were at the plaintiff's house, defendant Collins told him that he took the plaintiff's wife and slapped her up against the barn and she groaned right out. The defendants, without inquiring of the witness respecting his testimony on the former trial, offered to show by the stenographer that, at the former trial, the witness testified that Lovell, at another time and place, told him that he, Lovell, took Mrs. McKinstry, on the occasion in question, and kicked her across the barn floor. No foundation was laid by inquiries of the witness for the introduction of this testimony, and the same was properly excluded. It was permissible for the plaintiff to show the physical condition of his wife before the injury complained of, as indicated by her acts and appearance, also her condition after the injury; and, in so far as appears, there was no error in the rulings of the Court upon questions relating to her condition, nor does it appear that there was error in receiving opinion evidence based upon the facts which the evidence tended to show respecting her symptoms and conditions. *State v. Hayden,* 51 Vt. 296; *Foster's Executors v. Dickerson,* 64 Vt. 254, 24 Atl. 253; *McKinstry v. Collins and Lovell,* 74 Vt. 147, 52 Atl. 438.

It appeared from the cross-examination of the plaintiff that he had entered a plea of guilty of an assault upon defendant Collins on the occasion in question, and that he testified on the former trial, that, when he did so, he understood he was pleading to a charge for resisting an officer. Subject to the defendants' exception, the plaintiff was allowed to testify to the circumstances under which he entered the plea and what he then understood his plea of guilty referred to. In this there was no error. The fact that the plaintiff had pleaded guilty to a charge of resisting an officer, or of assaulting Collins, on the occasion in question, tended to discredit the testimony given by him; and, as bearing upon the force and weight to be given to his plea of guilty, it was competent to show the circumstances and conditions under which he entered

the plea, and his understanding of the nature of the charge
to which he entered a plea of guilty. *Laflam* v. *Missisquoi
Pulp Co.*, 74 Vt. 140, 52 Atl. 526; *State* v. *Lockwood*, 58 Vt.
378, 3 Atl. 539.

As tending to show that the plaintiff's wife died of pneu-
monia, the defendants offered in evidence a certified copy of
the record of the certificate of her death, in which was stated,
among other things, that the cause of her death was pneu-
monia. The offer was excluded and the defendants excepted.
In this there was no error. Since we held in this case that
such certificates were evidence of the cause of death, as reported in 74 Vt. 147, the Legislature has changed the law, by
No. 44 of the Acts of 1902, which provides that no public
record of births, marriages or deaths required by law to be
kept, nor any certified copy thereof, shall be competent evidence in the trial of any suit now or hereafter pending to
prove any fact stated therein, except the fact of birth, marriage or death. There is no vested right in a rule of evidence.
Such rules only affect the remedy, and it is within the constitutional power of the Legislature to modify or limit their
effect, as was done by the act in question. 6 Am. & Eng.
Ency. Law, 2 Ed. 950; *Richardson* v. *Cook*, 37 Vt. 605; *State*
v. *Welch*, 65 Vt. 55, 25 Atl. 900.

The Court instructed the jury to answer the following
question: "Did Collins have a completed bond before he delivered the colt to Lovell?" To this question the jury answered, "No." The defendants excepted to the Court submitting this question to the jury. The Court could, in its
discretion, take an answer to this question, so that it could
be seen whether the instruction, for the purposes of the general verdict, respecting the taking of a bond before delivering
the property to the plaintiff, if wrong, harmed the defendants.

If the jury had found that the bond was seasonably taken, the instruction, for the purposes of the general verdict, would have been harmless. The jury having found that a bond was not taken before the property was delivered, reversible error appears, if it was not the duty of Collins to take a bond before delivering the property. If it was his duty to take a bond before delivering the property, the general verdict and judgment are not affected by the question and answer; and the same are immaterial. The important inquiry is whether there was error in the instruction to the jury upon this subject, for the purposes of the general verdict. The Court told the jury, that, if Collins delivered the colt to Lovell without first taking a bond, he was not proceeding regularly and the writ was no protection. To this instruction the defendants excepted.

The Court also instructed the jury, that, in order to replevy the colt, the law required Collins to take possession of it, so that it could be appraised or its value agreed upon, and then take a bond from the plaintiff to the defendant; that the law required him to do this before turning the colt over to the plaintiff; that, if he did this, or in good faith intended to take such bond before turning the colt over to the plaintiff, he was proceeding regularly; and that he had a right, if he was proceeding regularly, to take the colt into his possession in the first place, in order to make an appraisal of it or have an agreement as to its value. The instruction excepted to presents the question of whether it is necessary for an officer, when serving a replevin writ, to take a bond from the plaintiff in the writ to the defendant before delivering the property replevied to the plaintiff. V. S. 1472, requires an officer, before serving a replevin writ, to take a bond from the plaintiff to the defendant. This imposes upon him the duty of

tàking a bond before he delivers the property to the plaintiff.·
His doing so after the property had been delivered is not
taking a bond before serving the writ, and is not a compliance
with the statute.   When the property has been delivered to
the plaintiff, the service of the writ, so far as it relates to the
transfer of the property from the possession of the defendant
to the possession of the plaintiff, is completed, and the property has been replevied.   In *Miller* v. *Cushman*, 38 Vt. 598,
the Court, in holding that the bond should be given before
the replevin is completed, said: "The fair construction of the
officer's return would place the appraisal and giving of the
bond, as they should be, subsequent to the taking of the property from the defendant and prior to its delivery to the plaintiff."

In *Eastman* v. *Barnes*, 58 Vt. 330, 1 Atl. 569, TAFT, J.,
in delivering the opinion of the Court, said: "The security
taken by way of bond in replevin is a substitute for the property, and the defendant is entitled to such security at the
time his property is taken; if he does not get it then, he never
may; and the defect cannot be cured by filing a bond subsequently."   In *Walcott* v. *Mead*, 12 Met. 516, it is held that
the officer may commence the service of a writ of replevin
before taking a bond from the plaintiff, doing only so much,
however, as is necessary to effect an appraisement of the
value, preparatory to taking a bond.   He has no authority for
delivering the property to the plaintiff to be taken into custody, until the plaintiff has given the bond required by the
statute; but the writ may be delivered to the officer, and he
may begin to execute it, proceeding only so far as is requisite
to enable him to take a proper bond.   The form for a replevin writ prescribed in V. S. 5417, form 11, commands the
officer to replevy the property and deliver it to the plaintiff

in the writ, provided he give a bond in double the value of the property, with a sufficient surety or sureties, to prosecute his replevin, pay such costs and damages as the defendant may recover against him, and to return the property in case such shall be the final judgment. This command requires him to take a bond before delivering the property to the plaintiff. He is not to deliver the property unless such bond is given, and, if he does so, he disregards the direction of his process. The giving of a bond is a condition upon which the lawfulness of the replevin depends. An officer, in the execution of his process, is bound to observe the commands of the law, whether expressed in the process itself or in the general law applicable to its execution; and an officer who, after taking property from the defendant in the replevin writ, delivers it to the plaintiff without first taking a bond from the plaintiff to the defendant, cannot justify his act in doing so under his process. *Wright* v. *Marvin*, 59 Vt. 437, 9 Atl. 601; *Ellis* v. *Cleveland*, 54 Vt. 437; *Driscoll* v. *Place*, 44 Vt. 252; *White & Co.* v. *Allen*, 30 Vt. 484; *Dearborn* v. *Kelley*, 3 Allen 426; *Moors* v. *Parker*, 3 Mass. 310; 18 Ency. Pl. & Pr. 617.

The defendants insist that there was no evidence in the case to submit to the jury upon the question of whether Collins had a completed bond at the time he delivered the property. It does not appear that this precise question was raised in the Court below. It does not appear that the defendants asked for such a ruling, nor that they excepted because the Court did not so rule. But the defendants did request the Court to charge, that the sufficiency of the writ or bond is not to be tried in this case; that, if there was any defect or insufficiency in the writ or bond in the replevin case, that question should have been tried in that case; and that the return on the writ imports absolute verity and cannot be inquired into or contradicted in this case. These requests were

properly denied. No question was raised respecting the sufficiency of the writ or bond. The question was whether the
bond was seasonably taken, and the officer's return was not
conclusive upon that question, notwithstanding the plaintiff
was a party to the process on which the return was made.
The return on the writ showed that Collins had served the
writ in the manner the law requires, and as he was commanded to do by the precept, and was therefore conclusive in
the replevin suit, as between the parties to that suit. *Barrett
v. Copeland,* 18 Vt. 67; *Windham* v. *Chester,* 45 Vt. 459;
Bank v. *Downer,* 29 Vt. 332; *Witherell* v. *Goss & Delano,* 26
Vt. 748. But the return is not conclusive in the case at bar.
The officer who made it is a party defendant. He seeks to
justify an alleged assault under the process upon which the
return is made. His return was *prima facie* evidence in his
favor, but it was open to contradiction by the plaintiff, notwithstanding the plaintiff was a party to the process on which
the return was made. *Barrett* v. *Copeland,* 18 Vt. 67.

The defendants asked for the following instruction:
"That the legal presumptions are that Collins did not commit any assault, and that he discharged his duty in the serving of his process as he was commanded in his process to do,
and that presumption stands with him until it is overcome by
evidence." To the refusal of the Court to comply with this
request, the defendants excepted. This request is sound in
law. That part of it which asked for an instruction, that it
is presumed that Collins did not make an assault, states a rule
of general application in civil cases, where a person is charged
with fraud, dishonesty or crime. In the case at bar, the
defendants were charged with an assault and battery, which,
under our statute, is a criminal offense. Such being the nature of the charge, there was a legal presumption that the

defendants were innocent, and the jury should have been told
that the presumption existed. *Child* v. *Merrill,* 66 Vt. 308.
The defendants did not ask for an instruction that the law
presumes that Collins did not commit an assault because he
was an officer; they asked for no more than the ordinary instruction in such cases. Presumption of innocence, in this
class of cases, means that it is presumed that the defendant
did not commit the act charged. *Bradish* v. *Bliss,* 35 Vt. 328;
Currier v. *Richardson,* 63 Vt. 620. It is presumed the contrary not appearing, that sworn public officers, acting under
process, perform their duty as commanded by the general law
and their process; and this rule applies when public officers
seek to justify their acts, under process, in legal proceedings
to which they are parties. The defendants, in effect, asked
for such instruction. The issue presented by the evidence
called for the instruction. As we have seen, the general law
and the process under which Collins sought to justify his acts
made it his duty to take a bond from the plaintiff to the defendant before delivering the property to the plaintiff. He
could not lawfully deliver the property without first taking a
bond. It appeared that a bond was taken and seasonably returned with the writ to the Court, and the property replevied
and delivered to the plaintiff in the replevin suit. The plaintiff's contention was that the claimed justification was not a
defense, because, as he claimed, the bond was not taken before
the property was delivered to the plaintiff. This was a material issue and was found in favor of the plaintiff. It being
the duty of Collins to take a bond before delivering the property, and the lawfulness of the replevin being dependent upon
his doing so, and it appearing that a bond was taken and the
property delivered, it is presumed, until the contrary appears,
that he did his duty as commanded by his process and season-

ably took the bond. The request upon this subject, when read
in connection with the issue made on the trial, does not call for
more than this. It is limited to duties enjoined by the process. The only issue made respecting these duties was whether
the bond was taken before the property was delivered to the
plaintiff. Upon this issue, the defendants were entitled to the
benefit of the presumption; and the denial of the request was
error. *Bank* v. *Tucker,* 7 Vt. 134; *Insurance Co.* v. *Wright,*
60 Vt. 515, 12 Atl. 103; *Chandler* v. *Spear,* 22 Vt. 388; *Mc-
Kinstry* v. *Collins and Lovell,* 74 Vt. 147, 52 Atl. 438; *Drake*
v. *Mooney,* 31 Vt. 617; *Fairbanks* v. *Benjamin,* 50 Vt. 99;
Brock v. *Bruce,* 59 Vt. 313, 10 Atl. 93; *Sargeant* v. *Sunderland,* 21 Vt. 284; *Jewett* v. *Guyer,* 38 Vt. 209; *Nofire* v.
United States, 164 U. S. 657; *Hartwell* v. *Root,* 19 John.
345, 10 Am. Dec. 232; *Jackson* v. *Shafer,* 11 John. 517. In
22 Am. & Eng. Ency. Law, 2 Ed. 1267, many cases are cited
in support of the rule, that the general presumption is that
public officers perform their official duty and that these official acts are regular, and where some preceding act or pre-
existing fact is necessary to the validity of an official act, the
presumption in favor of the validity of the official act is
presumptive proof of such preceding act or pre-existing fact.

Judgment reversed, and cause remanded.

In Re Nahum F. Wheelock's Will.

October Term, 1903.

Present: Rowell, C. J., Tyler, Start, Watson, and Stafford, JJ..

Opinion filed February 13, 1904.

Wills—Proponent—Legatee as Witness—Testamentary Capacity—Decree of Probate Court—Prima Facie Evidence.

The proponent of a will, who is also a legatee, but is not an attesting witness, is competent to testify to the circumstances attending its execution.

When a will was executed after the maturity of the testator, and it appears that there had been no change in his mental capacity since he reached maturity, evidence tending to show his mental condition at any time since that period, or within a reasonable time prior thereto, has a tendency to show his capacity at the time the will was executed.

Letters of a testator are admissible to show his knowledge of the contents of his will.

An adjudication of the Probate Court that one is *non compos*, while it remains in force, is *prima facie* evidence of his insanity, and of his incapacity to make a will.

Appeal from a Decree of the Probate Court refusing to establish an instrument as the will of Nahum F. Wheelock. Ella A. Burgess, proponent. Loie Smith and Mabel Lifinaman, contestants.

Trial by jury at the December Term, 1902, Bennington County, *Munson*, J., presiding. Verdict and judgment for the proponent. The contestants appealed.

It appeared that none of the attesting witnesses saw the testator sign the instrument in question; but that they witnessed what purported to be his signature in his presence and in the presence of each other.

The proponent, Ella A. Burgess, now married, is named as a specific and residuary legatee in the will by the name of Ella A. Galusha. The contestants are two nieces of the testator.

The will is dated July 9, 1888, was made on that day, and the testator died in May, 1901, at the age of fifty-nine years. It appeared that the testator from his birth, or early infancy, was crippled and deformed so that he never walked; that he was almost helpless physically; that he had a defective utterance, so that it was very difficult to understand him; that he could read, write and spell, and had some knowledge of other common school branches; that he had a good memory; played cards and checkers, and liked music. The attesting witness and the proponent were the only persons who testified as to the execution of the will.

Batchelder & Bates and *W. B. Sheldon* for the contestants.

It is against public policy that the legatee should testify. *Ames* v. *Parrott*, 87 Am. St. R. 538; *Stevens* v. *Leonard*, 77 Am. St. R. 467.

The jury should have been instructed that the decree of the Probate Court adjudging the testator *non compos* is *prima facie* evidence of incapacity. *Stone* v. *Damon et al.*, 12 Mass. 487; *Breed et. al.* v. *Pratt*, 35 Mass. 115; *Will of Slinger*, 72 Wis. 22; *Leonard* v. *Leonard*, 31 Mass. 280; *White* v. *Palmer*, 4 Mass. 147; *Harrison* v. *Bishop*, 131 Ind. 161.

Barber & Darling and *Waterman & Martin* for the proponent.

The proponent, though a legatee, was a competent witness. *Foster's Executors* v. *Dickerson et al.*, 64 Vt. 233; *In Re Buckman's Will*, 64 Vt. 313; *Clark* v. *Clark*, 54 Vt. 489.

Whether evidence offered is too remote, is for the court, and its decision is not reversible in Supreme Court. *Dover v. Winchester,* 70 Vt. 418; *Maggi v. Cutts,* 123 Mass. 535; *Dale's Appeal,* 57 Conn. 127, at 143.

WATSON, J. Under exception by the contestants the proponent, a special and residuary legatee under the will, was allowed to testify (in contradiction of the testimony of the attesting witnesses), that at the time the will was executed, one of the attesting witnesses in the presence of the others and when looking at the will, said "Nahum's name is on the will and we never saw him put it there," and that then he said to the testator, "Is this your will and is this your signature?" To which the testator answered, "Yes, sir," and that then the attesting witness put his name on the will.

It is argued that to allow a legatee to testify to the execution of the will is improper as against public policy. At common law in the probating of a will a legatee thereunder was incompetent to testify. This, however, was solely on the ground of pecuniary interest in the outcome of the action. 1 Underhill on Wills, § 192; 4 Kent's Com. (11th Ed.) 598.

Since such disqualification has been removed by statute it is no more against public policy to allow a legatee to testify as a common witness on all questions arising in the probation of a will than it is to allow any other person interested in the result of a suit to give testimony therein. In either case the only reason why it could be against public policy is the interest of the witness, and that ground is no longer available.

In *Foster's Exrs. v. Dickerson,* 64 Vt. 233, 24 Atl. 258, subject to contestants' objection and exception, one of the legatees under the will was permitted to testify on behalf of the proponents on all the material issues in the case. The objection made was that the legatee was a party to the issue raised by the pleadings and on trial and that the deceased testatrix was the other party thereto, and that consequently the witness was not competent by reason of the provisions of R. L. 1002, 1003. The witness was held to be competent. In Kentucky, where they have a statute removing disqualification because of interest, it has been held that thereby all litigants in this kind of an action are put on an equal basis as witnesses, and that a devisee may testify generally in the probating of a will. *Williams* v. *Williams,* 90 Ky. 28. See also *Martin* v. *McAdams,* 87 Tex. 225.

The exceptions state that there was no evidence of any special or marked change in the testator's mental condition or characteristics at any particular period of his life after he attained the ordinary age of maturity. His capacity under consideration was therefore such as he had always naturally possessed since arriving at that age. Any evidence tending to show his mental condition and natural capacity within that period or within a reasonable time before, as he was approaching it, had a tendency to show his capacity at the time the will was executed. All the evidence received on that question, including the letters written by the testator, had such tendency, and there was no error in its reception. *Foster's Exrs.* v. *Dickerson,* before cited. Some if not all of the letters were also admissible as evidence of the testator's knowledge of the contents of the will. *McAuley* v. *Western Vt. R. R. Co.,* 33 Vt. 311.

It appears that the testator was under guardianship as *non compos* at the time the will was executed. The contestants requested the Court to charge in short that the adjudication of the Probate Court in this regard and the appointment of the guardian was *prima facie* evidence of the fact that the testator was *non compos* and incapable of taking care of himself and property at the time of the execution of the will.

Upon this question the Court charged that the fact that the testator was so under guardianship by order of the Probate Court could afford no test for the determination of the question of the testator's capacity; and that in disposing of the issues submitted for the jury's determination they should consider the facts and circumstances of the testator's guardianship in connection with the other circumstances and conditions of his life, but should give them no effect beyond this. An exception was taken to the non-compliance with the request and also to the charge as given upon that question. Thus the question of what weight such an adjudication shall have as evidence bearing upon the mental condition of a testator in the establishment of his will is fairly presented.

The adjudication of a Court of competent jurisdiction that a person is *non compos,* and incapable of taking care of himself and property, is in the nature of a judgment *in rem* upon matters of public interest and concern to which no one can strictly be said to be a stranger, and it is evidence of the facts determined against all the world.   3 Taylor Ev. sec. 1174; 1 Greenl. Ev. sec. 556.

The fact, however, that a person has been adjudged *non compos* and placed under guardianship as such does not of necessity show that a will made by him while that adjudication is in full force and during the pendency of the guardianship is not a good will, "for," says Lord Chancellor COT-TENHAM in *Cooke* v. *Cholmondeley,* 2 Macn. & G. 18, "it is very possible that there may have been a period during which it was competent for the testator to make a will, and that such a will might be valid, though the commission existed. The existence of the commission is, no doubt, a circumstance of extreme suspicion, and one which gives rise to the strongest presumption against the validity of the will; but this presumption is nevertheless capable of being rebutted." Accordingly, it is the rule of law in England and in this country that such an adjudication while it remains in full force is *prima facie* evidence of the testator's insanity and incapacity to make a will. It follows that the contestants were entitled to a charge according to their request in this respect. The charge given was not a compliance therewith, and the exception must be sustained. 1 Jarm. Wills (5th Am. Ed.) 72; 2 Greenl. Ev. § 690; *Breed* v. *Pratt*, 18 Pick. 115; *Crowninshield* v. *Crowninshield*, 2 Gray, 524; *Hamilton* v. *Hamilton*, 10 R. I. 538; *Harrison* v. *Bishop*, 131 Ind. 161, 31 Am. St. Rep. 422; *Estate of Johnson*, 57 Cal. 529; *In Re Fenton's Will*, 97 Iowa, 192; *In Re Gangwere's Est.*, 14 Pa. St. 417.

Judgment reversed, and cause remanded.

JAMES B. LAWRIE, ET AL. *v.* W. H. SILSBY, ET AL.

October Term, 1903.

Present: ROWELL, C. J., TYLER, MUNSON, STAFFORD, and HASELTON, JJ.

Opinion filed February 13, 1904.

Riparian Rights—Prescription—Question of Fact—Corporation—Organization—Articles of Association—Signing—Capacity to Sue.

The presumption of a grant from long continued enjoyment arises only where the person against whom the right is claimed could have lawfully interrupted or prevented the exercise of the supposed right.

Persons who, for more than forty years, under a claim of right, have taken water by a pipe from a brook on a riparian lot to their sev-

eral nonriparian farms, have not thereby acquired the right to do
so as against an upper riparian owner.

Persons who, for more than forty years, under a claim of right, have
taken water by a pipe from a brook on a riparian lot to their
several nonriparian farms, have acquired a prescriptive right to
do so as against the owner of said riparian lot, although the water
was taken, in the first instance, by license of said owner, it appearing that such license was unlimited in point of time.

The nonriparian grantees of a riparian owner of the right to take
water from a brook for nonriparian use can maintain an action
in their own name against an upper riparian proprietor for polluting the water to their damage.

Riparian owners are entitled, as against each other, to a reasonable
use of the water of the stream.

Whether the use of the water of a stream by a riparian owner, is reasonable, is a question of fact.

Since Chapter 85, of the Compiled Statutes provided for incorporation
by written articles "subscribed by the members," such subscription was a condition precedent to incorporation.

Since Chapter 85 of the Compiled Statutes provided that corporations
created thereunder, "when organized," should be capable to sue
and be sued; unless organized, such corporation cannot be sued,
though its articles are subscribed by its members.

APPEAL IN CHANCERY, Washington County.　Heard at
Chambers on bill, answer, master's report, and exceptions
thereto. *Start,* Chancellor. Decree, *pro forma* for the orators.
The defendants appealed.

The master reported that prior to the year 1854, the then
owners of the property in the Ox Bow District joined together
in laying an aqueduct from the stream at a certain point in
the Lawrie lot to their respective farms and buildings, and
shared in the expense and ownership thereof, and thereby conveyed water from said stream to said farms and buildings for
domestic and farm uses; that said farms and buildings were
thereafterwards so supplied with water, for the purposes
named, until, in the year 1854, the owners of said aqueduct
wishing to have their respective rights better defined and

understood and enforceable in law between themselves, their heirs and assigns, did then adopt articles of association under the laws of this State. The master sets forth the articles of association so adopted, but they do not appear to have been signed.

On the 17th day of October, 1887, the defendant, William H. Silsby, became the sole owner in fee of the Hale lot, which is situated immediately north of the Lawrie lot, and between that time and the year 1890, said Silsby cut and removed from the Hale lot most of the timber growing thereon and converted the land into pasture in which he afterwards kept thirty to forty head of cattle and horses, all of which had access to the brook in question, which flowed south through the Hale lot and across the Lawrie lot.

On the 21st day of November, 1894, said Silsby leased for the term of ninety-nine years to the defendants, E. T. Bailey and A. W. Silsby, a portion of the land lying on said stream running through the Hale lot to be flowed and used for a private fish pond and for trout only. The lessees were to control the land for a distance of thirty feet back from the water's edge all around said pond. They also had the right to control the stream running into said pond up as far as they might desire towards its source for the purpose of hatching and protecting trout therein.

In the fall of 1894 said lessees erected a dam across said stream near the southerly boundary of the Hale lot, and by means of the same the water has been set back and forms a pond, the area of which is between six and seven acres, with an average depth of over six feet, and containing, in round numbers, nearly 14,000,000 gallons of water. In the construction of said dam a spillway was provided at its top through which it was expected that the natural stream would flow after the dam was once filled, but much of the time since its completion, through loss of water from the pond by leakage of the dam and evaporation, the surface of the water has been considerably below the spillway, and at such times the water that has flowed from the dam in the natural bed of the stream below that point, has been only such water as has escaped through said leakage.

The master finds that by reason of the storage of water in said pond, the water that flows therefrom has at all times since the dam was completed been decidedly inferior to the water in the brook; that in wet seasons, when the dam overflows, the water is of better quality than in drier seasons when it does not overflow, and when by standing in the pond it becomes to a greater or less extent stagnant. The opinion states the other facts.

Smith & Smith for the orators.

The orators have the right to have the water of the stream continue to flow in its natural channel unimpaired in quality and undiminished in quantity to any material degree, except to satisfy natural wants. Kent. Com., Vol. 3, 439; *Chapman* v. *Rochester,* 1 L. R. A. 296; *Bealey* v. *Shaw,* 6 East. 208; *Evans* v. *Merriweather,* 4 Ill. 495, 38 Am. Dec. 106.

After a stream has run in an artificial channel for the length of time required to gain title to land by adverse possession, the proprietors on the banks of the artificial stream have all the rights which they would have if they were riparian proprietors on a natural stream. *Shepardson* v. *Perkins,* 58 N. H. 354; *Major* v. *Chadwick,* 11 Ad. & El. 571, 39 E. C. L. 169; *Watkins* v. *Peck,* 13 N. H. 360; *Williams* v. *Wadsworth,* 51 Conn. 277; *Sutcliffe* v. *Booth,* 32 L. J., Q. B. 136.

Rights in a stream may originate in grant or in prescription, and these may be acquired either by riparian or non-riparian proprietors. Angell on Watercourses, § 224; Kent Com. Vol. 3, pp. 441-444; *Shrewsbury* v. *Brown*, 25 Vt. 197; *Tracey* v. *Atherton*, 36 Vt. 503; *Perrin* v. *Garfield*, 37 Vt. 304; *Ford* v. *Whitlock*, 27 Vt. 265; *Wilcox* v. *Wheeler*, 47 N. H. 488; *Finch* v. *Resbridger*, 2 Ver. 390; *Matthewson* v. *Hoffman*, 6 L. R. A. 349; *Woodbury* v. *Short*, 17 Vt. 387; *Belknap* v. *Trimble*, 3 Paige 577; *Murchie* v. *Gates*, 78 Me. 300.

Equity is the proper forum to abate a nuisance. Enc. Pl. & Pr., Vol. 14, 1118; Am. & Eng. Enc. Law, Vol. 10, 844; *Ullbricht* v. *Eufaula Co.*, 4 L. R. A. 572; *Barton* v. *Union Cattle Co.*, 7 L. R. A. 457; *Canfield* v. *Andrews*, 54 Vt. 1; *Coffin* v. *Cole*, 67 Vt. 226.

Dunnett & Slack, and *R. M. Harvey* for the defendants.

The bill should have been dismissed for want of proper parties. The water system, as the report finds, is the property of the Oxbow Aqueduct Co. Said corporation is a necessary party. Story, Eq. Pl. § 72; *Poore* v. *Clark*, 2 Atk. 515; *Sturges & Douglass* v. *Knapp*, 31 Vt. 1; *Shaw* v. *R. R. Co.*, 5 Gray 162; *Stevens* v. *Austin*, 3 Met. 474; Thompson, Corp. § 4471; *Smith* v. *Hurd*, 12 Met. 371; *Taylor* v. *Homes*, 127 U. S. 489; *Detroit* v. *Dean*, 106 U. S. 537; *Lane* v. *School Dist.*, 10 Met. 462; *Byers* v. *Coal Co.*, 14 Allen 470; *Hoe* v. *Wilson*, 9 Wall. 501; *Smith* v. *Bartholomew*, 24 Vt. 369.

None of the orators are riparian owners except Lawrie. Therefore only Lawrie has any of the rights incident to riparian ownership. Gould on Waters, § 148; *City of Emporia* v. *Soden*, 37 Am. Rep. 265; *Stein* v. *Burden*, 60 Am. Dec. 465; *Gardiner* v. *Newburg*, 7 Am. Dec. 526; *Platt* v. *Johnson*, 8 Am. Dec. 233.

The defendants have injured no one, they have merely exercised the rights which the law has given them. *Tyler* v. *Wilkinson,* 4 Mason 400; *Gould* v. *Boston Duck Co.,* 13 Gray 442; *Dumont* v. *Kellogg,* 18 Am. Rep. 102; *Pitts et al.* v. *Lancaster Mills,* 13 Met. 156; *Davis* v. *Gretchell,* 50 Me. 602; *City of Springfield* v. *Harris,* 4 Allen 494; *Barre Water Co.* v. *Carnes,* 65 Vt. 626; *Wood* v. *Edes,* 2 Allen 578; *Snow* v. *Parsons,* 28 Vt. 459; *Barnard et al.* v. *Shirley,* 135 Ind. 547; *Hazelton* v. *Case,* 5 Am. Rep. 715; *Pool* v. *Lewis,* 5 Am. Rep. 526; *Thurber* v. *Martin,* 2 Gray 394.

RowELL, C. J. The orators, who take water by a pipe from a brook on what is called the Lawrie lot, and conduct it to their several nonriparian farms and buildings for domestic and farm uses, have not thereby acquired a prescriptive right to do so as against the defendants, who own the riparian land next above the Lawrie lot, called the Hale lot, though the water has been taken long enough in point of time, for the law of this State is, as well as of many if not most of the other states, and of England, that the presumption of a grant from long-continued enjoyment arises only where the person against whom the right is claimed could have lawfully interrupted or prevented the exercise of the subject of the supposed grant. *Shumway* v. *Simons,* 1 Vt. 53; *Norton* v. *Volantine,* 14 Vt. 239; *Hoy* v. *Sterrett,* 2 Watts. 327, 27 Am. Dec. 313; *Holsman* v. *Boiling Springs Bleaching Co.* 14 N. J. Eq. 335; *Vliet* v. *Sherwood,* 35 Wis. 229; *Nelson* v. *Butterfield,* 21 Me. 220; 28 Am. & Eng. Ency. Law, 1st ed. 1005; *Stockport Waterworks Co.* v. *Potter,* 3 H. & C. 300, 325; *Chasemore* v. *Richards,* 7 H. L. Cas. 349, 370; *Webb* v. *Bird,* 13 C. B. N. S. 841; *Sturges* v. *Bridgman,* .11 Ch. D. at page 855.

Here, neither the defendants nor their predecessors in title could lawfully have interrupted nor prevented the taking of the water, as it does not appear that it infringed their rights.

Murchie v. *Gates,* 78 Me. 300, 4 Atl. 698, and *Holker* v. *Porritt,* L. R. 8 Ex. 107, and L. R. 10 Ex. 59, on which the orators rely to support their claim of a prescriptive right, are not in point, for there natural streams had been divided so that part of the water flowed in artificial channels, and the law of natural watercourses was applied to the artificial channels, and the plaintiffs were regarded as riparian proprietors the same as though they abutted on the natural branch of the stream; though in the Exchequer Chamber the judgment in *Holker* v. *Porritt* was affirmed on different ground.

The orators, therefore, having no prescriptive right against the defendants, must stand on whatever other rights they have against them. The orator, James B. Lawrie, owns the Lawrie lot, and has ever since 1870, and must stand on his right as such owner. The defendants do not question the right of the other orators as against Lawrie to take the water as they do, but they say nothing as to the legal quality of the right, and the orators claim that in the circumstances it will be presumed to rest in grant, and we are inclined to think that this is the true view of the matter. It appears from the report that prior to the year 1854, the then owners of the orators' farms and buildings, one of whom was H. N. Chamberlin, the then owner of the Lawrie lot and of the said Lawrie's farm, joined together in laying the aqueduct in question, and thereby took water from the brook to their respective farms and buildings for domestic and farm uses, and shared in the expense and ownership of said aqueduct; that said farms and buildings were thus supplied with water until the year 1854, when the owners of said aqueduct, wishing to have their rights therein better defined and understood, and better enforceable among themselves, their heirs and assigns, adopted written articles, purporting to be under ch. 85 of the Comp. Sts., whereby they undertook to form themselves into a corporation under the name of the Ox Bow Aqueduct Company, for the purpose of bringing water by aqueduct from the hill westerly of the "Ox Bow" where most convenient, each agreeing to pay his proportion of the expense, and the cost of keeping in repair to the point where each took the water from the main branch, each putting in and maintaining his own branch, and whereby the number of shares that each, or his assigns, should be entitled to, was fixed, and subjected to assessment from time to time for building and repairing the aqueduct. And water has ever since been, and still is, taken from said brook by means of said aqueduct, to the farms and buildings of the orators for the purposes and uses aforesaid.

Although it appears clearly enough that water was thus taken in the first instance by license of Chamberlin, the then owner of the Lawrie lot, yet it appears with equal clearness that that license was unlimited in point of time, and so understood by all the parties thereto, and that the water has been taken and used for all these forty years and more under a claim of right. This being so, the fact that the use began by permission did not prevent the acquisition of a prescriptive right to take as against the owners of the Lawrie lot. *Arbuckle* v. *Ward*, 29 Vt. 43; *Blaine* v. *Ray*, 61 Vt. 566, 18 Atl. 189.

But is this prescriptive right sufficient to enable the orators, other than Lawrie, to maintain this bill in their own names? It is not, unless a grant to them from an owner of the Lawrie lot would be sufficient, for they can prescribe for

no more than he could grant, as prescription is based upon a
supposed grant. This raises the question whether a nonriparian grantee of a riparian proprietor, of a right to take
water from the stream for nonriparian use, can maintain an
action in his own name against an upper riparian proprietor
for polluting the water of the stream to his damage. It has
been expressly held in England that he cannot; that though
the grant is good against the grantor, it does not enable the
grantee to sue in his own name a riparian proprietor other
than his grantor for interfering with his right. This is put
upon the ground that the rights of a riparian proprietor in
respect to the water are derived entirely from his possession of
land abutting on the stream, and are so annexed to the soil
that they cannot be granted away apart from the land as far
as other riparian proprietors are concerned. *Stockport Water-
works Co.* v. *Potter,* 3 H. & C. 300; *Ormerod* v. *Todmorton
Mill Co.,* L. R. 11 Q. B. 155 Cf.; *Kensit* v. *Great Eastern
Railway* Co., 27 Ch. D. 122. In *Nuttall* v. *Bracewell,* L. R. 2
Ex. 1, it was held that the plaintiff was a riparian proprietor
in respect of a goit; but Pollock, C. B., and Channell, B.,
adhered to the ground of their judgment in the *Stockport
Waterworks* case, and said that if a riparian proprietor is
bound to abstain from interfering with nonriparian grantees
of riparian proprietors, as well as from interfering with riparian proprietors themselves, it would well nigh destroy his
rights altogether, for that can hardly be called a right that
is subject to an indefinite restriction, unascertained and practically unascertainable. They considered that the rights of a
riparian proprietor with respect to the stream are limited only
by the rights of persons in a similar or an analogous position
with themselves. The Master of the Rolls said in *Ormerod*
v. *The Todmorden Mill Co.,* that though the law of flowing

water is a part of the common law of England, it exists only as among riparian proprietors, and does not extend to those whose lands do not abut on streams and rivers.

But in this country it is held in some jurisdictions that an incorporeal right to water may be granted in gross or made appurtenant to other land, and that the grantee may sue in his own name for a disturbance of his right. Thus, in *St. Anthony Falls Water Power Co.* v. *The City of Minneapolis*, 41 Minn. 270, a riparian owner of part of an island in the Mississippi River just above the Falls, sold other land of his not bordering on the river, and with it granted a right to take water from the river for use thereon, which the grantees did by means of a canal, and the defendant succeeded to their rights. It was objected that as the city had no land abutting on the river, it was not a riparian owner, and had no riparian rights. But the court said it was entirely immaterial whether the defendant's rights were riparian or conventional; that it had rights, for the disturbance of which it had a right of action; that it was unimportant whether it was held that the provision in the grantor's deed in regard to a canal amounted to a division of the river into two courses, or whether, what seemed to be more in accordance with principle and common sense, it was held that a riparian owner may grant a part of his estate not abutting on the stream, and, as appurtenant thereto, a right to draw water from the stream for use on such land.

In *Goodrich* v. *Burbank*, 12 Allen, 459, it was held that an assignable right in gross to take water from a spring on land conveyed could be reserved to the grantor, his heirs and assigns. The court said that water itself may not be the subject of property, but that the right to take it, and to have pipes laid in the soil of another for that purpose, and to

enter upon the land of another to lay, repair, and renew such
pipes, is an interest in the realty, assignable, discernable, and
devisable; that there are many cases in Massachusetts recognizing the right to take water from a millpond as a distinct
and substantive right, without restriction as to its use at any
particular place; and that it was unable to distinguish between
a right to take water from a pond by means of a canal for the
purposes of power, and a right to take water from a spring
for domestic purposes.   Judge Curtis said in *The Lonsdale*
. *Co.* v. *Moies,* 21 Monthly Law Reporter, 658, a case in the
U. S. Circuit Court concerning water rights in the Blackstone
River, that incorporeal rights may be inseparably annexed to
a particular messuage or tract of land by the grant that creates them, or may be granted in gross, and afterwards, for
the purpose of enjoyment, be annexed to a messuage or land,
and then severed therefrom by a conveyance of the messuage
or land without the right, or a conveyance of the right without the land.   This court said substantially the same thing in
Rood v. *Johnson,* 26 Vt. 64, 71, when construing a grant of
a water right in a river, thus: "The land is conveyed, and the
grantor might, had he chosen, have reserved the use of all
the water to himself, or he might have conveyed the use of
all or a part of it as a mere incorporeal hereditament, and
retained the fee of the land in himself, notwithstanding the
maxim that one cannot convey the water separate from the
land."

In *Poull* v. *Mockley,* 33 Wis. 482, a grant to one and
his heirs and assigns forever of a right to take water from a
well on the grantor's land, was held to create an easement in
gross, and to be assignable by the grantee.   The court followed the Massachusetts cases, and said it saw no substantial reason why such an easement is not assignable.

In *Hill* v. *Shorey*, 42 Vt. 614, it was held that a reservation in a deed, "of the right of taking all the waste water as it now runs into the tub on said premises by aqueduct" from a spring thereon, was a reservation of an interest and a right in the spring itself to the extent named. It is said in Washburn on Easements, 4th ed., 14 and 15, that where water is, as it may be, the subject of sale in gross as a thing of value, it does not seem to be violating any rule of law to regard it as a species of *profit a prendre,* and therefore a subject of separate grant; and that although it might be difficult to raise a prescriptive right of inheritance in the privilege of an aqueduct by personal enjoyment independent of its use in connection with some estate, and although a right to the enjoyment of water from a well or a spring or a river may be gained by custom, since no part of the soil or freehold proper is thus carried away any faster than it is ordinarily supplied from natural sources, yet, after all, it is an interest in land; and that, as said in *Goodrich* v. *Burbank,* above cited, there is no distinction between a right to take water by a canal from a pond for the purposes of power, and the right to take it from a spring in a pipe for domestic purposes.

It would seem to follow that if the right to take water from a spring or a stream is an interest in the land itself, that such right is grantable as a right in gross or appurtenant, and is assignable, descendable, and devisible; and such, we think, has always been the view entertained and practiced upon in this State. Situated as we are, with so many springs and streams of pure water on which our people are largely dependent for their domestic needs, we think this doctrine best adapted to our local situation and circumstances. We hold, therefore, that the other orators, as well as Lawrie, can maintain the bill in their own names if the defendants have infringed their rights. But what are their rights as against the defendants?

Each riparian proprietor has a right to use the water of the stream for his own natural wants, and for the like wants of his family and his beasts. Many of the authorities say that for these purposes he may use all of it if necessary. But the logical result from the correlative rights of riparian proprietors would seem to be that each must use his own right so as not to deprive the others of an equal enjoyment of their same rights. And this is the view taken in *Chatfield* v. *Wilson,* 31 Vt. 358, and *Barre Water Co.* v. *Carnes,* 65 Vt. 626, 27 Atl. 609. The same view is taken in *Elliot* v. *Fitchburg Railroad Co.,* 10 Cush. 191. It would seem to follow that reasonable use is the only limit that can be set to the exercise of these rights. This is the rule in New Hampshire, where they repudiate the English doctrine, and hold it to be a question of fact whether the use of the water made by a riparian owner for his own purposes or for sale to others for non-riparian purposes is, in all the circumstances, a reasonable use. *Gillis* v. *Chase,* 67 N. H. 161, 31 Atl. 18. Sometimes the law will say what is a reasonable use. Thus, they hold in New Jersey that the sale of a right to take water for use on non-riparian lands is unreasonable as matter of law, if thereby another riparian proprietor sustains palpable damage. *Higgins* v. *Flemington Water Co.,* 36 N. J. Eq. 538. But if the use is lawful and beneficial, it must be deemed to be reasonable, and not an infringement of the rights of other riparian owners to whom it occasions no actual and perceptible damage. *Elliot* v. *Fitchburg Railroad Co.,* 10 Cush. 191, 197. There a riparian owner granted to the defendant a perpetual right to divert all the water of the stream to its non-riparian premises, where it supplied its locomotive engines with water.

The court said that the grantor and the grantee together held
the whole right, and that the case was to be considered as
though the defendant owned the land. This case is like that
in this respect. Here the taking of the water by the orators
is lawful and beneficial, and does not alter the rights of the
defendants nor do them any actual and perceptible damage.
Therefore their use must be deemed reasonable as to the defendants. But the use the defendants are making of the water
is found to damage the orators to some extent, and therefore
it cannot be said as matter of law, in the circumstances, to
be a reasonable use. Hence it is a question of fact for the
master, and he has not passed upon it, and the case will have
to go back to him.

We are asked to deny an injunction because the damage
is so small to the orators, and growing smaller all the time,
and the master thinks that the water in the defendants' pond,
the creation of which is complained of, may purify itself from
objectionable taste and odor in ten years, though probably a
longer time will be required to render it tasteless and odorless
as it leaves the pond; and because an injunction will hurt the
defendants more than it will help the orators. But as the case
has got to go back for further findings, this question is reserved.

It is objected that the bill cannot be maintained because
not brought in the name of The Ox Bow Aqueduct Company.
But this objection cannot be sustained, because it does not
appear that the company was ever incorporated and organized. The statute provided that associations thereunder should
be formed by written articles, "subscribed by the members."
It fairly appears that these articles were not subscribed by
the members, for the report professes to set out the articles
in their very words, and no signatures are attached. Substantial compliance with the terms of a general incorporation

law is a prerequisite to the formation of a corporation under it. 1 Morawetz, Corp. 2d ed., § 27.

Again, the statute provided that corporations created thereunder, "when organized," should be capable to sue and be sued. It does not appear that said association was ever organized, and therefore it would have no capacity to sue even though the articles had been subscribed.

Reversed and remanded with mandate.

H. C. LEONARD and CLARK HOLDEN v. A. J. SIBLEY, ADMR.

October Term, 1903.

Present: ROWELL, C. J., MUNSON, START, WATSON, STAFFORD, and HASELTON, JJ.

Opinion filed February 13, 1904.

Trustee Process—Judgment—Final—Interlocutory.

When, in an action by trustee process, judgment by default is rendered against the principal defendants, and the case is continued for assessment of damages, and also as to the trustee and claimant, such judgment is interlocutory merely, and final judgment may be rendered against said defendants at a subsequent term, and, by special leave of court, execution thereon may issue, though the liability of the trustees is not yet determined.

WRIT OF ERROR to review a judgment rendered for the defendants in error at the March Term, 1903, Washington County, *Stafford,* J., presiding.

The assignments of error are: (1) That the court should not have continued the original suit for assessment of damages, since said suit was for a sum certain, the action being debt on judgment. (2) That the court should not have entered judgment against the defendants in the original suit at the September Term, 1902, since judgment by default had already been entered at the March Term, 1889. (3) That the court should not have granted execution against the defendants at the September Term, 1902.

Audita querela was also brought by the plaintiffs against the defendant, to set aside said judgment. Trial by court at the March Term, 1903, Washington County, *Stafford*, J., presiding. Judgment that the supersedeas be vacated, that the respondent is not guilty, and that he recover his costs. The plaintiffs excepted.

The exceptions and the writ of error, being designed for the same purpose, were heard together.

When final judgment was rendered against the defendants the case was entered "with the court as to trustee and claimant." The opinion states the other facts.

John W. Gordon and John Senter for the plaintiffs in error.

The judgment rendered in the original case at the September Term, 1902, was a void judgment. *Stone* v. *Seaver*, 5 Vt. 542; *Sutton et al.* v. *Sutton et al.*, 10 Vt. 87; *Potter* v. *Hodges et al.*, 13 Vt. 239; *Chase* v. *Scott*, 14 Vt. 77; *Lincoln* v. *Flint*, 18 Vt. 247; *Tittlemore* v. *Wainwright*, 16 Vt. 173; *Griswold* v. *Rutland*, 23 Vt. 324; *Perry* v. *Moore*, 57 Vt. 509; *Johnson et al.* v. *Plimpton*, 30 Vt. 420.

If execution should issue before the final disposition of the case as to the trustees, it should be an execution founded upon the judgment of the March Term, 1889, and should recite that judgment. *Wilson et al.* v. *Fleming*, 16 Vt. 649; *Rice et al.* v. *Talmage*, 20 Vt. 378.

A judgment *nunc pro tunc* cannot be entered unless the case be in such a condition on the day to which the judgment is to relate back, that final judgment could then have been rendered. 1 Black on Judgments, § 131; *Rugg* v. *Parker,* 7 Gray 172; *Balch et ux.* v. *Shaw,* 7 Cush. 282.

The judgment rendered at the March Term, 1889, was final. Freeman on Judgments, §§ 330-332; 2 Bouvier's Law Dic. 28; *Loring* v. *Illsley,* 1 Cal. 28; *Clements* v. *Berry,* 11 How. 398; *Turner* v. *Plowden,* 23 Am. Dec. 596; *Com.* v. *Baldwin,* 26 Am. Dec. 33; *Rawdon* v. *Rapley,* 58 Am. Dec. 370; *Bank* v. *Hall,* 41 Am. Dec. 41; *Mills* v. *Hoag,* 31 Am. Dec. 271; *Bank* v. *Dobson,* 127 Cal. 208; *State* v. *R. R. Co.,* 16 Fla. 708; *Shepard* v. *Brenton,* 20 Iowa 41.

H. C. Shurtleff for the defendant.

Final judgment against the principal debtor was ordered by the court. If any error was committed in so doing it was error of the court and *audita querela* does not lie to correct such errors. *Little* v. *Cook,* 1 Aik. 363; *Weeks* v. *Lawrence,* 1 Vt. 437; *Dodge* v. *Hubbel,* 1 Vt. 491; *Stone* v. *Seaver,* 5 Vt. 549; *Suttons* v. *Tyrrell,* 10 Vt. 87; *Parker* v. *Hodges,* 13 Vt. 239; *Chase* v. *Scott,* 14 Vt. 77; *Tittlemore* v. *Wainwright,* 16 Vt. 173; *Betty* v. *Brown,* 16 Vt. 669; *Griswold* v. *Rutland,* 23 Vt. 324; *School Dist.* v. *Rood,* 27 Vt. 214; *Perry* v. *Morse,* 57 Vt. 509.

The case was properly continued for assessment as long as the liability of the trustee and claimant remained unsettled. *Jones* v. *Spear & Tr.,* 21 Vt. 426; V. S. 1386; *Spring* v. *Ayer,* 23 Vt. 518; *Passumpsic Bank* v. *Beattie,* 32 Vt. 315; *Bank* v. *Downer,* 29 Vt. 332; *Hapgood* v. *Goddard,* 26 Vt. 404.

An assessment of damages may take place at any convenient time. *Sheldon* v. *Sheldon & Tr.,* 37 Vt. 152; *Webb* v.

Webb, 16 Vt. 636; *Brown* v. *Irwin,* 21 Vt. 72; *Yatter* v. *Miller,* 61 Vt. 147; *Shepard* v. *Charter,* 4 T. R. 275; *Green* v. *Hearne,* 3 T. R. 301; *Nelson* v. *Sheridan,* 8 D. & E. 395.

WATSON, J. This case is here on writ of error. The original action against the plaintiffs in error was by trustee process with a declaration of debt on judgment, and was returnable to and entered in the County Court at the December Term, 1889. At that time the plaintiffs in error made no appearance; whereupon judgment was rendered against them by default, a claimant of the funds in the hands of the trustee entered in the suit, and a commissioner was appointed to determine and report to the court the liability of the trustee and the right of the claimant. The cause was then continued for the assessment of damages and as to the trustee and the claimant. It was so continued from term to term until the September Term, 1902, when final judgment against the plaintiffs in error was ordered, with leave to take out execution forthwith. The damages were assessed, final judgment rendered, and execution issued accordingly.

The errors assigned are that, since the action was debt on judgment, it was for a sum certain and that the continuation of the cause after the March Term, 1889, for the assessment of damages, the rendering of judgment against the plaintiffs in error at the September Term, 1902, the grant of leave to issue execution on said judgment, and the issue of the same were contrary to and without authority of law.

It is urged that when the judgment by default was rendered it was for a sum certain, to be computed by the clerk of court, and that it was a final judgment. Also that the rendition of judgment at the September Term, 1902, was error, for the reason that the former judgment was still in force and at most nothing remained to perfect it but the assessment of the damages, which, it is contended, should have been inserted in the records *nunc pro tunc.* Was the judgment of 1889 final, or was it only interlocutory?

From the fact that a declaration is debt on judgment it does not necessarily follow that a judgment by default is final. Under the common law of England, where the action was brought on a judgment, the plaintiff was generally considered entitled to a writ of inquiry, after a judgment by default, to recover interest by way of damages for the detention of the debt. 1 Tidd's Prac. (3rd Am. ed.) 573. Yet it was not the universal practice to award such a writ. In some instances a reference was made to the secondary or to the prothonotary to assess the damages, and in later years this seems to have become the prevailing practice. *Holdipp* v. *Otway,* 2 Saund. 106 and Notes; *Webb* v. *Webb,* 16 Vt. 636; *Smith* v. *Vanderhorst,* 1 McCord, (S. C.) 328.

Black on Judgments, § 21, says: "A final judgment is such a judgment as at once puts an end to the action by declaring that the plaintiff has or has not entitled himself to recover the remedy for which he sues. * * * * * A judgment which is not final is called 'interlocutory.' That is, if the amount of the recovery or damages remain to be ascertained by a writ of inquiry or other judicial method of computation, then the judgment is merely interlocutory, until such amount is settled and entered on the record."

Bouvier's Law Dictionary says: "Interlocutory judgments are such as are given in the middle of a cause upon some plea, proceeding or default which is only intermediate, and does not finally determine or complete the suit. Any judgment leaving something to be done by the court, before the rights of the parties are determined, and not putting an end to the action in which it is entered, is interlocutory."

In *Collins* v. *Paddington,* 5 Q. B. D. 368, it is said by Baggallay, L. J., that where any further step is necessary to perfect an order or judgment it is not final but interlocutory.

By statutory provision when judgment is rendered otherwise than on the verdict of a jury, the judges of the court may, by themselves, by the jury in court, by report of the clerk, or by the report on oath of a person appointed by the court, ascertain the sum due. R. L. 1178, V. S. 1411. In the case under consideration, the court directed an assessment by the clerk, and in connection therewith ordered that the cause be continued for assessment of damages, and as to the trustee and claimant. As regards the damages, the effect of this order was that they should be ascertained by the clerk at the term to which the case was thus continued, unless there should be a further continuance for that purpose. After the damages were so assessed it then devolved upon the court to give final judgment thereupon at such time as the circumstances of the case should require. Hence, the action was not finally determined or completed in that respect. Further judicial action of the court was necessary to be directed to the question before final judgment could be entered of record.

Our holdings here are consonant to the rules of law governing the practice in actions by trustee process before laid down by this court. In such actions the judgment against the principal defendant in the suit, even though it be for a sum certain, does not make a final end of the case as to him, so that an execution can issue against him before the case has been determined as to the trustee.

In *Jones* v. *Spear*, 21 Vt. 426, the action was assumpsit for money had and received, and the trial was by the court. At the trial the plaintiff sought to recover only on a promissory note for one hundred dollars with interest. Judgment was rendered for the plaintiff to recover the amount due upon the note. At a subsequent term, the trustee moved to be discharged for the reason that judgment had been rendered against the principal defendant and that the suit was thereby ended, as to the defendant, at the former term. The motion was overruled and, on exception by the trustee, the case was heard in this court. Upon a careful consideration of the decisions of this court hitherto made bearing upon the question, it was held that the case was not ended as to the principal defendant, nor could he be considered as out of court or disconnected with the case by having judgment rendered against him; but that such judgment must lie until the case should be legally determined as to the trustee. It is not conceivable how a judgment by default in an action of debt on judgment can be more specifically for a sum certain than was the judgment in that case for the amount due on the note. See also *Hapgood* v. *Goddard,* 26 Vt. 401.

We think it clear that the judgment of 1889 was merely interlocutory, that considering the status of the case as to the trustee and claimant, the continuance from term to term for assessment of damages was peculiarly fitting, and that at the September Term, 1902, final judgment was properly rendered of that term. It is equally clear in practice in this State that when final judgment against the principal debtor has been entered, execution may issue thereon by special leave of the court, while the action is still pending and undetermined as to the trustee. *Spring* v. *Ayer & Tr.,* 23 Vt. 516; *Bank* v. *Beattie,* 32 Vt. 315.

The question whether a writ of error will lie to review a judgment by default was not presented in argument nor have we considered it in the disposition of the case.

The action of *audita querela* between the same parties was heard in connection with this case. It involves, however, no questions that have not directly or indirectly been determined on the writ of error. Whether *audita querela* will lie we do not consider.

The judgment is affirmed in both cases.

W. L. CURRIER and E. F. NORCROSS *v.* THE TOWN OF BRIGHTON, and TOWN SCHOOL DISTRICT.

October Term, 1903.

Present: ROWELL, C. J., MUNSON, START, WATSON, STAFFORD, and HASELTON, JJ.

Opinion filed February 13, 1904.

Town School District—Directors—Control by District—Evidence—Town Meeting—Record.

A town school district cannot be controlled by its directors in the matter of paying a debt contracted by them as the statutory agents of the district.

In an action against a town and its town school district to recover a debt contracted by the school directors and assigned to the plaintiff, a certified copy of the record of the warning of an annual meeting of the town and the proceedings of said town meeting, showing that the meeting voted to pay said debt to the plaintiff, is admissible.

ASSUMPSIT for wood sold and delivered. Pleas, the general issue, and tender before suit. Trial by jury at the October Term, 1903, Essex County, *Munson, J.,* presiding. On motion, the court directed a verdict for the plaintiffs. Judgment on verdict. The defendants excepted. The opinion states the facts.

Dale & Amey for the defendants.

The school directors are the statutory agents of the school district and not subject to the control of the district. *School Dist.* v. *Harvey*, 56 Vt. 556; *Mason* v. *School Dist.*, 20 Vt. 491; *Chittenden* v. *Waterbury*, 56 Vt. 551; *Cobb* v. *Pomfret*, 63 Vt. 648; *Wait* v. *Ray*, 67 N. Y. 36.

J. W. Redmond for the plaintiffs.

A town may be liable upon a *quantum meruit.* *Rowell* v. *School Dist.*, 59 Vt. 658; *Brown* v. *School Dist.*, 55 Vt. 42; *Daggett* v. *Mendon*, 64 Vt. 323; *Union, etc., Co.* v. *School Dist.*, 20 L. R. A. 136.

The district can control the school directors in the matter of paying a bill contracted by them. *Sheldon et al.* v. *Stockbridge*, 67 Vt. 303; *Bates* v. *Bassett*, 60 Vt. 536; *Lucia* v. *Eaton*, 60 Vt. 537; *Kimball* v. *School Dist.*, 28 Vt. 8; *Richardson et ux.* v. *School Dist.*, 38 Vt. 602.

ROWELL, C. J. This is assumpsit for wood sold and delivered by the plaintiff Currier. Pleas, the general issue and tender before suit. The wood was bought for the district by the school directors; but they refused to draw an order on the district treasurer to pay for it, because they claimed it was not according to the contract. Currier made out a bill for the wood, and gave an order on the district for its payment to the plaintiff Norcross. In the warning for the annual town meeting in 1903, there was an article to see if the town would vote to pay said bill to Norcross, and the meeting voted to pay it to him. The court admitted in evidence a certified copy of the record of the warning and the proceedings of said meeting, to which the defendant excepted, and said that it did not care to go to the jury on any question, and that if the record was admissible at all, it was of binding force upon the town and determined its liability. Thereupon the court directed a verdict for the plaintiffs, to which the defendant excepted. Hence the only question is, whether the record was admissible at all, and the defendant contends that it was not, because the matter was wholly within the statutory jurisdiction of its school directors, and that therefore the town had nothing to do with it. But the purchase of the wood by the directors created a debt against the town district, and in the matter of paying it the district could not be controlled by the directors, for in respect of that they were not the statutory agents of the town, any more than under the old school district system the prudential committee was such agent of the district in respect of paying debts that he had created against the district, and that he was not such agent is shown by *Richardson* v. *School District,* 38 Vt. 602, which fully recognized the right of the district to deal with the matter of paying a teacher whom the prudential committee had wrongfully discharged. So we think the record was admissible to show that the town had the wood, and as tending to show its value, but whether conclusive or not upon the town we do not inquire, for its counsel said it was conclusive if admissible at all, and the court acted upon that in directing a verdict.

Judgment affirmed.

MARY ANN BAILEY v. GEORGE BAILEY.

October Term, 1903.

Present: ROWELL, C. J., TYLER, MUNSON, STAFT, WATSON, and
HASELTON, JJ.

Opinion filed February 13, 1904.

Divorce—Alimony—Pension.

Upon a decree of divorce *a vinculo* for the fault of the husband, it
is proper for the court, in fixing the amount of alimony the husband shall be required to pay, to consider his pension from the
United States as part of his financial resources.

PETITION FOR DIVORCE, with prayer for alimony. Bill
granted and alimony decreed at the June Term, 1903, Caledonia County, *Stafford*, J., presiding. The petitionee excepted.

Harland B. Howe and *Marshall Montgomery* for the
petitionee.

The court had no jurisdiction to decree petitionee's pen-
sion to the petitioner because it was not yet owned by him,
but was to be acquired subsequently. Bishop, Mar. and Div.,
Vol. 2, §§ 857-887; *Feighley* v. *Feighley*, 61 Am. Dec. 375;
Cochrane v. *Cochrane*, 42 Neb. 612; *Van Orsdal* v. *Van
Orsdal*, 67 Iowa 35; *Harrison* v. *Harrison*, 56 Am. Dec. 227;
Buckminster v. *Buckminster*, 38 Vt. 248; Am. & Eng. Enc.
Law, Vol. 2, pp. 98, 124.

May & Simonds for petitioner.

Orders in divorce cases are not founded upon contracts.
Andrews v. *Andrews*, 62 Vt. 495.

A decree for alimony is based upon the husband's income;
and his resources and other helpful facts are taken into ac-

count in determining the amount. Stewart, Mar. & Div. §
373; *Haywood* v. *Clark,* 50 Vt. 617; *Rozelle* v. *Rhodes,* 2 Am.
St. Rep. 591.

WATSON, J. On dissolution of the marriage for the
cause of intolerable severity, the court decreed to the petitioner as permanent alimony the sum of four hundred dollars
payable, one hundred dollars on the 20th days of October,
1903, January, April, and July, 1904, respectively, with interest after maturity, if not paid, and made the same a charge
upon the petitionee's interest in certain real estate. The petitioner was also decreed all the articles of personal property
and the household furniture then in her possession. It was
further decreed that the petitionee should pay to the clerk of
the court, for the benefit of the petitioner, the sum of thirty-
six dollars on the 15th day of October, 15th day of January,
15th day of April, and the 15th day of July annually thereafter, until further order of court, as a continuing alimony.
In the making of this last order the court took into consideration the pension of twenty-four dollars per month which the
petitionee receives from the United States government for
disabilities resulting from his service as a soldier in the Civil
War, holding as a matter of law that the court might properly
consider that as a part of his financial resources. To this
holding the petitionee excepted. Beyond this no exception
was taken, and our consideration of the case is confined accordingly.

The Revised Statutes of the United States, § 4747,
provides that "No sum of money due, or to become due, to
any pensioner, shall be liable to attachment, levy, or seizure,
by or under any legal or equitable process whatever, whether
the same remains with the Pension Office, or any agent or
officer thereof, or is in the course of transmission to the pen-

sioner entitled thereto, but shall inure wholly to the benefit of such pensioner."

It is contended that by force of this section the court has no power to award pension money not received by the husband at the date of the decree, as alimony to a divorced wife. But this is not the question. The question is, had the court a right, as a matter of law, to consider such a pension as a part of the petitionee's financial resources?

The exemption under the law covers pension money only during its transmission to the pensioner. When it has been received by him, it has inured wholly to his benefit, within the meaning of this statute. Then, to the same extent as money from other sources, it is subject to attachment, levy, and seizure as opportunity presents itself. *McIntosh* v. *Aubrey*, 185 U. S. 122, 46 L. Ed. 834. And so, in effect, was the holding of this court in *Martin* v. *Hurlburt*, 60 Vt. 364, 14 Atl. 649.

Nor did the fact that it was neither property in hand nor the income of such property render its consideration improper. A husband's faculties are his capabilities of maintaining a family, ordinarily consisting of his income from whatever source derived, and they, with all the other circumstances surrounding the parties, should be taken into consideration when alimony or other annual allowance is decreed to be paid by the husband to the wife. 2 Bish. M. & D. §§ 1005, 1006, 1017. See, also, *Hedrick* v. *Hedrick*, 128 Ind. 522; *Tully* v. *Tully*, 159 Mass. 91; *Eidenmuller* v. *Eidenmuller*, 37 Cal. 364; and *Holmes* v. *Holmes*, 29 N. J. Eq. 9.

Judgment affirmed.

TYLER, J., dissents.

ARTHUR MORRISETTE v. CANADIAN PACIFIC RAILWAY CO.

May Term, 1903.

Present: TYLER, MUNSON, START, WATSON, and STAFFORD, JJ,

Opinion filed February 15, 1904.

Master and Servant—Negligence—Injury to Servant—Dangerous Premises—Switches—Foreign Law—Enforcement— Comity—Pleading— Evidence—Experts—Opinion—Construction of Rule—Exceptions—Scope.

A question, which is not raised by the objection and exception taken in trial court, will not be considered in the Supreme Court.

The law of Canada that contributory negligence does not bar the right of recovery but operates only to reduce the damages, relates to the right of action, not to the remedy.

Comity requires us to enforce the law of a foreign state, however unlike our own, unless it be either criminal or penal, or contrary to pure morals or abstract justice, or its enforcement would be of evil example to our people.

In a suit brought in Vermont by a resident of Canada against a Canadian corporation for injuries received there, the right of action is governed by the law of Canada; and, under an exception to the admission of evidence concerning the Canadian law on the ground that the case is governed by the law of Vermont, the Supreme Court will not consider whether the case should have been dismissed because, under the circumstances, a resort to our tribunals was needless and embarrassing.

One who is a practical railroad man and understands the mechanism and operation of switches, though not an engineer, is competent to testify that he knows of no reason why a certain switch might not have been set in a different place.

In an action by a brakeman for injuries caused by being struck from the side of a freight car by a switch alleged to have been negligently placed too near the track, it is proper, as bearing on the assumption of risk, to allow the plaintiff to show, by observations and measurements made after the accident, the position and relative distance of stirrups and grab-irons on cars of the same general character as those operated by him during his service.

When the evidence tends to show that all "two throw" switches were mounted with lanterns of a uniform size, and that the switch in question was a "two throw" switch; as tending to show the size of the lantern on the switch in question, it is proper to allow a witness to state his judgment of the size of "two throw" switch lanterns, and to allow another witness who had measured such a lantern to state its dimensions.

The rule of a railroad company providing that "conductors and brakemen of freight trains approaching stations must be out on their trains at least one mile from stations, and must remain until station is passed," is equally applicable to all trains approaching a station whether about to stop or not.

In an action by a brakeman for injuries caused by being struck from the side of a freight car by a switch alleged to have been negligently placed too near the track, there is no presumption of negligence on the part of the defendant from the mere happening of the accident.

In a suit brought in Vermont by a resident of Canada against a Canadian corporation for injuries received there, it is not error to refuse to instruct the jury that if the plaintiff failed to establish that the Canadian law was settled, and settled as he alleged, and different from the law of Vermont, then it was not to be considered.

An exception to a portion of the charge as given is not sufficient to cover an objection to the failure of the court to charge.

CASE for personal injuries.   Plea, the general issue. Trial by jury at the September Term, 1902, Orleans County, *Haselton*, J., presiding.   Verdict and judgment for plaintiff. The defendant excepted.

This case has been once before in the Supreme Court. See 74 Vt. 232.

The plaintiff was unable to tell what car in the train he was attempting to mount when he was struck by the switch. The opinion states the other facts.

F. E. Alfred and *W. W. Miles* for the defendant.

The plaintiff in his declaration alleged "that said injury arose solely because of said negligence of the defendant, and

without any fault on the part of the plaintiff." Having thus
alleged his lack of negligence the plaintiff must prove the
same. *Barber* v. *Essex*, 27 Vt. 69; *Walker* v. *Westfield*, 39
Vt. 246; *Bovee* v. *Daniels*, 53 Vt. 183; *Melendy* v. *Ames &
Co.*, 62 Vt. 14; *Baker* v. *Sherman*, 73 Vt. 26; Gould's Pleading, Ch. 3, §§ 35-41; *Deragan* v. *Rutland*, 58 Vt. 128; *Dixon*
v. *Ramsay's Exrs.*, 3 Craunch 319; *Scoville* v. *Canfield*, 14
Johns 338; *Pickering* v. *Fisk*, 6 Vt. 102; *Suffolk Bank* v.
Kidder, 12 Vt. 464; *Harrison* v. *Edwards*, 12 Vt. 648.

The foreign law upon which the plaintiff rests his case
permits a recovery notwithstanding contributory negligence.
This law is opposed to public policy, is demoralizing to juris-
prudence, is contrary to our own law, and should not be en-
forced by our courts.   Rorer on Inter-State Law, pp. 4-5;
Story on Conflict of Laws, §§ 557-571-572; Dicey on Conflict
of Laws, p. 660, rule 176; *Pierce* v. *O'Brien*, 129. Mass. 314;
Green v. *Buskirk*, 7 Wall. 138; *Canaga* v. *Taylor*, 70 Am.
Dec. 62; *Blanchard* v. *Russell*, 13 Mass. 6; *Wheelwright* v.
Depeyster, 1 Johns. 470; *Smith* v. *McAtee*, 92 Am. Dec. 641;
Texas & Pac. Ry. Co. v. *Richards*, 68 Tex. 375; *St. Louis
R. R. Co.* v. *McCormick*, 71 Tex. 660; *Richardson* v. *R. R.
Co.*, 98 Mass. 85; *Higgens* v. *R. R. Co.*, 155 Mass. 176;
Anderson v. *R. R. Co.*, 57 Wis. 321; *Dennick* v. *R. R. Co.*,
103 U. S. 11; *McLeod* v. *R. R. Co.*, 58 Vt. 727; *Burns* v.
R. R. Co., 113 Ind. 169; *Cincinnati, etc., R. R. Co.* v. *Mc-
Mullen*, 177 Ind. 439; *Vawter* v. *R. R. Co.*, 84 Mo. 679.

The plaintiff was not competent to give an opinion as to
whether the switch could have been set in a different place.
Lester v. *Pittsford*, 7 Vt. 161; *Clifford* v. *Richardson*, 18 Vt.
620; *Crane* v. *Northfield*, 33 Vt. 124; *Sturgis et al.* v. *Knapp
et al.*, 33 Vt. 531; *Oakes* v. *Weston*, 45 Vt. 430; *Bixby* v.
M. & St. J. R. R. Co., 49 Vt. 123; *Stevenson* v. *Gunning's
Est.*, 64 Vt. 612; *Sias* v. *Consolidated Lighting Co.*, 73 Vt. 35-

J. W. Redmond and *E. A. Cook* for the plaintiff.

To justify the court in refusing to enforce a right of action which accrued under the laws of another state, because against the policy of our laws, it must appear that it is against good morals or natural justice or that for some other such reason the enforcement of it would be prejudical to the general interests of our citizens. *Dennick* v. *R. R. Co.,* 103 U. S. 11; *McLeod* v. *R. R. Co.,* 58 Vt. 727; *Herrick* v. *Minneapolis, etc. Co.,* 47 Am. Rep. 771; *Chicago, etc. R. R. Co.* v. *Rouse,* 44 L. R. A. 410; *Boston & Maine R. R. Co.* v. *McDuffey,* 79 Fed. 934; *Ill. Cent. R. R. Co.* v. *Ihlenberg,* 34 L. R. A. 393; *Northern P. R. Co.* v. *Babcock,* 154 U. S. 190; *Hovis* v. *Richmond, etc. R. R. Co.,* 91 Ga. 36; *Rich* v. *Saginaw, etc. Co.* (Mich.) 93 N. W. 632; *Brewster* v. *Chicago, etc. R. R. Co.* (Iowa), 86 N. W. Rep. 221; *Atchison, etc. R. R. Co.* v. *Moore,* 29 Kan. 632; *Ill. C. R. Co.* v. *Harris,* (Miss.) 29 So. Rep. 760; *Walsh* v. *R. R. Co.,* 160 Mass. 571; *Louisville, etc. Co.* v. *Whitlow,* 41 L. R. A. 614; *Clark* v. *Russell,* 97 Fed. 900; *Bridger* v. *Asheville, etc. R. Co.,* 27 S. C. 456; *East Tenn. etc. R. Co.* v. *Lewis,* 89 Tenn. 235.

Under the declaration in this case, the right of action, and the liability of the defendant, is governed wholly by the law of Canada. *LeForrest* v. *Tolman,* 117 Mass. 109; *Buckles* v. *Ellers,* 37 Am. Rep. 156; 56 L. R. A. 194, note.

STAFFORD, J. The plaintiff was a brakeman upon one of the defendant's freight trains, and claimed to have been injured through the negligence of the company in maintaining a switch too near the track, so that when he was attempting to mount a moving car he struck against it and was knocked off.

The accident occurred in the Province of Quebec, and the declaration, treating the law of the province as matter of

fact, alleges that the defendant as employer of the plaintiff
owed him the care and oversight which the good father of a
family owes to his children and was bound to guard him even
against his own mistakes and thoughtlessness; that neither ·
assumption of risk nor contributory negligence constituted a
bar to the right of recovery, but operated only to reduce the
damages.

The defendant objected to any and all evidence of the law
of Quebec, upon the ground that as it was alleged in the declaration, it was "in direct conflict with the law of Vermont, and
related not to the right of action but solely to the remedy."
The objections stated were overruled, an exception was allowed, and the plaintiff introduced evidence in support of his
allegations. Under this exception the defendant, in this Court,
presents the objection that the plaintiff should not have been
permitted to make good his declaration touching the law of
the province on the subject of contributory negligence because
he had also alleged that the defendant was in fact wholly free
from fault,—that having made the latter allegation he was
bound to prove it. This question is not raised by the objection and exception and is not considered.

It is next objected that evidence as to the law of contributory negligence was inadmissible because it related not
to the right of action but only to the remedy. But we think
it related clearly to the right of action. By the laws of Vermont it was a bar; by the laws of Canada, as the evidence in
question tended to show, it was not a bar.

It is further objected that the Canadian law, as alleged,
although neither criminal nor penal, is so different from ours
that we ought not to administer it. Comity does not require
us to take up and enforce the law of a foreign state which is
contrary to pure morals, or to abstract justice, or to enforce

which would be contrary to our own public policy. The law we are considering is not claimed to be open to either of the first two objections but is claimed to be open to the third, because it is so different from the law of Vermont. Some states have adopted this view, declining to administer foreign laws unless closely analogous to their own. *Mexican National Ry. Co. v. Jackson,* 89 Texas, 107; *Anderson v. M. & St. P. Ry. Co.,* 37 Wis. 321; *Richardson v. N. Y. C. R. Co.,* 98 Mass. 85. But we believe the sounder opinion is that a court should not, in otherwise proper cases, refuse to adopt and apply the law of a foreign state, however unlike the law of its own, unless it be contrary to pure morals, or abstract justice, or unless the enforcement would be of evil example and harmful to its own people and therefore inconsistent with the dignity of the government whose authority is invoked. Judged by that test the ruling was correct. *Herrick v. Minneapolis, etc. Co.,* 31 Minn. 11, 47 Am. Rep. 771; *Higgins v. R. Co.,* 155 Mass. 180; *Dennick v. R. Co.,* 103 U. S. 11; *McLeod v. R. Co.,* 58 Vt. 727, 6 Atl. 648; *Chicago & E. I. R. Co. v. Rouse,* 178 Ill. 132, 44 L. R. A. 410.

It is still further objected that in the circumstances of this case, a resort to our tribunals was so needless and so embarrassing that the County Court should have refused to entertain the complaint. See *Western Ry. Co. v. Miller,* 19 Mich. 306; *Gardner v. Thomas,* 14 Johns. 134. The defendant is a Canadian corporation, the plaintiff is a resident of Canada, and there the accident occurred. The courts of the Dominion were open to the plaintiff, the witnesses could there have been compelled to attend and testify in person, a view could have been ordered if necessary, and the governing law would have been determined by judges, without the necessity of a tedious and perplexing trial by jury to settle the law as a question of fact. Without saying what might or ought to have been done if a motion to this effect had been made at the outset of the case, we do not feel at liberty at this time and under this exception to say that the proceeding should have been dismissed. The exception was merely to the admission of evidence concerning the law of Canada on the ground that the case was governed by the law of Vermont,—a position that cannot be sustained. *Morrisette* v. *Pacific Ry. Co.,* 74 Vt. 232, 52 Atl. 520.

The court found that the plaintiff, although not an engineer, was "a practical railroad man," upon evidence "that he had had experience as a yard man and brakeman, and in operating various switches, and had knowledge of what a switch rod is, what its connections are, and how it works in connection with the switch to move the rails so as to change the track"; and thereupon permitted him to testify that he knew of no reason why the switch in question, which stood between the main line and the siding, could not have been set on the other side of the main track and on the other side of the platform, in what the plaintiff claimed would have been a safer place. To this the defendant excepted, and still urges that only an engineer could be an expert upon such a question. We cannot accede to this view. An engineer's opinion might indeed be of more value, but one having the plaintiff's experience might properly be found, and we must suppose was found, by the court, to be better able than men in general to form an opinion upon the subject. He might be able to see at once some objection to the proposed change which the inexperienced man could not see; and if he could in fact see no objection it would be some evidence that none existed; indeed it might be strong evidence that no very obvious objection existed. If other objections did exist, which only an expert of wider experience and more thorough training could understand or discover, the field was open to the defendant and was in fact entered and improved by it.

The plaintiff claimed that when he was struck by the switch, or the lantern on top of the switch, he was in this position: his feet on the stirrup at the bottom of the side of the car, his hands "hold of the grab-iron." The defendant claimed that the relative position of the stirrup and grab-iron were such that he could not in that way have swung out far enough from the car to have been struck. It also claimed that if the accident did occur in that way the risk was obvious and was assumed. The accident happened April 3, 1900. On January 2, 1901, Mr. Cook, one of the plaintiff's counsel, visited the place and watched a long freight train draw in upon the same siding, and observed the cars in respect of grab-irons and stirrups and their distance from each other. He had been in the habit of noticing in the same respects the cars that had been passing over the road for several years, and testified that these were of the same general character as those. The plaintiff was with Mr. Cook on January 2d, and his testimony was that the cars in the train which they watched were, in part at least, such as he had had to operate through the years of his service, and such as were in the train at the time he was injured. Upon this basis Mr. Cook was permitted to testify to the distance between the grab-iron and the stirrups on the cars in that train, and to explain the point at which the stirrup was attached in respect of being under or flush with or projecting beyond the side of the car. It is claimed by the plaintiff that no exception was really taken to this testimony, but as we read the bill and the transcript we consider that the question was saved. The testimony was admitted as bearing on the assumption of risk. We understand the evidence referred to above as fairly tending to show that the cars which Mr. Cook observed and described were such cars in respect of grab-irons and stirrups as the plaintiff's duty required him to mount from day to day, and the description of them was therefore properly presented to the jury to aid them in determining whether the plaintiff was to be considered as having assumed the risk of such an accident as befell him. It was really a description of the place where he had to work, and, considering the shifting and changing character of the objects with which he had to deal, was perhaps as certain and definite in its nature as could be expected. Whether it was admissible for any other purpose, it is not necessary to decide.   See *Hoskinson* v. *Central Vt. R. Co.*, 66 Vt. at 626, 627, 30 Atl. 24.

The plaintiff having testified that at the time he was injured there were in use upon the defendant's road "two-throw" and "three-throw" switches, and that the switch where he was hurt was a "two-throw," and that the lanterns upon such were of uniform size, was properly allowed to state his judgment of the size and shape of a "two-throw" switch lantern; and Mr. Cook, who was shown one of these by the plaintiff, and measured it, was properly allowed to testify to the measurement.

At the time of the accident the plaintiff was serving as front brakeman upon a freight train of twenty and more cars moving westerly. The accident occurred in the station yard at Lennoxville. The next station west of Lennoxville is Sherbrooke. Plaintiff's train was ordered to stop at Lennoxville and there meet and pass a train coming from the west. Consequently it drew in upon the siding. Beyond the station building was a highway crossing, which the law of the province required should not be obstruced by trains for more than

five minutes at a time. So the plaintiff claimed that as his
train approached the station building he got off and inquired
of the man in charge whether the train they were to meet had
already left Sherbrooke; because he knew that if it had, there
would be no occasion to cut the train, whereas, if it had not,
there would be, for it would be more than five minutes before
the expected train would arrive. Thus he claimed that he
was acting in the line of his duty in dismounting and in attempting to remount the moving train, while the defendant
claimed that he was bound to have remained on top of the
car, at his post, at least until the train came to a full stop.
In support of its position the defendant offered a rule contained in a book which the plaintiff and other employees had
from the defendant prescribing their duties. The rule is:
"107· Conductors and brakemen of freight trains approaching stations must be out on their trains at least one mile from
station, and must remain until station is passed. (See Rule
69.)" Rule 69 therein referred to is: "Flag stations. All
trains must approach flag stations, or stations not furnished
with semaphores, very cautiously, expecting to find main line
occupied at such stations, whether they be stopping places on
time table or not, and must pass cautiously through side
tracks and large yards and over switches. Mixed and freight
trains must not exceed a rate of six miles per hour through
places above specified." It was shown that, in the railroad
business, "station" means the whole tract within the limits of
the station yard, and not the buildings merely, or the immediate vicinity where they are located. It also appeared that
Lennoxville was not a flag station, nor one "not furnished
with semaphores." The trial court, taking both rules into
consideration, held the offered rule immaterial and inadmis-

sible on the ground that it applied only to trains that were to pass without stopping.

The rejected rule was a direction from the master to the servant, couched in general terms equally applicable to all trains approaching a station, whether about to stop or not. The reason of the thing would require the brakeman to be out on the car when approaching the yard as much in one case as in the other. It would not be supposed that he would remain in the caboose. It is not necessary or proper to treat it as an iron-bound order, not to be varied from in any circumstances, but rather as a general direction that when approaching a station and until the station is passed, the brakeman's post of duty is "out on the cars." He might have to leave it for a moment to perform his brakeman duties. The jury might even find as a fact that he was right in leaving his post to make such an inquiry as was made on the present occasion. But the question is whether the rule was not admissible as a general order to be considered in connection with any others that might apply and with all the circumstances? In this view it might fairly be taken to mean that for a mile before reaching the limits of the station yard, and until the yard limits were passed in leaving the station, the brakeman's duty was to be out on the cars unless some immediate and more imperative duty required him to be absent for the time being. In the present case the jury might have found, if they had had this rule before them, that even if the plaintiff did need to leave his post to make the inquiry he did not need to leave it until the train stopped, and so might have failed to find that he was acting in the line of his duty when he got hurt. It seems to us that the rule should have been admitted.

The defendant presented eighteen requests to charge. The thirteenth and fifteenth were treated as complied with.

To the refusal to comply with the others exception was taken. Most of these were requests to charge, as the substantive law, that the case was governed by the law of Vermont, and so were properly refused. The first and seventeenth, however, demand separate consideration.

The first was, "There is no presumption of negligence from the mere happening of the accident." This touched a rule of evidence and so properly appealed to the law of the forum. It was not in terms complied with, although it was a correct statement of the law as applied to the case in hand. Yet the omission is not necessarily error if the charge as a whole conveys the same impression, and it certainly does. We cannot think that any juror after listening to it could entertain any idea that negligence could be inferred from the mere fact that the accident happened. The jury were told that to recover the plaintiff must prove that he was knocked off by the switch, that he was acting in the line of his duty at the time, and that the defendant was guilty of negligence in maintaining the switch where it was,—that the burden was on the plaintiff to make out each one of these propositions by a fair balance of testimony. If it was necessary for the plaintiff to prove that the defendant was guilty of negligence, even after proving that the plaintiff was knocked off by the switch in the performance of his duty, then of course the negligence was not proved by the mere fact that he was so knocked off. There could have been no doubt in the minds of the jury upon that point.

The seventeenth request was that if the plaintiff failed to establish that the Canadian law was settled and settled as he alleged and different from the law of Vermont, then it was not to be considered. The request as drawn was properly refused. The question, what the law of Canada was, was made an issue of fact and was to be tried and decided like any other. It was for the plaintiff to make out that it was substantially as alleged. If he failed to do so, he failed in his case, regardless of what the law of Vermont might be. If the charge permitted the plaintiff to recover under a different rule of Canadian law than the one he had alleged, no exception was taken in that respect.

In regard to the question of the defendant's negligence in maintaining the switch where it was, the court told the jury to take into consideration all of the evidence bearing upon what the situation was; whether the switch could have been moved and whether, if it could not, the tracks could have been spread apart. Exception was taken in these words: "To the charge with reference to whether the defendant was negligent in not spreading its tracks further apart, and also, in connection with that, to what the court said as to whether this switch could have been maintained in any other position or a safer place." It is urged that "it was error not to have called attention to all the important considerations indicating negligence on the part of the defendant, having called attention to a part"; that the portion of the charge excepted to was misleading as indicating that the question of negligence depended upon the mere question whether the switch could have been moved or the tracks spread apart, whereas there was no question but that these things might have been done and the real question was whether such change would have made the place safer to work in.

We observe first that the exception was not to the omission to call attention to other facts, but to the charge as given. The defendant well says that of course the switch could have been moved or the tracks spread apart. Then it is not to be supposed that the jury understood the words in the narrow sense of whether the change was physically possible, but in the broader sense of whether it was practicable and demanded by the rule of obligation which should be found by the jury to exist under the Canadian law. Such was the evident meaning as shown by the context, wherein the jury were directed to consider "all of the evidence bearing upon what the situation was."

The remaining exception is to the supposed omission to charge "with respect to the effect of the law of Canada if found to be as claimed by the defendant—that contributory negligence constitutes a bar to the right of recovery." We find no such omission in the charge as first given, and after the exception was taken a more explicit statement was made to which no exception was reserved.

Reversed and remanded.

PEOPLE'S NATIONAL BANK, ET AL. *v.* HALL & BUELL; FIRST NATIONAL BANK, ETC. *v.* SAME; NATIONAL COMMERCIAL BANK *v.* SAME.

January Term, 1904.

Present: ROWELL, C. J., MUNSON, START, WATSON, STAFFORD, and HASELTON, JJ.

Opinion filed February 15, 1904.

Partnership — Nonresident Partner—Jurisdiction — Substituted Service—Promissory Note—Absent Maker.

In an action against two as partners, when only one resides in the State, and neither the firm nor the other defendant has property here, if personal service is made on the resident defendant, and substituted service, under V. S. 1641-1643, made on the other defendant, the court has acquired no jurisdiction of the firm or of the absent defendant.

When such action is assumpsit on a note signed by both defendants, the writ will not abate, but the suit will be sustained against the resident defendant, under V. S. 1174.

ASSUMPSIT on a promissory note.   Heard on what amounts to a demurrer to a plea in abatement, at the September Term, 1903, Chittenden County, *Tyler,* J., presiding. Judgment that the court has jurisdiction of the firm, and plea dismissed.   The defendant excepted.   The opinion states the facts.

Powell & Powell and *Alfred Hall* for the defendant.

Service upon a firm must be either *in personam* or *in rem.*   There has been neither in this case.   *Pennoyer* v. *Neff,* 95 U. S. 714; *Nat. Bank* v. *Peabody,* 55 Vt. 496; *St. John* v. *Holmes,* 32 Am. Dec. 602; *York Bank's Appeal,* 36 Pa. 460.

Judgment cannot be rendered against one member of a partnership.   The partnership debt is entire against the firm and judgment must also be entire against the firm.   *Hall* v. *Williams,* 17 Am. Dec. 356; *Buffum* v. *Ramsdell,* 55 Me. 252; *Richards* v. *Walton,* 12 Johns. 434; *Rangeley* v. *Webster,* 11 N. H. 299; *Newburg* v. *Numshower,* 23 Am. Rep. 769; *Tittlemore* v. *Wainwright,* 16 Vt. 173; *Starbird* v. *Moore,* 21 Vt. 529; *Franks* v. *Lockey,* 45 Vt. 395; *Whitney & Titus* v. *Silver,* 22 Vt. 634.

Brown & Taft and *Mower & Peck* for the plaintiffs.

At law both the separate and joint creditors of a partnership may attach separate or joint property and sell it upon execution in satisfaction of their judgment, without regard to the equities of the debtors.   *Bardwell* v. *Perry,* 19 Vt. 292.

Substituted service upon a nonresident is valid. *Hogle* v. *Mott,* 62 Vt. 255; *Jones* v. *Dillihanty,* 68 Vt. 490; *Beech* v. *Abbott,* 6 Vt. 586.

STAFFORD, J. The question is whether these three actions ought to abate. The situation is the same in all. The firm of Hall & Buell did business at Bay Mills, Michigan. Hall resides in New York; Buell, in Vermont. There is no property of the partnership in Vermont, but there is property of Buell. The plaintiffs bring action against Hall and Buell as partners, cause Buell's property to be attached and personal service to be made on him, and cause substituted service to be made upon Hall without the State upon the theory that Hall stands as he would if his own property or the property of the firm had been attached. Hall does not appear. Buell appears specially and in the name of the firm pleads in abatement to the jurisdiction of the court over the partnership. A stipulation is filed by which nearly all the facts averred in the plea are admitted, and thereupon the County Court adjudges that it has jurisdiction of the firm and dismisses the plea. The only question presented to us is whether the facts above recited show that the court was without jurisdiction for want of service upon Hall.

It was not a case for substituted service. There was no basis for it, because no property had been attached in which Hall had any interest. V. S. 1641-1643, which provides for notice to an absent defendant as a foundation for proceeding to judgment and execution against property attached in this State, have no application to a case like the present. There being no personal service upon Hall and no ground for the attempted service by delivery of copies without the State, the court had no jurisdiction of Hall, nor of the firm. See *Woodruff* v. *Taylor,* 20 Vt. 65; *Price* v. *Hickok,* 39 Vt. 292;

Natl. Bank v. *Peabody,* 55 Vt. 492; *Pennoyer* v. *Neff,* 95
U. S. 714, 732; Freeman on Judgments, 2d Ed., §§ 566, 567;
Cobanne v. *Graf,* 87 Minn. 510, 92 N. W. 461, 94 Am. St.
722.

But it does not follow that the plea should have pre-
vailed. V. S. 1174 provides that when a bond, note or other
contract has been executed by two or more persons jointly
and one or more of them resides without the State, an action
may be sustained thereon against the party residing in the
State. The present action is general assumpsit in the common counts, with specification of a note signed "Hall & Buell,"
and comes fairly within the statute. It might have been commenced against Buell alone and may still be lawfully sustained against him. The question, then, is, whether a defendant may have a writ abated for want of service upon his
co-defendant when the court has jurisdiction to proceed to
judgment against him individually. That question must, we
think, be answered in the negative.

The judgment of the County Court in so far as it over--
ruled the plea was correct, but in so far as it adjudged that
the court had jurisdiction of the firm, was erroneous, and so

Judgment is reversed, plea overruled, and cause remanded.

H. A. JACKSON *v.* B. A. HUNT.

January Term, 1904.

Present: ROWELL, C. J., TYLER, MUNSON, START, WATSON, and
STAFFORD, JJ.

Opinion filed February 15, 1904.

Contract—Breach—Liquidated Damages—Offset—V. S.
1159.

When it has been agreed between plaintiff and defendant that the
former shall sell and deliver to the latter a specified quantity of
logs each year, and that if the required quantity is not delivered
in any year, the price for that year's delivery shall be reduced by
a specified sum, such reduction is liquidated damages for such non-
delivery.

V. S. 1159 prohibits the recovery in offset of damages arising from a
breach of contract committed after suit brought thereon.

GENERAL ASSUMPSIT to recover the value of logs sold
and delivered. Pleas, the general issue, payment, and declaration in offset. Trial by court at the December Term, 1903,
Lamoille County, *Haselton,* J., presiding. Judgment for the
plaintiff. The defendant excepted. The opinion states the
facts.

B. A. Hunt for the defendant.

Courts construe contracts, not make them. 19 Vt. 202;
44 Vt. 395.

R. W. Hulburd and *G. M. Powers* for the plaintiff.

When parties to a contract provide for the payment of
an amount fluctuating with the extent of the breach, it is generally regarded as manifesting an intention to liquidate the
damages. 19 Enc. Law, (2 ed.) 413; *Kilbourne* v. *Lumber*

Co., 55 L. R. A. 275; *O'Brien* v. *Pipe Works*, 93 Ala. 582;
Kemp v. *Ice Co.*, 69 N. Y. 45; *Louis & Co.* v. *Brown*, 7 Ore.
326; *Williams* v. *Vance*, 30 Am. Rep. 26; *Westerman* v.
Means, 12 Pa. St. 97; *Cushing* v. *Drew*, 97 Mass. 445; *Jones*
v. *Binford*, 74 Me. 439; *Williams & Co.* v. *Vance et al.*, 9
S. C. 344; *Dunlop* v. *Gregory*, 10 N. Y. 241; *Martin* v. *Mining Co.*, 114 Fed. 553; *Lumber Co.* v. *Ison*, 23 Ky. 80; *Bor-
ley* v. *McDonald*, 69 Vt. 309.

STAFFORD, J. The plaintiff is seeking to recover the
price of logs delivered to the defendant under a written contract. The contract is that he shall deliver all the merchant-
able timber standing upon his certain lot,—one hundred thousand feet, or more, the first year, and at least four hundred
thousand each succeeding year; and that the price shall be
$6.25 per M, unless he fails to deliver the required amount
in any given year, in which case it shall be twenty-five cents
per thousand less for the quantity delivered in that year; provided, however, that any excess above the required quantity
delivered in a previous year shall be added to the deficient
quantity of the later year in determining the question of deficiency. The plaintiff delivered somewhat more than the
required amount the first year and considerably less than the
required amount in the second year and in the third year.
The defendant settled with the plaintiff for the first year and
paid him at the full rate. He settled with him for the second
year and paid him at the reduced rate. For the third year
the parties have not settled, and the plaintiff had judgment
below for the balance unpaid upon that year's delivery at the
reduced rate, after deducting damages for improper piling.
The defendant claimed that he should be allowed a further deduction as damage for failure to deliver the stipulated quantity in the second and third years, and offered evidence in

support of his claim, which was excluded on the ground that
.such damages were provided for by the contract itself in the
stipulation for a reduced price. The question is on the cor-
.rectness of this ruling.

It may be asked, what *was* the discount for, if it was not
to compensate for shortage in quantity? The defendant's
suggestion is that it was to compensate him for starting his
mill to saw an insufficient supply. But that is only naming a
special element of damage due to shortage, and there is nothing to show that the discount was intended to refer to that
element more than to any other. The parties having agreed
upon a certain sum as compensation, they must abide by it.

The ruling is sustained by the cases cited in the plain-
tiff's brief, which are closely analogous. *Louis & Co. v.
Brown,* 7 Oregon, 326; *Kemp* v. *Knickerbocker Ice Co.,* 69
N.Y. 45; *O'Brien* v. *Anniston Pipe Works,* 93 Ala. 582; *Kil-
bourne* v. *Burt & Brabb Lumber Co.* (Ky.) 55 L. R. A. 275;
Williams v. *Vance,* 9 S. C. 344, 30 Am. Rep. 26, and note.

The defendant urges as a reason why this construction of
the contract should not be adopted, that it leaves the defendant without remedy in case no lumber at all is delivered.
That does not follow. The contract is drawn in contemplation
of an honest attempt to fulfil it and provides a compensation
for shortage while the contract is being operated under. We
do not say that the compensation by way of discount would
have any application in case of a total breach or a repudiation.
That question is not here involved.

The defendant also claimed damages in set off by reason
of an alleged breach and total repudiation occurring after
action brought. But such could not be recovered in this suit.
V. S. 1159.

Judgment affirmed.

MARSHALL R. MASON v. SILAS MASON'S EXECUTORS.

January Term, 1904.

Present: ROWELL, C. J., TYLER, START, WATSON, STAFFORD, and
HASELTON, JJ.

Opinion filed February 15, 1904.

Partnership—Decedent's Estate—Administration—Bill in Equity—Parties—Sole Heir.

No reason appearing why the matter should not follow the common
course of regular administration, the sole heir of an intestate,
though there be no creditors, cannot maintain a bill in equity to
reach the assets of the decedent's estate; but the suit must be
brought by the administrator.

APPEAL IN CHANCERY. Heard on demurrer to the bill
at the December Term, 1902, Bennington County, *Munson,*
Chancellor. Demurrer sustained, and bill adjudged insufficient. The orator appealed. The opinion states the case.

Arthur P. Carpenter for the orator.

Wherever a fiduciary relation exists, the right to an action in equity is well settled. *Barnes* v. *Dow,* 59 Vt. 531;
Hale v. *Hale,* 4 Humph. 183; *Dyckman* v. *Valiente,* 42 N. Y.
549; *Suydam* v. *Bastedo,* 40 N. J. Eq. 433; *Tateum* v. *Ross,*
150 Mass. 440.

Whenever it appears that no other heir or creditor is
interested they need not be joined as parties. *Bellows* v.
Sowles, 57 Vt. 411.

O. E. Butterfield for the defendants.

Where a party has an ample remedy at law, his action
must be at law and not in equity. *Currie* v. *Rosebrookes,* 48
Vt. 34; *Durkee* v. *Durkee,* 59 Vt. 70.

The administrator of Marshall S. Mason has a full remedy against Silas Mason's executors under our statutes. V. S. 1451-1452; *Newell* v. *Humphrey*, 37 Vt. 268; *Park* v. *McGowan*, 64 Vt. 173; *Porter* v. *Wheeler*, 37 Vt. 281.

STAFFORD, J. Silas Mason and his son Marshall were partners in trade for two or three years, and then Marshall died. His father wound up the business and turned the assets into money which he held thereafter until his own death, nearly twenty years later. An accounting would have shown a considerable sum due to Marshall at the time of his death. The orator is the son and only heir of Marshall and, being a minor, brings this bill by his mother, as next friend, against the defendants as executors of Silas's will. The orator is informed and believes that papers and books of account of the partnership, showing the true state of affairs, are in the defendants' hands, and he asks that the defendants be enjoined from putting them beyond his reach; that an account may be taken, and a decree rendered against them for the balance that would have belonged to his father. Marshall owed no debts at his decease and left no will. There is an administrator upon his estate, but he is not a party to this proceeding. In the Court of Chancery the bill was held insufficient on demurrer, and dismissed; and the case is here on appeal from that decree.

The bill cannot be maintained by the heir. The statute confers upon the administrator the right to bring all actions at law and suits in equity that may be necessary to enable him to collect the assets. The fund here sought to be reached would be assets. He has given his bond, and is responsible to the orator for the collection of this fund. The orator cannot thus take the administration into his own hands. If the defendants are liable, they have a right to insist upon settling that liability with the administrator, the officer appointed by law. V. S. 2445; *Robinson* v. *Swift*, 3 Vt. 377, 384.

We do not say that circumstances might not exist which would entitle the heir to maintain the bill,—such as fraud, collusion or the danger of irretrievable loss. But no such circumstances are alleged to exist here, and no reason appears why the case should not follow the common rule of orderly administration.

Decree affirmed and cause remanded.

FRANK E. KIMBALL *v.* DOMINICK COSTA.

October Term, 1903.

Present: ROWELL, C. J., TYLER, START, WATSON, STAFFORD, and HASELTON, JJ.

Opinion filed February 15, 1904.

Conditional Sale—Memorandum of Lien—Defective Note— Additional Security.

The figures upon the margin of a note may be referred to for the purpose of removing any ambiguity, or even to supply the amount, when that has been wholly omitted in the body of the instrument.

A conditional sale note payable to F. E. Kimball or order, for the "sum of F. E. Kimball .... dollars, $50. payable August 9, 1902, and $50. every two months thereafter until note is paid," and having $385. written in the upper left hand corner, is a note for $385. payable as indicated.

In trover for the conversion of property described in a lien note it is immaterial that a third person had given plaintiff a chattel mortgage upon other property, and had stated in the mortgage that he had purchased the property described in the lien note; that the mortgage was given as additional security for the payment of that note, and in consideration of the plaintiff's forbearing to take possession of, and foreclose on, the property described in the note.

TROVER to recover the value of horses. Plea, not guilty. Trial by jury at the June Term, 1903, Orange County, *Munson,* J., presiding. Verdict ordered for the plaintiff. Judgment on verdict. The defendant excepted.

The exceptions state that, "it was conceded by the parties that the horses were at the time of the alleged conversion of the value of $300; that the interest to date of trial would be $8.00 in addition; that there was proper demand and refusal before the suit was begun; that the defendant admitted the conversion of the property, provided the plaintiff made out a proper and legal title thereto; that the defendant had no actual notice of any lien or claim upon the property on the part of the plaintiff at the time of the purchase of the horses by the defendant, and that the only notice he then had was the notice which the record of the town clerk of Waterford showed; that the defendant paid full value for the horses before he had any actual notice of any lien on the property; that the note was properly recorded in the town clerk's office within the statutory period of thirty days."

The defendant claimed that the whole case showed that the plaintiff could not maintain the action, and asked that he be nonsuited. The court overruled this objection, to which the defendant excepted. The defendant claimed that the so-called conditional sale showed that if any sum was due, it was only $100, and if such was the law, then the County Court had no jurisdiction. The court held to the contrary, to which ruling the defendant excepted.

Upon the undisputed facts as stated, the court held that
the defendant was liable, as matter of law, for the sum of
$308, and ordered a verdict for that sum, and rendered judg-
ment upon said verdict, to which rulings and judgment the
defendant excepted.

H. A. Farnham and *May & Simonds* for the defendant.

The note in question is a note either for $50 or $100,
and its construction is a matter of law for the court, and
parol evidence was incompetent. *Witty* v. *Mich., etc. Ins. Co.*,
8 L. R. A. 365; *Ives* v. *Bank,* 84 Mass. 236; *Nugent* v. *Ro-
land,* 12 Martin (La.) 659; *Corgan* v. *Frew,* 39 Ill. 31; *Nor-
wich Bank* v. *Hyde,* 13 Conn. 279.

This being a note for either $50 or $100, the County
Court had no jurisdiction. *Jeffers* v. *Pease et al.,* 73 Vt. 215;
Clark v. *Stoughton,* 18 Vt. 50; *Com.* v. *Bailey,* 2 Am. Dec. 3.

Smith & Smith for the plaintiff.

It is not necessary that the instrument should contain
any marginal figures, provided that the amount payable is
properly expressed at length in words in the body, and in that
case the words control, and the marginal figures are not a
part of the instrument. *Garrard* v. *Lewis,* 10 Q. B., Div. 30;
37 Eng. Rep. 375; Story, Bills, par. 42; Chitty, Bills, p. 170;
Daniel, Neg. Ins. § 86; Addison, Contracts, § 224; *Sanderson*
v. *Piper,* 5 Bing. N. C. 425; 35 Eng. C. L. R. 162; *Payne* v.
Clark, 19 Mo. 152; *Mears v. Graham,* 8 Blackf. 144.

But where there is an imperfection or omission in the
statement of the amount in the body of the instrument, that
imperfection or omission is aided by the figures in the margin.
Chitty, Bills, pp. 170, 182; Daniel, Neg. Ins., § 86, notes
5 and 6; *Rex* v. *Elliott,* 2 East's P. C., 951; *Hutley* v. *Mar-*

shall, 56 L. T., N. S. 186; *Sweetzer* v. *French,* 13 Metcalf, 262; *Petty* v. *Fleispel,* 31 Tex. 169; *Corgan* v. *Frew,* 39 Ill. 31; *Coolbroth* v. *Purinton,* 29 Me. 469; *Wittey* v. *Mich. Mut. Life Ins. Co.,* 123 Ind. 411; *Hubert* v. *Grady,* 59 Tex. 503; *Strickland* v. *Holbrook,* 75 Cal. 268; *Wittey* v. *Life Ins. Co., supra.*

The effect of the written contract is to be collected from all within the four corners of the instrument. Chitty, Cont. p. 83; *Warrington* v. *Early,* 2 El. & Bl. 763; Daniel, Neg. Inst. § 149.

When it is apparent on the face of a written instrument that a mere clerical error has been made therein the courts will correct such error by construction. *Weed* v. *Abbott,* 51 Vt. 609; *Richmond* v. *Woodard,* 32 Vt. 833; *Wood* v. *Cochrane,* 39 Vt. 544; *Gray* v. *Clark,* 11 Vt. 583; *Thrall* v. *Newell,* 19 Vt. 202.

TYLER, J. This action is trover for the conversion of two horses. The defendant admitted the conversion, provided the plaintiff had a legal title to the property.

It appeared that the plaintiff had made a conditional sale of the horses to one Lawrence, and in proof of a lien reserved he introduced in evidence, subject to the defendant's exception, a memorandum of the sale with a certificate of the town clerk that it had been duly recorded. It reads:

"$385. NEWBURY, VT., June 9, 1902.

Lien Note.

For value received, I hereby promise to pay F. E. Kimball or order the sum of F. E. Kimball —— dollars, $50 payable August 9, 1902, and $50 every two months thereafter until note is paid, with interest annually, payable at the National Bank of Newbury, Wells River, Vt.

This note is given for one chest mare and one chest horse, one Ryan wagon, and four harnesses known as the Lowd harnesses, and one pole known as the Ryan pole, this day conditionally sold and delivered by F. E. Kimball to me, and said property is to be and remain the property of the said F. E. Kimball until said note is fully paid.

V. V. LAWRENCE."

The defendant afterwards bought the horses of Lawrence and paid their full value, with no other notice of the lien than what appeared by the record.

V. S. 2290 provides that no lien reserved on personal property sold conditionally and passing into the hands of the conditional purchaser shall be valid against attaching creditors or subsequent purchasers, unless the vendor of such property takes a written memorandum, signed by the purchaser, witnessing such lien, and the sum due thereon, and causes it to be recorded, etc.

The only question in the case is whether the writing signed by Lawrence was a sufficient memorandum to meet the requirements of the statute.

The writing of the name, "F. E. Kimball," after the words, "the sum of," was clearly a clerical error, and the name in that place should be read out of the note. The question then is whether the figures, "$385," in the margin can be employed to give an interpretation to the note, which, upon its face, does not contain a promise to pay any definite sum, except $50, which evidently was the first installment of the principal. Can the marginal figures be resorted to for the purpose of ascertaining the principal?

The authorities are not fully in accord in respect to the use of marginal figures in interpreting the body of the note. Where the note is written in plain, unambiguous terms these figures have no use other than convenience of reference, which was the primary purpose in placing them upon the note. In some jurisdictions it is held that the figures form no part of the note. *Bank* v. *Hyde*, 13 Conn. 279; *Smith* v. *Smith*, 1 R. I. 398; 53 Am. Dec. 652; 4 Enc. of Law, 130 and notes. It was held in *Prim & Kimball* v. *Hammel*, 134 Ala. 652; 92 Am. St. R. 52, that the alteration of the marginal figures was not a material alteration of the note for the reason that they were not a part of the instrument.

It is well settled that when there is a variance between the amount expressed in words and the marginal figures, the words must control.

In *Sweetser* v. *French*, 13 Metc. 262, the promise was "to pay three hundred" and there being in the margin "$300," the note was held good for that sum. In *Witty* v. *Mich. Mut. Life Ins. Co.*, 123 Ind. 411; 18 Am. St. R. 327, the number of dollars was left blank in the body of the note, but "$147.-70" appearing in figures in the margin, it was held that they should be taken as the amount intended to be paid. In the same direction are *Petty* v. *Fleishel & Smith*, 31 Tex. 169; 98 Am. Dec. 524, and *Corgan* v. *Frew*, 39 Ill. 31; 89 Am. Dec. 286.

Other cases hold that everything appearing upon a promissory note at the time of its delivery is to be regarded as a part of the note. *Bank* v. *Freency*, 12 So. Dak. 156; 76 Am. St. R. 594 and notes.

It cannot be maintained that, inasmuch as one sum of $50 and perhaps two sums of that amount are described in the body of the note as definite sums to be paid, they are to control and cannot be changed by the figures in the margin. The $50 payments are clearly installments of a principal sum that is not described in the body of the note, and the same rule should apply as in cases where the sum to be paid is left entirely blank.

While the authorities differ about filling the blank with the amount indicated by the marginal figures, the weight of authority favors it.   It is concisely stated in the note to *Witty* v. *Mich. Mut. Life Ins. Co.* as follows: "Notes should express the sum for which they are given in the body of the instrument; but an omission of the sum will not be fatal or render the note invalid if the true amount can be gathered from other parts of the writing. * * * A defect existing in the amount stated in the body of the note, the figures upon the margin may be referred to for the purpose of removing any ambiguity, or even to supply the amount, which has been wholly omitted in the body of the instrument." Mr. Freeman, however, admits that there are authorities that refuse to adopt this rule.

Daniel on Neg. Instr., 5th ed. § 86, as to the sums payable in promissory notes, says in substance, that it is usually specified in figures in the upper, or lower, left hand corner of the instrument, as well as in writing in the body of it; that these marginal figures are really not a part of the instrument, but merely a memorandum of the amount; that the marginal figures were probably added at a very early date in order that the amount of the bill might strike the eye immediately, and was in fact a note, index or summary of the contents of the bill which followed. Quoting directly from this section: "Where a difference appears between the words and figures, evidence cannot be received to explain it; but the words in the body of the paper must control; and if there is a difference between printed and written words, the written must control. If the words are so obscurely written or printed as to be indistinct, the figures in the margin may be referred

to to explain them. If by inadvertence the amount is expressed in figures only, it will suffice."

The words, three hundred and eighty-five dollars, should
be read into the body of the note. The defendant had no
right to understand that $50 or $100 was all there was to be
paid. The figures in the margin were notice to him of the
amount for which the note was given. The judgment below
for three hundred dollars, the value of the horses at the time
of the conversion, was correct.

On Nov. 6, 1902, Orvill V. Lawrence, a son of the
maker of the lien note, gave the plaintiff a chattel mortgage
upon *other* property, and stated in the mortgage that he had
purchased the property described in the lien note; that the
mortgage was given as additional security for the payment of
that note and in consideration of the plaintiff's forbearing to
take possession of and foreclose on the property described in
the note for the space of one week thereafter. The plaintiff's
taking this mortgage did not affect his prior lien and was
an immaterial fact in the case.

Judgment affirmed.

BANKERS' LIFE INSURANCE CO. *v.* FREDERICK G. FLEET-
WOOD, and JOHN L. BACON, INSURANCE COMMISSIONERS.

May Term, 1903.

Present: TYLER, MUNSON, START, WATSON, and STAFFORD, JJ.

Opinion filed February 29, 1904.

*Insurance—Reserve Liability—Basis of Computation—In-
surance Commissioners—Discretion.*

Under Nos. 73, 76, Acts 1902, a foreign life insurance company which issues one year term policies with an option of renewal, has the right
in computing its "reserve liability," to value the first year's insurance made on such policies as term insurance.

Neither § 1, No. 76, nor No. 77, Acts 1902, has so enlarged the discretion of the insurance commissioners as to permit them to insist
that the re-insurance reserve which such company must have before allowed to do business in this State, shall be determined upon
some other valuation of such policies.

PETITION FOR MANDAMUS brought to the Supreme Court
for Washington County, and heard on demurrer to the petition at the May Term, 1903.

The petition alleged that the petitioner is a life insurance
company duly incorporated under the laws of the State of
New York; that on the 31st day of December, 1902, when a
final report is required from it by the laws of Vermont, it had
a capital stock of $100,000, fully paid in cash, invested in
securities readily convertible into cash, and in addition thereto
it had assets equal in value to its liabilities, reckoning the
re-insurance reserve as a liability; that it held funds in secure
investments equal to its reserve liability above all its other liabilities; that on the 17th day of February, 1903, the petitioner
made application for a license for one year from April 1, 1903,
and filed with its application a report of its financial condition

in which its assets were stated to be $1,060,787.41; that among its liabilities was included the petitioner's valuation of its policies issued prior to January 1, 1903, as of December 31, 1902, in which they are construed and valued as one year term policies upon the actuary's tables of mortality with four per cent. interest, amounting to $777,752; that this valuation was duly certified by the New York Department of Insurance as being accurate according to the laws of that State; that the respondents made a valuation of the same policies disregarding the provision for a one year term, using the same mortality tables and rate of interest which raised the valuation to such a sum that the petitioner's assets were not equal to its liabilities; that the petitioner admits its assets are not equal to its reserve liability above all other liabilities on respondents' construction of its policies; that the respondents admit the petitioner's assets are equal to its reserve liability above all other liabilities on petitioner's construction of its policies; that the respondents refused to accept the petitioner's valuation contained in its financial report, although duly certified by the New York Insurance Department, for the reason that its valuation of its policies therein contained is on the one year principle, and accordingly refused it a license.

B. F. Fifield for the petitioner.

This case is between the same parties, involves the construction of the same policies, and is upon substantially the same state of facts as arose when this case was here before. 73 Vt. 1. That case is decisive of this. To the same effect is *Rosenplaenter* v. *Provident, etc. Soc.*, 91 Fed. 728; *McDougall* v. *Assur. Soc.*, 135 N. Y. 551; *Baldwin* v. *Provident, etc. Assur. Soc.*, 47 N. Y. 463.

The Insurance Commissioners have no discretion because of recent statutes to insist upon any different valuation. *Peck*

v. *Powell,* 62 Vt. 296; *Hendlee* v. *Cleveland,* 54 Vt. 142; *Beard* v. *Townsend,* 26 Vt. 670; 51 Cal. 339; 41 Mo. 226; 78 Ill. 389; 10 Wend. 285; 81 Cal. 542; 79 Mich. 364; 76 Cal. 550.

William B. C. Stickney for the respondents.

MUNSON, J., (for a majority.) This case is between the same parties, touches the construction of the same policy, and stands upon the same facts, as that disposed of in *Bankers' Life Insurance Co.* v. *Insurance Commissioners,* 73 Vt. 1, 48 Atl. 435. But certain statutes relating to the duties of the Insurance Commissioners have been enacted since that case was decided, and it is claimed that these have so changed the law as to require a different disposition of the case now submitted.

Under V. S. 4178, as it read when the former case was determined, a foreign joint stock life insurance company could not do business in this State unless it had, in addition to the required capital, "assets equal in amount to its outstanding liabilities," reckoning "the premium reserve on life risks based on the actuaries' tables of mortality, with interest at four per cent., as a liability." As amended by No. 73, Acts of 1902, the above clause reads as follows, "assets equal in value to its outstanding liabilities, reckoning the reinsurance reserve as a liability"; and the omitted direction for computing the reserve is embodied, with modifications and further provisions, in No. 76, Acts of 1902.

The act of 1902 provides for computing the net value of all outstanding policies issued before January first, 1903, upon the basis of the actuaries' tables of mortality, with interest at four per cent.; and for computing the net value of all outstanding policies issued after December thirty-first, 1902, upon the basis of the American experience table of mortality, with interest at three and one-half per cent.; and for charging the company with the value of a certain annuity "in every case where the actual premium charged for an insurance is less than the net premium for such insurance computed according to" the respective tables and rates aforesaid; and declares that the "aggregate net value so ascertained" of all the policies of the company "shall be deemed its reserve liability."

It was considered in the case already decided that the only requirement regarding the computation of the premium reserve was that it be based upon certain tables of mortality and the prescribed rate of interest. We are now to inquire whether the present law calls for anything more.

The rule established by the act of 1902 is given to ascertain the "reserve liability" of the company. It makes the "net value" of the policies the measure of this reserve liability, and prescribes the method of computing the net value. The term used in the former law was "premium reserve" instead of "reserve liability," but it is not necessary to inquire whether "reserve liability" is anything different, for whatever it may be, it is declared to be the same as net value, and the method of arriving at net value is given. The term "net value" is an addition, but it is not necessary to consider what this would ordinarily imply, for its scope in this connection is determined by a specific rule. The result of the problem cannot be enlarged by giving it a different name if the process of computation remains the same. The elements of the computation are the tables of mortality, the rates of interest, and the addition of the value of an annuity when the premium charged for an insurance is less than the net premium as determined by those tables and rates. The last is an additional provision, but it is not claimed that this has any bearing upon the question now in issue. So the computation depends entirely upon the tables of mortality and the rate of interest, as it did when our former decision was made. Nor do we find anything new affecting the application of the rule. It is said in the petitionees' brief that the present law provides for a computation of the net value of all outstanding policies of life insurance upon a prescribed basis, without making any distinction between policies providing for a preliminary one year term with an option for renewal, and any other class of policies. This is equally true of the former law; which, after prescribing rules relating to fire, health, accident and marine risks, provided for a computation of the reserve on "life risks." This term covered the company's policies of life insurance without distinction as to classes, and left nothing to be added by saying *all* the policies. All policies were considered in our former opinion, but were valued for what they were construed to be. If the Legislature intended to require that policies construed by the court as term policies should be valued as if they were not, it has failed to make its intention manifest.

It remains to consider whether the discretion of the commissioners has been so enlarged as to permit them to require a different valuation. The provisions that the commissioners shall grant a license when they "are satisfied" that the company has complied with certain requirements, and may renew such license as long as they consider the company "safe and entitled to public confidence," and may revoke the license if the company violates any of our laws relating to insurance companies,—which are the only provisions referred to by the petitionees in their argument upon the question of discretion,—were all in existence when our former decision was made. The question of discretion as affected by the first of these provisions was specially considered in the opinion. The only subsequent provisions touching the discretion of the commissioners are those found in § 2 of No. 76, Acts of 1902, and in V. S. 4205 as amended by No. 77, Acts of 1902. The only one of these that can possibly be claimed to give a further discretion in the matter under consideration is that contained in the amendment to V. S. 4205. This section formerly authorized the commissioners to visit and examine the "condition and affairs" of a foreign insurance company when they had reason to doubt its solvency. The section as amended authorizes the commissioners to do this when they determine it to be prudent, and provides that "such examinations shall include a computation of the reinsurance reserve." It may be doubted if the section as amended covers more than the original provision, for an examination of the "condition and affairs" of a company to determine its solvency must necessarily include some ascertainment of its reserve. But if the amendment authorizes an ascertainment of the reserve in some manner not contemplated by the original act, it certainly does not authorize a computation regardless of the statutory rules.

The phraseology of the statute of 1902 is that of the Massachusetts law, under which it is held by the Supreme Court of the State that the rulings of the commissioner made in good faith must be accepted as final; and it is a general rule that when one State adopts the statute of another its courts will give that statute the construction it has received in the State from which it is taken. But this rule cannot be considered applicable when the transcribed statute is substituted for provisions already construed by the courts of the State making the adoption, and the new law is found to be substantially the same as the old.

The law remaining unchanged in the respects considered, the case must be disposed of in accordance with our former decision.

Judgment that the prayer of the petition is granted, and that a mandamus issue directing the commissioners to grant a license as prayed for; without costs.

METROPOLITAN STOCK EXCHANGE *v.* LYNDONVILLE NATIONAL BANK.

May Term, 1903.

Present: TYLER, MUNSON, START, STAFFORD, and HASELTON, JJ.

Opinion filed February 29, 1904.

Pleading — Replication, De Injuria — Corporation — Ultra Vires—Estoppel—Judicial Notice—Acts of Congress.

In an action of assumpsit against a corporation, to a plea of *ultra vires* the replication *de injuria* is bad.

The acts of Congress are not facts to be alleged and proved in the state courts. They are a part of the law of which the state courts take judicial notice.

In an action of assumpsit against a corporation, the plea that the defendant was a national bank, and without authority to make the contract declared upon, is good.

Contracts which are *ultra vires* in the strict sense, are wholly void, not merely voidable; and therefore they cannot be ratified.

A corporation cannot be estopped from making the defense of *ultra vires*.

GENERAL AND SPECIAL ASSUMPSIT. Pleas, (1) the general issue, (2) *ultra vires.* Replication to second plea, *de injuria.* Heard on demurrer to replication to second plea, at the December Term, 1902, Caledonia County, *Watson,* J., presiding. Judgment, that the demurrer be sustained, and the replication is insufficient. The plaintiff excepted.

The first special count alleged that the defendant upon good and valid consideration moving from the plaintiff to the defendant, entered into the following written contract with the plaintiff: "We hold for you (the plaintiff) two thousand five hundred and twenty-seven dollars ($2,527.00), to be yours (the plaintiff's) on delivery of one hundred shares of United States Rubber—meaning one hundred shares of the stock of the United States Rubber Co."; that relying on this agreement the plaintiff purchased for the defendant one hundred shares of this stock, and sent the certificates to the defendant with a demand draft for $2,527.00; that defendant refused to accept the stock, returned the certificates, and refused to pay the draft; that the price of this one hundred shares had depreciated $600 since the purchase; that plaintiff lost by this depreciation, and the expense of purchasing the stock and sending same with the draft to the defendant, the sum of $610.00; that by reason of said written contract the defendant became liable to pay the plaintiff this sum.

The second special count is substantially the same as the first, except that it does not quote the written contract, but alleges that the defendant "in consideration that the plaintiff would, within a reasonable time thereafter, purchase certain shares of the United States Rubber Company's stock, to wit, one hundred shares, and would deliver the same to the defendant bank, the defendant bank faithfully and in writing, promised to pay the plaintiff $2,527.00 in cash on the delivery of said shares of stock."

The substance of the second plea, which concludes with a verification is stated in the opinion. The replication to said plea is as follows:

"And the said plaintiff, as to the plea of the said defendant by it secondly above pleaded, saith that it, the plaintiff, by reason of anything by the said defendant therein alleged, ought not to be barred from having or maintaining its aforesaid action against the defendant, because it says that the said defendant of its own wrong, without the cause by the said defendant in its said second plea above alleged in that behalf, disregarded its said promise and agreement and did not accept and pay said draft, but held the same and said one hundred shares a long time and then refused to and did not accept and pay the said draft and keep the one hundred shares of stock, but returned the certificate of the stock to the plaintiff as aforesaid, whereof the plaintiff hath in said second count complained against the defendant; without this that at the time of making said promises and undertakings they were beyond the power of the defendant to make, and therefore void against it; and this the plaintiff prays may be inquired of by the country."

May & Simonds for the plaintiff.

The defendant has pleaded the United States Statutes. It must prove those statutes. *Morrisette* v. *C. P. R.*, 74 Vt. 232; *Burke* v. *R. R. Co.*, 1 Cliff. 308; No. 2161, Fed. Cas. 99 Mass. 388; *Crogate's Case*, 8 Coke, 66; 1st Smith's Leading Cases, 53.

Ultra vires must be specially pleaded. *Griesa* v. *Mass. Ben. Asso.*, 133 N. Y. 619.

When a contract with a corporation has been executed by one of the parties the other will not be permitted to plead *ultra vires*. *Holmes Co.* v. *S. Co.*, 127 N. Y. 252; *State Bld. Co.* v. *R. Co.*, 17 Am. Rep 702; Clark, Contracts, 286; 63 N. Y. 63; Thompson, Cor. §§ 6015-6018; Morse on Banking, (3rd ed.) § 731.

Dunnett & Slack for the defendant.

A national bank has the right to plead its want of power, that is, to assert the nullity of an act which is *ultra vires. Wiley* v. *First Nat. Bank of Brattleboro,* 47 Vt. 546; *California Nat. Bank* v. *Kennedy,* 167 U. S. 362; *Burrows* v. *Niblack,* 84 Fed. 111; *Concord First Nat. Bank* v. *Hawkins,* 174 U. S. 364.

If the replication is the replication *de injuria* it is a general traverse of all the facts set forth in the plea. This replication, however, is not the replication *de injuria. Henderson* v. *Withy et al.,* 2 Durnf. & East 576; *Hanna* v. *Rust et al.,* 21 Wnd. 149; *Chandler* v. *Roberts,* 1 Doug. 58; *Day* v. *Bank,* 13 Vt. 102.

HASELTON, J.   This was an action of general and special assumpsit.   Special counts, two in number, set out promises and undertakings on the part of the defendant regarding a transaction in respect to shares of the United States Rubber Company, and a breach of such promises and undertakings resulting in damage to the plaintiff.

The defendant filed pleas, the second of which was in brief to the effect that the supposed promises and undertakings set out in the declaration related solely to an alleged supposed purchase by the defendant from the plaintiff of such shares, and that at the time in question the defendant was a national bank without power or authority to make such alleged purchase.

To this plea the plaintiff filed a replication which, though somewhat like a special traverse, is in its general structure and purpose a replication *de injuria.*   It contains the characteristic allegation that, "The said defendant of its own wrong, without the cause by the said defendant in its said second plea above alleged in that behalf disregarded its said promises and agreement."   To this replication the defendant demurred.

The demurrer was sustained and the replication adjudged insufficient.

The replication *de injuria*, though peculiarly applicable in actions of tort, is, under a rule of practice now grown familiar, allowable in actions of assumpsit to meet a plea which merely sets up matter of excuse for the non-performance of a promise or undertaking.   But the plea of *ultra vires* here interposed denies the making of the alleged agreement on the ground that the plaintiff could not make it.   In the nature of things, it is no reply to such a plea to allege that the defendant of its own wrong and without the cause alleged in the plea disregarded its promise and agreement.

This replication closes with a denial that the alleged promises and agreement of the defendant were beyond its power to make.   It is argued in behalf of the plaintiff that this is a traverse of fact, the ground of the argument being that as the states of the union are foreign to each other, so the Federal government and each state are foreign each to the other and that a statute of one is a fact to be pleaded and proved in the courts of the other if there relied on.   But in each state the acts of the Legislature of that state and the acts of Congress operate alike upon every one and alike claim recognition and due application by the courts.   The public statutes of the general government are no more facts to be alleged and proved in the courts of a state than are the public statutes of that state.

Under our complex system there are in every state two bodies of statutory law equally entitled to direct recognition. When questions relating to bankruptcy, naturalization, the national banking system, coinage and currency, patents, interstate commerce, the postal system, copyrights, internal revenue, and other proper matters of congressional legislation are before the state courts, the public acts of Congress on those subjects are not facts to be proved, but the courts and all concerned must take notice of them precisely as they must take notice of the public acts of their own state Legislature.

If in this case an attempt is made to treat the replication as something else than that for which it was obviously intended, difficulties are presented which cannot fairly be met. The result is that the replication is adjudged bad.

The question now arises whether or not the plea is good; for it is a truism that a bad replication may be a sufficient answer to a bad plea. The plea is good in form, and, whatever conflict of decisions there may have been formerly or may be now, we have no hesitation in saying that it is good in substance, and we so hold. *Concord National Bank* v. *Hawkins,* 174 U. S. 364; *California Bank* v. *Kennedy,* 167 U. S. 362; *McCormick* v. *Market Bank,* 165 U. S. 538; *Central Transportation Co.* v. *Pullman Car Company,* 139 U. S. 24.

Counsel for the defendant having in their brief referred to and quoted from *Wiley* v. *National Bank of Brattleboro,* 47 Vt. 546, this court takes occasion to point out that that case and *Whitney* v. *National Bank of Brattleboro,* 50 Vt. 389, are expressly disapproved by the Supreme Court of the United States in *National Bank* v. *Graham,* 100 U. S. 699.

With regard to contracts which are *ultra vires* in the strict sense, the sound doctrine is that they are wholly void and not merely voidable; that the corporation is under a perpetual disability to make them; that, therefore, there can be no ratification by the corporation, and that a corporation cannot be estopped from making the defense of *ultra vires* when it is sued for non-performance on its part. The denial of corporate existence, and the claim that a corporation has not proceeded in the way or through the officers designated by law, are defenses that stand on a different and much narrower ground than the defense of *ultra vires* in its full and proper sense.

In some cases a corporation which has received the benefit of an *ultra vires* contract may be recovered from on a *quantum meruit* without reference to the attempted contract. In some cases a corporation may be liable in an action of tort for acts connected with or growing out of an attempted *ultra vires* contract. In some cases directors or officers of a corporation may make themselves liable in an attempt to fix ˙ upon the corporation a liability with which it cannot under the law be charged. It may be said, too, in passing that directors of corporations do well to heed the right of the government which has created them to act properly and efficiently with reference to usurpations of power on the part of its creations.

Whether, if the facts in this case are as alleged in the plaintiff's declaration, the plaintiff, under a different state of pleadings, has a remedy in this action, or whether he has a remedy in some other action against this defendant or against some other defendant or defendants, are questions not considered.

Judgment affirmed, and cause remanded.

ASA C. FULTON, ET AL. *v.* JOHN A. ALDRICH, ET AL.

January Term, 1904.

Present: ROWELL, C. J., TYLER, MUNSON, START, WATSON, STAFFORD, and

HASELTON, JJ.

Opinion filed February 29, 1904.

Mortgage—Foreclosure—Taxes—Payment by Mortgagee.

The last owner of real estate on the first day of April in any year
continues liable for the taxes legally assessed thereon in that
year regardless of subsequent conveyances.

Though taxes legally assessed upon real estate are a first lien thereon,
such lien is not enforceable while the last owner on the first day of
April in the year of such assessment has personal property from
which the tax can be collected.

A tax on real estate does not become a fixed incumbrance thereon until
the officer charged with the collection does some official act indicating an intention to pursue the land.

If mortgagees after foreclosure, and before the equity of redemption
has expired, upon the mortagor's refusal to do so, pay the taxes
assessed upon the land, and no official act has then been done to
charge the land with such taxes, they act as mere volunteers, and
on redemption of the land the mortgagor is not chargeable with
the amount so paid.

APPEAL IN CHANCERY. Heard on demurrer to the bill
at the December Term, 1903, Orange County, *Start,* Chancellor. Decree, *pro forma,* sustaining the demurrer and dismissing the bill. The orators appealed.

The bill alleged, in addition to the facts stated in the
opinion, that soon after he redeemed the property, Aldrich
mortgaged the same to defendant, Sarah A. Jenkins; that both
she and Aldrich, prior to the execution of said mortgage, had
notice that the orators had paid the taxes.

The prayer was that the defendants be decreed to pay the orators the amount of the taxes they had paid, with interest and costs, and in default thereof, that they be foreclosed from all right and equity in the mortgaged premises.

William Batchelder for the orators.

All persons having an interest in property subject to an incumbrance by which their interest may be prejudiced, have a right to free the property from such incumbrance by payment of the debt, and be subrogated to the rights of the creditors against the property. 2 Story Eq. Juris. § 1227; Mosier's Appeal, 56 Pa. St. 80; *Bank* v. *North,* 4 Johns. Ch. 370.

Taxes legally assessed upon land are a lien thereon. *Williams* v. *Hilbin,* 35 Me. 547; *Staples* v. *Fox,* 45 Miss. 667.

A prior mortgagee upon payment of the taxes due upon the property is subrogated to the lien of the taxes upon the premises as against the mortgagor. Jones, Mort. 1080, 1134; *Kortright* v. *Cady,* 23 Barb. 497; *Pratt* v. *Pratt,* 96 Ill. 184; *Bank* v. *Danforth,* 80 Ga. 66.

To wait until the time for paying the taxes to the town treasurer has elapsed, and the taxes have been put into the collector's hands, would mean a loss of four per cent. discount. The orators were not obliged to lose this amount. *Allen* v. *Burlington,* 45 Vt. 202; *Stowe* v. *Stowe,* 70 Vt. 609; *Sidenberg* v. *Ely,* 90 N. Y. 263; *William* v. *Townsend,* 31 N. Y. 414.

David S. Conant and *R. M. Harvey* for the defendants.

Under our statutes the mortgagor is owner of real estate for the purpose of taxation. *Wilson* v. *Marsh,* 34 Vt. 352, 363.

This case does not differ in principle from the case where one of several notes secured by mortgage has been left out of the decree. If it was left out voluntarily the mortgage security so far as that note is concerned is lost. *Noyes* v. *Rockwood,* 54 Vt. 647.

For taxes paid by a mortgagee after foreclosure he has no remedy. *Spencer* v. *Levering,* 8 Minn. 461; *Northwestern Mut. Ins. Co.* v. *Allis,* 23 Minn. 337; Desty, Tax. Vol. 2, 745.

Where there is no promise to pay the taxes by the mortgagor there should be no claim for subrogation. *Manning* v. *Tuthill,* 30 N. J. Eq. 29.

It does not appear that the payment of taxes was secured by the original mortgage. *Bryant* v. *Clark,* 45 Vt. 483.

MUNSON, J. The statute requires that real estate be set in the list to the last owner thereof on the first day of April. The last owner on that day remains liable for the taxes, regardless of subsequent transfers. A mortgagor is deemed the owner for purposes of taxation until the mortgagee takes possession. V. S. 368, 369. *Pitkin* v. *Parks,* 54 Vt. 301.

Taxes legally assessed upon real estate become a first lien upon the property, but that lien is not enforceable if the owner has personal estate from which the tax can be collected. In default of personal property, the collector may extend his warrant upon any land in the State owned by the delinquent. V. S. 478, 487. A tax is held not to become a fixed incumbrance upon the land until the officer charged with the collection does some official act that indicates an intention to pursue the land. *Hutchins* v. *Moody,* 34 Vt. 433; *Cummings* v. *Holt,* 56 Vt. 384.

The orators obtained a decree of foreclosure against the defendant Aldrich, and requested him to pay the taxes assessed on the mortgaged premises, and upon his refusal to do so made payment thereof to the treasurer in time to save the discount. This was long before the equity expired, and the defendant afterwards redeemed the property.

The bill cannot be maintained. The orators were not justified in treating the taxes as an incumbrance upon the mortgaged premises. The officer might have enforced collection upon other property of the delinquent, personal or real, and the taxes never have become a charge upon this particular estate. Nothing had been done that made the taxes a fixed incumbrance upon the land, and in paying them when they did the orators were merely volunteers.

Decree affirmed and cause remanded.

JOHN E. TRACY v. GRAND TRUNK RAILWAY CO.

January Term, 1903.

Present: TYLER, MUNSON, WATSON, and HASELTON, JJ.

Opinion filed February 29, 1904.

Statute of Limitations—Extension of Period—Previous Action—Commencement—Failure of Service—Unavoidable Accident—Evidence—Motion to Dismiss.

The inquiry under a motion to dismiss relates only to what appears of record.

For most purposes, if not for all not relating to the Statute of Limitations, an action is not commenced until process is served.

Under the general provisions of the Statute of Limitations, the time of issuing the writ is the commencement of the action, provided due service follows, but not otherwise.

When a writ is issued with the purpose on the part of the plaintiff to have it served and proceeded with, and service thereof fails through unavoidable accident, the suit is commenced within the meaning of V. S. 1214, which is an exceptional provision of the Statute of Limitations.

A writ "fails of sufficient service," within the meaning of V. S. 1214, when there is an utter failure of service.

When the evidence tends to show that a writ was issued within the period of limitations, and the next day plaintiff's attorney in another county sent the writ by mail to the clerk of the county court, with a letter requesting him to approve the bail and forward the writ to the plaintiff's local attorney by next mail; that the clerk complied with the request, but when the writ reached the office of the latter attorney he was away from home, but returned in about a week, when twelve days still remained for service; that he did not find the writ, and knew nothing of it until long after the time for service had expired, when it was discovered in a pigeonhole with matter relating to an official position held by the attorney, which had come in envelopes of the same size; that the attorney had assumed that his associates in the other county would attend to the service of the writ; that there was no doubt he acted in good faith; such evidence tends to show that the failure of service in question resulted from "unavoidable accident" within the meaning of V. S. 1214.

Oral evidence is admissible to show why a writ failed of sufficient service, although said writ was entered in court, and on motion, was dismissed for lack of seasonable service.

Though evidence be undisputed, yet, if it affords ground of opposing inferences of fact in the minds of reasonable men, it is for the jury to consider.

When the evidence relied upon to show certain facts is wholly oral, and there is no concession that the facts were what the oral evidence tends to show, the question cannot be taken from the jury except by a ruling, as a matter of law, against the party on whom the burden of proof rests.

CASE for personal injuries. Pleas, the general issue and Statute of Limitations. Replications, similiter and plea in confession and avoidance of the plea of the Statute of Limitations. Issue joined on said last named plea. Trial by jury at the October Term, 1902, Essex County, *Start*, J., presiding.

Verdict and judgment for the plaintiff. The defendant excepted.

All the facts stated in the opinion as to why the first writ was not seasonably served and returned were proved by oral evidence received subject to the objection and exception of the defendant. The opinion states the case.

C. A. Hight, L. L. Hight and *Chamberlain & Rich* for the defendant.

The court should have granted the defendant's motion for a verdict on the ground that the issue as to whether an action had been commenced within six years had already been heard and finally adjudicated in favor of the defendant. *Porter* v. *Gile, et al.*, 47 Vt. 620; *Dowling* v. *Polack*, 18 Cal. 626; *Leese* v. *Sherwood*, 21 Cal. 152; *Zoller* v. *McDonald*, 23 Cal. 136; Black on Judgments, (last ed.) §§ 691, 692, and cases in notes; *Welter* v. *Schetten*, 46 N. W. Rep. 201, 203; *Mayhy* v. *Henry*, 83 N. C. 298; *Dwight* v. *St. John*, 25 N. Y. 203; *Blanchard* v. *Webster*, 62 N. H. 467; *Wilson* v. *Otis et al.*, 71 N. H. 483; *Boyle* v. *Kansas City*, 51 Mo. 454; *Scribner* v. *Surch*, 39 Mich. 98; *Cooper* v. *Reynolds, Lessee*, 10 Wall. 308; *Cromwell* v. *Sac County*, 94 U. S. 551; *Nesbitt* v. *District*, 144 U. S. 610; *Commissioners* v. *Platt*, 79 Fed. 567; *Outram* v. *Morewood*, 3 East. 246; Freeman on Judgments, § 16.

In ordinary cases the action is not commenced until the writ is served. *Stanley* v. *Turner*, 68 Vt. 315; *Randall* v. *Bacon*, 49 Vt. 20; *Howard* v. *Bartlett*, 70 Vt. 314; *Burlington* v. *Traction Co.*, 70 Vt. 491; *Day* v. *Lamb*, 7 Vt. 426; *Chapman* v. *Goodrich*, 55 Vt. 354.

On plaintiff's evidence the court should have adjudged as matter of law that the first writ did not fail of service by reason of unavoidable accident. *Scott* v. *School Dist.*, 67 Vt.

150; *Marble v. Hinds,* 67 Me. 205; *Packard v. Swallow,* 29
Me. 458; *Donnell v. Gatchell,* 38 Me. 218; *Hayes v. Stew-
art,* 23 Vt. 623; *Poland v. R. R. Co.,* 47 Vt. 73; *Bullock v.
Dean,* 12 Met. 15.

May & Simonds for the plaintiff.

The question raised by the issue joined on the replication to the plea of the Statute of Limitations was for the
jury, although the evidence was uncontradicted. *Barber v.
Essex,* 27 Vt. 62; *Vinton v. Schwab,* 32 Vt. 612; *Willard v.
Dow,* 54 Vt. 188.

Defendant can raise the question of *res adjudicata* only
by plea. *Dunklee v. Goodenough,* 63 Vt. 459.

The former judgment on motion to dismiss only estab-
lished that the service and return were defective. *Jericho v.
Underhill,* 63 Vt. 85; Herman, Estop. Vol. 1, p. 112; *Riggs v.
Pursell,* 74 N. Y. 378; *Leonard v. McArthur,* 52 Vt. 439;
Gusten v. Carpenter, 51 Vt. 585.

HASELTON, J. This was an action on the case tried by
jury in the Essex County Court. A verdict for the plaintiff
was returned, and judgment was rendered thereon. The cause
of action was alleged to have accrued April 22, 1894. The
writ was dated September 20, 1900. The defendant's pleas
were the general issue and the Statute of Limitations. The
exceptions taken and relied on relate solely to that part of
the case involving the Statute of Limitations. To the defendant's plea of the statute the plaintiff replied, admitting that this action was brought more than six years after
the cause of action accrued, but alleging that before the expiration of that period, that is, April 16, 1900, he commenced a
suit against the defendant for the same cause of action, and
that the writ therein failed of sufficient service by unavoidable

accident; that the former suit was returnable, and was returned, to the Essex County Court and that at the September
Term, 1900, of said Court, said former suit was determined
against the plaintiff solely because of such failure of sufficient
service.

The plaintiff claimed that the case was brought within
V. S. 1214 which provides that "if, in an action commenced
within the time limited by the statute, the writ fails of sufficient service or return by unavoidable accident" the plaintiff
may within one year after the determination of the original
suit commence a new action for the same cause. In support
of his claim the plaintiff, without objection, introduced in
evidence the record of the former proceedings.   This record
showed the date of the former writ, April 16, 1900, service on
August 11, 1900, docketing August 13, 1900; and that at
the September Term, 1900, of said Court the defendant appeared specially and moved to dismiss for reasons stated as
follows:

"1· Because it appears upon the face of the record that
said action has never been legally commenced, and is not now
legally pending before this court.

2. Because it appears upon the face of the record that
the writ and process filed in said action was not served
within twenty-one days from the date of said writ as required
by law.

3. Because it appears upon the face of the record that
said process was not entered and docketed in the county
clerk's office on or before the expiration of twenty-one days
from the date of issuing the same.

4. Because the defendant named in said action has never
been legally served with process in said action, and the court
had no jurisdiction over the said defendant by virtue of said
action or process."

The record further recites that "after full hearing of said motion the court dismissed said action."

After the introduction of this record the plaintiff was allowed, subject to objection and exception on the part of the defendant, to introduce oral evidence for the purpose of showing why the writ in the original action was not served and returned within the twenty-one days limited therein.

The defendant claims that the very question upon which this oral evidence was received had been adjudicated in the former case after full hearing upon the merits. This contention is based upon the facts that the motion to dismiss presented, as the first ground for dismissal, that said former action had never been legally commenced, that a full hearing was had upon the motion, and that the court assigned no ground for dismissal, but sustained the motion generally.

But the inquiry under a motion to dismiss relates only to what appears of record. *Arel* v. *Centebar,* 73 Vt. 238, 50 Atl. 1064; *Alexander* v. *School District,* 62 Vt. 273, 19 Atl. 995; *State* v. *Johnson,* 72 Vt. 118, 47 Atl. 398; *Johnson* v. *Williams,* 48 Vt. 565; *Bliss* v. *Smith,* 42 Vt. 198; *R. R. Co.* v. *Bailey,* 24 Vt. 465; *Culver* v. *Balch,* 23 Vt. 618. A full hearing upon such a motion means only a full hearing of such matters as are within the scope of the motion. In the defendant's brief it is stated that "in order to decide whether or not the action had been legally commenced it would be proper and necessary for the court to determine, among other things, whether or not the writ was properly made and dated; whether or not it was made and sued out with the intention of immediate service; as it was not served until more than three months after the proper time for service it would be necessary for the court to pass upon the question as to why it was not served; whether the plaintiff after making the writ had as matter of law or as matter of fact so acted as to abandon the suit." But, clearly, several matters are enumerated in the above quotation about which nothing appears in the record on which this motion to dismiss was granted, and which therefore under the practice in this State cannot be presumed to have been determined on a motion to dismiss. The presumption rather is that judgment on the motion passed on the clear and sufficient grounds for dismissal appearing of record and pointed out in the motion. It is suggested in argument that the oral evidence, taken under objection and exception and set out in the bill of exceptions herein, shows that the hearing on the motion to dismiss the former action was not confined to what appeared of record. But an examination of the evidence referred to merely shows certain questions in line with this suggestion. The answers to these questions are such that they fall short of being testimony to sustain the suggestion.

At the close of the evidence in this case the defendant moved the court to direct a verdict in its favor. This motion was overruled and the defendant excepted. The grounds of this exception were such that the basis was laid for the consideration not only of the claim already discussed but also of other claims, one of which is that it appears from the evidence introduced that the former action was never legally commenced. It is unquestionable that for most purposes, if not for all not relating to the Statute of Limitations, an action *in personam* is not treated as commenced until process is served. *Burlington* v. *Traction Co.*, 70 Vt. 491, 41 Atl. 514; *Howard* v. *Bartlett*, 70 Vt. 364, 40 Atl. 825; *Stanley* v. *Turner*, 68 Vt. 315, 35 Atl. 321; *Randall* v. *Bacon*, 49 Vt. 20. Under the general provisions of the Statute of Limitations the time of issuing the writ is regarded as the commencement of an action, if due service follows and not otherwise. *Chapman* v. *Goodrich*, 55 Vt. 354; *Randall* v. *Bacon*, 49 Vt. 20; *Kirby* v. *Jackson*, 42 Vt. 552; *Day* v. *Lamb*, 7 Vt. 426. But V. S. 1214 is an exceptional provision of the Statute of Limitations, and the part of it under consideration is meaningless if an action cannot be commenced within the true interpretation of the statute unless service of the writ is made, for it in unmistakable terms applies to actions commenced which fail of service. A suit is commenced within the meaning of V. S. 1214 when the writ is issued with the purpose on the part of the plaintiff of having served and proceeded with, although the writ fails of service or of sufficient service, provided it so fails through unavoidable accident. Any other holding would be obnoxious both to the spirit and to the letter of the section in question.

We come now to the question, raised by the defendant's motion for a verdict, whether the evidence considered together tended to show that the writ in the former suit failed of service by unavoidable accident. That that writ failed of service there can be no question. It had failed of service when the period of twenty-one days after April 16, 1900, had expired. What was done with the writ in the August following went for nothing. But a case in which there is an utter failure of service is as much within the contemplation of the statute in question as a case in which something is done towards service, but not enough to amount to legal service. No service is insufficient service. See *Bullock* v. *Dean*, 12 Met. 15; *Marble* v. *Hinds*, 67 Me. 203.

The plaintiff's evidence tended to show facts which may be stated in narrative form as follows: The plaintiff's attorneys were Bates, May & Simonds of St. Johnsbury in Caledonia County, and Porter H. Dale of Island Pond in the

county of Essex. The writ in question was issued April 16,
1900, and the next day plaintiff's counsel in St. Johnsbury
sent the same, by mail, to the clerk of the Essex County Court
at Guildhall. With the writ counsel enclosed a letter requesting the clerk to approve the bail, if good, and to forward the
writ to Porter H. Dale at Island Pond by next mail. The
clerk received the writ, approved the bail and forwarded the
writ as requested, on the 18th day of April, in an envelope
properly addressed and stamped. At that time 19 days remained for service. Mr. Dale was then away from home, but
returned in about a week, that is, when a period of some
12 days still remained for service. Upon his return he did
not find the writ and knew nothing about it until some time
in the following August, just before the attempted service was
made, when his attention was called to the matter by Mr.
May who, in setting cases for trial in the Essex County
Court, discovered that the writ had not been returned, and
immediately wrote Mr. Dale about the matter. Thereupon
search was made and the writ was found in a pigeon-hole in
Mr. Dale's office. Mr. Dale was deputy collector of customs
at Island Pond and the envelope with the writ in it was found
with official mail which had come in envelopes of the same
general kind to which that belonged that contained the writ.
There was another government officer in Mr. Dale's office
who had authority, in his absence, to open and examine official
mail. How the writ became pigeonholed can, however, only
be conjectured. Mr. Dale assumed that his associates in St.
Johnsbury would attend to and were attending to the service
of the writ, but that fact was not the reason why he did not
receive the writ. The testimony left no room for doubt that
he was acting in good faith as one of the attorneys for the
plaintiff, and that if he had actually got the writ he would

have attended to its service. The proximate cause of the failure of service was the fact that a writ duly mailed at Guildhall on the 18th of April, to Mr. Dale at his residence and
place of business at Island Pond, did not get into the hands
of Mr. Dale within the next 19 days, but was in some way
mislaid in his office. This evidence tended to show an unavoidable accident, unless counsel, prior to the expiration of
the time of service, were wanting in due diligence in respect
to the matter.

Two cases arising under statutes like ours are much in
point and will be briefly reviewed. The first of these is cited
both by the plaintiff and by the defendant, and the second is
cited by the defendant.

In *Bullock* v. *Dean*, 12 Met. 15, it appeared that the
plaintiff sued out a writ 16 days before the time when his
cause of action would be barred by the Statute of Limitations.
In this writ the defendant was described as of the town of
Taunton, which had been his former residence, although he
had resided elsewhere for about two years. The writ was
placed in the hands of an officer proper to make service in the
town of Taunton, who was not able to find the defendant,
and so the writ failed of service. The court held that the
writ failed of sufficient service by reason of unavoidable accident, and that a second suit brought within one year after the
determination of the first was maintainable.

In this case the court treat the creditor as not wanting in
due diligence, although, of course, after the failure of service,
the creditor and the court could see how the mistake or accident could have been prevented. The phrase "unavoidable
accident," the court says, "must have a reasonable construction, and does not mean to limit the case to a cause which
no possible diligence could guard against, but an unforeseen

cause, preventing the service of the writ where due diligence has been used by the creditor to commence his suit seasonably by the due and ordinary course of law."

The scope of the case of *Bullock* v. *Dean* can be understood only by reading the statement of the case in connection with the opinion of the court.

The defendant relies largely upon the case of *Marble* v. *Hinds,* 67 Me. 203. In that case the plaintiff sought to avoid a plea of the Statute of Limitations by setting up in substance that he sued out a writ against the defendant one day before the expiration of the statutory period of limitation; that after keeping the writ in his hands two months and twelve days he mailed it to an officer at so late a time that, if there was no delay in the mails, and the officer received the writ immediately upon its arrival at the postoffice, he would have but one day and a fraction of another in which to make service; that the officer did not receive the writ in season for service and that so the writ failed of service.

In this case counsel for the defendant did not attack the case of *Bullock* v. *Dean,* but distinguished it. The court on its part refers, with apparent approval, to the Bullock case and quotes from the opinion. Then, in distinguishing the case before it, the Maine Court says: "Here is no failure by unavoidable accident. The plaintiff claims that his writ was made on September 2, 1874. The writ if then made, remained in the hands of the plaintiff or his attorney until November 14th following. There was ample time in which the service could have been made. It was gross neglect on the plaintiff's part that the writ was not sooner forwarded. That cannot be deemed unavoidable accident which could have been so easily avoided. The risks of the probable absence of the deputy sheriff from home on the last day of service and of the possible miscarriage of the mail were unnecessarily and negligently incurred." The two cases are clearly distinguishable and are in entire harmony. The Maine case was obviously beyond the help of the doctrine which saved the case of *Bullock* v. *Dean*.

We think that these two cases are both good law and that from them a definition can be drawn as to what constitutes "unavoidable accident" within the meaning of that phrase as used in V. S. 1214; and we hold that the evidence here tended to show a failure of service by reason of unavoidable accident; that the failure of Mr. Dale to receive the writ within 19 days after it was mailed to him by the county clerk of his county was something which could not reasonably be foreseen. The writ was sent by the county clerk in the same way in which jurors are summoned, under the law of this state, not less than ten nor more than twenty days before the opening of the term at which they are required to appear. In so important a matter as the summoning of jurymen the law regards the possibility that a juryman will not within ten days actually receive the summons mailed to him from his county seat as too slight to call for any other mode of service..

In this case it can now be seen that steps might have been taken which would have prevented the accident in question. After every accident not such as the law terms an Act of God, ways can be pointed out in which the accident could have been avoided; and an accident may be unavoidable within the meaning of the statute in question and still fall short of being an "Act of God."

Our holding is that the evidence in this case tended to show that the failure of service in question resulted from "unavoidable accident" in that it tended to show that neither the plaintiff nor his attorneys nor any one for whose conduct the plaintiff was responsible was lacking in the exercise of such due and reasonable diligence as the business in hand called for.

Whether the writ in the former suit was taken out with the intention of having it served, and whether there was an abandonment of the former suit, are questions which this court treats as fairly raised by the exception to the overruling of the motion for a verdict; and it is held that the evidence tended to show that such writ was sued out with the intention named and that there was no abandonment of the former suit.

All the oral evidence that was received under objection and exception was admissible, and the defendant was not entitled to have a verdict directed in its favor.

In charging the jury, the trial court gave a definition of the phrase "unavoidable accident." To this the defendant took an exception, but in argument this exception was waived. This court has, therefore, no occasion to consider the adequacy of that definition, nor to attempt a comprehensive and precise definition of the phrase. All has been said in that regard that is necessary to a disposition of the questions presented by the case as argued.

The defendant also excepted to the submission of the question of unavoidable accident to the jury on the ground that as the evidence was not in dispute the question was one of law for the court. It sometimes happens that though the evidence is undisputed it is such as to afford ground for opposing inferences of fact in the minds of reasonable men. When the evidence is of such a character it is for the jury to consider it. However, it seems unnecessary to consider whether the evidence here was of such a character or not. Since, as we have already seen, the tendency of the evidence was such that the court could not rule as matter of law, that there was no unavoidable accident, the defendant cannot complain because the trial court, instead of ruling as matter of law against it on this point, submitted the question of unavoidable accident to the jury.

Besides the evidence relied on to show unavoidable accident was oral, and so far as appears there was no concession that the facts were what this oral evidence tended to show. The issue was to the jury and without such a concession the question could not be taken from the jury except by a ruling as matter of law against the plaintiff, the party on whom the burden of proof rested.   Such ruling the tendency of the evidence would not permit.

Judgment affirmed.

EDWARD F. BROWNELL *v.* PATRICK J. RUSSELL.

October Term, 1903.

Present: ROWELL, C. J., TYLER, MUNSON, START, WATSON, and STAFFORD, JJ.

Opinion filed February 29, 1904.

Chief of Police—Removal—Constitutional Law—Rule of Police Department—Reasonableness.

The chief of police of a city is a "police officer," and a "member of the police force" within the meaning of a rule adopted by the police department to secure the good conduct and efficiency of the police force.

The officers elected in the organization of party caucuses, and the positions filled by the action of those caucuses, are not such officers and offices as are contemplated by the eighth article of the Constitution of the State of Vermont.

A rule of the police department of a city forbidding members of the police force to be delegates to or members of political caucuses, or to take part in any political canvass, is a reasonable exercise of the power to make rules for the government of the police force.

When the chief of police of a city acts as chairman of a caucus, and as chairman of a political meeting, he is guilty of official misconduct sufficient to justify his removal from office, on the ground that he has thereby violated a rule enacted by the police department forbidding members of the police force to be delegates to or members of political caucuses, or to take part in any political canvass.

When a rule of the police department of a city forbids police officers to do a specific act, and the board of examiners, upon charges preferred against him, finds that the chief of police has done the forbidden thing, they cannot control the effect of their finding by also reporting that they find him not guilty of the charge.

COMPLAINT for a writ of *quo warranto* brought to the Supreme Court for Chittenden County at its October Term, 1903, and then heard on an agreed statement. The opinion states the facts.

J. E. Cushman for the relator.

Under the city charter the mayor cannot remove the relator except for the causes therein defined, which are merely declaratory of the common law on that subject. *Rex. v. Richardson*, 1 Burr. 517; *People ex rel. Munday v. Board, etc.*, 72 N.Y. 445; *People ex rel. Simms v. Fire Com'rs*, 73 N.Y. 437; *People ex rel. Keech v. Thompson*, 94 N. Y. 451.

The cause must be one which touches the qualifications of the officer for the office. *State v. Hawkins*, 44 Ohio St. 98; *State ex rel. Haight v. Lin*, 34 N. J. L. 14; *Ayers v. Newark*, 49 N. J. L. 170; *People v. Grant*, 12 Daly (N. Y.) 294.

The examiners found the relator not guilty of the two charges upon which the mayor bases his order of removal, the decision of the examiners will not be reviewed by this Court. *State v. Prince*, 45 Wis. 613; Throop Pub. Officers, §§ 394,

396; *Tainter* v. *Lucas*, 29 Wis. 375; *Gager* v. *Supervisors*, 47 Mich. 167; *Hamtramck* v. *Holihan*, 46 Mich. 127; *Patton* v. *Vaughan*, 39 Ark. 211; *U. S.* v. *Oliver*, 6 Mackey, 47; *Oliver* v. *City*, 69 Ga. 165.

J. A. Brown for the respondent.

The wisdom of the mayor in respect of the removal is not for review here. Throop Pub. Officers, pp. 386-387.

MUNSON, J. The charter of the city of Burlington requires the appointment of a board of police examiners, and provides that this board, with the approval of the mayor, "shall make rules for the government of the police force." Number 13 of the rules established under this provision, after recognizing the right of suffrage, declares that "no member will be permitted to be a delegate or representative to, or member of, any political or partisan convention or caucus, or take any part in any political canvass."

Section 213 of the charter provides that "whenever it shall appear to the mayor that any member of said force is or has been derelict in his official duty, or is guilty of any misconduct in his private or official life," the mayor may suspend such member pending an investigation by the board of examiners, and that the board, upon the written request of the mayor, shall investigate whatever charges are made "and report the facts found by them relative thereto in writing to the mayor"; and, by the same section, the mayor is given power to remove or suspend such member, "when found guilty, or when recommended for dismissal or suspension by said board."

In February, 1903, and until the proceedings now under consideration, the relator was the chief of police. On the first day of July, 1903, the mayor presented to the police examiners written charges against the relator, charging among other things that on the fourteenth day of February, 1903, the relator, in violation of Rule 13, "took part in a certain political caucus in ward two in said city, and acted as chairman of said caucus"; and further, that on the twenty-eighth day of February, 1903, the relator, in violation of said rule, "acted as chairman, and was one of the speakers, at a political meeting held in St. John's Hall * * in said city." It appears from the agreed statement that the political caucus referred to as held in ward two was a caucus to nominate Republican candidates for ward officers to be supported at the ensuing election, and that the relator was a legal voter in that ward.

The charges above stated were specifically reported upon as follows: "The police examiners find that said Brownell acted as chairman of a political caucus held on or about the 17th day of February, but did not take part therein in violation of said Rule number 13, and they find him not guilty of said charge"; and "find that said Brownell was present at a political meeting held in St. John's Hall on or about the 28th day of February, 1903, and acted as chairman, but was not one of the public speakers at that meeting, and took no part therein in violation of said Rule number 13, and they find him not guilty of said charge." The mayor considered that his charges were sustained by these findings, and revoked the relator's appointment and put the defendant in his place.

It is urged in behalf of the relator that Rule 13 does not apply to the chief of police. The arguments advanced in support of this claim are based upon the arrangement and classification of the rules relating to the police department, and upon certain changes in phraseology occurring in recent amendments to the charter. We do not consider it necessary to take up these matters in detail. Nothing is suggested that leads us to doubt that the chief of police is a "police officer," a "member of the police force," and amenable to the rules adopted to secure the good conduct and efficiency of the force.

The relator refers to the eighth article of our Constitution, which declares that all freemen "have a right to elect officers, and be elected into office"; and insists that under this article he had a "right to attend the caucus in question and be elected to office therein." If the scope of the provision were held to be as claimed, it is possible that the acceptance of an appointment, with this rule in force, would be a waiver of the constitutional right. But it is not necessary to inquire as to this, for it is clear that the officers elected in the organization of party caucuses, and the places filled by the action of those caucuses, are not such officers or offices as are contemplated by the article in question.

The argument that this is too small a matter to be accounted such a dereliction or misconduct as would bring the relator within the mayor's power of removal, is not applicable. This is not a charge brought under a general provision requiring faithful service and good conduct, but a charge of the violation of a specific requirement. The breach of such a requirement is necessarily official misconduct, and the only question here is whether the rule itself was such as the board was authorized to adopt.

It is doubtless true that the restrictions imposed must be a reasonable exercise of the power granted, and have some just relation to the end in view. It seems to us that the provision in question satisfies these requirements. We think the removal of the police force from the field of active politics is calculated to promote the efficiency of the force and the purity of municipal government, and that the rule adopted imposes no greater restriction than is reasonably necessary to the accomplishment of this purpose.

But it is said that the board has found the relator not guilty. This is a conclusion of the examiners which has no support in the facts they have reported. When the rule forbids the doing of a particular thing, and the doing of that thing is found by the examiners, they cannot control the effect of their finding by saying that the doer is not guilty. The report of the examiners justified the mayor in taking action, and the extent of the penalty was a matter for his discretion.

Petition dismissed with costs.

WILMINGTON SAVINGS BANK *v.* CHARLES H. WASTE.

January Term, 1904.

Present: ROWELL, C. J., TYLER, START, WATSON, STAFFORD, and
HASELTON, JJ.

Opinion filed March 16, 1904.

*Promissory Note—Forgery—Evidence—Comparison of
Handwriting—Cross-examination—Hearsay.*

In an action on a promissory note, the defendant, who claims his signature to have been forged, may, on cross-examination of either an expert on nonexpert witness, show such witness signatures conceded or proved to be genuine; but this is the limit of comparison.

In an action on a promissory note, to which defendant claims his signature has been forged, when a witness for the plaintiff testifies in chief that in his opinion the signature in question is the defendant's, it is error to allow the defendant on cross-examination, to show the witness sheets of paper with defendant's name several times written thereon, and require him to select therefrom those signatures which in his opinion are genuine. It is also error to allow such papers to go to the jury.

In action on a promissory note to which the defendant claims his name has been forged by one Hall, another signer thereof, it is error to allow the defendant to put in evidence a sheet of paper with his name several times written thereon, and two other sheets of paper each with two other names several times written thereon, which were all found at the house of said Hall, in a desk where he kept his papers, a year and a half after the note in question was signed; there being no evidence tending to show that these names were in Hall's hand writing, or that any of them resembled defendant's signature.

In an action on a promissory note payable to a bank, and claimed by the defendant to be a forgery, it is error to allow the defendant to testify that the plaintiff's clerk said to him, when he called to see the note, that it was in the office of an attorney "with the other forged notes."

GENERAL ASSUMPSIT, with specification of a promissory note, special plea alleging that defendant's signature is a forgery. Trial by jury at the April Term, 1903, Windham County, *Munson*, J., presiding. Verdict and judgment for the defendant. Plaintiff excepted.

The note in suit is for $150.00, is joint and several, payable to the plaintiff, or order, dated June 18, 1900, and purports to be signed by Clara I. Hall, Israel L. Hall, and the defendant.

The only plea or notice filed by the defendant is as follows:

"And the said Charles H. Waste by Charles S. Chase, his attorney, comes and defends the wrong and the injury, when, etc., and says that the said Wilmington Savings Bank ought not to have and maintain its aforesaid action thereof against him, because he says he did not sign said supposed note in the plaintiff's declaration or specifications mentioned, and that the signature attached to said note, which purports

to be his signature, is a forgery. And of this the said Charles
H. Waste puts himself upon the country for trial."

The exceptions state that "the defendant was called as
witness in his behalf and testified that some time after the
failure of Israel Hall he went to the Wilmington Savings
Bank, that the treasurer was away, but that one C. C. Barlow,
clerk of the bank, was in, and he asked to see the note in
question, and that Mr. Barlow thought it was across the way
in Mr. Butterfield's office with the other forged notes. The
plaintiff objected and excepted to the testimony of the defendant as to what Mr. Barlow told him. J. H. Goulding, the
treasurer of the Wilmington Savings Bank, was called as a
witness by the defendant and testified, subject to the plaintiff's objection and exception, that he supposed that Israel
Hall was in the insane asylum when the note in question was
put in the hands of plaintiff's attorney for collection, and that
previous to making demand upon Mr. Waste the plaintiff
held other paper of Israel Hall's; that there came a time when
there was a crisis in the affairs of Israel Hall in the fall of
1901; that he learned of the arrest of Mr. Hall, and that immediately thereafter there was a critical examination of the
paper held by the plaintiff, upon which the name of Israel Hall
appeared; that it might have been a year after that examination before the note in controversy was placed in their attorney's hands for collection; that at, and after, the examination
above referred to, the officers of the bank had suspected that
certain of the paper in said bank presented there and dis-
counted by Israel Hall, and alleged to be signed by Israel
Hall and others, and then held by the bank, were forged; that
he had such suspicion and that the other bank officers expressed such suspicion in his presence and hearing; that
neither he nor any of the bank officers, to his knowledge,

ever had any suspicion as to the genuineness of defendant's signature upon the note in question."

O. E. Butterfield for the plaintiff.

The papers whereon were several times written the name of the defendant were clearly inadmissible. A signature to be used as a standard of comparison must be conceded, or established by proof. *Baker* v. *Mygatt*, 14 Iowa 181; *Winch* v. *Norman*, 65 Iowa 186; *Clark* v. *Wyatt*, 15 Ind. 271; *Shorb* v. *Kinzie*, 80 Ind. 500; *U. S.* v. *McMillan*, 29 Fed. 247; *Sartor* v. *Billinger*, 59 Tex. 411; *Ort* v. *Fowler*, 31 Kans. 478; *Richardson* v. *Newcomb*, 21 Pick. 315; *Costello* v. *Crowell*, 133 Mass. 352; *Depue* v. *Place*, 7 Pa. St. 428; *Cohen* v. *Fuller*, 93 Pa. St. 428; *Pavey* v. *Pavey*, 30 Ohio St. 603; *Rowell* v. *Fuller*, 59 Vt. 688; *Nodin* v. *Murray*, 3 Camp. 228; *Cohen* v. *Fuller*, 93 Pa. St. 123; *Com.* v. *Eastman*, 1 Cush. 189; *Griffiths* v. *Ivery*, 11 A. & E. 322; *Bank* v. *Robert*, 41 Mich. 710; *Howard* v. *Patrick*, 43 Mich. 121; *Masey* v. *Farmer's Nat. Bank*, 104 Ill. 327; *Rose* v. *First Nat. Bank*, 91 Mo. 399.

The evidence relative to the papers found in Hall's house was inadmissible. 1 Cowen & Hill's Notes, 428, 475; 1 Greenl. Ev. § 52; Stark. Ev. Part IV. 380.

Charles S. Chase and *Clarke C. Fitts* for the defendant.

Because of defendant's plea denying signature the burden of proving same was on the plaintiff. *Bank* v. *Adams*, 70 Vt. 139; *Gregory* v. *Tomlinson*, 68 Vt. 413; *Stevenson* v. *Gunning*, 64 Vt. 614.

So far as appears the papers with defendant's name several times written thereon were used in cross-examination solely to test the capacity of the witness as an expert. This court will so construe the exceptions as to uphold the judgment of the trial court. *French* v. *Ware*, 65 Vt. 338; *Conway* v. *Fitzgerald*, 70 Vt. 103.

The test with the signatures was a fair one. *Thomas* v. *State*, 103 Ind. 419.

It is not opposed to the reasoning of this court. *In Re Barney's Will*, 71 Vt. 221; *Redding* v. *Redding's Estate*, 69 Vt. 508; *Bridgman* v. *Corey*, 62 Vt. 11.

But it does not appear that the witness was able to distinguish between the handwriting of the defendant and other parties. So if there was error it is harmless. *State* v. *Buckman*, 74 Vt. 313; *McKindley* v. *Drew*, 71 Vt. 138; *In Re Diggins*, 68 Vt. 200.

The evidence relative to the papers found at Hall's house was properly admitted. *State* v. *Doherty*, 72 Vt. 390; *Dover* v. *Winchester*, 70 Vt. 418; *Morrill* v. *Palmer*, 68 Vt. 1.

TYLER, J. This action is assumpsit brought to recover the amount due upon a promissory note, purporting to have been signed by Clara I. Hall, Israel L. Hall and the defendant, and payable to the plaintiff; defense, that the note was not signed by the defendant, and that his name upon it was a forgery.

I. The plaintiff called Martin A. Brown as a witness, who testified that he was familiar with the signature of the defendant, that he had seen him write, and that in his opinion the signature upon the note was the defendant's. In cross examination the defendant showed the witness a paper which had the name "C. H. Waste" written upon it ten times, in connection with an offer to show later in the trial that certain of the signatures upon the paper were the defendant's. The defendant was permitted to cross-examine the witness as to whether in his opinion any of the ten signatures were in the defendant's handwriting, and if so, which ones; whether any of them were not in the defendant's handwriting, and how many handwritings there were upon the paper. The defendant showed the witness two other papers of the same character and used them for the same purpose, and the three papers were admitted in evidence.

In cross-examination it was competent for the defendant, for the purpose of testing the correctness of the witness' judgment, to show him signatures of the defendant conceded or proved to be genuine, but this was the limit of comparison. *Sanderson* v. *Osgood*, 52 Vt. 309; *Rowell* v. *Fuller*, 59 Vt. 688, 10 Atl. 853; *Costello* v. *Crowell*, 133 Mass. 352. The defendant examined the witness as though he were an expert, when he was not. His testimony was directly upon the question whether or not the signature upon the note in suit was genuine. But if the witness had been an expert the rule required that a standard of comparison should be established before he could be examined by the use of signatures made for the purpose of the trial. Abbott's Trial Ev. (2nd ed.) 488, 489. It appears that the signature upon another note in evidence was conceded to be the defendant's, but the exceptions do not show that it was used in the cross-examination. The witness was required to select from the three papers the genuine signatures of the defendant, and then the papers went to the jury. It was error both to permit this course of examination and to allow the papers to be submitted to the jury.

II. The money for which the note was given was loaned to Israel L. Hall, the second signer upon the note, and the defendant claimed that his name was forged by Hall. As tending to establish this fact a witness, Collins, was called by the defendant and allowed to testify that he was a near neighbor of Hall and had done considerable business with him, had seen him write and knew where his desk was; that after Hall's

arrest, which was a year and a half after the note was signed,
he went to Hall's house, looked over his desk and papers and
there found a sheet of paper with the defendant's name written several times upon it, and two other sheets with two
other names written several times upon them, respectively,
but that he could not tell in whose handwriting the names
were.   Another witness, who was with Collins, testified to
the same facts.   With no evidence tending to show that
these names were in Hall's handwriting, nor that they resembled the defendant's signature, this evidence was placed before
the jury for the apparent purpose of inviting them to believe
that Hall had at some time practiced writing the defendant's
name.   This evidence should have been excluded.

III.   It was error to permit the defendant to testify
that the plaintiff's clerk said to the defendant, when he called
to see the note, that it was in the attorney's office "with the
other forged notes."   This evidence got before the jury the
opinion of the clerk that this note was forged.

IV. The testimony of the plaintiff's treasurer that the bank
officers made an examination of other notes, and that they had,
and had expressed, suspicions that some of them which purported to have been signed by Hall and others, were forged,
was hearsay as to the other officers, and was irrelevant to the
issue in the case. The testimony of the treasurer that neither he
nor any of the officers had any suspicion that the note in suit
was forged did not cure the error. If the jury believed that the
bank officers suspected that Hall had forged other paper, they
would more readily believe, and upon incompetent testimony,
that he forged the note in controversy.

All the evidence considered was admitted under the plaintiff's objection and exception.

Judgment reversed and cause remanded.

CONGREGATIONAL CHURCH OF CHESTER, ET AL. *v.* CHESTINA
CUTLER.

October Term, 1903.

Present: ROWELL, C. J., TYLER, MUNSON, START, and WATSON, JJ.

Opinion filed April 1, 1904.

*Wills—Conditional Bequests—Condition Subsequent—Church
—Incorporation—Demurrer in Answer—Waiver—Evidence—Harmless Error.*

A demurrer for want of equity, incorporated in the answer to an
amended bill, is waived unless brought on to hearing before the
case is heard on its merits.

When, after probate of a will giving certain money to a church upon
condition, the church applies to the Probate Court for an order
directing the fund to be paid to the church, and thereupon the
court orders that a trustee be appointed to hold and manage the
fund for the church, this is not a conclusive determination that
the church is not entitled to the fund.

A church which was within the scope and intent of a statute passed
in 1814, providing that any number of persons before then voluntarily associated for the maintenance of religious worship under a
statute passed in 1797, should be a body corporate and have all the
powers incident to corporations, is a valid corporation, though it
subsequently made an ineffectual attempt to incorporate under a
later statute.

A condition annexed to a bequest to a church, that its officers, or a
committee of the church chosen for that purpose, should annually
visit the grave of the testatrix and give it such care and attention as she would under like circumstances, is a condition subsequent.

When a condition is annexed to a bequest to a church, and a bill
brought by the church to construe the bequest alleges, and the
answer denies, an intention on the part of the orator to comply
with the condition, it is not error for the master to allow the
officers of the church to state what their intention has been and is,
in respect of complying with said condition.

When a bequest to a church is not conditioned upon a vote of acceptance, proof of such a vote by the society is harmless.

APPEAL IN CHANCERY. Heard on bill, answer, master's report and exceptions thereto, at the December Term, 1901, Windsor County, *Stafford*, Chancellor. Decree for the orators. The defendant appealed.

The defendant, Chestina Cutler, is administratrix, with the will annexed, of the estate of Sarah L. Cutler, is sister of the testatrix and her residuary legatee under said will.

The orator, Atwood Sargent, is the trustee appointed by the Probate Court in 1894 to hold and manage the legacy for the benefit of the church. He accepted the trust and the fund was paid over to him.

The bill alleges that the church has performed the condition annexed to said bequest, "if they correctly apprehend the meaning of said condition; but the same is uncertain and ambiguous and said beneficiary is willing and anxious to comply with said condition when its true intent can be ascertained and declared"; that said Chestina Cutler has hindered and annoyed the church and its officers in various ways in respect of performing said condition, and that she "is endeavoring to secure a forfeiture of said trust against equity and good conscience"; and prays for the construction of said will and the direction of the court so that it may be able to give the grave of said testatrix such care as she would give under like circumstances, and that the said Chestina be prohibited from vexing the orator with any further suits for obtaining a forfeiture of said trust until the true meaning and intent of said testatrix in her will has been declared by this court; and that said Chestina Cutler be enjoined from prosecuting further her appeal from the judgment and decree of the Probate Court now pending in Windsor County Court.

The master found that the orator, the Congregational
Church of Chester, is the legatee to which the bequest in question was made; that in 1894 application was made to the
Probate Court for the district of Windsor for an order upon
the defendant as administratrix to pay over to the Congregational Church of Chester the one thousand dollars bequeathed
to it in said will of Sarah Cutler; that said court upon hearing held that a trustee should be appointed to hold and manage said fund, and appointed the orator, Atwood Sargent,
such trustee; that Mr. Sargent at once invested the money
and has collected the interest on the investment and expended
it annually in strict compliance with the terms and conditions
of said will; that while the defendant held the fund no interest
or income was paid on the bequest under the will; that on
July 14, 1897, the defendant presented her petition to said
Probate Court praying that said trustee render his account of
said trust, and pay over to the defendant, as residuary legatee
under the will, said sum of $1,000 with interest thereon dur-
ing the time it has been in his hands; that after several hear-
ings and adjournments the court made an order from which
the petitioner therein, the defendant in this suit, appealed to
the Windsor County Court, where said cause is still pending;
that in May, 1900, the Congregational Church of Chester
made petition to said Probate Court to have the trustee discharged and said legacy paid over to the church to be held
as provided in said will; that in June, 1900, said Atwood Sargent resigned as trustee, and filed his account in said court;
that afterwards said account was allowed, said resignation
accepted, and the Congregational Church of Chester appointed
trustee of said fund; that from these orders Chestina Cutler
appealed and said appeal is still pending in Windsor County
Court; that the officers of the church have visited the grave
more frequently than the will requires, and have in good faith

given it such care and attention as they understand was required. The decree appealed from was, among other things, "The clause in question is construed to mean that this lot should receive the care and attention customarily given such lots in the same cemetery, including, besides the annual visit specified, the keeping the grass mown, the grave occasionally decorated with flowers and the stone' work clean and well set.

It is considered that the question now pending in the County Court upon the defendant's appeal from the Probate Court touching the custody of the fund, whether a trustee should be appointed or the church itself administer the trust, is a question properly to be determined in that. proceeding."

W. W. Stickney, J. G. Sargent, Homer L. Skeels and *George L. Fletcher* for the orators.

It is sufficient to show corporative existence by prescription or presumption. *Searsburg Turnpike Co.* v. *Cutler,* 6 Vt. 315; *Bank of Manchester* v. *Allen,* 11 Vt. 302; *Sherwin* v. *Bugbee,* 16 Vt. 439; *Londonderry* v. *Andover,* 28 Vt. 424; *Society of Middlesex* v. *Davis,* 3 Met. 133; *Methodist Episcopal Society* v. *Lake,* 51 Vt. 353; *Methodist Episcopal Union Church* v. *Pickett,* 19 N. Y. 485.

A demurrer incorporated in an answer must be heard before trial, or it is waived. *State* v. *Massey,* 72 Vt. 214.

Gilbert A. Davis for the defendant.

The non-performance of a condition subsequent will defeat the title to what is claimed under such condition. *Archerly* v. *Vernon,* Comyn's Rep. 513; *Beauben* v. *Cardigan,* Ambler's Rep. 533; *Chauncey* v. *Graydon,* 2 Aik. 619; *Fry* v. *Porter,* 1 Mod. 314; *Burgess* v. *Robinson,* 3 Meriv. 9; *Philips* v. *Bury,* Show P. C. 50; *Bertie* v. *Lord Falkland,* 2 Trienan 221; *Lady Ann Fry's Case,* 1 Ventr. 200.

The Probate Court has ample authority to decree this fund to the church, if it is entitled thereto. *School Dist.* v. *Sheldon,* 71 Vt. 95; *Mitchell* v. *Blanchard,* 72 Vt. 85.

If an estate is given on condition, the performance must be within a reasonable time. 2 Jarman on Wills, 513; *Carter* v. *Carter,* 14 Pick. 424; *Ross* v. *Tremaine,* 2 Metc. 495; *Drew* v. *Wakefield,* 54 Me. 291, 8 U. S. Dig. 694; *Ward* v. *Patterson,* 46 Penn. (10 Wright) 372; *In Re Hodge's Legacy,* 16 Law Rep. Eq. 92.

When a bequest becomes ineffectual for any cause, the residuary legatee takes the property. *Drew* v. *Wakefield,* 54 Me. 296, 14 U. S. Dig. 343; *Vick* v. *McDaniel,* 4 Miss. (3 Howard) 337; *Taylor* v. *Lucas,* 4 Hawks (N. C.) 215.

MUNSON, J. The bequest of Sarah L. Cutler to the orator, the Congregational Church of Chester, was on the following condition: "That the officers of said church, or a committee of said church chosen for that purpose, shall annually visit my grave, and give it such care and attention as I would give under like circumstances." The bill prays, among other things, for such direction of the Court of Chancery as will enable the orator properly to perform this condition.

The defendant insists that the Probate Court has power to construe the will, and that the bill should be dismissed for this reason. The action taken below precludes the raising of this question. A demurrer was incorporated in the answer to the amended bill, but this was not brought forward for hearing, and was treated as waived.

The corporate existence of the orator is denied. The master reports that this church has records, more or less perfect, covering a period of one hundred and twenty-eight years, but that the first articles of association contained therein were adopted in 1859. The statute then in force required that the first meeting be notified, organized and held in the manner prescribed in the articles of association. Comp. Stat. ch. 85, § 6. The articles of 1859 contain no provision regarding the notification of the first meeting, and this omission left the action then taken without a statutory basis. So we proceed to inquire as to the previous status of the organization.

By a statute passed in 1797, and continuously in force until after 1824, it was provided in substance that any number of persons might associate for the purpose of hiring a minister and erecting a house of worship, and might make contracts, and purchase, hold and transfer property for the benefit of the association. By an act passed in 1814, it was further provided that persons voluntarily associating under the act of 1797 should be a body corporate and politic for the purposes contemplated in that act, and have all the powers incident to corporations. We have then a statute authorizing persons to associate for the maintenance of religious worship, and a later statute making the persons thus associated corporations with the powers incident thereto. It sufficiently appears from the master's findings that the plaintiff organization has been in existence and supporting public worship from a time prior to 1814, and it is to be presumed that the organization has been maintained since 1814 under the statute of that date. Nothing more is required to establish its corporate existence. *Methodist Episcopal Society* v. *Lake*, 51 Vt. 353. That existence was not lost by the attempt to organize under the later statute.

In 1894 the church applied to the Probate Court for an order upon the defendant as administratrix to pay to the church the amount of this legacy, but the court held that a trustee should be appointed to hold and manage the fund for the church, and appointed as such trustee the orator Sargent.

The fund was then paid to the trustee, and he held it and paid over the avails to the church until 1900, when he resigned and the church itself was appointed trustee. The defendant appealed from the order making this appointment, and the appeal is still pending. We find nothing in this to support the defendant's contention that the decree of 1894 was a conclusive determination that the church is not entitled to this fund. The trustee was appointed upon the theory that the church was entitled to it, and the question raised by the subsequent appointment of the church to hold and administer it, is saved by the decree below for determination in the probate appeal.

The answer and the argument proceed upon the theory that the condition upon which the legacy was given is a condition precedent, and that the orator has not yet obtained, and is not now entitled to receive, the legacy. The provision, if it be treated as a condition, is clearly a condition subsequent; and if the question of forfeiture can be raised upon the pleadings, the claim cannot be sustained upon the findings of the master.

It was not error to permit the officials of the church to state what their intention had been and was as regards the care of the grave. The bill alleges, and the answer denies, an intention on the part of the orator to comply fully with the conditions of the bequest.

The defendant objected to the offer of a book of church records on the ground that it was not sufficiently authenticated. The facts reported regarding the custody and recognition of the book were sufficient to justify its admission.

The report says that the records of the society meetings were received subject to the defendant's objection and exception "so far as they are hereinafter referred to." The only further reference is to the record of a meeting in which it was voted to accept this bequest, and this record was specially objected to for that the bequest was to the church and not to the society. It is.not necessary to the determination of this question that we consider the findings of the master in regard to the relations of the church and the society. The bequest was not conditioned upon there being any vote of acceptance by the legatee, and proof of such a vote by the society was immaterial and harmless. The only requirement is that the officials or a committee of the church visit and care for the grave, and the report shows that all done in this respect has been done by the officials of the church.

Decree affirmed and cause remanded.

ADEN C. TEMPLETON *v.* CAPITAL SAVINGS BANK & TRUST CO.

January Term, 1903.

Present: TYLER, MUNSON, START, STAFFORD, and HASELTON, JJ.

Opinion filed April 5, 1904.

Attachment—Securing Property—Officer's Fees—Indorsement on Writ—Time of Recovery.

A sheriff may recover directly from the plaintiff his expenses in keeping attached property which the plaintiff released from attachment before the termination of the suit.

The right of a sheriff to recover of the plaintiff his expenses in keeping attached property which the plaintiff released from attachment before the termination of the suit, and his reasonable charges for securing property after the completion of services and the return of the writ, is not dependent upon such items being indorsed on the writ as part of his fees.

A sheriff's charges for securing and keeping the attached property, which the plaintiff has released from attachment, may be recovered of the plaintiff before the termination of the suit in which the attachment issued.

GENERAL ASSUMPSIT by an officer to recover his fees. Plea, the general issue. Trial by court at the September Term, 1902, Washington County, *Watson*, J., presiding. Judgment for the plaintiff. The defendant excepted.

The items in dispute are the following:

Cash paid for feeding six horses, attached at Calais.. $4.00
Cash paid for keeping six horses 67 days at 50 cents
per day for each horse.. ... ... 201.00
Officer's services securing property at Groton.. ... .. 5.00

In respect of these items the court found that subsequent to the making of the attachment, and after the writ was returned and docketed, the attorney of the plaintiff in that suit— the defendant in this—learned that the horses attached were about to be taken into the State of New Hampshire; that thereupon he directed the officer to secure the horses; where-upon the officer went to Groton, with assistance, and took the horses into his possession; that his charge of $5.00 therefor is reasonable, that after the officer had thus taken the horses into his possession, and had been to the expense of $201.00 for their keeping, the attorney for the plaintiff in that suit— of the defendant herein—being convinced.that the horses were covered by valid chattel mortgage held by parties in New Hampshire, directed the officer to release the horses from attachment, which he did and delivered them to said New Hampshire parties. The opinion states the other facts.

J. T. Deavitt and *Edward H. Deavitt* for the defendant.

Senter & Senter for the plaintiff.

A lien is destroyed if possession is surrender. *Jacobs* v. *Latour*, 15 E. C. L. 389; *Johnson* v. *Edson*, 2 Aik. 299; *Felker* v. *Emerson*, 17 Vt. 101.

Officers may recover of the attaching creditor a reasonable sum for time, service and expense incurred in keeping and caring for the property. *Addington* v. *Sexton*, 17 Wis. 337, 84 Am. Dec. 745; *Tarbell* v. *Dickinson*, 3 Cush. 345; *Campbell* v. *Phelps*, 1 Pick. 61.

MUNSON, J. The plaintiff, a deputy sheriff, sues to recover his fees and charges for serving the writ and securing and keeping attached property in a suit brought by the Savings Bank, defendant herein. The officer received the writ from the attorney for the bank, and attached some horses on it by lodging a copy in the clerk's office. After the writ was returned and docketed, he took the property into his possession in pursuance of instructions given him by the attorney. The horses were afterwards demanded by the holders of two chattel mortgages; and the attorney examined these claims, and thereupon directed the officer to release the property from attachment, which was immediately done. The officer's charges for copies and travel, properly itemized, were entered upon the writ when it was returned. His charges for securing and keeping the property have not been indorsed in any form. The suit is still pending.

The defendant claims that an officer's fees and charges are an incident of the suit in which the services are rendered, and cannot, in the absence of an arrangement for earlier payment, be recovered in advance of their adjustment in that suit; that the expense of keeping attached property is a charge against the debtor, and can be recovered of the creditor only upon a special undertaking; that in any event this plaintiff's charges for securing and keeping property cannot be recovered because not indorsed upon the writ.

V. S. 5366 provides that "for securing property attached on mesne process a sheriff * * shall be allowed a reasonable sum as fees, subject to the revision and allowance of the court." V. S. 1111 provides that "the officer serving process shall indorse thereon his fees and charges, * * * otherwise his fees shall not be allowed." The defendant refers to these sections, and cites in connection with them, *Dean* v. *Bailey,* 12 Vt. 142; *Felker* v. *Emerson,* 16 Vt. 653; *Houston* v. *Howard,* 39 Vt. 54; and *Harrington* v. *Hill,* 51 Vt. 44.

It is said in *Dean* v. *Bailey,* that when personal property is attached it is to be kept at the expense of the debtor, and that if the debtor settles with the creditor, so that no execution comes into the officer's hands, the officer may sustain an action against the debtor for the keeping. This case is referred to in *Felker* v. *Emerson* as holding that the rule in regard to property attached on mesne process is the same as that prescribed by the statute in the case of property taken upon execution—that it "shall be safely kept at the expense of the debtor." In *Houston* v. *Howard,* the attaching officer brought trespass against a claimant of the property attached for unlawfully removing it, and was held entitled to recover as damages an amount equal to the debt, costs and interest due upon the execution for the satisfaction of which the property was held. The officer's fees were originally returned in gross, but the items were endorsed before judgment was entered. The defendant insisted that these could not be included, but the court held their allowance proper, at least as against the defendant, he not being a party to the execution and standing in relation to the property as a trespasser. It is held in *Harrington* v. *Hill* that an officer selling property on execution is liable to the execution debtor for money retained as fees when the fees were not itemized in his return.

It is also said of the statute requiring the indorsement, "It can hardly be claimed that this language does not make the indorsement of his fees in the manner specified a condition precedent to his right to demand payment of them from the plaintiff in the process, or to retain them out of money of the defendant which may come into his hands, on the process." In distinguishing the case from *Houston* v. *Howard*, the opinion refers, among other things, to the fact that in that case the officer had amended his return of fees so as to comply with the statute.

On the other hand, the plaintiff cites *Felker* v. *Emerson*, 17 Vt. 101; *McNeil* v. *Bean*, 32 Vt. 429; and *Baldwin* v. *Shaw*, 35 Vt. 273. In the first of these cases, the owner of attached property, who had settled the suit, recovered in trover against the officer, who had refused to give up the property until paid for the keeping. It is said in the opinion that an officer making an attachment is the agent and servant of the plaintiff, and has an imperfect lien upon the property, which will be perfected by the recovery of final judgment, but which may be lost by a failure to prosecute or by the rendition of an adverse judgment; and that if the plaintiff settle the suit the officer will have the same claim upon him for his charges that he would have had if the lien had been lost by a final judgment in favor of the debtor. In *McNeil* v. *Bean*, the avails of the execution sale were applied first in satisfaction of the officer's charges for keeping the property during the pendency of the suit, although they had not been taxed and included in the judgment, and this application was sustained. The court considered that inasmuch as the statute did not expressly require that such costs be taxed, or forbid their payment from the avails of the sale unless so taxed, the general and long continued practice to treat such charges as a lien upon the property when the attaching party recovered judgment, might properly be permitted to determine the construction. The court intimated, however, that there was but little reason for treating these charges differently from other costs, and that but for this practice it might be considered better to require that they be taxed and included in the judgment. In *Baldwin* v. *Shaw,* the officer charged to the creditor the commission allowed for levying an execution, when the property was taken from him by a replevin suit so that there was no sale; and it was claimed that this fee could only be obtained from the avails of property sold. But the court considered that if the creditor employed an officer to do this service, and he was prevented from getting his pay from the proceeds of a sale on execution without fault on his part, the creditor must pay him.

It is evident that this officer has lost the opportunity to obtain his charges from the avails of an execution sale of the property, and this through the act of the bank and without any fault on his part. It seems equally clear that the creditor cannot require the officer to look to the debtor for his pay, when he has deprived the officer of the security which he held for the satisfaction of his claim as against the debtor. It must follow in such a case, whatever the holding may be where the lien is still subsisting, that the officer is entitled to look directly to the plaintiff for the payment of his charges, and that the question of the debtor's liability for the keeping is one for adjustment between the creditor and the debtor.

We are next to inquire whether the officer's recovery of the expense of the keeping is dependent upon its being returned as a part of his fees. Our latest discussion regarding the recovery of fees is that contained in *Harrington* v. *Hill,* and the views there expressed may seem inconsistent with the result arrived at in the earlier case of *McNeil* v. *Bean.* But it does not appear that the charges in *Harrington* v. *Hill* included anything for the care of property, and if they did not there is nothing in the case that conflicts with *McNeil* v. *Bean*. In the latter case the court stated the defendant's claim to be that charges for keeping are like other taxable costs, which cannot be taken out of the avails of the sale unless taxed and included in the judgment; and the disposition of the case was a distinct holding that these are not like other costs. If held to be different from other costs as regards a satisfaction through the lien, we see no reason for holding otherwise when demand is made of the plaintiff upon his discharge of the lien. The practice spoken of in *McNeil* v. *Bean* has now continued under the sanction of that opinion nearly half a century longer, and the reasons then advanced in support of the construction adopted must be quite as potent in favor of a retention of that construction. There has been no change in the phraseology of the statute upon which to base a change of holding.

But the charges considered in *McNeil* v. *Bean* were for the keeping of property. Included in the plaintiff's bill is a separate item for securing the property. This was for assistance in taking possession of the property subsequent to the making of the attachment and the return of the writ. The law formerly provided that certain classes of personal property, not easily removable, might be attached by lodging a copy of the writ in the clerk's office, but in all other cases it was necessary to take the property into possession. G. S. ch. 33, §§ 25, 27. As the law now stands all personal property may be attached by copy, and it is provided that when property has been attached by copy, the officer "shall thereafter remove the property so attached or take it into his possession whenever the care, safety or preservation of the property so requires." V. S. 1103, 1105. The statute seems to admit of a reasonable distinction between the securing of property to perfect the attachment, and the securing of it subsequent to the completion of the service. In the latter case it is done in the necessary care of the property, and naturally goes with the keeping rather than with the service. The justness of this distinction is also indicated by the fact that the writ is not in the officer's hands when the subsequent charges accrue. We hold that charges incurred in securing property subsequent to the completion of the service and return of the writ, may be recovered without having been indorsed.

It remains to inquire whether the suit is premature. It is a frequent, and perhaps the usual, practice of officers to leave their right to demand payment from the creditor in abeyance until the termination of the suit, and if the plaintiff recovers and execution issues, to deduct their fees and charges from the amount collected. The language of some of our opinions is evidently due to the court's recognition of this practice; but we find no intimation in any case that the officer cannot proceed against the creditor until the suit is ended. If there is any exception as regards charges for the keeping of property still under attachment, the charges in this case are not within it. It is plainly implied in *Carlisle* v. *Soule*, 44 Vt. 265, and in *Dix* v. *Batchelder*, 55 Vt. 562, that an officer may require the payment of his fees before taking a writ for service. If the officer may insist upon having his fees in advance, it may well be held that when he waives this right he is entitled to demand his fees as soon as the work is done. There is nothing in a waiver of prepayment that can justify the inference of an agreement to wait until the final determination of the suit. It is not necessary that the officer await the event of the suit in order that his fees may be approved by taxation if the plaintiff recovers. It is evident that in speaking of an allowance by the court, the statute does not refer solely to an allowance by the court where the suit is pending. The amount of fees recoverable can be ascertained in any court where the question arises, as will be seen by a reference to our cases where fees have been collected or over-charges recovered. Even when the fees have been taxed and allowed against the debtor, this is not treated as a conclusive determination of the amount as between the officer and the creditor. *Johnson v. Burnham,* 22 Vt. 639. We find no obstacle in the way of a present recovery.

Judgment affirmed.

I. N. Chase *v.* H. S. Soule.

January Term, 1904.

Present: Rowell, C. J., Tyler, Munson, Watson, and Stafford, JJ.

Opinion filed April 29, 1904.

Contract of Indemnity—Consideration—Common Owners of Personalty—Rights of Co-Owners.

The plaintiff and defendant become common owners of a stallion when the former sells the latter a half interest therein, and it is agreed that the plaintiff shall have the possession and management of the property; that each is to share equally in all expenses and in the profits and losses; and that when either is dissatisfied the plaintiff is to propose what he will give for the defendant's interest or take for his own.

One of two co-owners of personal property cannot sell the other's interest therein without his consent.

Although the plaintiff and the defendant were co-owners of a horse, the fact that the defendant requested the plaintiff, who was anxious to accept an offer to purchase the animal, to refuse the offer, and when asked on cross-examination if plaintiff had the right to dispose of the horse, said, "I suppose so," tends to show that at the time of said offer he understood that the plaintiff had the right to sell the horse.

SPECIAL ASSUMPSIT on a contract of indemnity. Pleas, the general issue, and declaration in offset. Trial by jury at the March Term, 1901, Chittenden County, *Start*, J., presiding. Verdict and judgment for the plaintiff. The defendant excepted.

This case was argued in the Supreme Court at the May Term, 1903. At the January Term, 1904, upon an order to that effect, it was again argued upon the question, "was it claimed by the plaintiff, at the trial, that the defendant gave him authority to sell the horse, or that there was any agreement between them to that effect?"

At the time defendant purchased the half interest in the stallion and took a bill of sale thereof, the parties made and executed the following agreement:

"It is further understood and agreed that I, H. S. Soule, shall pay for Marion Wilkes' keeping while he is standing in the stud at I. N. Chase's stable, one-half of five dollars as my share, and one-half of other necessary expenses and while he is campaigning I shall share equally the expense, and share equally the profits or loss from service fees and what is earned, if any, while he is campaigning, and when either is dissatisfied, said I. N. Chase shall say what he will give or take for the other's interest."

The opinion states the other facts.

W. H. Fairchild and *Brigham & Start* for the defendant.

The title to this property was a tenancy in common. The parties had formed a non-trading partnership. The plaintiff could not sell the defendant's interest in the horse without his consent. Hence there was no consideration for the defendant's promise of indemnity. *Goell* v. *Morse*, 126 Mass. 480; *Walker's Admr.* v. *Walker's Est.*, 66 Vt. 285; *Dowling* v. *Ex. Banks*, 145 U. S. 512; *Smith* v. *Sloan*, 19 Am. Rep. 757; *Fudge* v. *Bashnell*, 26 Am. Rep. 183; *Welch* v. *Clark*, 12 Vt. 681; *Irwin* v. *Williar*, 110 U. S. 497; *Ham* v. *Newton City Bk.*, 32 Kan. 522; *Blaker* v. *Sands*, 29 Kan. 551; *M'Nair* v. *Wilcox*, 121 Pa. 437, 126 Mass. 470.

A promise to do what one is bound by law to do is *nudum pactum.* 20 Mass. 93; 64 Vt. 387; 40 Vt. 25; 67 Am. St. 271; 77 Am. Dec. 685; 127 Mass. 31; 21 Atl. 749.

V. A. Bullard and *R. E. Brown* for the plaintiff.

The contract in question is one of indemnity. *Beanon* v. *Russell*, 20 Vt. 205; *Carr* v. *Whaley*, 23 Ala. 821.

The consideration of defendant's promise was that plaintiff should not accept the offer for the horse; that he should not insist that the horse be sold; that the defendant should have the right to sell the horse when he saw fit; the plaintiff gave up his right to terminate the horse contract by an offer to give or take.

The promises between the plaintiff and defendant were mutual and concurrent, the plaintiff to refrain from selling the horse or insisting that he be sold, the defendant to save the plaintiff from loss for so doing. Mutual promises are sufficient consideration for each other. *Sinclaire* v. *Blanchard*, 17 Vt. 464; *Black* v. *Peck*, 11 Vt. 484; *Hildreth* v. *Academy*, 29 N. H. 227; *Perry* v. *Blackmore*, 32 Vt. 7; *Weilds* v. *Nichols*, 17 Pick. 538.

TYLER, J. In February, 1895, the defendant purchased of the plaintiff, for five hundred dollars, a half interest in a trotting stallion then owned by the plaintiff and of which, by the mutual understanding of the parties, the plaintiff was to have the possession and management. A bill of sale was given by the plaintiff to the defendant, and at the same time and as part of the transaction, the parties made and signed an agreement in respect to paying the expenses of keeping the horse, which agreement contained a clause providing that if either party should become dissatisfied the plaintiff should propose what sum he would give for the defendant's interest or take for his own.

In the following August the plaintiff claimed to have received an offer of six thousand dollars for the horse which he desired to accept. The defendant was opposed to the sale, wished to hold the horse for a higher price, and verbally guaranteed that the plaintiff should suffer no loss if he refused the offer. On the same occasion the defendant loaned the plaintiff sixteen hundred dollars, the latter being in want of money and having expected to obtain it from a sale of the horse. In consideration of the guaranty the plaintiff refused the offer. In February, 1896, at the plaintiff's suggestion the defendant drew up and signed a writing as evidence of the loan and guaranty, and the defendant then, as a part of that transaction, cancelled the stipulation in the former writing in respect to the offer to "give or take." The parties continued common owners of the horse until January, 1900, when, having become nearly worthless, he was sold at auction by the plaintiff for eighty dollars.

The plaintiff sues upon the verbal guaranty, alleging in his declaration the common ownership, the offer of six thousand dollars, his authority and right to sell for himself and the defendant, the defendant's request that the offer be rejected, the guaranty, the rejection of the offer at the defendant's request and in reliance upon the guaranty, and the consequent loss and damage.

The defense was that the professed offer was fictitious and that the guaranty was obtained by fraud. This was the only question of fact submitted to the jury in relation to the guaranty.

The defendant submitted four requests to the court for instructions to the jury, but only the following one need be considered here:

"That the plaintiff had no legal right to sell the horse, and that his agreeing not to do what he had no legal right to do was no consideration for an undertaking or promise on the part of the defendant."

The case comes here upon the defendant's exceptions to the refusal of the court to direct a verdict and to comply with his requests to charge.

The plaintiff's foregoing the offer of six thousand dollars for the horse was a sufficient consideration for the defendant's guaranty, if the plaintiff, from the nature of the ownership, had a legal right to make the sale, or if the defendant, at some time during the ownership, had given him such authority.

The parties were common owners of the horse, and neither could sell his co-tenant's interest without the other's consent. *Goell* v. *Morse,* 126 Mass. 480; *Walker's Admr.* v. *Walker,* 66 Vt. 285, 29 Atl. 146; *Irwin* v. *Williar,* 110 U. S. 499; *Dowling* v. *Banks,* 145 U. S. 512. The guaranty, therefore, was without a consideration resting upon the ground of a legal right in the plaintiff to make the sale because of the common ownership. It was a guaranty to the plaintiff against loss for refusing an offer that he had no legal right to accept. The plaintiff does not controvert this rule of law, but contends that the facts in the case show that the defendant gave him authority.

It was competent for the plaintiff to prove, under the allegations in the declaration, that the defendant, at some time during the common ownership, gave him authority to sell the horse. Upon an examination of the record we cannot say that conferred authority was not claimed by the plaintiff, nor that there was no evidence to support such claim, though neither party testified directly to that fact. The fact that the defendant requested the plaintiff not to sell the horse and gave him a guaranty against loss if he would refuse the offer of six thousand dollars tended to show that he then understood that the plaintiff had a right to make the sale, either because he had given him authority, or that such authority was incident to the common ownership. Presumably he would not have made the request and given the guaranty if he had understood that the plaintiff had no right to make the sale. His action was consistent with the idea of authority acquired by the plaintiff by law or by the defendant's consent. The defendant's answer, "I suppose so," to the cross-question, whether Chase had the right to enter the horse for races or dispose of him, also tended in the same direction.

The request to charge was not sound because the evidence referred to was in the case and tended to show that the plaintiff derived authority from the defendant to make the sale, and the record does not show that it was not so claimed in argument. For the same reason the court could not have complied with the defendant's motion for a verdict.

Judgment affirmed.

T. E. ANGELL v. E. R. FLETCHER, ET AL.

October Term, 1903.

Present: ROWELL, C. J., TYLER, MUNSON, START, WATSON, and
HASELTON, JJ.

Opinion filed April 29, 1904.

Ejectment by Mortgagor—Possession—Eviction—Sufficiency of Evidence—Certified Execution—V. S. 1505.

In an action of ejectment the evidence recited in the opinion is sufficient to support a finding that the plaintiff took possession of the premises and was ejected by the defendant.

When the plaintiff prevails in an action of ejectment by a mortgagee against the mortgagor, a certified execution may issue.

V. S. 1505, prohibiting an execution to issue against the body, has reference only to the action for betterments.

EJECTMENT by a mortgagee. Plea, the general issue. Trial by court at the March Term, 1903, Washington County, *Start*, J., presiding. Judgment for the plaintiff. The defendant excepted.

Upon the evidence recited in the opinion the court found that the plaintiff had taken possession of the premises, and had been evicted by the defendant, and rendered judgment for the plaintiff for the seizin and possession of the premises, and against Fletcher and the Kimballs, for $155.36, as damages by way of mesne profits and costs; and adjudged that the cause of action arose from the wilful and malicious act of the defendants, and that they ought to be confined in close jail. Thereupon the defendant applied for an order staying execution, on the ground that the plaintiff claimed title to the premises by a deed of mortgage, the condition of which had not been performed, under V. S. 1493-1494, and asked to have the sum equitably due the plaintiff on said mortgage ascertained. Whereupon the court did ascertain the sum so equitably due the plaintiff, and made an order as to the times the several instalments thereof should be paid, which, if complied with would stay execution, and if complied with in full, the judgment for possession, damages and costs be vacated.

The defendant claimed there was no evidence to support the finding that plaintiff was ever in possession, or that he was evicted by the defendants, or any evidence upon which to base a close jail execution, and excepted to the judgment of the court in those respects. The opinion states the other facts.

Bullard and *Morse* for the defendants.

There is no evidence that plaintiff took possession. Possession should be taken by a distinct and unequivocal act. *Hopper* v. *Wilson*, 12 Vt. 695.

There was no evidence in the case that at the time suit was brought the defendants were rightfully in possession. Rob. Dig. Vol. 1, p. 465, § 52.

Taylor & Dutton for the plaintiff.

The judgment for seizin and possession was right. After condition broken a mortgagee is entitled to possession. *Wilson* v. *Hooper, et al.*, 13 Vt. 653; *Morey, Admr.* v. *McGuire*, 4 Vt. 327; *Lull* v. *Matthews*, 19 Vt. 322; *Langdon* v. *Paul*, 22 Vt. 205; *Hager* v. *Brainerd et als.*, 44 Vt. 294; *Fuller* v. *Eddy*, 49 Vt. 11; *Hamblet* v. *Bliss*, 55 Vt. 535; *Oakman* v. *Walker*, 69 Vt. 345; V. S. 1498; *Pierce* v. *Brown*, 24 Vt. 165.

Ejectment is a tort action, and properly followed by a certified execution. No actual malice need be found. *Sheeran* v. *Rockwood*, 67 Vt. 82; *Barnes* v. *Tenney*, 52 Vt. 557;

Boutwell v. *Harriman*, 58 Vt. 516; *Judd* v. *Ballard*, 66 Vt. 668; *Mullen* v. *Flanders*, 73 Vt. 95.

The awarding of a certified execution is matter of discretion. *Smith* v. *Wilcox*, 47 Vt. 537; *Hill* v. *Cox*, 54 Vt. 627; *Soule* v. *Austin*, 35 Vt. 515; *Sartwell* v. *Soules, et al.*, 72 Vt. 270.

MUNSON, J. The action is ejectment. The plaintiff is a mortgagee who claims to have taken possession of the mortgaged premises after condition broken. The defendants claimed on trial that there was no evidence tending to show that the plaintiff was ever in possession or was evicted by defendants, and excepted to the order granting a close jail certificate.

It appeared that one McKinstry had been looking after the house for defendant Fletcher, the mortgagor, and had had charge of the key, and that plaintiff had got the key of him two or three times before the occasion in question to go in and look the house over. The plaintiff testified that on the last occasion he merely asked for the key, without saying what he wanted it for or promising to return it; that he unlocked the door and went into the house, having with him one McCloskey, to whom he then and there rented the house and delivered the key; that he saw a stove in the house, but nothing else; that they took nothing out of the house and put nothing in; that two or three days later he went there and found the house occupied by defendants Kimball as tenants of defendant Fletcher. McKinstry, after giving his version of the procurement of the key, testified that he went to the place where plaintiff had left the key on previous occasions, and did not find it, and that he got it from somebody afterwards. There was no evidence, except as it may be gathered from the above statement, tending to show that any

of the defendants, or McKinstry, knew what the plaintiff and
McCloskey had done at the house as above stated. The court
found that the plaintiff took possession of the premises and
was evicted by the defendants. It is thought by a majority,
the writer of the opinion dissenting, that there was evidence
tending to show a sufficient taking of possession by the plaintiff and eviction by the defendants. This being so, the finding of the court below is conclusive, and the case presented
is one in which a close jail certificate could properly be
granted.

The claim that the granting of a certified execution is
prohibited by V. S. 1505 is based upon a misapprehension
as to its meaning. The judgment there referred to is that
rendered in the action for betterments provided for in sections 1501-2, and the defendant referred to is the defendant
in the declaration for betterments. This will be made plain
by a reference to the first section of the betterment act of
1800, which contains the provisions as they stood before revision.

Judgment affirmed.

HARRIET A. HARE *v.* THE CONGREGATIONAL SOCIETY OF
FERRISBURG.

October Term, 1903.

Present: ROWELL, C. J., TYLER, MUNSON, START, WATSON, and
STAFFORD, JJ.

Opinion filed April 29, 1904.

*Wills—Consideration—Life Estate with Power to Sell—In-
terest of Remainderman.*

A bequest to two persons, and the survivor of them, of the use of
certain estate, with the power of sale by them, or the survivor of

them, of as much of the estate as may be needed for their support, should the use prove insufficient, with remainder over to the defendant, gives the defendant a vested remainder in said estate, which is liable to be divested by the exercise of the power of sale, but which cannot be divested in any other manner.

When a testator bequeathed to his wife and daughters the use of his estate for life with remainder, subject to a power of sale in two of the life tenants, over to the defendant, the third life tenant, in respect of her having temporarily waived her right to share in the estate so that a sale of the property was thereby avoided, was a mere volunteer as to the defendant, and is not entitled to an equitable lien on the property as against defendant's remainder interest.

APPEAL IN CHANCERY. Heard on demurrer to the bill at the June Term, 1903, Addison County, *Haselton,* Chancellor. Demurrer sustained and bill dismissed. The orator appealed. The opinion states the case.

Brown & Taft for the orator.

The Court of Chancery alone has jurisdiction of the subject matter of this bill. The Probate Court does not have general equity powers. *Mann* v. *Mann's Est.,* 53 Vt. 55; *Goff* v. *Robinson,* 60 Vt. 641; *Davis* v. *Eastman,* 66 Vt. 651; *Heirs of Adams* v. *Adams,* 22 Vt. 50; *Leonard* v. *Leonard's Exr.,* 67 Vt. 318.

The Court of Chancery has exclusive jurisdiction of equitable liens. Pomeroy Eq. Jur. (2 ed.) Vol. 1, §§ 137, 165.

E. J. Ormsbee and *Joel C. Baker* for the defendant.

The Court of Chancery has nothing to do with the settlement of decedent's estate in this state. *Angus* v. *Robinson,* 62 Vt. 60; *Blair* v. *Johnson,* 64 Vt. 598; *Re Hodge's Estate,* 63 Vt. 661; *School Dist.* v. *Sheldon,* 71 Vt. 95; *Bickford* v.

Bickford, 68 Vt. 525; *Boomhower* v. *Babbitt,* 67 Vt. 327; *Mitchell* v. *Blanchard,* 72 Vt. 85; *Ward* v. *Congregational Soc.,* 66 Vt. 490.

Only the donees of the power of sale could affect the defendant's interest. *Cheney's Exr.* v. *Stafford,* 76 Vt. 16.

MUNSON, J. George P. Fraser bequeathed to his wife Harriet and his daughter Rebecca, and to the survivor of them, the use of all his estate; and authorized a sale by them, or the survivor of them, of as much of the estate as might be needed for their support, if the use proved insufficient. This bequest was subject to the further provision that if his daughter Harriet should become a widow, she should share equally with his wife and daughter Rebecca in the use of his estate during the time she remained a widow. The defendant is the residuary legatee.

The daughter Harriet, the oratrix, became a widow about two years after the testator's death, and remained such until after the death of her mother and sister, which occurred some years later. The estate consisted of a small farm, and the mother and daughter Rebecca carried this on; but the income was insufficient for their support, and the oratrix temporarily waived her right to a share of it. The power of sale conferred upon the deceased devisees not having been exercised, the oratrix prays that a sale be now decreed, and that the proceeds be applied in liquidation of her interest thus waived and contributed. The right to have this done is claimed upon the ground of an equitable lien.

The will gave defendant a vested remainder in this property, which was liable to be devested by an exercise of the power of sale conferred upon the holders of the life estate. It could be defeated in no other manner. The donees of the power could not charge the defendant's interest by a lien of

any description. Nor can the court subject it to a lien upon
any general ground of equity. An equitable lien arises only
where there is some personal obligation or duty to be enforced. If the facts alleged are such that the law can imply
an obligation of repayment on the part of the deceased devisees, this affords no basis upon which the interest of the
defendant can be reached. The failure to exercise the power
of sale, although beneficial to the defendant, was not due to
any action on its part; and as to the defendant the oratrix
must be considered a mere volunteer.

Decree affirmed and cause remanded.

SADIE FOSS *v.* ISAAC STANTON.

January Term, 1903.

Present: TYLER, MUNSON, START, STAFFORD, and HASELTON, JJ.

Opinion filed May 16, 1904.

Landlord and Tenant—Covenant to Repair—Justice Eject-
ment—Life Tenancy—Real Covenants—Right of As-
signee—Breach Before Assignment.

The proceeding given by V. S. 1560, and commonly called "justice
ejectment," is available though the tenancy be for life, provided
it is created by contract.

When by the terms of a lease the lessee is to keep the premises in
good repair, a notice to repair given by the landlord to the tenant
need not state the particulars and extent of the repairs required.

A lessee's duty to the lessor under a covenant in the lease requiring
the lessee to keep the premises in good repair, is measured by the
condition of the property at the beginning of the term.

A lessee's duty to the assignee of the lessor, under a covenant in the
    lease requiring the lessee to keep the premises in good repair, is
    measured by the condition of the property at the time of the
    transfer.

A covenant by a tenant to keep the premises in good repair runs with
    the land, and though the assignee of the lessor can maintain an
    action for a breach accruing after the transfer, he cannot do so
    for one which occurred before.

JUSTICE EJECTMENT. Plea, the general issue. Trial
by court at the September Term, 1902, Washington County,
Watson, J., presiding. Judgment for the plaintiff. The defendant excepted. The opinion states the facts.

J. P. Lamson for the defendant.

Frank Plumley and *John G. Wing* for the plaintiff.

No notice to quit is necessary. *Chamberlain* v. *Dona-
hue*, 45 Vt. 50; *Rich* v. *Bolton*, 46 Vt. 84.

The plaintiff had the title when the suit was begun, and
when it was tried. This is sufficient to enable him to maintain an action. *Beach* v. *Beach*, 20 Vt. 83; *Edgerton* v. *Clark*,
20 Vt. 264; *Gibson* v. *Seymour*, 3 Vt. 565.

MUNSON, J. The defendant is in possession under a
written instrument by which the premises were let to him
and his wife "to hold for the term of their and each of their
natural lives." The proceeding is that ordinarily spoken of
as justice ejectment. We have no case of this kind where
the tenancy in question was for more than a term of years.
The defendant contends that the remedy is not available when
the tenancy is for life.

There is nothing in the language of the statute that suggests any distinction between tenancies. The remedy is given
when one in possession of demised premises under a written or

parol lease remains in possession, without right, after the determination of the lease by its own limitation, or after the breach of a stipulation contained in the lease. The relation of landlord and tenant is that which subsists by virtue of a contract for the possession of lands, at will, for a definite period, or for life. The contract employed in the creation of this relation is called a lease, and with reference to this the parties are designated as lessor and lessee. Tenancies for years and for life may both be created by will, and in such cases the statute would apply to neither. The distinction called for by the statute is not between tenancies for life and lesser estates, but between tenancies created by contract and those arising otherwise.

We find nothing in our decisions that suggests a different view. It is said that the proceeding is analogous to, and contains all the elements of, an action of ejectment; that it is given as a summary remedy for the recovery of demised premises, and is designed to avoid the expense and delay attendant upon the prosecution of an action of ejectment; that it is available only against one whose rightful possession was that of a technical lessee, and who remains in possession after the expiration or forfeiture of his lease. *Middlebury College* v. *Lawton,* 23 Vt. 688; *Hadley* v. *Havens,* 24 Vt. 520; *Davis* v. *Hemenway,* 27 Vt. 589; *Pitkin* v. *Burch,* 48 Vt. 521; *Baldwin* v. *Skeels,* 51 Vt. 121.

The question here is whether the lease has been forfeited. The only breach relied upon is the failure to repair the buildings. The lessees covenanted, among other things, to keep the premises in good repair, and surrender them at the end of the term in the same condition as when taken, ordinary wear and providential damage excepted. It was further provided that if the lessees should refuse for the space

of three months to fulfill the covenant of the lease, the lessors
might re-enter. More than three months before the bringing
of the suit, the plaintiff notified the defendant to repair the
buildings or quit the premises.

The plaintiff holds the reversionary interest by virtue of
a quit-claim deed from Dorman W. and Wilma M. Cole, executed October 6, 1900. The lease was given by the Coles
September 21, 1891. The shed was so far gone at the date
of the lease that it was not worth repairing. The house and
barn were then old and very much out of repair, and they
have since grown gradually worse as a natural result of that
condition. The roof of the house became more and more
dilapidated, and leaked badly. The window lights became
loose because of the condition of the putty, and let in the
cold. The sills of the barn rotted away, and the floor of the
stable pitched towards the manger. The defendant made no
repairs on the buildings before the suit, except to put two or
three planks in the stable.

It was not necessary to the sufficiency of the notice that
it state the particulars and extent of the repairs required. The
notice given called, in legal effect, for such repairs as it was
the lessee's duty to make under the provisions of the lease.
All parties in interest are supposed to know the effect of the
covenants, and the lessee was to determine for himself
whether, and how far, he had come short of meeting the requirement.

The covenant was to keep the premises in good repair—
not to put and leave them in good repair. The lessee's duty
to the lessor under this covenant is to be measured by the condition of the property when taken. But when the lessor takes
no advantage of a failure to keep in repair, and afterwards
conveys his interest, the lessee's duty to the assignee is to

be measured by the condition of the property at the time of the transfer. The covenant to repair runs with the land, and the plaintiff can sue for any breach occurring after she took the title. But the deed gave her no right to proceed for a prior breach. Neither a right of entry nor a right of action can be transferred. Co. Cop. § 60. *Trask* v. *Wheeler,* 7 Allen 109.

The plaintiff acquired the reversion in October, 1900, and brought this suit in February, 1901. The case finds the condition of the buildings at the date of the lease, nine years before, describes a subsequent gradual deterioration, and gives in detail the resulting impairments. But the case does not show when these conditions were reached with reference to the date of the plaintiff's deed, and nothing appears from which it can be said that the deterioration subsequent to the transfer was more than the ordinary wear of buildings such as these were at the time of the transfer. The plaintiff's notice, given twelve days after she received her deed, was in effect a requirement that the defendant make good the failure to keep in repair during the years preceding her acquirement of the reversion. The defendant's failure to do this did not constitute a breach for which the plaintiff can claim a forfeiture.

Judgment reversed and judgment for defendant.

Town of Searsburg *v.* Town of Woodford.

January Term, 1904.

Present: Rowell, C. J., Tyler, Munson, Start, Watson, Stafford, and
Haselton, JJ.

Opinion filed May 21, 1904.

Towns—Boundaries—Prescription Line—V. S. Chap. 140.

Although the lines of our states cannot be changed by prescription or
    otherwise, without the consent of Congress, if thereby the political
    power and influence of the state enlarged would be increased, yet,
    where the running of a boundary line has no such effect, a line
    may be established by prescription, though variant from the orig-
    inal grant.

The proceeding given by V. S. Chap. 140, for establishing town lines,
    confines this Court to locating and establishing the true division
    line,—the charter line—between the towns.

It is doubtful whether, under the Constitution of this State, the Legis-
    lature can confer upon the judiciary the power to establish any
    division line between towns other than the charter line.

Petition brought to the Supreme Court for Bennington
County at its October Term, 1901, under V. S. Chap. 140,
for the establishment of the division line between the towns
of Searsburg and Woodford. Heard at the January Term,
1904, on report of commissioners. The opinion states the
facts.

O. E. Butterfield and *Waterman & Martin* for the petitioner.

The authority of the commissioners is confined to locating the charter line. *Elphick* v. *Hoffman,* 49 Conn. 331.

The rule as to prescriptive rights does not apply to towns
or other political bodies. *R. I.* v. *Mass.,* 15 Pet. 233; *Hacker*
v. *Sterling,* 36 Pa. St. 423; *Corinth* v. *Newbury,* 13 Vt. 496;

White v. *Fuller*, 38 Vt. 193; *State* v. *Young*, 46 Vt. 565; *Goodman* v. *Myrick*, 5 Or. 65; *Edwards County* v. *White County*, 85 Ill. 390; *Hubbard* v. *Newton*, 52 Vt. 346; *Somerset* v. *Glastenbury*, 61 Vt. 449; *Pitman* v. *Albany*, 34 N. H. 577; *Greenville* v. *Mason*, 57 N. H. 385; *Freeman* v. *Kenney*, 15 Pick. 44; *Middleboro* v. *Taunton*, 2 Cush. 406.

There is no Statute of Limitation applying to this proceeding. *State Treasurer* v. *Weeks*, 4 Vt. 215.

Batchelder & 'Bates for the petitionee.

The line so long acquiesced in should be established as the division line. *Rhode Island* v. *Massachusetts*, 4 Pet. 261; *Handon* v. *Russell*, 28 N. H. 3; *Proprietors of Enfield* v. *Day*, 2 N. H. 520; *Chatham's Petition*, 18 N. H. 227; *Wells* v. *Iron Co.*, 48 N. H. 491; *State* v. *Young*, 46 Vt. 565.

The petitioner and petitionee are in the same county, so neither the county nor the state are affected. *Kellogg* v. *Smith*, 7 Cush. 375; *Shenney* v. *Waltham*, 8 Cush. 327; *Forest River Lead Co.* v. *Salem*, 165 Mass. 193.

ROWELL, C. J.   This is a petition to this Court under chapter 140 of the Vermont Statutes, for the appointment of commissioners to locate and establish the division line between said towns. Commissioners were appointed at a former term, and make their report at this term, in which they locate and establish the division line between said towns where it is fixed by their charters, "unless the court should hold as matter of law that the line to which said towns have heretofore claimed and exercised jurisdiction must control, and that the line fixed by the charters must give way to said line of claim and occupation." As to this occupation line, the commissioners find that a little over a hundred rods east of said charter line, and nearly parallel with it, there is an ancient line of marked trees, made some hundred and thirty years ago, traceable through the town of Searsburg as they find it, and part way through the town of Readsboro on the south, and into the town of Somerset on the north; that for a great many years, and for so long a time that no witness could recollect otherwise, the parties hereto and their inhabitants have recognized said last-mentioned line as the town line, and that in Searsburg the allotments of the town were made to said line, and that Woodford had maintained the highways to said line, and placed all the land west of it in her grand list, and collected taxes thereon, and that the deeds of conveyance of lands between said lines had been recorded in the town clerk's office in Woodford, and that said easterly line had been recognized in all ways as the true town line, and had never been questioned by Searsburg in any legal proceeding until this petition was brought.

The defendant claims that Searsburg cannot now be allowed to claim that the jurisdictional line, so long acquiesced in by her, shall be rejected and the charter line set up, because Woodford has acquired a prescriptive right to the jurisdictional line, which, therefore, ought to be established as the division line.

It is undoubtedly true as a general proposition that the doctrine of prescription is applicable to boundary lines between independent states and nations as well as between individuals. *Indiana* v. *Kentucky,* 136 U. S. 479; *Virginia* v. *Tennessee,* 148 U. S. 503. But the lines of our states cannot be changed by prescription nor otherwise without the consent of Congress, if thereby the political power and influence of the state enlarged would be increased, and thus the full and free exercise of Federal authority be encroached upon. *Virginia* v. *Tennessee,* 148 U. S. 503, 520. And this consent is necessary because the Federal Constitution provides that no state shall, without the consent of Congress, enter into any agreement or compact with another state. But the running of a boundary may have no effect upon the political influence of either state; it may simply serve to mark and define that which actually existed before, but was undefined and unmarked. In that case an agreement for running the line, or its actual survey, would in no respect displace the relation of either state to the general government, and therefore would not require the consent of Congress. In those circumstances, a line that had been run out, located, and marked upon the earth, and afterwards recognized and acquiesced in by the parties for a long time, would be conclusive, even if it were ascertained to be somewhat variant from the courses given in the original grant; and the line so established would take effect, not as an alienation of territory, but as a definition of the true and ancient boundary. *Virginia* v. *Tennessee,* 148 U. S. 503, 520, 522.

But we think that the statute under which this proceeding is brought, confines the Court to locating and establishing the true division line, the charter line, between the towns. It provides that selectmen, when instructed by a vote in town meeting to cause any "division line of the town to be located," shall notify the selectmen of other towns interested, to meet to agree upon such line; that if the line is not thus agreed upon, a petition may be brought to this Court for the appointment of commissioners "to establish the line," who shall hear the parties and "establish such line"; and that if their report is accepted, the selectmen of either town may cause it, and the judgment of the Court thereon, to be lodged for record in the clerk's office of the several towns, and that thereupon the line so established shall be the division line between such towns.

It seems clear that the statute contemplates that the charter line is the one to be located and established; not necessarily absolutely and precisely according to the charter, which might in some cases be quite impracticable and perhaps impossible, but as nearly according to the charter as it reasonably can be. And indeed the statute received substantially that construction in *Somerset v. Glastenbury,* 61 Vt. 449, 17 Atl. 748. There it was objected that it was the duty of the commissioners to establish the true line, the line as originally located, and that the report should show that they had done so; but that from anything in the report they might have established the line, not where it was, but where they thought it ought to be. But the Court said they had performed the duty imposed upon them by the statute; that they had heard the parties, their witnesses and counsel, and as the result of such hearing and their own personal examination of the premises, had made up their minds as to the true location of the line and established it accordingly, which was just what the statute contemplated, and that it was hard to see how they could have followed more closely both its letter and its spirit.

A line so established would take effect, not as a transfer of territory, though somewhat variant from the charter line, but as a definition of that line.

There is another thing that makes strongly against giving the statute a broader construction. The Constitution confers upon the Legislature the power to "constitute towns, boroughs, cities, and counties," and this power necessarily includes the power to alter their boundary lines at pleasure. But this power is essentially political and governmental and not judicial, and the Constitution provides that "the legislative, executive and judiciary departments shall be separate and distinct, so that neither exercise the powers properly belonging to the other." Any substantial change of the charter boundaries of towns would necessarily enlarge or diminish their municipal jurisdiction, and to that extent would constitute an amendment of their charters. It has been held that the Legislature cannot delegate this power to the judicial courts. That the courts can determine what are the corporate limits already established, and whether what are claimed by the authorities to be such limits are such, and may inquire whether the Legislature has exceeded its authority, all which implies an existing law applicable to the matter in hand, and an administration of that law; but that for the courts to change charter boundaries would be, not to declare rights under the law, but to make a law, amending and changing a previous statute as to the extent of territory over which the particular municipal government shall obtain. *City of Galesburg* v. *Hawkinson,* 75 Ill. 152; *People* v. *Town of Nevada,* 6 Cal. 143; 1 Dill. Municip. Corp. § 183. See, also, Cooley's Const. Lim., 6th ed., 119, note 1.

It being doubtful, therefore, to say the least, whether the Legislature can delegate to the judicial courts the power materially to change the charter boundaries of towns, the statute will not be construed as intending to do that, in the absence of language clearly indicating such intent.

Judgment that the report of the commissioners is accepted; that the charter line therein established as the division line between the towns is, and shall be, the division line between them; and that the petitioner recover its costs.

TOWN OF READSBORO *v.* TOWN OF WOODFORD.

January Term, 1904.

Present: ROWELL, C. J., TYLER, MUNSON, START, WATSON, STAFFORD, and HASELTON, JJ.

Opinion filed May 31, 1904.

Towns—Corporate Existence—Charter—Legalized by Acquiescence.

When a town has for more than one hundred years, with the consent of the State, assumed and exercised the powers and privileges of a town, the validity of its charter cannot be questioned.

PETITION brought to the Supreme Court for Bennington County at its October Term, 1901, under V. S. Chap. 140, for the establishment of the division line between the towns of Readsboro and Woodford. Heard at the January Term, 1904, on report of commissioners.

The line in controversy and the questions in respect thereof are the same as in *Town of Searsburg* v. *Town of Woodford, ante.* The opinion states the facts.

O. E. Butterfield and *Waterman & Martin* for the petitioner.

Batchelder & Bates for the petitionee.

ROWELL, C. J. The case is essentially like *Searsburg* v. *Woodford, ante,* except that here the validity of the plaintiff's charter, which covers the disputed strip, is called in question. Said charter was granted on the 24th day of April, 1770, to John Reade and his associates, by Cadwallar Colden, Lieutenant Governor and Commander-in-Chief of the Province of New York, and was signed, "Clarke," and not otherwise, and it does not appear who "Clarke" was. The land granted was thereby created into a township by the name of Readsboro, upon the inhabitants of which were conferred all the powers, authorities, privileges, and advantages theretofore given and granted to, or legally enjoyed by, all, any, or either of the King's other townships within said province; and it was thereby ordained and established that there should be forever thereafter in said township certain officers, elected and chosen yearly out of the inhabitants thereof.

In 1781, a tract of land four miles square was taken from the north end of Readsboro by this State, and created into the town of Searsburg; but the rest of Readsboro has been permitted to remain as chartered by New York.

Readsboro offered in evidence a certified copy of her charter from the office of the Secretary of State of the State of New York, to the admission of which the defendant objected, for that the Colonial Governor of New York could not grant charters of townships in the New Hampshire Grants; and for that said copy was not properly certified, as it bore the signature of "Clarke," instead of the signature of the Lieutenant Governor. But the copy was admitted, and the defendant now objects that said charter is no charter, and can have no force nor effect as such, as it is signed by no authority authorized to grant the same, and that the government of New York, at the time the instrument is dated, had no authority to issue a charter within the territory now constituting Vermont, but was expressly prohibited therefrom by an order of the King in Council; that consequently the boundaries of Readsboro extend only to the line of actual occupation, at least as against any prior occupancy of Woodford; that as far as Readsboro has exercised jurisdiction, it has been recognized as a town, and those boundaries have become fixed; but beyond that it cannot go.

But the defendant cannot attack the legality of Readsboro's charter. When a municipal corporation has assumed
under color of authority, and exercised for a considerable
time with the consent of the state, the powers and privileges
of such corporations, a private party in private litigation cannot question the legality of its existence. 1 Mod. Law Municip. Corp. § 59; 1 Dill. Municip. Corp. 4th ed., § 43a; Cooley,
Const. Lim., 7th ed., 363, 364. This proposition is supported
by all the cases on the subject.

Thus, in *Shapleigh* v. *San Angelo*, 167 U. S. 646, 651,
it is said to be the general rule that the state, being the creator
of municipal corporations, is the proper party to impeach the
validity of their creation; that if the state acquiesces in the
validity of a municipal corporation, its corporate existence
cannot be collaterally attacked. So in *Graham* v. *City of
Greenville*, 67 Texas, 62, 67, it is said that if a municipality
has been illegally constituted, the state alone can take advantage of the fact and in a proceeding instituted for the purpose
of testing the validity of its charter. In *The Inhabitants of
Fredericktown* v. *Fox*, 84 Mo. 59, the defendant offered to
show that the plaintiff was not a corporation. But the court
would not permit it, and said that such a question should be
raised by the state itself, and that a private person cannot
directly nor indirectly usurp this function of the government.

Nor can the state itself question the legality of a municipal charter after long acquiescence in its validity. Thus,
The People v. *Maynard*, 15 Mich. 463, was *quo warranto*
against the defendant for intruding into and usurping the
office of county treasurer, based upon the claimed unconstitu-
tionality of a certain county act. The court said that if the
question had been raised immediately, it was not prepared to
say that it would have been altogether free from difficulty;

but that inasmuch as the state of things in question had been
acted upon for ten years, and been recognized as valid by all
parties interested, it could not be disturbed; that in public
affairs, when the people have organized themselves under
color of law into the ordinary municipal bodies, and have
gone on year after year raising taxes, making improvements,
and exercising the usual franchises of such corporations, their
rights are properly regarded as depending quite as much on
the acquiescence as on the regularity of their origin, and that
the corporate standing of the community could no longer be
open to question. So in *State* v. *Leatherman*, 38 Ark. 81,
the court would not allow the State on *quo warranto* after
nine years of acquiescence to question the legal existence of
a town corporation, the proceedings to incorporate which had
been had before a court without jurisdiction to entertain them.
There are many more cases to the same effect, but it is unnecessary to refer to them.

Readsboro has assumed and exercised the powers and
privileges of a town for more than a hundred years with the
consent of the State, whereof we take judicial notice, as it is
shown by divers public statutes, passed from time to time
since 1797, when, for the first time, she was included by name
in Bennington County as one of the towns thereof. Her charter, therefore, has long since become legalized by recognition
and acquiescence.

*Judgment that the report of the commissioners is ac-
cepted; that the charter line therein established as the division
line between the towns is, and shall be, the division line between them; and that the petitioner recover its costs.*

E. E. RICE & COMPANY v. FREDERICK C. KENNEDY.

January Term, 1903.

Present: ROWELL, C. J., TYLER, MUNSON, WATSON, STAFFORD, and
HASELTON, JJ.

Opinion filed May 21, 1904.

Corporations—Liability of Directors—V. S. 3724.

V. S. 3724, making directors, who assent to the creation of corporate
indebtedness exceeding in amount two-thirds the capital stock
actually paid in, personally liable for the excess, applies only to
corporations by voluntary association.

V. S. 3724 never applied to corporations created by special acts of the
Legislature, except while No. 79, Acts 1886, was in force, which act
was repealed by the revision of 1894.

When, on demurrer to a declaration, the county court sustained the
demurrer, adjudged the declaration insufficient, and passed the
case to the Supreme Court before final judgment, and the Supreme
Court affirms the judgment of the county court, and the plaintiff
can gain nothing by any amendment to the declaration, the Supreme Court will render final judgment.

DEBT, under V. S. 3724, against Frederick C. Kennedy,
as director of the Burlington Woolen Co., a corporation organized and existing under a special act of the Legislature of
this State, for goods sold and delivered to said corporation.
Heard on a general demurrer to the amended declaration at
the September Term, 1902, Chittenden County, *Start*, J., presiding. Demurrer sustained, and declaration adjudged insufficient. The plaintiff excepted. The opinion states the material allegations of the declaration.

Joseph T. Stearns and *Robert L. Raymond* for the plaintiff.

No. 79, Acts of 1886, not only made R. L. 3291,—now
V. S. 3724—apply to the Burlington Woolen Co., but re-

pealed the charter provision as to directors' liability. *Barton Nat. Bk.* v. *Atkins,* 72 Vt. 33.

That provision of the charter was then gone forever, and the repeal of No. 79, Acts of 1886, did not revive it.

It may well be held that No. 79, Acts of 1886, was not necessary; that R. L. 3291,—now V. S. 3724—of its own force applied to all specially chartered corporations. *Farr* v. *Brackett,* 30 Vt. 344; *State* v. *Smith,* 63 Vt. 201.

This action is properly brought at law. 3 Thomp. Corp. § 4178; *Gaffney* v. *Colvill,* 6 Hill (N. Y.) 567.

A single director may bring an action in behalf of himself alone in states where an action at law is the proper remedy. 3 Thomp. Corp. §4320; *State Bank* v. *Andrews,* 18 N. Y. Supp. 167.

Actions of a similar nature have, with one exception, been brought at law in this State. *Field et al.* v. *Haines et al.,* 28 Fed. 919; *Windham Prov. Inst.* v. *Sprague,* 43 Vt. 502; *Nat. Bk. of Rutland* v. *Paige's Exr.,* 53 Vt. 452; *Cady et al.* v. *Sanford et al.,* 53 Vt. 632; *Corey* v. *Morrill et al.,* 61 Vt. 598; *Farr* v. *Briggs' Est.,* 72 Vt. 225; 3 Thomp. Corp. § 4317.

The exception referred to is *Bassett et al.* v. *St. Albans Hotel Co.,* 47 Vt. 313, where it was held that the action should not be in equity.

W. L. Burnap for the defendant.

V. S. 3724 does not apply to corporations organized by special act of the Legislature.

If V. S. 3724 is available against the defendant, suit must be for the benefit of all the creditors. One creditor cannot reap all the advantage given by the statute. *Windham*

Prov. Inst. v. *Sprague,* 43 Vt. 502; *Buel* v. *Warner,* 33 Vt. 570.

The cause of action under this statute is not cognizable at law, but in equity. *Bank* v. *Atkins,* 72 Vt. 33; *Cushing* v. *Perot,* 34 L. R. A. 737; Thomp. Corp. § 3435; *Mich. Sav. Co.* v. *Fidelity Co.,* 87 Fed. 113; *Patterson* v. *Lynde,* 106 U. S. 519; *Flash* v. *Conn.,* 108 U. S. 371; *Terry* v. *Little,* 104 U. S. 216; Thomp. Corp. § 3368; *McCusick* v. *Seymour,* 50 N. W. 1114; *Farmers' Loan & Trust Co.* v. *Funk,* 68 N. W. 939; *Pickering* v. *Hastings,* 76 N. W. 587; *German Nat. Bk.* v. *Far. Bank,* 74 N. W. 1086; *Gianella* v. *Bigelow,* 71 N. W. 111; *Attorney-Gen.* v. *Guardian Ins. Co.,* 77 N. Y. 272; *Story* v. *Furman,* 25 N. Y. 221.

WATSON, J. The amended declaration shows that the Burlington Woolen Company was organized in 1863 under a special charter,—No. 61, Acts of 1862,—and thenceforth did business thereunder with such amendments thereto as may have been made by general legislation, until it went into the hands of a receiver on the 21st day of February, 1898. Section 5 of the charter provided that "the sum of one hundred thousand dollars, of the capital stock of said company, shall be paid in before said company shall contract any debts; and the indebtedness of the company shall at no time exceed two-thirds of the capital actually paid in; and if at any time the indebtedness of said company shall exceed that amount, the directors and stockholders shall be personally holden for such excess to the creditors of the company; and no part of the capital stock of said company actually paid in shall be withdrawn or diverted from the business of the company, until all the indebtedness and liabilities of the company shall have been fully satisfied." By section 6, the act was subject to any and all general laws of this State applicable to similar acts of incorporation, not inconsistent therewith, and the act was under the control of any future Legislature. By No. 79, Acts of 1886, all private corporations so organized were made subject to the provisions of certain sections of the Revised Laws, among which were sections 3291 and 3292. Section 3291 reads: "One-half of the capital stock shall be paid in before the corporation contracts debts, and no part of it shall be withdrawn or diverted from the proper business of the corporation; and no debts shall be contracted by the corporation exceeding in amount two-thirds of the capital stock actually paid in; and any director assenting to the creation of such indebtedness shall be personally liable for the excess"; and section 3292, "The stockholders in the corporation shall be individually liable to its creditors to an amount equal to the amount of stock held by them respectively, for contracts and debts made by such company, until the whole amount of stock fixed by the company is paid in." The act of 1886 was a revision of the entire subject matter of section five of the charter, was intended as a substitution therefor, and the latter was impliedly repealed thereby. *Barton National Bank* v. *Atkins,* 72 Vt. 33, 47 Atl. 176.

In 1892, the statutory law respecting corporations by voluntary association was generally taken into consideration by the Legislature, resulting in the enactments of No. 60 of the laws of that year, by which chapter 153 of the Revised Laws, of which section 3291 formed a part, was expressly repealed. Section 21 of this act contains the provision that "no debts shall be contracted by the corporation exceeding in amount two-thirds of the capital stock actually paid in; and a director assenting to the creation of such indebtedness shall be personally liable for the excess." This is the same provision contained in section 3291, and with the immaterial change of a single word it is in the same language.

Under the revision of 1894, the same provision in substance was placed in section 3724 of Vermont Statutes, upon which this action is based.. No question is made, nor could there be, but that this provision as contained in R. L. 3291, has thus been a continuing one in the law to the present time. But the defendant contends that the Burlington Woolen Company was subject to it only so long as the act of 1886 remained in force, and this contention we think is sound.

The provision upon which the plaintiff has declared, as contained in section 3291 of the Revised Laws, in section 21, No. 60, Acts of 1892, and in section 3724 of the Vermont Statutes, in itself, applies only to corporations by voluntary association. It never had any application to private corporations organized under special acts of the Legislature except as they were made subject to it by the law of 1886. Under the revision of 1894 that act was expressly repealed from and after the first day of August, 1895. V. S. 5463. With that act thus repealed, such corporations ceased to be subject to the provision in question in the general law, and directors are not liable under that provision for any excess of indebtedness subsequently contracted by the corporation.

The allegations in the amended declaration show that the indebtedness from the Burlington Woolen Company to the plaintiff was contracted after the 17th day of November, 1897, hence the statute declared upon gives him no right of action.

In the trial court the demurrer was sustained, the amended declaration adjudged insufficient, and the cause passed to this Court before final judgment. Inasmuch, however, as the statute upon which the action is based gives the plaintiff no right of action, he can gain nothing by any amendment to the declaration which might properly be made if the case were

remanded. In these circumstances, final judgment will be
rendered here.

*The judgment of the County Court is affirmed, and judg-
ment that the defendant recover his costs.*

WILLIAM L. SCOVILLE *v.* JAMES W. BROCK.

October Term, 1903.

Present: ROWELL, C. J., MUNSON, START, WATSON, and HASELTON, JJ.

Opinion filed May 21, 1904.

*Guardian and Ward—Final Account of Guardian—Settle-
ment—Bill to Vacate—Demurrer—Laches of Ward—
Statute of Limitations—V. S. 2810.*

The record of judicial proceedings is not conclusive in a proceeding
  brought expressly to vacate them for fraud.
When the Probate Court specifically decrees to a minor certain stocks
  and bonds of nonresident corporations, as his interest in his
  father's estate, his guardian should not be charged with a breach
  of duty merely because he did not refuse to receive said securities as his ward's interest in said estate, and demand cash.
On demurrer to a bill brought to set aside the allowance of the final
  account of a guardian by which certain securities were decreed
  to his ward, the allegations that the defendant, contriving and
  intending to deprive the orator of his rights in the premises, and
  with intent to prevent him from calling the defendant to account
  for his breach of trust as guardian, represented that he had used
  all due care in managing orator's estate; that, as the investments
  had been made before the securities came into his hands, he was
  under no duty to change them; that loss by depreciation of the
  securities was without his fault, and that he had fully performed
  all the duties of his trust; and the orator, fully believing and
  relying on these false representations, did not object to receiving

his property in the form in which it was offered to him, sufficiently
set forth fraud on the part of the guardian.

A bill against the orator's former guardian for a breach of trust,
which alleges that it was defendant's duty to have sold certain
stocks and bonds of nonresident corporations in which the estate
was invested, for which there was a market in Vermont, and that,
if defendant had exercised ordinary care, he would have ascertained that such investments were injudicial and were likely to
become worthless, as they subsequently did, is not objectionable
for want of equity on the ground that if defendant had ascertained these facts, and had then attempted to sell the securities
without disclosing to the purchaser what he knew, he would have
been guilty of fraud, and if he disclosed all he knew no one would
buy; because he could have offered them for sale at the purchaser's risk, under the rule of *caveat emptor.*

As against the orator, who seeks to set aside the allowance of the final
account of his former guardian for fraud, time does not necessarily
begin to run when the confidential relation ends, but only when
the influence of that relation ceases to operate upon him so he
can act independently of it.

BILL IN CHANCERY. Heard on demurrer to the amended
bill at the September Term, 1902, Washington County, *Stafford,* Chancellor. Demurrer sustained, and bill dismissed.
The orator appealed. This case has been once before in the
Supreme Court. See 75 Vt. 243.

In respect of the defendant's alleged breach of duty in
not refusing to receive the securities in question, besides what
is said in the opinion, the bill merely states that, about September 1, 1890, defendant was appointed guardian of the
orator, who was then seventeen years of age; that on September 19, 1890, by decree of the Probate Court for the district of Washington, the stocks and bonds mentioned in the
opinion were specifically decreed to the orator out of the
estate of his father; that the defendant, as guardian of the
orator, immediately thereafter received said securities from
the administrator of said estate; that it was the duty of the

defendant, as such guardian, "not to have received or accepted
the orator's property in such unlawful and objectionable investments in stocks and bonds." The opinion sufficiently
states the other allegations of the bill.

William L. Scoville and *Edward H. Deavitt* for the
orator.

The Court of Chancery has original jurisdiction of all
cases of this kind. *Wade* v. *Pulsifer*, 54 Vt. 45; Woerner
Guardians, § 160; Perry Trusts, § 1, 802; *Brown* v. *Est.
of Sumner*, 31 Vt. 671.

The decree of the Probate Court allowing the final account of the defendant, as guardian, cannot be attacked collaterally except for causes which render it void. Fraud does
not render a judgment void, but is merely the ground of relief in equity. Black, Judgments, § 245; *Porter* v. *Gile*, 47
Vt. 620; *Doolittle* v. *Hilton*, 28 Vt. 819; *Probate Court* v.
Winch, 57 Vt. 282; Van Fleet Collateral Attack, § 826; *Probate Court* v. *Slason*, 23 Vt. 306; Bispham Eq. 198; *Delaney*
v. *Brown*, 72 Vt. 344.

The defendant was bound to disclose to his ward all the
facts and circumstances which he himself knew or ought to
have known which would enable the orator exactly to com-
prehend the character of the act which he did in refraining
from casting the loss upon the guardian, and to know what
were his legal rights. Bispham Eq. § 283; *Harvey* v. *Clarke*,
4 Russ. 34; *Willan* v. *Willan*, 16 Ves. 72; *Sturge* v. *Sturge*,
12 Beav. 229; *Lloyd* v. *Atwood*, 2 De G. & J. 614; Bispham,
§§ 280-293 inc.; *Tate* v. *Williamson*, L. R. 2 Ch. 61; *Smith*
v. *Kay*, 7 H. L. Cas. 771; *Coward* v. *Hughes*, 1 Kay & J.
443; *McCarthy* v. *Decaix*, 2 Russ. & M. 614; *Regenell* v.
Sprye, 8 Hare 221; *Hylton* v. *Hylton*, 2 Ves. Sr. 547; *Bur-*

rows v. *Wallis*, 2 De G. M. & G. 233; *Hugenin* v. *Baseley*, 14 Ves. 273; *Hunter* v. *Atkins*, 3 Myl. & C. 135; *Gregory* v. *Orr*, 61 Miss. 307.

It was the duty of the defendant to have refused to receive the stocks and bonds, and to have demanded cash. Woerner Guardians, § 160; Perry, Trusts, § 1; *Mills* v. *Hoffman*, 26 Hun. 594.

He certainly should have endeavored within a reasonable time to get the securities into a form approved by law. In retaining the investment he acted at his peril. Bispham Eq., § 139; Lewin Trusts, ch. 14, § 5; *Powell* v. *Evans*, 5 Ves. 859; *Tebbs* v. *Carpenter*, 1 Madd. 298; *Clough* v. *Bond*, 3 Milne & Cr. 496; *Lowson* v. *Copeland*, 2 Brown C. C. 156; *Hemphill's Appl.*, 18 Pa. 303; Perry Trusts, §§ 493, 440, 465; *Mills* v. *Hoffman*, 26 Hun. 594; *Kinmouth* v. *Brigham*, 5 Allen 270; *Baskin* v. *Baskin*, 4 Lans. 90; *Goodwin* v. *Howe*, 52 How. Prac. 134.

The stocks and bonds were improper and unlawful investments of trust funds. *Hemphill's App.*, 18 Pa. 303; *Gray* v. *Fox*, 1 N. J. Eq. 259; *King* v. *Talbot*, 40 N. Y. 76; Lewin on Trusts, § 5; *Powell* v. *Evans*, 5 Ves. Jr. 859; *Tebbs* v. *Carpenter*, 1 Madd. 298; *Ormiston* v. *Olcott*, 84 N. Y. 359; *Kinmouth* v. *Brigham*, 5 Allen 270; *Armfield* v. *Brown*, 73 N. C. 81; Bispham Eq., § 145; *Potter* v. *Hiscox*, 30 Conn. 508; *McClosky* v. *Gleason*, 56 Vt. 264; *Kimball* v. *Reding*, 31 N. H. 352; *Judge* v. *Mathes*, 60 N. H. 433.

M. E. Smilie for the defendant.

ROWELL, C. J. This is a bill to impeach a decree of the probate court allowing the final account of the defendant as guardian of the orator, because of the alleged fraud of the defendant in procuring the orator's approval of said account.

When the case was here before—75 Vt. 243, 54 Atl. 177—
the bill was held bad on demurrer because the allegations that
said approval was obtained by fraud were not followed by
averments sufficient to carry the effect of the alleged fraud
into the decree, and the sufficiency of the allegations of fraud
was not considered. Since then the bill has been amended,
and alleges that said decree was made solely by reason of
said approval, and without consideration by the court of any
other facts and circumstances, and without any consideration
whatever by the court.

The bill is again demurred to, and it is objected that the
allegation that said decree was made solely by reason of said
approval and not otherwise is not well pleaded, as it contra-
dicts the record set out in the bill, which shows that the defendant swore to the justness and truth of his account before
the probate judge himself. But the rule as to the conclusiveness of the record of judicial proceedings does not apply when
process is brought bearing directly upon them for the purpose of vacating and setting them aside for fraud. In such
cases the record may be contradicted. *Godfrey* v. *Downer*,
47 Vt. 653.

It appears from the bill that on September 19, 1900, the
probate court specifically decreed the property in question
to the orator, then a minor, as legatee under his father's will;
that the property consisted of divers shares of the capital
stock and the debenture bonds of various banks and trust
companies in Iowa and Missouri, and was received by the
defendant soon after his appointment as guardian and immediately after the making of said decree, from the administrator *de bonis non* with the will annexed of said estate.

It is alleged in the bill, and urged in argument, that it
was the duty of the defendant to refuse to receive the stock
and bonds from the administrator, and to demand cash in-

stead. But it is impossible, on the allegations of the bill, to charge him with a breach of duty in this respect.

It is further objected that the allegations of fraud are not sufficient. We take no note of the allegations in paragraph 17 of the bill, for they are bad for generality. Those in paragraph 19 are, that the defendant, contriving and intending to deceive and defraud the orator of his rights in the premises, and with intent to prevent him from calling the defendant to account for his breach of trust as guardian, told the orator that he had used all due care and diligence in and about the orator's estate; that as the investments had been made before the securities came into his hands, he was under no duty to change them, and that the losses occasioned by their depreciation were without his fault, and that he had fully performed all the duties of his trust. The bill then goes on to allege that the orator fully believed and relied upon the truth of said representations, and believed that the defendant had disclosed to him all the facts necessary to inform him of the full extent of his rights and remedies in the premises, and believed that the defendant had committed no breach of trust for which he could be called to account, and so did not object to receiving his property in the form in which it was offered to him, and approved the defendant's account.

It is contended that these declarations of the defendant were but expressions of his conclusions of law, and that such general statements of opinion are not fraudulent, especially as it is not alleged that the defendant did not honestly believe them to be true. But the allegation is that they were made with intent to deceive the orator, and that they did in fact deceive him, in respect of his rights; and this the demurrer admits. It is also alleged, in effect, in the last amendment, that said statements were not true. But if these statements

are to be treated as conclusions of law, as contended, yet such
representations cannot be made with impunity in respect of
matters pertaining to a fiduciary relation existing between the
parties concerning which, as here, the declarant had superior
knowledge and means of knowledge, for he knew what he
had done or omitted to do, while the orator knew nothing
about it. 1 Big. Fraud, 1st ed., pp. 264, 488. The bill further
alleges that when the defendant presented his final account to
the orator for his approval, he knew, and had known for several months, that the securities in question were of little or no
value, and that loss thereon must be sustained by him or the
orator, and that to avoid loss to himself, he took advantage
of his relation to the orator and of his influence over him,
and thereby obtained said approval from him, which he would
not have given but for the withholding of said information
by the defendant. These allegations are sufficient to induce
the court to inquire into the matter on its merits, for the law
is extremely watchful to prevent a guardian from taking any
advantage immediately on his ward's coming of age and at
the time of settling his account and delivering up his trust,
because undue advantage may be taken. It is not necessary
that actual fraud should have been practiced; it is enough
that there was an opportunity to practice it. *Hylton* v. *Hylton,* 2 Ves. 549; *Wade* v. *Pulsifer,* 54 Vt. 45.

It is objected that the bill is without equity, for although
it alleges that the defendant might, by the exercise of proper
diligence, have sold the securities for from ten to thirty per
cent. above their par value, yet it also alleges that they had no
value nor quotation in the large stock markets of the United
States, and that their salability in and around Montpelier,
where the defendant lived, was due to the fact that certain
unscrupulous and dishonest persons interested in the cor-

porations issuing said securities had created a "boom," or an abnormal demand therefor, fraudulently, and with intent to deceive those who invested their property therein: that said abnormal demand had no sound business foundation, but rested in the well-known tendency of people to invest in something that promises large returns, and that at the time the defendant received said securities, said corporations were managed in a grossly extravagant, and in some cases in a fraudulent and dishonest, manner by the officers thereof; that it was widely believed at the places where said corporations were located that they were conducted for the purpose of defrauding Eastern investors who had been induced to put money into their securities; that the large dividends paid by them were paid out of capital and not out of earnings; and that said corporations had knowingly made loans on real estate grossly in excess of its value; that the affairs of said corporations, from the time of the appointment of the defendant until their final bankruptcy, were conducted so extravagantly, fraudulently, and dishonestly that had the defendant gone to the places where said corporations were located and made personal investigation of their business standing, he would have been satisfied as a man of sound discretion, ordinary business prudence and intelligence, that the orator's funds then invested in said securities were not safely and profitably invested, and that it was his duty to convert said securities into cash forthwith, and to reinvest the same safely and profitably according to law. The bill further alleges that the situation afforded the defendant no means of compelling repayment of the capital sums of the orator's property invested in said securities, had it at any time appeared to him that such sums were unsafely invested.

This is a pretty thorough impeachment of the value of these securities, and shows that they were really worth little or nothing when they came into the defendant's hands, and the bill alleges that they were worth nothing when he turned them over to the orator. It also alleges that they could not have been enforced against the companies, and had no value on 'Change. The only complaint is that the defendant should have taken the tide at the flood, and sold when the "boom" was on in and around Montpelier. But the defendant says, that charging him with all the bill alleges he would have found out about the securities had he done his duty, he could not have sold them without disclosing to the purchaser what he knew, without committing an actionable fraud himself, which he was not bound to do, and that if he disclosed what he knew, he could not have sold at all. But suppose that is so, still he could have offered them for sale at the purchaser's risk, under the rule of *caveat emptor,* and we cannot say as matter of law that he could not have sold in that way. The inference that he could have, from all that is alleged, is neither too remote, indefinite, nor contingent to form an element of recovery. Indeed the demurrer must be taken as admitting that he could have sold in some legitimate way, for that is the fair import of the allegation, which must be construed to mean such a sale, supposing the pleader to have intended his pleading to be consistent with itself. *Royce* v. *Maloney,* 58 Vt. 437, 5 Atl. 395.

Whether he could have safely sold the stock without disclosing what he is to be charged with knowing about it, we do not decide. Some cases make a distinction between the sale of the capital stock of a going concern and the sale of commercial paper or other obligations for the payment of money, in respect of the duty of the seller to disclose his knowledge of the corporation's or the maker's insolvency. *Rothmiller* v. *Stein,* 143 N. Y. 581.

If the orator was dissatisfied with the defendant's account as settled and allowed by the probate court, the statute gave him four years to apply to said court for a re-examination and correction of it, as he resided out of the State at the termination of the trust. But he made no such application, and alleges that the defendant did not tell him that he could, and that he did not discover his rights till shortly before he brought his bill, which was eight years after he came of age and after the making of said decree; but why he did not sooner discover them is not alleged, unless, possibly, by vague and uncertain inference. The defendant contends that the orator ought to have discovered his rights sooner, and that, as he sets forth no reason why he did not, he is barred by the lapse of the statutory time for applying for a re-examination of the account, and by the lapse of the statutory period limiting actions at law for fraud. But this defense cannot be availed of by demurrer, because, if for no other reason, time did not necessarily begin to run against the orator when the confidential relation ended, but only when the influence of that relation ceased to operate upon him so he could act independently of it, and the bill does not show when that was, unless it shows that it was shortly before the suit was brought, but not how shortly before. *Wade* v. *Pulsifer,* 54 Vt. 45, 65; Benjamin's Principles of Contracts, 84; 18 Eng. Ruling Cases, 357.

Demurrer overruled, bill adjudged sufficient, and cause remanded.

E. L. BASS *v.* H. J. RUBLEE.

January Term, 1904.

Present: ROWELL,. C. J., TYLER, START, WATSON, STAFFORD, and
HASELTON, JJ.

Opinion filed May 21, 1904.

Contract under Seal—Modification by Simple Contract—Evidence—Sufficiency—Motion for Verdict—Demurrer to Evidence—Effect—Requisites—Joinder in Demurrer—Practice in Supreme Court—Final Judgment—Remanding.

In an action on a simple contract which modified, in respect of the time of delivery, a contract under seal for the sale and delivery of lumber, when the plaintiff testifies that it was mutually agreed between him and the defendant that the time of delivery should be extended and their correspondence tends to confirm this; it is error to direct a verdict for the defendant on the ground that there is no evidence of any agreement between the parties to extend the terms of the original contract.

A motion for a verdict is in the nature of a demurrer to the evidence, and, in respect of the view to be taken of the evidence, is governed by the same rules. But the required technicalities of such demurrer do not appertain to a motion for a verdict.

On a motion for a verdict the court is strictly confined to a determination of whether there is evidence from which, if taken to be true, and excluding the effect of all modifying evidence, it can be reasonably inferred that the fact affirmed exists.

On overruling a motion for a verdict, no judgment is rendered against the moving party.

Though it is a long established rule of the Supreme Court to finally dispose of cases brought there on exceptions, it is part of the same rule that, if the decision of that Court places the case in such, a state that either party has the right to a trial by jury, the case will be remanded.

When, on a bill of exceptions, the Supreme Court holds that the county court erred in granting defendant's motion for a verdict, and the evidence bearing upon the question involved consists of oral tes-

timony, correspondence between the parties, their actions for six
months, together with inferences to be drawn from circumstances,
the defendant should not be deprived of an opportunity of a jury
trial, and the case will therefore be remanded.

Such a case should be remanded, even if defendant's motion for a verdict be treated as governed by the law applicable to a demurrer to
the evidence, for the defendant cannot oblige the plaintiff to join
in such demurrer so as to dispense with the verdict of a jury,
unless he distinctly admits on the record every fact which the
plaintiff's evidence tends to prove, and every inference legitimately deducible from such evidence.

SPECIAL ASSUMPSIT on a simple contract in modification of a contract under seal for the sale and delivery of lumber. Plea, the general issue with notice. Trial by jury at
the June Term, 1903, Orange County, *Munson*, J., presiding.
At the close of the plaintiff's evidence a verdict was ordered
for the defendant. The plaintiff excepted. The opinion states
the case.

M. M. Wilson and *Darling & Darling* for the plaintiff.

The defendant's motion admits all the facts which plaintiff's evidence tends to prove, and all inferences that can be
legitimately drawn therefrom. *Walcott* v. *Met. Life Ins. Co.*,
64 Vt. 221; *Varnum* v. *Higgins*, 65 Vt. 416; 6 A. & E. Enc.
Pl. & Pr. 693; *Dickey* v. *Schreider*, 3 S. & R. 413; *Pawling*
v. *U. S.*, 4 Cranch 219. No question could have been made,
even on demurrer, but that assumpsit is the proper action.
Briggs v. *R. Co.*, 31 Vt. 211; *Smith* v. *Smith*, 45 Vt. 433;
Sherwin v. *R. Co.*, 24 Vt. 347.

If it was error to direct a verdict, this Court should render
final judgment for the plaintiff. *Snow* v. *Carpenter*, 54 Vt.
17. The only reason that could exist for remanding the case
would be to have the facts established. *Peach* v. *Mills*, 13

Vt. 504; *Porter* v. *Smith,* 20 Vt. 344; *Chandler* v. *Spear,* 22 Vt. 388.

But that reason cannot apply in this case, for defendant's motion for a verdict is equal to a demurrer to the evidence, and is governed by the same rules. *Latremouille* v. *R. Co.,* 63 Vt. 336; Thompson Trials, § 2267.

When evidence has been demurred to, all facts and inferences which are fairly deducible therefrom are thereby established; and it only remains for the court to apply the law to those facts, as to a special verdict or agreed statement. 6 A. & E. Enc. of Pl. 441; *Cocksedge* v. *Fanshaw,* 1 Doug. 118; Tidd's Prac. 866; *Gibson* v. *Hunter,* 2 H. Bl. 209; *Davis* v. *Steiner,* 14 P. St. 275; *Fray* v. *DeCamp,* 15 S. & R. 227; *Ross* v. *Vaughn,* 4 Yeats' 54; *Minear* v. *Halloway,* 56 Ohio St. 148; *Stephens* v. *Hix,* 38 Tex. 656; *Harwood* v. *Blythe,* 32 Tex. 803; 2 Steph. Nisi Prius, 1791.

Because the defendant, at the time he entered into the contract, knew that the plaintiff had a contract with another person for the sale and delivery of the lumber purchased, the measure of damage is the profit which would have accrued to the plaintiff if the defendant had performed his contract. *Rahm* v. *Deig,* 121 Ind. 283; *Carpenter* v. *First Nat. Bank,* 119 Ill. 352; *Works* v. *Mitchell,* 114 Mich. 29; *Robinson* v. *Hyer,* 35 Fla. 544; *Messmore* v. *N. Y. Lead & Shot Co.,* 40 N. Y. 422; *Booth* v. *Rolling Mill Co.,* 60 N. Y. 487; *Jordan* v. *Patterson,* 67 Conn. 473; *Cockburn* v. *Atlantic Lumber Co.,* 54 Wis. 619; 1 Suth. Dam. 34, (Vol. 1, 2 ed., §52); Sedgw. Dam. 144 to 169; *Borries* v. *Hutchinson,* 18 C. B. N. S. 44; *Hadley* v. *Baxendale,* 9 Ex. 341; *Dunlop* v. *Higgins,* 12 Jur. (Pt. 1) 295.

M. P. Maurice and *Emmet McFeeters* for the defendant.

The modification claimed was not proved, therefore the proper action in this case is covenant instead of assumpsit. *Sherwin* v. *Rutland & Bur. R. Co.*, 24 Vt. 347; *Barker* v. *Troy & Rut. R. Co.*, 27 Vt. 766; *King* v. *Lamoille R. Co.*, 51 Vt. 369; *McKay* v. *Darling*, 65 Vt. 639; 4 "Cyc." 323.

WATSON, J. The declaration is special assumpsit in three counts severally declaring on a written contract dated February 13, 1901, sealed and subscribed by the plaintiff and the defendant, whereby the defendant promised and agreed to furnish to the plaintiff in the cars at East Berkshire in the month of June, 1901, certain specified lots of maple lumber to be paid for by the plaintiff as therein stipulated. It is further alleged that subsequently the parties by mutual agreement not under seal extended the time for the delivery of the lumber without setting a time limit therefor, and that in pursuance of the contract so modified as to time, thereafter between the dates in the several counts alleged, the defendant delivered to the plaintiff a portion of the lumber specified in the agreement and received payment therefor. Then follow allegations of the defendant's breach of the contract in neglecting and refusing, though requested, to deliver the balance of the lumber, etc.

At the close of plaintiff's opening evidence, the defendant moved for a verdict on the grounds that (1) there was no evidence of any agreement between the parties to extend the terms of the contract beyond its original stipulation; and (2) there was no evidence of such an extension as is set up in the writ. The motion was granted *pro forma*, to which plaintiff excepted.

The record shows that the plaintiff testified in effect that the defendant could not get the lumber out in June, the time specified in the original contract; that in June they mutually agreed that, since the lumber could not be ready to ship until in the fall, the time should be extended till fall; and that then they would survey and ship the lumber when it was ready. The subsequent correspondence between the parties, and their actions regarding the lumber tended to show the same thing. Since there was evidence to go to the jury on the question whether the original contract was modified as claimed by the plaintiff, it was error to order a verdict.

If the second ground stated in the motion could be considered as covering a variance, if any there be, between the time for the performance of the modified contract as alleged, and that which the evidence tends to show, we do not so consider it, for it appears from the record that it was not so treated by the defendant in the court below, and it is not so treated in his brief here.

It is urged by the plaintiff that if it was error to direct a verdict, he is entitled to final judgment in his favor in this court. Hereon it is argued that the motion for a verdict was equivalent to a demurrer to the evidence, and is governed by the same rules, referring to *Latremouille* v. *Bennington & Rutland Ry. Co.*, 63 Vt. 336, 22 Atl. 656. There in discussing the defendant's motion for a verdict, made at the close of the evidence, it is said that "such a motion is like a demurrer to the whole evidence, on the ground of its insufficiency to warrant a verdict for the plaintiff if one should be found. The motion could not be entertained, if, as the case stood, there was any evidence tending fairly and reasonably to support the claim of the plaintiff. If the verdict was to be determined by an inference, to be made by the jury from facts, any of which was more or less in dispute, the disputed fact, or facts, were to be determined, and the inference made by the jury. So long as any fact from which such inference is to be made, is in doubt or dispute, the inference is dependent, partly upon the fact to be determined by the jury. It is not wholly a question of law."

A motion for a verdict is considered in law as in the nature of a demurrer to the evidence, and to the extent in the Latremouille case indicated, that is, to the mode of viewing the evidence, it is governed by the same rules. But the required technicalities of the demurrer and the procedure incident thereto have no place when the court is moved to direct a verdict. The province of the court on such a motion is not to weigh the evidence and ascertain where the preponderance is; but it is limited strictly to determining whether there is, or is not, evidence from which, if believed, it may reasonably be inferred, in legal contemplation, that the fact affirmed exists, excluding the effect of all modifying or countervailing evidence; and on overruling the motion, no judgment is rendered against the moving party. *Bartelott* v. *International Bank*, 119 Ill. 259.

In the case before us, a modification of the original contract is essential to be shown to the maintenance of the action. The evidence bearing on that question consists of oral testimony, correspondence between the parties, and their actions covering a period of six months or more of time, together with inferences to be drawn from the circumstances disclosed by the evidence. A jury trial is most appropriate for the settlement of the facts involved, and the defendant should not be deprived of an opportunity therefor. While it is a long established rule of practice in cases brought into this Court upon exceptions to finally dispose of the case here, it is a part of the same rule that when a jury trial becomes necessary, or if the decision of this Court places the case in such a state that either party has a right to a trial by jury, the cause will be

remanded. *Peach* v. *Mills,* 13 Vt. 501; *Porter* v. *Smith,* 20
Vt. 344.

Nor could the result be different were the defendant's
motion treated as a demurrer to the evidence, and determined
by the law governing under that practice; for some of the
technical requirements were not complied with. The object
of such proceedings is not to bring before the Court an investigation of facts in dispute, nor to consider and weigh the
force of testimony, and the presumptions and inferences arising from the evidence. The only purpose of such a demurrer
is to refer to the court questions of law arising from the facts
ascertained. Where the parol evidence is loose and indeterminate, which may be urged with more or less effect to a
jury; or if the evidence is of circumstances, and is meant to
operate beyond the proof of the existence of those circumstances and to conduce to the proof of the existence of other
facts, the defendant cannot demur to the evidence and insist
on the jury's being discharged from giving a verdict, and
oblige the plaintiff to join in the demurrer, without distinctly
admitting upon the record, every fact, and every conclusion,
which the plaintiff's evidence conduced to prove. This was
not done. When the facts are not thus admitted upon the
record, and there has been a voluntary joinder in demurrer
leaving the facts unsettled and indeterminate it is deemed a
sufficient reason for refusing judgment on the demurrer.
Furthermore, there is no joinder of demurrer on the record,
without which no final judgment can properly be rendered.
With the case standing in this way, it is the settled practice
to award a new trial on the ground that the issue between
the parties, in effect, has not been tried. 2 Tidd's Pr. (3
Am. ed.) 865-866; *Gibson* v. *Hunter,* 2 H. Black. 187; *Fowle*

v. *The Common Council of Alexandria,* 11 Wheat. 320, 6 L.
ed. 484; *Crowe* v. *People,* 92 Ill. 231.

The pro forma judgment is reversed and cause remanded.

A. O. VITTY *v.* ROSILL A. PEASLEE'S ESTATE.

May Term, 1904.

Present: ROWELL, C. J., TYLER, START, WATSON, STAFFORD, and
HASELTON, JJ.

Opinion filed May 21, 1904.

*Claim Against Decedent's Estate—Evidence—Burden of
Proof—Charge of Court.*

In assumpsit against a decedent's estate, when the estate contends that
the claimant should be charged with $3,500 in offset, as the pro-
ceeds received by him from the sale of her farm, and he claims
he has fully accounted for the money, and that he has, at the
decedent's request, paid $1,000 of it to her daughter, it is proper
to allow the claimant to put in evidence a paper signed by the
decedent, which states that she had settled with her son, and had
given him $1,000 from her estate, and that, "to make it equal,"
she thereby gave her daughter the same sum.

In such a case the charge of the court that if the money is shown
into the claimant's hands, the burden is on him to account for it
as having been paid to the decedent, or disposed of in accordance
with her directions, is a sufficient statement of the law of the
matter.

APPEAL from the decision of commissioners on the claim
presented by A. O. Vitty against the estate of Rosil A.
Peaslee and the claim of Joseph C. Enright, the administrator, in offset thereto. Declaration in general assumpsit, with

specifications of yearly charges for board, washing, and attention covering a period of six years previous to decedent's death. Plea, the general issue and declaration in offset. Trial by jury at the December Term, 1903, Windsor County, *Munson*, J., presiding. Verdict and judgment for the claimant. The appellant excepted.

It appeared that the administrator had declined to appeal, and that the appellant is Moses R. Peaslee, the only son of the intestate.

Gilbert A. Davis for the appellant.

The burden was on the claimant to show that decedent was fully informed that he had received $3,500 for the farm, and the court should have so instructed the jury. *Clark* v. *Moody*, 17 Mass. 145; 1 Am. Lead. Cases, 694, 706; *Dodge* v. *Perkins*, 9 Pick. 368; *McMahan* v. *Franklin*, 35 Mo. 55; *Gallup* v. *Merrill*, 40 Vt. 137; 1 Am. & Eng. Enc. L. 372, 373; 1 Story's Eq. Juris. § 1462 to § 1468.

The amount claimant had received from the sale of the farm was a fact peculiarly within his knowledge, and for this reason the burden is on him. Best Ev. § 274; Greenl. Ev. § 79; Starkie Ev. 589.

W. B. C. Stickney and *E. R. Buck* for the claimant.

ROWELL, C. J. The only questions made relate to the set-off pleaded to the claimant's demand. The appellant and the claimant's wife are the children and sole heirs of the intestate.

The appellant's testimony tended to show that in 1897 the claimant, as the intestate's agent, sold a farm of hers for $3,500 and received the price in money, and this is the matter of set-off. The claimant contended in rebuttal that he fully

accounted for the money to the intestate, and claimed, as it
seems from the exceptions, that he paid a thousand dollars
of it to his wife at the intestate's request; and as tending to
prove that, he offered in evidence part of a paper writing,
signed by the intestate and dated June 12, 1899, which stated
that she had settled with her son and given him towards his
share $1,000 of her estate, which she called an advancement,
and that, "to make it equal," she thereby gave to her daughter
the sum of a thousand dollars. The testimony was admitted,
to which the appellant excepted, for that it was allowing the
intestate's declarations to be shown as to money given to
another person not a party to this suit. But the paper was
clearly admissible, as it tended to show, in connection with
the other testimony in the case, that the thousand dollars
therein referred to as given to the defendant's wife was a
part of the farm money, and the court left it to the jury to
say on the whole evidence whether it was or not, and whether
it was actually delivered to her, to which the appellant did not
except.

The appellant requested the court to charge that if it
was found that the claimant received the farm money as the
intestate's agent, the burden was on him to show that the
intestate was fully informed of the amount received, and to
establish that he fully accounted for and paid over to her the
whole of it. The court charged that if the money was shown
into the claimant's hands, the burden was on him to account
for it as having been paid to the intestate or disposed of in
accordance with her directions. This was a substantial compliance with the law of the subject.

Judgment affirmed. Let a certificate go down.

A. G. COOLIDGE, TRUSTEE IN BANKRUPTCY, v. LAMSON
AYERS.

January Term, 1904.

Present: ROWELL, C. J., TYLER, START, WATSON, and STAFFORD, JJ.

Opinion filed May 21, 1904.

Bankruptcy—Preference—Sale by Preferred Creditor—Voidability—Innocent Purchaser—Warranty of Title—Estoppel—After-Acquired Title.

When one, with express warranty of title, sells personal property which
he does not own, his title thereto subsequently acquired inures to
the benefit of the vendee by estoppel.

When a debtor executes to his creditor a release, with full knowledge
that the creditor has taken certain attachable property belonging
to the debtor, and within the following month is adjudged a bankrupt, this transfer constitutes a preference within the U. S. Bankruptcy Act, 1898.

When a bankrupt's preferred creditor sells property, the transfer of
which created the preference, to a third person, the latter's title
thereto is not voidable, under the U. S. Bankruptcy Act, 1898, if
he purchased in good faith, without notice, and for valuable consideration.

Whether such third person did so purchase is, under the evidence in
this case, a question for the jury,

A party is entitled to have the whole case submitted to the jury,
either for a general verdict, or for such special findings as will
be determinative of the case.

TROVER for a piano. Plea, the general issue. Trial by
jury at the September Term, 1903, Rutland County, *Munson*,
J., presiding. Judgment for the plaintiff on special verdicts.
The defendant excepted.

This case came to the county court on appeal from the
city court for the city of Rutland. The opinion states the
case.

Joseph Enright and *Edward R. Buck* for the defendant.

The trustee cannot follow the property into the hands of a *bona fide* purchaser. Collier Bankr. (3 ed.) 357-369; *In Re Mullins*, 4 Am. B. Rep. 224; Brandenburg Bankr. (2 ed.) 731.

Butler & Moloney for the plaintiff.

It follows from the special verdict that the McPhail Piano Cớ. never owned the piano, so the defendant was the mere bailee of McClure, and converted it when he refused to deliver same to the plaintiff. *Gleason* v. *Beers*, 59 Vt. 323; *Swift* v. *Moseley*, 10 Vt. 208; *Cramton* v. *Valido Marble Co.*, 60 Vt. 302.

˙ The pretended sale by the McPhail Piano Co. did not amount to a conversion, and no action lies against the company. *Deering* v. *Austin*, 34 Vt. 330; *Amadon* v. *Myers*, 6 Vt. 308; *Lowery* v. *Walker*, 4 Vt. 76; *Clark* v. *Smith*, 52 Vt. 529.

McClure had no action against anyone except the bailee, after demand and refusal. *Swift* v. *Moseley*, 10 Vt. 208; *Spaulding* v. *Robbins*, 42 Vt. 90; *Hodges* v. *Clark*, 46 Vt. 418; *Babcock* v. *Culver*, 46 Vt. 715.

WATSON, J. In the fall of 1899, Marvin McClure caused the piano in question, which he then owned, to be placed in the house of the defendant. The piano was not then sold to the defenant, but McClure left it there in his possession for trial, hoping to sell it to him. In March, 1900, McClure, being largely indebted to the McPhail Piano Company, was requested by the manager of that company to turn out to it to apply on his indebtedness to the company sundry pianos in possession of various persons, of which pianos was the one in controversy. The testimony was conflicting as to whether in fact the pianos were turned out to the company. But it appeared that when McClure was so requested, the manager of the company told him that they should take possession of the pianos and apply the proceeds thereof to his account.

In June, 1900, the company's agent had an interview with the defendant wherein he represented that the company was the owner of the piano in question. Thereupon the defendant, acting in good faith and believing the said representation regarding the ownership of the piano to be true, bought it of the company and paid full value therefor. At the same time the company gave to the defendant a bill of sale guaranteeing the title.

In December, 1900, McClure, with full knowledge that the company had taken this and other pianos, executed to it a written release under seal of claims and demands against it, to which release was attached a list of the pianos taken by the company, including the one in question. McClure in January, 1901, was adjudged a bankrupt. Later the plaintiff was appointed trustee of the bankrupt estate, and he brings this action as such trustee to recover the value of the piano in the defendant's possession.

The case was submitted to the jury by three questions to be answered, namely: First, did the officer before serving the writ in the cause make a demand on the defendant for the piano in question? To which the jury answered, Yes. Second, did McClure, in March, 1900, turn out the piano in question to the McPhail Piano Company? This question was answered, No. Third, what was the value of the piano in question in December, 1902? The answer was $225. To the refusal of the court to submit the whole case to the jury, the defendant seasonably objected and excepted. Judgment was

rendered on the special findings for the plaintiff to recover
$225 with interest thereon from January, 1902, to which de-
fendant also excepted.

The second special finding shows that the company had
no title to the piano in June, 1900, consequently the company
conveyed no title to the defendant in its sale to him. This
sale, however, was with the company's express warranty of
title, and the subsequently acquired title by the company from
McClure inured to the benefit of the defendant by virtue of
estoppel. *Sherman* v. *The Champlain·Trans. Co.*, 31 Vt. 162.

Clearly the transfer by McClure to the company under
the circumstances shown by the record constituted a preference within the meaning of the bankrupt law, and the company had reasonable cause to believe that it was so intended.
Since the proceedings in bankruptcy were commenced within
four months thereafter, the preference was voidable by the
trustee and he could recover the property or its value from
the preferred creditor. Bankruptcy Act 1898, § 60.

The question then arises whether the defendant's title
acquired subsequently from the preferred creditor is voidable.
This depends upon whether the defendant took the property
under his purchase in good faith and without notice and for
a valuable consideration. If he did so take it, his title is not
voidable; but if he did not, his title is no more secure against
the trustee in bankruptcy than would be that of the preferred
creditor had he not transferred the property. Brandenburg
on Bankruptcy (2nd ed.) 731; *Rison* v. *Knapp,* 4 N. B. R.
349; *In re Mullen,* 4 Am. B. R. 224.

It is argued by the plaintiff that the fact that the defendant took a bill of sale of the piano, with warranty of title,
shows that he did not act in good faith and without notice in
making the purchase. In determining the force of this fact

as evidence either for or against the defendant, it must be considered in the light of the other circumstances in the case. The piano was left in the defendant's possession by McClure, the then owner. About three months later the McPhail Piano Company claimed to own it and sold it to the defendant, receiving full value therefor. Under these circumstances, a jury might say that the defendant took the bill of sale with warranty wholly for his own protection, and that it has no evidenciary significance in the manner claimed by the plaintiff. Whether the defendant took the piano from the company in good faith, without notice, and for a valuable consideration was a question of fact essential to the proper disposition of the case, and it should have been submitted to the jury. A party is entitled to have the whole case submitted either for a general verdict or for such special findings as will be determinative of the case. The defendant's exception to the refusal of the court to submit the whole case is therefore available, as is also his exception to the judgment.

Judgment reversed and cause remanded.

O. H. MOSSMAN *v.* WALTER BOSTRIDGE.

May Term, 1904.

Present: ROWELL, C. J., TYLER, START, and WATSON, JJ.

Opinion filed May 27, 1904.

Trespass—Plea in Justification—Sufficiency—Dogs—Hunting Deer—No. 108, Acts 1898—Construction.

In trespass for killing a dog, the plea that "on the day and date of the said supposed killing of said dog," it was found by the defendant hunting wild deer, sufficiently identifies the trespass attempted to be justified with that declared upon.

Under the provision of No. 108, Acts 1898, that "any person may lawfully kill any dog found hunting deer," the dog may be killed only while so hunting; so that a plea in justification, which merely alleges that "on the day" he killed it, the defendant found the dog hunting deer, is bad on general demurrer.

In order to warrant the killing of a dog found hunting deer, under No. 108, Acts 1898, the dog need not be of the variety therein named, nor need its owner or harborer have permitted it to run at large in the forests where deer inhabit. Those provisions relate only to the penalty of the statute.

TRESPASS for killing a dog. Pleas, the general issue, and plea in justification. Heard on general demurrer to the second plea, at the March Term, 1904, Orleans County, *Haselton*, J., presiding. Demurrer overruled, and plea adjudged sufficient. The plaintiff excepted, and the case was passed to the Supreme Court before trial on the merits. The opinion states the substance of the plea in question.

W. W. Miles and *W. M. Wright* for the plaintiff.

The plea is bad in that it does not confess the trespass alleged in the declaration. Chit. Pl. (14 Am. ed.) Vol. I, 501, Vol. III, 1096.

The plea is also bad in failing to allege that defendant killed the dog *while* hunting deer. *Simonds* v. *Holmes*, 15 L. R. A. 253; *Wells* v. *Head*, 4 Car. & P. 568; *Johnson* v. *McConnell*, 80 Cal. 545.

Albert W. Farman and *George B. Young* for the defendant.

ROWELL, C. J. This is trespass for killing a dog. The second plea, which follows the general issue, attempts to justify, and alleges that "on the day and date of the said supposed killing of said dog, said dog was by the defendant found pursuing, hunting, and chasing wild deer." To this plea the defendant demurs generally, and objects that it is insufficient because it does not confess a cause of action. Without considering whether the objection can be taken advantage of on general demurrer, it is clear that the plea gives good color in the words, "the said supposed killing of said dog," and consequently sufficiently identifies the trespass attempted to be justified with the one declared upon.

Baron PARKE says in *Earnstaff* v. *Russell,* 10 M. & W. 365, that there can be no doubt whatever that the word *supposed* is a sufficient admission of a cause of action; that it is the usual mode of pleading; and that he had seen instances without number where, after the general issue, a special plea followed professing to answer the supposed cause of action in ' the declaration mentioned. The word *supposed* is equivalent to *alleged,* and a sufficient admission of a cause of action. Note to *Gould* v. *Lasbury,* 1 C. M. & R. 254, Hare and Wallace's ed; Martin, Civil Proced. § 290.

The statute provides that any person may lawfully kill any dog found hunting deer. Sec. 3, No. 108, Acts of 1898. But the dog must be killed while thus hunting, and the plea is bad for not so alleging. We do not construe the statute to require, in order to warrant the killing of a dog found hunting deer, that the dog must be of the breed or variety named in the statute, nor that the owner or the harborer of the dog must have permitted it to run at large in the forests where deer inhabit. Those provisions relate to the penalty of the statute, and not to the right to kill a dog found hunting deer.

Judgment reversed, demurrer sustained, plea adjudged insufficient, and cause remanded.

THE BELLOWS FREE ACADEMY OF FAIRFAX, VERMONT, AND
THE TRUSTEES THEREOF, AND THE TOWN OF FAIRFAX
v. MARGARET B. SOWLES, EDWARD A. SOWLES, AND
SUSAN B. SOWLES.

May Term, 1903.

Present: TYLER, MUNSON, WATSON, STAFFORD, and HASELTON, JJ.

Opinion filed May 28, 1904.

*Wills—Conditioned Bequest—Acceptance—Trustees—Duties
and Powers—Injunction—Parties.*

When a bequest is made to a town on condition that, at a legally
warned meeting, it should vote to accept the bequest on the conditions named in the will, and should appoint five trustees to
take charge of the same; and the town at such meeting voted
"to accept the bequest," and appointed men "as trustees to receive
the property and carry out the purposes as named in the testator's will," such vote is a sufficient acceptance of the bequest on
the conditions named in the will.

When a bequest is made to a town in trust for the purpose of establishing an academy, and the will provides that the fund shall be
managed in a specified manner by trustees to be appointed by the
town, who should give bonds to the treasurer of the town, and
make report of their doings at each annual March meeting;
though after the trustees were appointed and had received the
fund, the Legislature passed a private law incorporating the academy and the trustees, and the trustees organized under the act,
this will not cause the bequest to go over, under a provision of the
will that, if the town should neglect or refuse to perform the
various conditions, or should divert any part of the fund from
the purpose of the trust the same should vest in a designated
person.

A will which gives shares of stock in a railroad company to a town
in trust for the purpose of establishing an academy, and which
provides that the dividends, "as far as practicable" shall be invested in said stock till the fund shall amount to a specified sum,
when a certain amount thereof shall be used in the construction
of buildings, does not mean that the fund shall be kept forever

in the stock of the same railroad company, but that when the fund, invested as directed, shall have increased to the extent specified, it may be re-invested, under the law pertaining to trust funds in general.

When, under the terms of a will giving certain shares of stock to a town in trust for the purpose of establishing an academy, trustees are elected by the town to receive and manage the property, and thereafter a private law is passed incorporating the academy and said trustees, a bill in equity subsequently brought by the town to restrain the executor of the testator from interfering with the sale of the stock, and which is sworn to by the trustees, one by one, is not demurrable on the ground that it is not in the name of proper parties, though said trustees are also therein named as trustees of the academy corporation, and that corporation is joined as orator.

APPEAL IN CHANCERY.   Heard on demurrer to the bill at the September Term, 1902, Franklin County, *Tyler*, Chancellor.   Demurrer overruled, *pro forma*, and bill adjudged sufficient.   The defendants appealed.   The opinion states the case.

E. A. Sowles for the defendants.

The Legislature cannot sanction a scheme of administration of a trust fund different from that prescribed by the donor. *Cary Library* v. *Bliss*, 151 Mass. 364; *Granville* v. *Mason*, 53 N. H. 515; *Thorp* v. *Fleming*, 1 Hous. 580; *Plimpton* v. *Jackson*, 15 Pa. St. 44; *Stanley* v. *Colt*, 5 Wall. 119; *Lackland* v. *Walker*, 151 Mo. 210; *Webster* v. *Morris*, 66 Wis. 396.

The directions given in an instrument of trust must be strictly followed, and are strictly construed. Perry Trusts, §§ 294, 460-475.

Alfred A. Hall and *Lee S. Tillotson* for the orator.

If the demurrer is not well founded, this Court should send down a mandate directing a final decree. *Bailey* v. *Holden, et al.,* 50 Vt. 14; *Stewart* v. *Flint,* 57 Vt. 216.

STAFFORD, J. This is a bill for an injunction, and the questions are raised by a demurrer to the bill which was incorporated in the answers and brought forward for hearing. It is claimed that the bill is insufficient for want of equity and for want of parties. It will be necessary to state the allegations rather fully.

When Hiram Bellows, late of St. Albans, died (Oct. 18, 1876) he left a will, made a few months before in part as follows: He gave in trust to his native town of Fairfax two hundred and fifty shares in the Chicago, Rock Island & Pacific Railroad Company of the par value of $100 each, the dividends upon which, as far as practicable, were to be invested in the same stock until the fund should amount to $250,000, for the purpose of establishing a free school in that town to be located on land thereinafter devised, and to be called The Bellows Free Academy of Fairfax, Vermont. The primary and higher branches of learning were to be taught therein and the children of indigent parents were to be preferred. Then followed a devise to the town, in trust, of a tract of land in Fairfax. Within one year from the time when notice of the bequest should be given by the executor to the selectmen of Fairfax, the town was to choose five competent and responsible men to serve as trustees of the funds and to control the land, the trustees to be chosen for terms of from one to five years respectively, and thereafter at each annual March meeting one trustee to be chosen for five years and all vacancies filled. The trustees were to give bonds to the treasurer of the town with ample sureties for the faithful discharge of their duties, upon failure to do which their places were to be vacant and others appointed in their stead. Said trustees were to take charge of the fund, which was to be called The Bellows Free Academy Fund, and make report of the same at each annual March meeting. They were to prevent the erection of any building on the premises until the funds should have accumulated to the sum of $250,000, but were to prepare the land as far as practicable by fencing and grading and setting out ornamental trees. When the funds should reach the sum named the trustees were directed to erect on the premises suitable buildings for the purpose aforesaid, expending in buildings, apparatus and library not to exceed $50,000, leaving $200,000 as a permanent fund, the interest of which was to be expended in procuring teachers and paying other expenses of the Academy. The bequest was made on condition that the town, at a legally warned meeting, within one year after receiving notice of this provision, should vote to accept the bequest upon the condition named and should appoint the trustees to take charge of the same. There was a further provision that if the town should neglect or refuse to perform the various conditions and stipulations, or directly or indirectly divert any part of the railroad shares or real estate or dividends, interest or avails thereof, "from the purposes and objects named in the will in the manner therein provided," said stocks, real estate, dividends, interest and avails should go to Margaret B. Sowles and her heirs forever.

The Margaret B. Sowles just named is the daughter of the testator. Her husband, Edward A. Sowles, is the executor of the will, and both are defendants hereto. The other defendant is their daughter.

Notice of the bequest was given to the town, and within one year thereafter, on the 6th day of March, 1877, at a legally warned meeting, the town "voted to accept the bequest of Hiram Bellows * *, * * to the town of Fairfax and appointed" five men for the specified terms "as trustees to receive the property and carry out the purposes as named in the testator's will." At each annual March meeting since, a new trustee has been chosen and all vacancies have been filled and bonds have been duly furnished. The trustees now holding office under the town's election are the individuals named in the bill as the trustees of the academy. The original trustees so elected, acting under the executor's advice, met, organized and received from him the stock, appointed him attorney to receive the dividends and left the certificates with him as such attorney. The executor had the land surveyed and put the trustees in possession and control, and it has remained in their possession and control or that of their successors ever since. They took charge of the funds and they and their successors have as far as practicable invested the dividends in shares of the same company. They have prevented the erection of any building on said land and have prepared it as directed.

At the session of the General Assembly of the State of Vermont for 1878, a private law was enacted (No. 164), entitled "An Act to Incorporate the Bellows Free Academy of Fairfax and the Trustees thereof." By that act such persons as might thereafter associate themselves together as trustees of the Bellows Free Academy of Fairfax or might have been or should thereafter be chosen or appointed as such trustees by that town in pursuance of said will, and their associates and successors in office, were constituted a body politic and corporate by the name of The Bellows Free Academy of Fairfax, Vermont, with all the rights, privileges and powers belonging to similar corporations for the purpose of instructing pupils as provided in said will, and with power to sue and be sued under the name aforesaid, and have a common seal. The corporation, or the trustees chosen by the town as required by the will, were empowered to make such by-laws, rules and regulations as were required by the terms of the will for the government of the corporation or said trustees, and their associates and successors, and for the establishment, control, endowment and government of the institution, and to take and hold by gift, grant, bequest, devise, purchase or otherwise property to any amount, the net annual income of which should not exceed $40,000, and to manage, control, use and dispose of the same for the benefit of the academy in a manner not inconsistent with, but in conformity to and in furtherance of, the provisions of said will. The corporation, or the trustees chosen by the town in accordance with the provisions of the will, or the town of Fairfax, were empowered to perpetuate the existence of the corporation or of the trustees and their associates and successors in office by the election of new trustees under the provisions of the will or otherwise, and the acts of the town done under or in pursuance of the provisions of the will were ratified and approved, and the town was empowered to carry out the provisions of the will.

This enactment was procured by Edward A. Sowles. The trustees elected by the town organized under the act and they and their successors in office elected by the town have maintained the organization, and the present trustees thus elected now constitute the same. They have made reports at each annual March meeting. The fund now consists of 1,348 shares of the capital stock of said railroad company, standing in the name of the town of Fairfax as trustee, and cash and other securities to about $18,000. The market value of the stock has fluctuated, but is now about $173 per share. It is probable that it will soon reach a point when a sale of it will make the fund to amount to $250,000. Believing which, the academy and the trustees thereof at a meeting duly called for that purpose, unanimously instructed one of their number to sell the stock at not less than $175 per share, a price which would make the fund of the required amount. The agent went to New York to execute his commission, when he was prevented by a telegram from Mr. Sowles to the transfer agent of the company requesting the latter to decline the transfer until after a vote of the town. The agent returned to Vermont and waited upon Mr. Sowles to learn the reason for his action, and was informed of various objections and claims which are not recounted here, as for the most part they are not now insisted upon. To obviate the objection suggested in the telegram a town meeting was warned for the purpose of authorizing or confirming a sale of the stock, and electing an agent to carry it out; but the date for the meeting had not arrived when the bill was filed. If the sale is delayed the stock is likely to depreciate in market value, and it may be a long time before the fund will again reach the required amount.

The orators believe upon good reason that if not restrained by injunction the defendants will hinder and impede the sale, and therefore ask that they be temporarily enjoined from so doing, and that upon final hearing the injunction be made perpetual. A temporary injunction was granted.

In the Court of Chancery there was a *pro forma* decree overruling the demurrer and adjudging the bill sufficient, and the appeal is from that decree.

The substantial objections made under the demurrer are:

(1) That the trust was not accepted by the town.

(2) That the gift over to Margaret B. Sowles has become operative by reason of the act of incorporation and the proceedings of the trustees thereunder.

(3) That there was no right to sell the stock.

(4) That the bill is not in the name of the proper parties.

(1) As to the first point it is enough to say that we regard the vote already recited as a sufficient acceptance of the bequest upon the conditions contained in the will.

(2) Has the gift over become operative? The will vests the title to the land and the stock in the town of Fairfax. The town is the real trustee. The trust is to be administered through five officers or agents, called trustees, to be elected and qualified as the will prescribes, whose course of dealing is also to some extent laid down by the testator. If the will had been silent as to the persons through whom the trust was to be administered, the case would apparently have fallen under V. S. 3034-3037, which provides for the management of such property by the Trustees of Public Funds. As already stated, the stock has been kept in the name of the town and has been managed by the trustees in the town's name, just as the statute requires shall be done in the case of property in the hands of the Trustees of Public Funds. V. S. 3035.

What has the town done or permitted that constitutes a diversion of the property from its true use and legal control? It does not appear that the town had the act passed nor that anything has been done with the fund by the trustees except what they ought to have done by the terms of the will. No outsider has meddled with the trust property or interfered with its management. The trustees have given bonds and made reports as required by the will. It may be said that they have attempted to make use of the act of incorporation which the defendant, Edward A. Sowles, procured, as he now says, unlawfully and against the right of his wife. But the title to the property has never been transferred to the corporation, nor has any attempt been made to transfer it. It is only the trustees elected by the town and duly qualified according to the will who have been associated together as the members of the corporation, and their decisions are alleged to have been unanimous. It may not be easy to point out any advantage in the act of incorporation, and we do not decide that it can be used at all in the administration of the trust. But neither is it easy to see what harm has yet been done or why the act should be treated as an attempt to divert the trust property until by reason of it, or in the name of it something has been done, or attempted, or left undone contrary to the provisions of the will.

(3) Neither do we see any merit in the claim that the trustees were attempting to divert the fund from the purposes of the trust in proceeding as they were to sell it at a price that would raise the fund to the amount it was required to reach before it could be used. The will does not mean that the fund shall be kept forever in the stock of the same railroad. To impute such an intention to the testator would be unreasonable and inconsistent with the language of the bequest. The requirement is that it shall be kept in that stock, as far as practicable, *until* it has reached $250,000. Thereafter, the intention evidently is that it shall be invested under the law pertaining to trust funds in general. The trustees were proceeding in strict performance of the testator's directions when they were obstructed by the defendants. It is the defendants, not the trustees, who are attempting to thwart his purpose.

(4) As to parties. The town is here seeking to carry out through its agents, selected as the will required, the trust reposed in it by the testator. As before remarked, the town is the real trustee. It is to the town's treasurer that the bonds are to be taken, and it is to the town the reports are to be made, and it is the duty of the town to oversee to some extent

the administration of the trust by its agents. We entertain no doubt that it was a proper party to a bill brought as this was to insure the execution of the trust according to the testator's purpose. The trustees, so called, elected by the town, have made oath to the bill one by one. It is true that they also name themselves as the trustees of the academy corporation, and that the corporation itself is joined as a party, but the bill itself clearly shows that the town is behind the proceedings with the concurrent action of the officers who are to administer the trust, as well as the selectmen and the agent for prosecuting and defending suits, who have also signed and sworn to the bill in behalf of the town. Whether the academy, or the trustees thereof under the act of incorporation, are proper parties to the bill, and whether the trustees have signed in proper form to make themselves orators in their capacity as trustees by the election of the town under the provisions of the will—these are questions which we do not consider important under this demurrer, for we have in the person of the town, acting through the officers aforesaid, a proper and sufficient party to the bill as an injunction bill to prevent threatened interference with the administration of the trust.

Decree affirmed and cause remanded.

O. V. Joslyn v. Taplin & Rowell.

May Term, 1904.

Present: Rowell, C. J., Tyler, Start, Watson, and Haselton, JJ.

Opinion filed May 28, 1904.

*Land Contract—Reservation of Crops—Vendee's Interest—
Foreclosure.*

Under a contract for the sale of land, wherein it is provided that the
vendor "reserves the ownership and control of all crops" grown
upon the premises till the notes given for the purchase money are
fully paid, the vendee has neither an equity of redemption nor any
other attachable interest in such crops while the notes are unpaid.

Said notes are not paid within the meaning of the contract, so as to
give the vendee any interest in such crops, merely because the
value of the premises, when the vendor obtained possession thereof,
under a decree in a proceeding brought by him to foreclose the
vendor's interest therein, exceeded the sum due on the notes and
the costs of foreclosure.

TROVER. Plea, the general issue. Trial by court at
the September Term, 1903, Orleans County, *Stafford*, J., presiding. Judgment for the plaintiff. The defendant excepted.

The trial court found that the defendant at the time of
trial was, and for ten years before had been, a deputy sheriff
within and for the County of Orleans; that on April 4, 1903,
an execution, issued on a judgment of the Orleans County
Court in favor of C. K. Colby, W. S. May, and William
Collison and against O. H. Hawkins, was placed in his hands,
as such deputy sheriff, for service on said O. H. Hawkins;
that, after making demand of said Hawkins, the defendant
levied said execution on fifty tons of hay which had been
attached on the original writ on the 19th day of August,
1902; that said execution was issued in season to charge said

hay so attached; that after said levy, and before the day fixed
for the sale on the execution, the defendants converted said
hay to their own use; that on July 5, 1889, James R. Collison
and said O. H. Hawkins entered into a written contract whereby Collison agreed to sell, and Hawkins agreed to buy, certain
land for $2,684, as evidenced by several promissory notes
signed by said Hawkins; that said contract contained the
following:

"The said party of the first part reserves the ownership
and control of all crops, produce, and products raised or
grown hereafter on said premises, until the notes below described are paid, with interest annually, in full"; that said
Hawkins occupied the premises described in said contract
from the date thereof till after September 9, 1902, and during that time cut and put into the barns on said premises the
hay in question, which was grown on said premises; that said
Hawkins was in possession of said premises and of said hay
when said attachment was made; that Hawkins failing to pay
his said notes, James R. Collison obtained a decree from the
court of chancery, dated September 9, 1901, foreclosing the
equity of redemption of said Hawkins in the premises, and
said decree became absolute September 9, 1902, when the
value of said premises was more than enough to pay the sum
due on said notes and the costs of foreclosure; that on the 8th
day of September, 1902, said James R. Collison sold the hay
in question to the defendants, who later moved it.

W. W. Miles and *W. M. Wright* for the plaintiff.

The relation of Hawkins and J. R. Collison was that of
mortgagor and mortgagee. *Whiting* v. *Adams,* 66 Vt. 679;
Davis v. *Hemenway,* 27 Vt. 589; *Paine* v. *McDowell &
Tucker,* 71 Vt. 28.

The defendants have obtained only Collison's interest in the hay. But growing crops do not pass to the mortgagee if severed before the decree becomes absolute. *Caldwell* v. *Aslop,* 17 L. R. A. 782; *Richards* v. *Knight,* 4 L. R. A. 453; *Jones* v. *Adams,* 50 L. R. A. 388; *Yeazel* v. *Emspaha,* 24 L. R. A. 449; Cooley Torts, p. 507 & *p. 434; Tiedman, Real Property, 324.

But the premises, under the facts found, paid the notes. *Loveland* v. *Leland,* 3 Vt. 581; *Thomas* v. *Warner,* 15 Vt. 110; *Paris* v. *Hulett,* 26 Vt. 308.

B. F. D. Carpenter and *F. W. Baldwin* for the defendants.

Hawkins never paid the notes. Hence, by the terms of the contract, he never owned the hay. *Batchelder* v. *Jenness,* 59 Vt. 104; *Bellows* v. *Wells,* 36 Vt. 599; *Fitch* v. *Buck,* 38 Vt. 683; *Walworth* v. *Jenness,* 58 Vt. 670; *Dickerman* v. *Ray,* 55 Vt. 65; *Smith* v. *Atkins,* 18 Vt. 461; *Baxter* v. *Bush,* 29 Vt. 465; *Cooney* v. *Hayes,* 40 Vt. 478; *Darling* v. *Robbins,* 60 Vt. 347.

When the decree became absolute, Collison became the sole owner of the real estate and of the crops. *Oakman* v. *Walker,* 69 Vt. 344; *Franklin* v. *Gorham,* 2 Am. Dec. 86; *Whitney* v. *Higgins,* 70 Am. Dec. 748; *Paris* v. *Hulett,* 26 Vt. 308.

WATSON, J. The land contract contained a provision whereby the vendor reserved the ownership and control of all crops, produce, and products thereafter raised or grown on the premises until the notes described therein should be fully paid. Within the meaning of that provision, the notes were never paid. Consequently the vendee never became the owner of the hay in question nor of any attachable interest therein. Under this reservation the vendor was the sole owner of the hay until he sold it to the defendants after the decree in the foreclosure proceedings respecting the land had become absolute. By their purchase the defendants became the owners thereof and were such at the time of the alleged conversion. The cases of *Batchelder* v. *Jenness,* 59 Vt. 104, 7 Atl. 279, and of *Dickerman* v. *Ray,* 55 Vt. 65, are authorities decisive of this question.

It is argued, however, that under the said reservation the parties to the contract stood in the relation of mortgagor and mortgagee respecting the crops, produce, and products, and that the vendee as such mortgagor had an attachable interest in the hay. In support of this contention the plaintiff relies upon *Whiting* v. *Adams,* 66 Vt. 679, 30 Atl. 32, where a land contract containing a similar reservation was involved. But there the vendor brought his bill to foreclose the vendee's equity of redemption not only in the land but in the property covered by the reservation also, thereby admitting in his pleadings in effect that the parties stood in the relation of mortgagor and mortgagee under the reservation. The vendor having made such a case by his bill was bound by it. *Thomas* v. *Warner,* 15 Vt. 110. Furthermore the parties agreed that such was their relation. "This admits," says the court, "that the defendant has an equity in all the property embraced in the contract sought to be foreclosed," and the case was treated accordingly. Hence the question now under consideration was not then before the court, and that case is not an authority thereon.

Since the vendee in the land contract had no attachable interest in the hay, the plaintiff acquired no lien thereon by his attachment as against the vendor or the defendants, his subsequent vendees. *Sanborn* v. *Kittridge,* 20 Vt. 632, 50 Am. Dec. 58.

It is found that the value of the premises which came to the vendor under the decree in the foreclosure proceedings, exceeded the sum due on said notes and the costs of foreclosure. The plaintiff claims that the notes were thereby fully paid, and that consequently the vendee then became the owner of the hay. But this could not be so unless he previously had an equity of redemption therein, which we have seen he did not have.

Judgment reversed, and judgment for defendants to recover their costs.

State *v.* Klondike Machine.

May Term, 1904.

Present: ROWELL, C. J., TYLER, MUNSON, START, WATSON, STAFFORD, and HASELTON, JJ.

Opinion filed June 1, 1904.

Gambling Devices—Seizure—Order of Destruction—Appeal —No 121, Acts 1898.

There is no right of appeal from the judgment of a justice of the peace ordering the destruction of a Klondike machine under No. 121, § 2, Acts 1898.

APPEAL from the judgment of a justice of the peace ordering the destruction of a Klondike machine upon a complaint brought before him under No. 121, § 2, Acts 1898, by the sheriff of Bennington County. Heard on motion to dis-

miss the appeal at the December Term, 1903, Bennington.
County, *Watson,* J., presiding. Judgment *pro forma* dismissing the appeal. The appellant excepted.

The Auto Machine Co. entered as claimant before the
justice, and is the appellant.

W. B. Sheldon for the appellant.

The proceeding at first was *in rem* but, when the appellant came in as claimant, it became a proceeding *inter partes.*
State v. *Adams,* 72 Vt. 255.

It never has been the policy of this State to take away
the right of appeal in criminal cases. *In Re Kennedy,* 55 Vt.
1; *State* v. *Peterson,* 41 Vt. 510.

J. J. Shakshober, State's Attorney, and *O. M. Barber* for
the State.

This proceeding is purely *in rem,* instituted to determine
the status of the property. *In Re Powers,* 25 Vt. 261; *Woodruff* v. *Taylor,* 20 Vt. 65; *Johnson* v. *Williams,* 48 Vt. 565;
Johnson v. *Perkins,* 48 Vt. 572; *State* v. *Intoxicating Liquor,*
55 Vt. 82; *State* v. *Barrels of Liquor,* 47 N. H. 375; *Barnat-
coat et al.* v. *Six Casks of Gunpowder,* 1 Met. 255; *Com.* v.
Intoxicating Liquor, 14 Gray 375.

A proceeding of this kind should be summary. It is in
the exercise of the police power, and unless the statute au-
thorizing the proceeding provides for an appeal, none lies.
Lincoln v. *Smith,* 27 Vt. 333; *Lawton* v. *Steele,* 119 N. Y.
134; S. C. 7 L. R. A. 134; *Grossman* v. *Oakland* (Ore.) 36·
L. R. A. 593; *Savannah* v. *Mulligan,* (95 Ga. 323), 29 L.
R. A. 303; *Lowry* v. *Rainwater,* 35 Am. Rep. 420; *State* v.
Conlin, 27 Vt. 318; *State* v. *Speyer,* 67 Vt. 502; *Indiana* v.
Robbins, (Ind.) 8 L. R. A. 438; *State* v. *Karstendiek,* (La.)

39 L. R. A. 520; *State* v. *Ford*, 41 L. R. A. 55; S. C. 85 Md. 465.

Since the statute provides for notice to the owner of the machine, all constitutional requirements are met. *Lincoln* v. *Smith*, 27 Vt. 333; *Lowry* v. *Rainwater*, 35 Am. Rep. 420; *Com.* v. *Dana*, 2 Met. 329; *Bobel* v. *People*, 173 Ill. 19; *State* v. *Peterson*, 41 Vt. 504.

MUNSON, J. No. 121, Acts of 1898, consists of three sections; of which the first imposes a penalty for keeping a Klondike machine in a place of public resort, the second provides for the seizure, condemnation and destruction of the machine, and the third gives justices jurisdiction of cases arising under the act. The question is whether there is a right of appeal in proceedings under the second section.

It is held that the general provision allowing appeals from the judgments of justices in civil causes applies only to cases falling within the ordinary jurisdiction of justices, and cannot be extended to cases arising under a special and extraordinary jurisdiction. *Griswold* v. *Rutland*, 23 Vt. 324. This decision is not directly in point here, for the proceeding under the second section of this act, while not strictly a criminal proceeding, must be classed with criminal cases. *State* v. *One Bottle of Brandy*, 43 Vt. 297. But we think the reasoning of the decision may properly be applied to a case of this character.

The general provision governing appeals in criminal causes allows respondents to appeal from justice judgments against them in all cases where the judgment is not rendered upon a plea of guilty. V. S. 1932. The prosecution of the keeper under the first section of the act of 1898 is in line with the ordinary jurisdiction of justices, and may properly be treated as within the general provision just cited. Moreover,

the third section of the act could not be construed as giving
the justice final jurisdiction of the prosecution of the keeper,
for to do so would make the provision unconstitutional. *State*
v. *Peterson*, 41 Vt. 504. But the proceeding under the second section of the act is not a matter of ordinary jurisdiction,.
nor fairly within the language of the general provision for
appeals; and the constitutional consideration does not require
that it be brought within that provision, for in these cases the·
claimant would not be entitled to a jury in the County Court.
State v. *Intoxicating Liquor, Smith Claimant*, 55 Vt. 82.

Section two provides that "if, upon hearing, it is found
.that such machine was seized in a place of public resort, the·
same shall be ordered destroyed, and the justice shall issue·
his warrant to carry such order into effect." If the Legislature had contemplated an appeal, it would doubtless have accompanied this provision with further sections regulating the
appeal, and have adapted the language of the provision to
the contingency of a final order in a higher court; as is done·
in the statute authorizing the destruction of intoxicating liquor.
But the claimant argues that inasmuch as that statute recog-·
nizes the right of appeal without directly conferring it, it must
be considered that the Legislature deemed the general provision for appeals applicable to proceedings of that character.
This can hardly be claimed, however, when the history of the·
enactment is considered; for the act as originally passed contained an express provision for an appeal, and this remained·
in the statutes until omitted from the revision of 1880. Acts·
1852, No. 24, § 14; G. S. ch. 94, § 24; R. L. § 3824.

We hold that no appeal lies from the order authorized
by the second section of this act.

Judgment affirmed.

STATE *v.* GEORGE RAYMO.

January Term, 1904.

Present: ROWELL, C. J., TYLER, MUNSON, START, WATSON, and
HASELTON, JJ.

Opinion filed June 2, 1904.

*Criminal Law—Mental Condition—Evidence—Declarations
· of Respondent—Self-Defense—Instructions.*

Declarations of a party in his own favor are not admissible, unless
they are a part of the *res gestae.*

Declarations of a person expressing mental suffering are admissible
when the mental state is a material fact to be proved; but the
statements of past suffering, or of the past cause of suffering, are
not admissible.

In a prosecution for an assault on B., wherein the respondent claims
he acted in self-defense, his declarations, made after prior assaults
of B. on him, that he was afraid of B.—afraid he would injure him,
etc., were no part of the *res* of such prior assaults, and are not
admissible.

In this case it was proper for the court, in explaining to the jury the
apprehension of danger a person must be in to justify him in
taking his assailant's life, to say that if the respondent did not,
at the time he was assaulted, anticipate more serious injury than
he actually received, that would not be the great and serious bodily
harm to which the law refers when it says that a man may take
his assailant's life rather than receive such injury.

INFORMATION filed at the respondent's request, for an
assault with intent to kill and murder. Plea, not guilty. Trial
by jury at the September Term, 1903, Orleans County, *Stafford,* J., presiding. Verdict guilty, and judgment thereon.
The respondent excepted.

The evidence of the respondent tended to show that, in
consequence of the blows he received from Bronson, "his nose
was swollen some, his right eye was nearly closed up and was
black and blue, his face was marked up and had blood on it."

But the exceptions further state: "Raymo took the stand in his behalf, and at that time, eight or nine days after the affray in question, his face and head showed no signs or marks of injury, and he did not claim he was then suffering in any respect from the blows he received from Bronson." The opinion states the other facts.

H. F. Graham and *F. C. Williams* for the respondent.

The declarations of the respondent should have been admitted. They were part of the *res* of the prior assaults. *People* v. *Davis*, 56 N. Y. 95; *Eything* v. *People*, 79 N. Y. 546; *Ohio, etc. R. Co.* v. *Stein*, 19 L. R. A. 733; *Hadley* v. *Carter*, 8 N. H. 40.

Perfect coincidence in time is not required to make declarations part of the *res gestae*. *Ala. etc. R. Co.* v. *Hawk*, 47 Am. Rep. 403; Wharton Crim. Ev. (9 ed.) §§ 262-291; *State* v. *Daley*, 53 Vt. 444.

Albert W. Farman, State's Attorney, for the State.

TYLER, J. This trial was upon an information which charged that the respondent, on October 13, 1903, made an assault upon Malcolm Bronson with intent to kill and murder him; trial, and conviction of a breach of the peace. The respondent's evidence tended to show that Bronson was the first assailant, and that the respondent used no more force than was necessary to repel him; that Bronson was unarmed; that the respondent had a pistol that he obtained two or three months before with which to defend himself in case of an attack by Bronson. In the affray both parties struggled for the possession of the pistol, which was discharged, the ball striking Bronson and wounding him. The question was whether the respondent used excessive force in his defence.

The respondent's evidence tended to show that Bronson had been in his family a considerable part of the time for several years; that the respondent had ordered him to leave the house, but he refused to go; that Bronson had assaulted him several times and severely bruised his face and had threatened his life; that Bronson was a lighter man than himself, but more athletic and that in all their affrays Bronson was victorious.

The respondent testified to these facts and to his fear of Bronson; that in the spring of 1903, after Bronson had assaulted him at his house, he went to the house of a neighbor named Humphrey, to hire a horse to drive to the state's attorney's office to make a complaint. Humphrey testified that the respondent was much excited, and the respondent offered to show further by him that he then told him that he was afraid of Bronson, afraid he would injure him, and afraid to return home, which offer was excluded subject to exception.

The respondent also offered to show that after Bronson had assaulted him on an occasion in December, 1902, he went to the house of his neighbor, Porter, for assistance. Faulkner, the only man whom he found there, testified that his face was bruised and bloody and that the witness went home with him. The respondent offered to prove by the witness that he then told him he wanted him to go home with him because he was afraid to return alone, as Bronson was there and had been pounding him, which offer was excluded subject to exception. The respondent lived upon a farm, but how far from these neighbors did not appear.

Proof of the respondent's declarations to Humphrey and Faulkner was offered as tending to show his fear of Bronson and his apprehension of bodily harm from him, and as bearing upon the question of excessive force used in the assault

for which he was on trial. It was competent for him to show
by proper evidence that he was in fear of Bronson, before
and at the time of the assault, by reason of Bronson's previous assaults upon him. The question is whether he could
prove his condition of mind by his own declarations made at
the times stated in his offers.

It is the general rule that declarations of a party in his
favor cannot be introduced in evidence. *Ellis* v. *Cleveland,*
55 Vt. 358. An exception to the rule is where the declarations are made as a part of the *res gestae,* otherwise the say-
ings of a party in his favor made at any time would be admissible, and the general rule would be abrogated.

The only case in this State upon which the respondent
relies is *State* v. *Daley,* 53 Vt. 442. There the respondent
was on trial for stealing a heifer; he admitted the taking, but
claimed that about three months before that time he lost a
heifer resembling the one taken, and that he took this one
supposing it was his. He offered to show that immediately
after the alleged loss he was hunting and inquiring for a lost
heifer; held, admissible for the reason that the inquiries were
a part of the *res* of the search.

That these declarations were not admissible as a part of
the *res* of the assaults that had, a short time before, been committed upon the respondent is well settled. In *State* v. *Carlton,* 48 Vt. 636, the statement of the wounded man as to where
the respondent shot him, made about two minutes after the
assault and about eleven rods distant from the place, was held
inadmissible.

It cannot be maintained, as contended, that these declarations of fear were admissible as expressive of the respondent's mental condition. It is the general rule formulated from
many authorities that declarations of a person expressing

mental feeling are admissible in evidence when the mental state is a material fact to be proved; but statements as to past sufferings or as to the past cause of the suffering are not admissible; 1 Greenl. Ev. § 102; Chase's Steph. Dig. of Ev. § 47, notes; Abbott's Trial Ev. 729; *Mut. Life Ins. Co.* v. *Hillmon,* 145 U. S.285; *Comm.* v. *Trefethen,* 157 Mass. 180; *Kidder* v. *Bacon,* 74 Vt. 275, 52 Atl. 322.

Another exception to the general rule that a party cannot make testimony for himself by proof of his own statements, is by some authorities stated to be, that where he is entitled to the benefit, in evidence, of a fact, or of an act done by himself, then his declaration made contemporaneously with the fact or act, and explanatory of its quality and motive, should also be admitted. But these offers did not fall within this exception, for the one made to Faulkner as characterizing his acts in seeking assistance and in going home included a statement that Bronson had pounded him, which was not admissible, as it was a mere narrative of a past event. *Knight* v. *Smythe,* 57 Vt. 529. The declaration to Humphrey, if made, was explanatory of no material act. In the circumstances the respondent could not supplement his own testimony about his fear of Bronson by proving his declarations made to these witnesses.

It is not necessary to decide whether there was error in the expression used by the court in the charge, to the effect that the respondent must have reasonably believed in his danger. The charge was amended in this respect and the law stated in such a way that no exception was taken.

In explaining to the jury the apprehension of danger that a person assaulted must be in to warrant him in taking his assailant's life, the Court remarked that if the respondent did not at the time anticipate more serious injury from Bron-

son than he actually received that would not be the great and
serious bodily harm which the law refers to when it says that
a man may take his assailant's life rather than receive such
injury. In this there was no error. It only illustrated the
rule of law that a person assaulted must be in great danger
or in apprehension of it to justify his use of a deadly weapon
in defence.

*Judgment that there was no error in the proceedings and
that the respondent take nothing by his exceptions.*

STATE v. FRED JEWETT.

January Term, 1904.

Present: ROWELL, C. J., TYLER, MUNSON, START, WATSON, STAFFORD,
and HASELTON, JJ.

Opinion filed August 2, 1904.

Game Law—Killing Deer.

No. 94, Acts 1896, prohibits the killing of deer at any time, except
during the last ten days of October in each year, and then only
deer having horns may be killed.

INDICTMENT for unlawfully killing wild deer. Heard
on demurrer to the indictment at the September Term, 1903,
Washington County, *Stafford,* J., presiding. Demurrer overruled, *pro forma.* The respondent excepted.

Lord & Carlton for the respondent.

The words of the statute, "as hereinafter provided," must
refer to the open season, the only words in the excepted clause

to which they could refer. This statute must be construed strictly. *State* v. *Broderick,* 61 Vt. 424; *Com.* v. *Fisher,* 17 Mass. 49; *U. S.* v. *Moulton,* 5 Mason 579; *U. S.* v. *Sheldon,* 2 Wheat. 119; *Law* v. *Kellmere,* 25 N. J. L. 522; McClain Crim. Law, § 83; *Todd* v. *U. S.,* 158 U. S. 282; *U. S.* v. *Lacher,* 134 U. S. 624.

John H. Senter, State's Attorney, for the State.

START, J. This case was heard on demurrer to the indictment, wherein it is charged that the respondent, on the 23rd day of October, 1903, one wild deer, without horns, did kill and destroy. The respondent contends that the killing of deer, with or without horns, during the last ten days of October in each year is not prohibited by No. 94 of the Acts of 1896.

Section one of the act prohibits the killing of deer, "except in the open season as hereinafter provided"; and no deer can be lawfully killed in this State, except as is thereafter provided by the act. The only permit thereafter given is found in section two, which provides that deer having horns may be hunted and taken in this State during the last ten days of October in each year, with this exception, the killing of deer is prohibited at all seasons of the year, and in the open season only deer having horns can be lawfully killed. The act does not provide for an open season for killing all kinds of deer. It only provides an open season for killing deer having horns. The words, "as hereinafter provided," found in the exception to the prohibited act, do not refer solely to the open season thereafter provided; they also refer to "deer having horns." Any other construction of the act would render these words meaningless and inoperative. The act fairly admits of a construction that will give effect to

these words, and when it is so read, it is clear that it provides that no deer shall be killed in this State, except that deer
having horns may be killed during the last ten days of October in each year; and that the killing of deer having no horns
is prohibited.   Therefore, the indictment, which charges that
the respondent killed a deer without horns, charges a statutory offense.

Judgment affirmed, and cause remanded.

L. G. HAMMOND'S ADMR. *v.* M. O. HAMMOND.

May Term, 1904.

Present: ROWELL, C. J., TYLER, START, STAFFORD, and HASELTON, JJ.

Opinion filed August 2, 1904.

*Statute of Limitations—Payment on Account—Evidence—
Interest—Annual Balances.*

The mere fact that decedent's books, in a long account against the
    defendant, show two charges against him for articles sold, one of
    25 cents each on January 5; one charge of 70 cents on September
    30; two charges, aggregating 45 cents on September 4; and on
    September 7, two credits, one of 45 cents for squash and one for
    $1.20 for butter, does not tend to show that either the squash or
    the butter was delivered in payment of any specific items of the
    account, so as to prevent its being a general credit thereon.
In assumpsit on a book account interest should be computed on the
    annual balance.

GENERAL ASSUMPSIT, with specification of book account.   Plea, the general issue.   Heard on the report of a
referee at the December. Term, 1903, Windsor County, *Mun-*

son, J., presiding. Judgment that the plaintiff recover 91 cents and interest.. The plaintiff excepted.

The referee reported that the decedent and the defendant were brothers; that the former was a merchant and the latter a farmer during all the time covered by the account, which was nearly thirty years; that the decedent's books of account were received in evidence without objection; that solely from an inspection of said books he found that the credits in question were intended to apply on the specific debit items named in the opinion, and not on the general account, and submitted to the court whether he was justified in so doing.

William W. Stickney, John G. Sargent, and *Homer L. Skeels* for the plaintiff.

When payments appear on an open account the law applies such payments to the earlier items of the account. 2 Greenl. Ev. 243; *Morgan* v. *Tarbell*, 28 Vt. 498; *Pierce* v. *Knight*, 31 Vt. 707; *St. Albans* v. *Faley*, 46 Vt. 448; *Crampton* v. *Pratt*, 106 Mass. 257; *Sunwich* v. *Fish*, 2 Gray 298; *Atkins* v. *Atkins*, 71 Vt. 422; *Jeffers* v. *Pease*, 74 Vt. 215.

Each item of payment takes the whole account out of the Statute of Limitations. *Abbott* v. *Keith*, 11 Vt. 525.

Butler & Moloney for the defendant.

There is nothing on the book to show that the credits in question were paid on the general account. *Robinson & Wiggins* v. *Doolittle*, 12 Vt. 249; *Hicks Est.* v. *Blanchard*, 60 Vt. 681.

An inspection of the account shows these items to have been specific payments. *Hodges* v. *Manley*, 25 Vt. 210; *Harris* v. *Howard's Est.*, 56 Vt. 695; *Abbott* v. *Keith*, 11 Vt. 525; *Chapman* v. *Goodrich*, 55 Vt. 356.

START, J. The important inquiry is whether the squash credited on the plaintiff's account at forty-five cents and butter at one dollar and twenty cents, under the date of September 7, 1895, are general credits. If they, or either of them, are such credits, the account is not barred by the Statute of Limitations, and the plaintiff is entitled to recover. The evidence, which it is claimed tends to show that these items were delivered in payment of specific items of the account, is as follows: There is a charge on the plaintiff's account of twenty-five cents for soda, and a like sum for sugar, under the date of January 5, 1895, and a charge subsequent to the credit of the butter, under the date of September 30, 1895, of seventy cents for salt, and these charges amount to one dollar and twenty cents; and there is a charge of thirty-five cents for coffee and ten cents for codfish, under the date of September 4, 1895, amounting to forty-five cents. If these facts tend to show that the squash and butter were delivered in payment of these items upon the debtor side of the account, then the referee so finds; otherwise he finds they are general credits upon the account.

These facts do not tend to show that the butter was delivered in payment of any specified item or items of the account. In amount it does not correspond with any one charge upon which it is claimed it should apply. In order to get a sum that will equal the credit, the referee goes back in the account some nine months to two items amounting to fifty cents, and forward to an item, subsequent to the credit, of seventy cents. In going back in the account, we find many charges of fifty cents to which the credit will apply equally as well as to the two items under the date of January 5, 1898. Also, there is a charge of one dollar and twenty cents on which the credit might apply without dividing it. In going forward in the account, we find an item of fifty cents for paper charged on the same day that the seventy cents for salt is charged. It is not probable that the parties intended the credit to apply upon anticipated transactions in part only, when the credit would just extinguish the indebtedness arising from that transaction. Under these circumstances, it will not be presumed that the parties intended to divide the credit and apply a part on particular charges that preceded it and a part on an indebtedness to thereafter accrue, when there was an existing indebtedness exceeding the credit on which it would naturally apply. There being no evidence tending to show that the butter was delivered in payment of any specific items of the account, it must be considered and applied as a general credit upon the account.

The referee computed interest on the annual balances. In this there was no error. *Langdon* v. *Caselton,* 30 Vt. 285.

Judgment reversed, and judgment for the plaintiff to recover the balance of account found due by the referee, on the basis that no part of the account is barred by the Statute of Limitations, with interest.

ALVIN J. FRENCH v. THE GRAND TRUNK RAILWAY CO.

May Term, 1904.

Present: ROWELL, C. J., TYLER, START, WATSON, STAFFORD, and
HASELTON, JJ.

Opinion filed August 2, 1904.

*Railroads—Person on Track—Injury—Contributory Negli-
gence—Last Clear Chance—Concurrent Negligence—
Request to Charge—Motion for Verdict.*

A request to instruct the jury that, on all the evidence in the case,
plaintiff is not entitled to recover, is, in effect, a motion for a verdict, and sufficiently states the ground thereof; and an exception
to its denial reserved the question whether, on the view of the
evidence most favorable to him, the plaintiff was entitled to have
the case submitted to the jury.

When the negligence of the plaintiff and that of the defendant are
concurrent and operative at the time of the injury, and each contributes to it, there can be no recovery.

Although when a person has reached a dangerous position where he
cannot help himself, and vigilance on his part will not avert the
injury, his negligence in reaching that position will not bar a
recovery, yet, if, when he reaches the dangerous position, a vigilant use of his faculties and powers will avoid the injury, and he
is negligent in that respect, such negligence at that point will prevent a recovery notwithstanding any negligence of the defendant.

A person, who is injured while crossing a railroad track by colliding
with the train just as he is taking the last step off the track, is
barred from recovery because his negligence is concurrent and
operative with any negligence on the part of the railroad company, when it appears that, if he has taken notice of the train,
even when he was in the middle of the track, he could have got
over in safety, and that he could have seen or heard the train, if
he had looked or listened.

CASE for personal injuries. Plea, not guilty. Trial by
jury at the October Term, 1903, Essex County, *Munson, J.,*

presiding. Verdict and judgment for the plaintiff. The defendant excepted.

The plaintiff testified that on the day of the accident, in going along the highway to his work after dinner, he came to a point where defendant's tracks crossed said highway at grade level; that this crossing is made up of eight separate tracks; that he started over this crossing and, after passing several tracks, found further progress blocked by defendant's train which extended several cars each side of the crossing; that no engine was attached to this train, and no engine was in sight; that he waited eight or nine minutes on the crossing for same to be unblocked; that then it was about one o'clock and he could wait no longer; that then he walked into defendant's yard, and beside said train till he reached the end thereof, then turned directly to the south, walked across the track on which the train stood, and approached the main line, which was the next track south; that, as he emerged from behind said train in approaching the main line, and before attempting to cross the same, he looked to the right and to the left, neither saw nor heard the train, and went right along.

The fireman testified that he saw plaintiff just as he was about to step upon the main line; that he shouted to him "Get out of the way!" and that then plaintiff was thirty feet from the engine.

The engineer testified that he heard the fireman shout, and that he leaned over to look through a window on the fireman's side to see what was the trouble; that he could stop the train within twenty-five or thirty feet but did not attempt to stop it until after the plaintiff was struck. The opinion states the other facts.

C. A. Hight and *L. L. Hight* for the defendant.

Plaintiff was guilty of negligence which caused, or helped to cause his injury. *Carter* v. *R. Co.*, 72 Vt. 190.

The doctrine of the last clear chance does not apply when the negligence of the plaintiff and that of the defendant are concurrent. *Batchelder* v. *R. Co.*, 57 Atl. 926; *Corson* v. *R. Co.*, 147 Pa. St. 219, 30 Am. St. Rep. 727; *Gahagan* v. *R. Co.*, 70 N. H. 441; *Davies* v. *R. Co.*, 70 N. H. 519.

J. W. Redmond and *E. A. Cook* for the plaintiff.

The request to charge "that on all the evidence in the case the plaintiff is not in law entitled to recover," if treated as a motion for a verdict, is defective in not stating the ground thereof. *German* v. *R. 'Co.*, 71 Vt. 70.

"When it became apparent that plaintiff was going upon the track, it was the duty of the defendant to do all it could to avoid injuring him," and, in default thereof, the plaintiff is entitled to recover notwithstanding his negligence. *Willey* v. *R. Co.*, 72 Vt. 120; *Davies* v. *Mann*, 10 Mess. & W. 546; *Inland, etc. Co.* v. *Tolson*, 139 U. S. 531; *Romick* v. *R. Co.*, 62 Iowa 167; *Denver, etc. Co.* v. *Dyer*, 20 Col. 132; *Donohue* v. *R. Co.*, 91 Mo. 357; 19 Eng. Rul. Cases, 206; 2 Thomp. Neg. 1157; *Baltimore, etc. R.* v. *Rifcowitz*, 43 Atl. .Rep. 762; *Isbell* v. *R. Co.*, 27 Conn. 393, S. C. 71 Am. Dec. 78; *Atwood* v. *R. Co.*, 91 Me. 399, S. C., 40 Atl. Rep. 67; *Rine* v. *Chicago, etc.R.*, 88 Mo. 392; *Cincinnati, etc. R.* v. *Kassen*, 49 Ohio St. 230, 16 L. R. A. 674; *Baltimore, etc. R.* v. *Few*, 93 Va. 82; *State* v. *Manchester, etc. R.*, 52 N. H. 528; *Sweeney* v. *R. Co.*, 6 N. Y. Supp. 528; *Tuff* v. *Warman*, 94 E. C. L. 583; *Radley* v. *Railway Co.*, 1 App. Cas. 754; *Bouwmeester* v. *R. Co.*, 63 Mich. 557; *Judson* v. *R. Co.*, 63 Minn. 248; *Magoon* v. *Boston & Maine R.*, 67 Vt. 177; *Trow* v. *R. Co.*, 24 Vt. 487; *Bemis* v. *Conn. & Pass. R.*, 42 Vt. 375.

START, J. The action is for the recovery of damages alleged to have accrued to the plaintiff by reason of being struck by an engine while attempting to cross the defendant's railroad track. The defendant requested the court to instruct the jury, "that on all the evidence in the case the plaintiff is not entitled to recover." This is, in effect, a motion for a verdict, and sufficiently states the ground of the motion; and, by excepting to the refusal of the court to comply with the request, the defendant has reserved for the consideration of this Court the question of whether, upon the most favorable view for the plaintiff of all the evidence, he was entitled to recover.

The plaintiff gave evidence tending to show, that he walked from the public crossing through the railroad yard of the defendant, along the side of a line of box cars some two hundred and thirty feet, and then passed the end of the line of box cars; that he looked to the right and left, went right along and attempted to cross the defendant's main line and, in so doing, was struck by the defendant's express train, coming from the west; that, as he passed the end of the box cars, he could see toward the west a distance of the length of two or three cars; and that he knew it was about time for the express to arrive and was dangerous to be on the track. The actual measurements of the surveyor, which were disputed only by estimates, from the position of a man stepping over the north rail, show that a person could see one hundred and eighty-eight feet along the north rail, and two hundred and twenty-three feet along the south rail. The train made a good deal of noise, and, upon the shout of warning from by-standers, the plaintiff did not quicken his pace in any way, but looked up, not in the direction of the approaching train, but in the direction of those who called to him; and, at the time he was struck, he was stepping over the last rail—had one foot over.

Upon these facts the plaintiff was not entitled to recover. There is no view of the evidence that relieves him from the charge of contributory negligence. He was in the possession of all his mental and physical faculties. He knew the express train was due. He was struck as he was stepping over the last rail. One step would have brought him to a place of safety. Assuming that he could see along the track over which the train was approaching for a distance of only the length of two or three cars, as testified by him, if he had had a regard for his own safety and looked and listened as he was crossing the track, he would have seen or heard the train, quickened his pace and reached a place of safety. If he had looked or listened before stepping upon the track, he would have heard or seen the train; and, if mindful of his safety, he would have stopped and avoided the collision. If he had quickened his pace when his attention was called to the approaching train, he could have saved himself. He was unencumbered and capable of easily hastening or checking his movements; and, if he had looked when he was in the middle of the track, he could have seen the engine in season to have stepped clear of danger. He could have seen the danger and avoided it at a time when it was too late for the defendant's servants to stop the train and avoid a collision. There was no time when the defendant's servants could have stopped the train and avoided the injury, in which the plaintiff could not have avoided being injured by a vigilant use of his eyes, ears and physical strength. It was his duty to make a vigilant use of these faculties up to the last moment when it was possible for him to do so. If he did not see or hear the train, if he did not heed the warning that was given him, it was because he was not mindful of his safety, when he was in a place that he knew was dangerous. It was because he was careless, and that carelessness continued until he was injured. His negligence was not a precedent negligence. He exposed himself to danger that was the beginning not the end of his negligence, and his negligence was the proximate cause of the injury.

The case of *Batchelder* v. *Boston & Maine R. R. Co.*, recently decided by the Supreme Court of New Hampshire, and reported in 57 Atl. 926, is very similar in its facts to the case at bar. The court, in holding that the plaintiff could not recover, said: "If it might be found from the evidence that the defendant would have discovered the plaintiff in time to prevent the accident if they had used ordinary care, it cannot be found that she would not have seen the train in time to escape injury, if she had used the same care. * * * So that the plaintiff's failure to use ordinary care to discover the approach of the train was, in any view of the case, a part of the cause of her injury; for her fault would not cease to be the cause and become merely the occasion of her injury, unless, in the series of events that resulted in the accident, a wrongful act of the defendant was subsequent in point of causation to her failure to use ordinary care to discover the train. The only complaint she makes is that the defendant failed to use such care to discover her in time to avoid the accident. It is clear that their failure to perform this duty concurred both in point of time and causation with her failure to use the same care to discover the train. There was no time when they could have discovered her in season to avoid injuring her, in which she could not have discovered the train in time to avoid being injured." In *Carter* v. *Central Vermont R. R. Co.*, 72 Vt. 190, 47 Atl. 797, it is held, that the duty to look and listen before crossing a railroad track includes the duty to do that which will make looking and listening reasonably effective; and, if a traveller, by the vigilant use of his eyes and ears, can discover and avoid injury and omits such vigilance, he is guilty of contributory negligence, and is chargeable with such knowledge of the approach of a train as he might have obtained by the exercise of that degree of care which, in circumstances of danger, he is bound to use.

The plaintiff relies upon the case of *Willey* v. *The Boston & Maine R. R. Co.,* 72 Vt. 120, 47 Atl. 398. It is true, that, by the rule there broadly and without qualification stated, the defendant would be liable, if, when it became apparent that the plaintiff was going upon the track, its servants did not do what they could to avoid injuring him, notwithstanding he was negligent; but this is not the true rule, or rather is not all there is to the rule. It is true, that, when a traveller has reached a point where he cannot help himself, cannot extricate himself, and vigilance on his part will not avert the injury, his negligence in reaching that position becomes the condition and not the proximate cause of the injury, and will not preclude a recovery; but it is equally true, that, if a traveller, when he reaches the point of collision, is in a situation to help himself, and by a vigilant use of his eyes, ears and physical strength to extricate himself and avoid injury, his negligence at that point will prevent a recovery, notwithstanding the fact that the trainmen could have stopped the train in season to have avoided injuring him. In such a case, the negligence of the plaintiff is concurrent with the negligence of the defendant, and the negligence of each is operative at the time of the accident. When negligence is concurrent and operative at the time of the collision and contributes to it, there can be no recovery.

Judgment reversed, and cause remanded.

GEORGE H. HUNT *v.* C. D. RUBLEE.

January Term, 1904.

Present: ROWELL, C. J., TYLER, START, STAFFORD, and HASELTON, JJ.

Opinion filed August 2, 1904.

Letting on Shares—Tenants in Common—Assumpsit.

In the ordinary case of letting a farm at the halves, the parties are tenants in common of the products of the farm.

Though defendant "sold, or otherwise disposed of" hay cut on his farm while plaintiff was carrying it on at the halves under a contract providing that no hay should be sold, but the stock should be increased to consume it, general assumpsit will not lie for the value of plaintiff's interest in the hay, it appearing that the parties have not adjusted all their rights under the contract, and it not appearing that defendant received money, or its equivalent, for the hay, or that any agreement has been made taking the hay out of the general account between the parties.

GENERAL ASSUMPSIT for the value of an undivided half of certain hay. Plea, the general issue. Heard on the report of a referee at the September Term, 1903, Franklin County, *Watson,* J., presiding. Judgment for the defendant. The plaintiff excepted.

The hay in question was left on the premises by the plaintiff at the expiration of the lease. The referee reports that "all matters in relation to said farm and the dealings in regard thereto, with the exception of certain matters regarding the sale of one hog and three calves and the surplus hay, had been settled between the parties; that there was no difference between the parties in regard to the hog and the calves, except as to the price at which the same should have been sold, and the amount the defendant was entitled to receive from the plaintiff as his just share thereof; that the plaintiff has been, and is ready and willing to pay to the defendant his interest in the calves and hogs sold, provided the plaintiff can be paid for his hay." The opinion states the other facts.

Farrington & Post for the plaintiff.

When the fact is found that defendant has plaintiff's money, the law creates the promise. *State* v. *St. Johnsbury,* 59 Vt. 332.

C. G. Austin & Sons for the defendant.

Since, under the contract, plaintiff and defendant are tenants in common of the hay, an action of account is the only proper remedy. *Bishop* v. *Dotey,* 1 Vt. 37; *Ganaway* v. *Miller,* 15 Vt. 152; *Kidder* v. *Rixford,* 16 Vt. 169; *Aiken* v. *Smith,* 21 Vt. 172; *Joy* v. *Walker,* 29 Vt. 257; *Cilley's Est.* v. *Tenney,* 31 Vt. 401; *LaPoint* v. *Scott,* 36 Vt. 609; *Albee* v. *Fairbanks,* 10 Vt. 314.

START, J. The action is assumpsit and is for the recovery of the value of one undivided half of sixteen tons of hay, which was cut on the defendant's farm while the plaintiff was carrying it on at halves. The lease provides that no hay shall be sold, but the stock shall be increased to consume it. It is found that the hay was sold, or otherwise disposed of, by the defendant. It is not found that he received any money or its equivalent therefor, nor can this be inferred from the facts reported by the referee. The parties were tenants in common of the hay and other products of the farm. *Willard* v. *Wing,* 70 Vt. 123, 39 Atl. 632; *Atkins* v. *Smith,* 21 Vt. 172; *Foster* v. *Kellogg,* 23 Vt. 308. It appearing that the parties have not settled and adjusted all of their rights respecting the common property, including the hay, and it not appearing that the defendant has received any money, or its equivalent, for the hay, nor that any agreement has been entered into whereby the hay has been taken out of the general account between the parties. the plaintiff cannot recover the value of his interest in the hay in an action of general assumpsit. *Albee* v. *Fairbanks,* 10 Vt. 314; *LaPoint* v. *Scott,* 36 Vt. 603.

Judgment affirmed.

Anna J. Luce *v.* F. V. Hassam.

May Term, 1904.

Present: Rowell, C. J., Tyler, Start, Watson, Stafford, and Haselton, JJ.

Opinion filed August 2, 1904

Negligence—Highways — Obstruction — Injury to Person Driving—Objection to Questions—Variance—Wagon— Definition—Exception to Charge—Too General.

When the ground of an objection to the admissibility of evidence is stated, the court is only required to pass upon the objection thus limited.

In an action for personal injury caused by defendant's negligently placing stones in a public highway, the fact that defendant claims there was a sidewalk at that point is not a sufficient reason for excluding the question asked plaintiff's witness, "What has been the use of the locality by persons with teams, where have they gone?"

The word "wagon" is synonymous with the word "carriage," and may be used to designate any wheeled vehicle intended to be drawn by horses.

There is no variance between the allegation in the declaration that the plaintiff, when injured was riding in a wagon, and the proof that she was then riding in a two-wheeled vehicle.

It is the duty of counsel to specify the particular points in the charge, or in the omission to charge, to which they except.

When the charge covers a variety of subjects and, with few exceptions, is considered to be correct, an exception "to the charge as given" is too general to be considered.

When there are twelve requests to charge, some of which are fully complied with, an exception "to the failure of the court to charge as requested, so far as there was such failure" will not be considered.

CASE for personal injuries. Plea, the general issue with notice. Trial by jury at the December Term, 1903, Windsor County, *Munson,* J., presiding. Verdict and judgment for the plaintiff. The defendant excepted.

The evidence of the plaintiff tended to show that on the evening of the day of the accident she was riding along the public highway in the village of Gaysville in the town of Stockbridge in a two-wheeled road cart drawn by one horse; that her husband was driving; that defendant had, a few days previous, set three stones,—described by plaintiff's witnesses as stone posts—at the edge of the sidewalk, and projecting about four inches beyond its edge into the travelled part of the highway at a point where two roads joined, making a sharp corner; that the stones projected out of the ground about a foot; that in attempting to turn said corner one of the wheels of the cart in which plaintiff was riding struck one or more of said stones, and she was thereby thrown out and injured.

The evidence of the defendant tended to show that a sidewalk had for many years existed along the margin of the highway at the point in question; that the sidewalk had been newly gravelled a short time before the accident; and that he placed the stones at the edge of the sidewalk, and within its limits, for the purpose of protecting its margin.

J. C. Enright and *E. R. Buck* for the defendant.

There was a fatal variance between the proof and the declaration. 1 Chit. Pl. 386; 5 Taunt. 534.

It was error to admit the testimony of Quimby. *Blodgett v. Royalton,* 17 Vt. 40; *Folsom v. Underhill,* 36 Vt. 580; *Bagley v. Ludlow,* 41 Vt. 425.

V. S. 4792 forbids driving on a sidewalk, and so plaintiff cannot recover. *Johnson v. Irasburg,* 47 Vt. 28; *McClay v. Lowell,* 44 Vt. 116.

William Batchelder and *Charles Batchelder* for the plaintiff.

There was no variance. A wagon is a wheeled carriage. But this was not a material allegation. It is sufficient if the proof agrees with the allegations in respect of those facts which are essential. Starkie Ev. 1527; Greenl. Ev. (14 ed.) § 56; *Allen v. Lyman,* 27 Vt. 20.

In respect of Quimby's testimony, defendant is limited to the objection stated. *Seguin v. Peterson,* 45 Vt. 255; *State v. Preston,* 48 Vt. 12; *Bartlett v. Cabot,* 54 Vt. 242; Thompson Trials, 693 and 698; Abbott's Civil Trial Brief, 245.

Exceptions to the charge must be specific. *Goodwin v. Perkins,* 39 Vt. 598; *Rowell v. Fuller,* 59 Vt. 688; *Morrill v. Palmer,* 68 Vt. 1; *Magoon v. Before,* 73 Vt. 231.

START, J. The action is case, and is for the recovery of damages alleged to have been caused by the wrongful and negligent act of the defendant in placing three stones in a highway over which the plaintiff was driving. The plaintiff called one Quimby and asked him the following question: "During the time you have lived where you say you now do, what has been the use of the locality at the Corner by the public with teams—where have they gone?" The defendant's counsel objected to this question and, on being asked to state the ground of his objection, said: "We claim there is a regular laid out sidewalk at that point, and regardless of what use the public made of it, they had no business on the sidewalk, and it makes no difference whether they have been on the sidewalk." The fact that the defendant claimed there was a sidewalk at the point in question, was not a sufficient reason for excluding the question; and, he having limited his objection to this fact, the court was only called upon to pass upon the limited objection thus made; and, as the objection disclosed no reason for excluding the question, the answer was properly taken. *State* v. *Nokes*, 70 Vt. 247, 40 Atl. 249; *Foster's Exrs.* v. *Dickerson*, 64 Vt. 246, 24 Atl. 253.

It is alleged in the declaration that the plaintiff, at the time she was injured, was riding in a wagon. The proof was that she was riding in a two-wheeled vehicle, and the defendant moved for a verdict on the ground of variance between the declaration and proof. The motion was properly overruled. The words wagon and cart are generic terms and mean almost any vehicle, whether used for the transportation of persons or property. The word wagon is synonymous with the word carriage and may be used to designate any wheeled vehicle intended to be drawn by horses. The vehicle in which the plaintiff was riding, at the time she received the alleged injury, was designated by the word wagon; and there was no material variance between the declaration and proof.

The defendant presented twelve requests to charge, and to the failure of the court to charge as requested, so far as there was such failure, and to the charge as given, excepted. These exceptions are qualified and too general. They do not point out any error in the charge as given, nor any omissions of the court to charge as requested. The words, "to the charge as given," is a general exception to an entire charge, covering a variety of subjects and relating to the law of negligence, contributory negligence, highways, sidewalks, and the rights and liabilities of owners of land adjacent to highways; and the exception to the refusal of the court to charge as requested is qualified and general. By the use of the words, "to the failure of the court to charge as requested, so far as there was such failure," the defendant, in effect, said to the court, if you have not complied with my requests, I except. This was not pointing out any error in the omission of the court to charge, nor was it an exception to an omission to charge that will be considered by this Court. The exception is also general, in that it refers to a large number of requests, very many of which it is conceded were complied with. It is the duty of counsel to specify the particular points in the charge, or in the omission to charge, to which they take exception. This Court will not consider a general exception to an entire charge, which, with few exceptions, is conceded to be correct; nor will it consider a general exception to the refusal of the court to charge as requested, when, as in this case, the requests are numerous, and some are fully complied with, while others are in part, or are disregarded. *Goodwin v. Perkins,* 39 Vt. 598; *Rowell v. Fuller,* 59 Vt. 688, 10 Atl. 853; *Morrill v. Palmer,* 68 Vt. 1, 33 Atl. 829; *Magoon v. Before,* 73 Vt. 231, 50 Atl. 1070.

Judgment affirmed.

INDEX.

ABATEMENT.

See "PARTNERSHIP," § 1.

Pending action held not cause for abatement of action subsequently brought. *Richardson* v. *Fletcher*, 206.

ACCIDENT AND MISTAKE.

See "JUDGMENT," § 2.

ACTION.

§ 1. Grounds and Conditions Precedent.

When parties refuse to perform a contract made for a term, the other party may sue immediately though he has then suffered no damage. *Parker* v. *McKannon Bros.*, 96.

It is a condition precedent to a right of action by one town against another for assisting a pauper, that the overseer of the plaintiff give notice to the overseer of the defendant of the "condition of such person." *Essex* v. *Jericho*, 104.

§ 2. Nature and Form.

The cause of action, given by V. S. 2359 against the executor of a will is different from that given against the custodian. *Richardson* v. *Fletcher*, 206.

§ 3. Commencement, Prosecution, and Termination.

For most purposes, an action is not commenced until process is served. *Tracy* v. *Ry. Co.*, 313.

ADVERSE POSSESSION.

See "WATERS AND WATER COURSES," § 2.

Adverse user avails only where the person against whom the right is claimed could have lawfully prevented its exercise. *Lawrie* v. *Silsby*, 240.

A town line may be established by prescription, though variant from the original grant. *Town of Searsburg* v. *Town of Woodford*, 370.

ALTERATION OF INSTRUMENTS.

The alteration of a duplicate order by an agent who holds it for transmission to the principal does not render it invalid. *Equitable Mfg. Co.* v. *Allen*, 22.

ANIMALS.

A plea in trespass for killing a dog *held* to sufficiently identify the trespass attempted to be justified with that declared upon. *Mossman* v. *Bostridge*, 409.

No. 108, Acts 1898, *held* to authorize the killing of a dog only while it is hunting deer, and a plea in justification on any other theory is bad. *Ibid.*

Under No. 108, Acts 1898, any dog, without regard to its breed, or whether permitted to run at large, may be killed while it is hunting deer. *Ibid.*

APPEAL AND ERROR.

§ 1. Presentation and Reservation in Lower Court of Grounds of Review.

To reserve available exception to the exclusion of testimony an offer must be made. *McKinstry* v. *Collins*, 221.

When the question of the competency of an expert witness was not raised at the trial it will not be considered. *Parker* v. *McKannon Bros.*, 96.

Question not raised in trial court will not be considered. *Morrisette* v. *R. Co.*, 267.

Exception to a portion of the charge as given does not cover an objection for failure to charge. *Ibid.*

A demurrer to a bill in equity is waived unless brought on to hearing before the case is heard on its merits. *Congregational Church of Chester* v. *Cutler*, 338.

A request to charge that, on all the evidence, plaintiff is not entitled to recover is equal to a motion for a verdict, and an exception to its refusal reserves the question of the sufficiency of the evidence. *French* v. *Ry. Co.* 441.

§ 2. Record and Proceedings Not in Record.

No fact will be assumed in aid of a mortgage which on its face is a marriage brokerage contract. *Jangraw* v. *Perkins*. 127.

To raise the question whether a master erred in his rulings his report must furnish the foundation for the question. *Sowles* v. *Sartwell*, 70.

A motion to recommit a master's report is addressed to the discretion of the chancellor. *Ibid.*

§ 3. Review.

In a suit to construe a conditional bequest, the admission of immaterial evidence *held* harmless. *Congregational Church of Chester* v. *Cutler*, 338.

§ 4. Determination and Disposition of Cause.

When the Supreme Court affirms a judgment adjudging the declaration insufficient, and plaintiff can gain nothing by amendment, Supreme Court will render final judgment. *E. E. Rice & Co.* v. *Kennedy*, 380.

Though it was error to direct a verdict for defendant *held* plaintiff was not entitled to final judgment in Supreme Court. *Bass* v. *Rublee*, 395.

No final judgment can be rendered in Supreme Court even on a technical demurrer to the evidence, when there is no joinder in demurrer in the record. *Ibid.*

When the decision of the Supreme Court leaves the case so that either party has a right to a trial by jury, the case will be remanded. *Ibid.*

A motion for a verdict resembles a demurrer to the evidence; but the required technicalities of such demurrer do not appertain to a motion for a verdict. *Ibid.*

AQUEDUCT.

See "PROPERTY."

ASSAULT AND BATTERY.

See "WITNESSES," § 2.

§ 1. Civil Liability.

Replication in assault and battery *held* not bad for duplicity. *Belknap* v. *Billings*, 54.

One may immediately repel an assault, using no more force than reasonably appears to him to be necessary. *Foss* v. *Smith*, 113.

In an action for assault on plaintiff's wife *held* entitled to show her
physical condition both before and after the assault. *McKinstry*
v. *Collins*, 221.

In an action for assault by an officer serving a writ of replevin, his
return thereon is not conclusive evidence in his favor. *Ibid.*

In an action for an assault the law presumes defendant innocent. *Ibid.*

In an action for an assault by an officer serving a writ of replevin, the
law presumes that he seasonably took the required bond. *Ibid.*

ASSIGNMENTS FOR BENEFIT OF CREDITORS.

One is not so interested that he may not be an assignee for the benefit of creditors because, as attorney, he had placed attachments
on the property subject to which the assignment was made. *Hilliard* v. *Burlington Shoe Co.*, 57.

A statutory assignment creates no invalidating preference by conveying the property subject to prior attachments. *Ibid.*

Such assignment is valid unless impeached in bankruptcy within four
months. *Ibid.*

It is not essential that a corporation's deed of assignment show on its
face the authority for its execution. *Ibid.*

ASSUMPSIT, ACTION OF.

See "CHATTEL MORTGAGES," § 1.

ATTACHMENT.

Under a contract of sale of land, reserving all produce grown thereon
till payment of purchase notes, *held* that the vendee acquired no
attachable interest in crops, the notes having been paid only by
foreclosure. *Joslyn* v. *Taplin and Rowell.* 422.

BANKRUPTCY.

§ 1.   Constitutional and Statutory Provisions.

The U. S. Bankruptcy Act does not suspend the operation of our
assignment law; but an assignment is good unless seasonably
impeached by bankruptcy proceedings. *Hilliard* v. *Burlington
Shoe Co.*, 57.

§ 2.   Rights, Remedies, and Discharge of Bankrupt.

A plea of discharge in bankruptcy need not state facts which gave
jurisdiction of the subject matter to the U. S. Dist. Court. *Bailey's Admr.* v. *Gleason*, 115.

A plea of a discharge in bankruptcy need not show that the debts sued on were provable in bankruptcy. *Ibid.*

But such plea must show that the debts sued on were scheduled, or that the creditor had notice of the bankruptcy proceedings. *Ibid.*

§ 3. Assignment, Administration, and Distribution of Bankrupt's Estate.

The title of a purchaser from a bankrupt's preferred creditor is not voidable, if he purchased in good faith, without notice, and for valuable consideration. *Coolidge* v. *Ayers*, 405.

Whether he did so purchase is a question for the jury. *Ibid.*

Transfer of property *held* a preference within U. S. Bank. Act. *Ibid.*

BANKS AND BANKING.

§ 1. National Banks.

A receiver of a national bank has the legal title to its assets, and may sue therefor at law in his own name in the state courts. *Fish* v. *Olin*, 120.

In assumpsit against a national bank the plea of *ultra vires held* good. *Metropolitan Stock Exchange* v. *Lyndonville Nat. Bank*, 303.

BILLS AND NOTES.

See "CORPORATIONS," § 5; "HUSBAND AND WIFE"; "PARTNERSHIP," § 1; "SALES," § 4.

§ 1. Requisites and Validity.

Reference may be had to figures on margin of note to remove ambiguity, or to supply amount. *Kimball* v. *Costa*, 289.

A defective note *held* sufficient. *Ibid.*

§ 2. Actions.

That, while one held a note as agent of the payee, he received and misappropriated money of the maker, does not tend to show payment. *Buck* v. *Troy Aqueduct Co.*, 75.

Evidence *held* inadmissible to prove that defendant's signature to a note was forged by another signer thereof. *Wilmington Sav. Bank* v. *Waste*, 331.

CARRIERS.

A company operating a street railway in one city *held*, on acquiring the railway of another company in another city, not obliged to issue transfers from one line to the other. *City of Montpelier* v. *Barre, etc. Co.*, 66.

CASES.

(Specially approved, criticised or distinguished.)

Bullock v. *Guildford,* 59 Vt. 517, *distinguished. In Re Joslyn's Est.*, 88.

Cross v. *Martin,* 46 Vt. 14, *explained. Davis* v. *Moyles,* 25.

Quimby & Rogan v. *B. & M. R. Co.,* 71 Vt. 301, *distinguished. Delphia* v. *R. Co.,* 84.

Sweat v. *Hall,* 8 Vt. 187, and *Ellsworth* v. *Hopkins,* 58 Vt. 705, each *distinguished. Spencer* v. *Stockwell,* 176.

Whitney v. *Nat. Bank of Brattleboro,* 47 Vt. 546, and *Wiley* v. *same,* *criticised. Metropolitan Stock Exch.* v. *Lyndonville Nat. Bank,* 303.

Willey v. *B. & M. R. Co.,* 72 Vt. 120, *explained. French* v. *Ry. Co.* 441.

CHARGE.

See "TRIAL," § 3.

CHARITIES.

§ 1. Creation, Existence, and Validity.

A vote by a town *held* a sufficient acceptance of a bequest on the conditions named in the will. *Bellows Free Academy* v. *Sowles,* 412.

The conduct of trustees under a will in organizing themselves under an act of incorporation *held* not to have caused the fund to go over to a certain person, under a provision of the will giving the trust funds over in case of any diversion of the fund from the purposes of the trust. *Ibid.*

§ 2. Construction, Administration, and Enforcement.

Trustees under a will *held* to have the right to sell the stock in which the trust funds were invested. *Bellows Free Academy* v. *Sowles,* 412.

A bill for an injunction to restrain interferences with trustees in the performance of their trust *held* not demurrable for want of proper parties plaintiff. *Ibid.*

CHATTEL MORTGAGES.

See "SALES," § 4.

General assumpsit *held* inapplicable to an action by mortgagee against mortgagor's vendee on his assumption of the original debt. *Miller* v. *Wilbur*, 73.

COLLATERAL INHERITANCE TAX.

See "TAXATION," § 2.

CONDITIONAL SALES.

See "SALES," § 4.

CONSTITUTIONAL LAW.

§ 1.　Construction, Operation, and Enforcement of Constitutional Provisions.

The preamble to the Constitution of 1777 refers only to lands held' under original charters from New Hampshire. *Davis* v. *Moyles*, 25.

§ 2.　Distribution of Govermental Powers and Functions.

The minimum fine of $300 prescribed by No. 90, § 68, Acts 1902, is. not so unjust as to warrant the Court in questioning the action of the Legislature; nor is the section unconstitutional because it fixes no maximum fine. *State* v. *Constantino*, 192.

It is doubtful whether the Ligislature can confer upon the judiciary the power to establish any division line between towns other than the charter line. *Town* of *Searsburg* v. *Town of Woodford*, 370.

§ 3.　Vested Rights.

There is no vested right in a rule of evidence. *McKinstry* v. *Collins*, 221.

§ 4.　Privileges or Immunities, and Class Legislation.

No. 123, Acts 1898, prohibiting the giving of coupons, etc., with property sold, *held* to violate Const. U. S. Amend. 14. *State* v. *Dodge*,. 197.

CONTRACTS.

§ 1.　Requisites and Validity.

A contract to hasten an intended marriage is a marriage brokerage contract and void. *Jangraw* v. *Perkins*, 127.

Mortgage *held* to be a marriage brokerage contract and void. *Ibid.*

An agreement by one or two co-owners of personal property to indemnify the other against loss if he would refuse an offer to purchase the property, *held* without consideration. *Chase* v. *Soule*, 353.

Under contract of sale of land, reserving all produce grown thereon till payment of purchase notes, *held* said notes are not paid, so as to give vendee any interest in crops, merely because the premises obtained by the vendor on foreclosure exceed in value the amount due on the notes and costs. *Joslyn* v. *Taplin & Rowell*. 422.

§ 2. Actions for Breach.

In an action for breach of contract for delivery of lumber *held* that it was a question for the jury whether there had been an extension of the time of delivery. *Bass* v. *Rublee*, 395.

CONTRIBUTORY NEGLIGENCE.

See "MASTER AND SERVANT"; "RAILROADS," § 2.

CORPORATIONS.

See "ASSIGNMENT FOR BENEFIT OF CREDITORS."

§ 1. Incorporation and Organization.

Under Comp. St. Ch. 85, association whose articles are not subscribed *held* not incorporated. *Lawrie* v. *Silsby*, 240.

Under same statute *held* association cannot be sued though its articles are subscribed. *Ibid.*

A religious association, organized under laws of 1797, *held* a corporation, though it subsequently made an ineffectual attempt to incorporate under a later statute. *Congregational Church of Chester* v. *Cutler*, 338.

§ 2. Corporate Name, Seal, By-laws, and Records.

Stockholders *held* to have changed, by unanimous consent, a by-law requiring five directors. *Buck* v. *Troy Aqueduct Co.*, 75.

A by-law requiring the assent of the directors to acts of executive committee does not require that transactions in the ordinary course of business should be specially authorized. *Roebling's Sons* v. *Barre, etc. Co.*, 131.

§ 3. Members and Stockholders.

In suit by a foreign receiver, declaration *held* to sufficiently show
that stockholders' statutory liability is a secondary asset of the
corporation available in payment of its debts, and that title to
same is in plaintiff. *King* v. *Cochran*, 141.

A stockholder of a foreign corporation, without notice thereof, is
bound by proceedings, in state of its domicile, assessing stockholder's liability, and this liability may be enforced in the state
of the stockholder's residence. *Ibid.*

§ 4. Officers and Agents.

Two of its board of three directors *held* to have bound a corporation,
without the consent or knowledge of the third. *Buck* v. *Troy
Aqueduct Co.*, 75.

The purchase of supplies for a corporation is a transaction in the
ordinary course of business and may be delegated by the directors to the executive committee. *Roebling's Sons* v. *Barre, etc.
Co.*, 131.

The directors of a corporation organized under a special charter
not liable, under V. S. 3724, for assenting to creating corporate
indebtedness exceeding two-thirds the capital stock actually paid
in. *E. E. Rice & Co.* v. *Kennedy*, 380.

V. S. 3724 applies only to corporations by voluntary association. *Ibid.*

§ 5. Corporate Powers and Liabilities.

It is not essential that the deed of a corporation show on its face the
authority for its execution. *Hilliard* v. *Burlington Shoe Co.*, 57.

A note signed with corporate name only *held* valid under the circumstances. *Buck* v. *Troy Aqueduct Co.*, 75.

Corporation's note *held* not invalidated by one of three directors acting in the transaction as agent for both borrower and lender.
Ibid.

The borrowing of money by a corporation to use in repairing its property, and giving its note therefor is an act in the transaction of
its ordinary business. *Ibid.*

Executive committee of a railroad corporation *held* to have power,
under its by-laws, to purchase feed wire. *Roebling's Sons* v.
Barre, etc. Co., 131.

Authority to purchase *held* conferred by a corporation's directors on
its executive committee by unanimous acquiescence in a course of
business. *Ibid.*

Replication *de injuria* to a plea of *ultra vires* held bad. *Metropolitan
Stock Exch.* v. *Lyndonville Nat. Bank*, 303.

A corporation cannot be estopped from making the defense of *ultra vires*. *Ibid*.

Contracts strictly *ultra vires* are void and cannot be ratified. *Ibid*.

COVENANTS.

Lessee's duty under covenant to repair is measured by condition of property at beginning of term. *Foss* v. *Stanton*, 365

Lessee's duty to assignee of lessor, under covenant to repair, is measured by condition of property at time of transfer. *Ibid*.

Covenant by tenant to repair runs with the land, but assignee of lessor can sue only for breach subsequent to transfer. *Ibid*.

CRIMINAL LAW.

See "INTOXICATING LIQUORS"; "CONSTITUTIONAL LAW," § 2.

DAMAGES.

See "OFFSET."

§ 1. Liquidated Damages and Penalties.

In a contract for sale of logs, the provision for reduced price if required quantity is not delivered liquidates the damages for such non-delivery. *Jackson* v. *Hunt*, 284.

§ 2. Measure of Damages.

Both past and prospective damage may be recovered for the breach of an executory contract. *Parker* v. *McKannon Bros.*, 96.

DEBTS.

See "DESCENT AND DISTRIBUTION."

DEEDS.

See "CORPORATIONS," § 5; "WATERS AND WATER COURSES," § 3.

DEFINITIONS.

"Furnish." *State* v. *Tague*, 118.

"Public use." *Stiles* v. *Newport*, 154.

"Wagon." *Luce* v. *Hassam*. 450.

DEMURRER.

To evidence, see "TRIAL," § 4.

DESCENT AND DISTRIBUTION.

Debts due resident decedents from nonresident debtors have their
situs in the place where the debtors reside, and are governed by
the law of that place. *In Re Joslyn's Est.*, 88.

DIVORCE.

Antenuptial contract *held* not to contemplate divorce for husband's
fault, nor to prevent court awarding permanent alimony. *Carter*
v. *Carter*, 190.

In fixing amount of alimony husband shall pay, court may consider his
pension from U. S. as part of his resources. *Bailey* v. *Bailey*,
264.

DOGS.

See "ANIMALS."

EJECTMENT.

In ejectment evidence considered, and *held* sufficient to support a finding that plaintiff took possession of the premises and was evicted
by defendant. *Angel* v. *Fletcher*, 359.

EQUITY.

See "CHARITIES," § 2; "PARTNERSHIP," § 2; "JUDGMENT," § 2; "LANDLORD
AND TENANT," § 3; "PARTIES"; "PLEADING," § 1.

A motion to recommit a master's report is addressed to the discretion
of the chancellor, and *held* not an abuse of discretion to refuse
to recommit. *Sowles* v. *Sartwell*, 70.

Orator is bound to show the amount of a payment properly chargeable to defendant. *Ibid.*

ESTATES.

Decedent's Estates, see "EXECUTORS AND ADMINISTRATORS," § 1.

ESTOPPEL.

See "TRUSTEE PROCESS."

When one, with express warranty of title, sells personal property
which he does not own, his subsequent title inures to the vendee
by estoppel. *Coolidge* v. *Ayers*, 405.

EVIDENCE.

See "APPEAL AND ERROR," §§ 1, 3; "ASSAULT AND BATTERY," § 1; "BILLS
AND NOTES," § 2; "CONSTITUTIONAL LAW," § 3; "EJECTMENT";
"EXECUTORS AND ADMINISTRATORS," § 1; "LIMITATION OF ACTIONS,"
§§ 1, 2; "MASTER AND SERVANT"; "SCHOOLS AND SCHOOL DIS-
TRICT"; "WILLS," §§ 1, 2, 3; "WITNESSES," §§ 1, 2.

§ 1. Judicial Notice.

Federal statutes need not be alleged and proved in state courts. *Metropolitan Stock Exch.* v. *Lyndonville Bank*, 303.

§ 2. Presumptions.

In an action by a brakeman for being struck from the side of a train
by a switch, there is no presumption of defendant's negligence
from the mere happening of the accident. *Morrisette* v. *R. Co.*,
267.

§ 3. Relevancy, Materiality, and Competency.

In an action for a breach of contract, evidence considered and *held*
admissible to show its value. *Parker* v. *McKannon Bros.*, 96.

Evidence *held* irrelevant to prove that defendant's signature to a note
was forged by another signer thereof. *Wilmington Sav. Bank* v.
Waste, 331.

§ 4. Declarations.

In laying the foundation for the receipt of evidence in matter of pedigree, the relation of the declarant must be shown by evidence
independent of the offered declarations. *Davis* v. *Moyles*, 25.

Declarations in matter of pedigree are inadmissible unless it appear
they were made *ante litem motam*. *Ibid.*

Declarations of a party in his own favor are not admissible unless a
part of the *res gestae*. *State* v. *Raymo*, 430.

Self serving statements of past suffering, or of the past cause of suffering are inadmissible. *Ibid.*

Declarations of respondent, after prior assault of B. on him, as to
fear of B. *held* not admissible on trial for assault on B. in which
B. was the first assailant. *Ibid.*

§ 5. Documentary Evidence.

A petition to the General Assembly, with report of a legislative committee, and private laws and official doings thereunder, are not
evidence of any fact therein recited. *Davis* v. *Moyles*, 25.

Private laws are evidence only against those who procured their enactment, and, in certain cases, the State. *Ibid.*

Recitals in a petition to the General Assembly for the granting of certain lands *held* inadmissible to show relationship between plaintiff and the original grantee of the lands, in the absence of any foundation. *Ibid.*

A record of judicial proceedings not conclusive in a proceeding to vacate them for fraud. *Scoville* v. *Brock*, 385.

§ 6. Parol or Extrinsic Evidence Affecting Writings.

In a suit for specific performance of one of two written options, parol evidence is admissible that neither was to have effect unless both were accepted. *Reynolds* v. *Hooker*, 184.

§ 7. Opinion Evidence.

A practical railroad man, though not an engineer, is competent to testify that he knows of no reason why a certain switch might not be set in a different place. *Morrisette* v. *R. Co.*, 267.

The cross-examination of a non-expert witness as to the genuineness of defendant's signature to a note *held* improper. *Wilmington Sav. Bank* v. *Waste*, 331.

When defendant claimed his signature to the note in suit was forged, it was error to permit the defendant to testify that plaintiff's clerk said to him, when he called to see the note, that it was in the office of an attorney "with the other forged notes." *Ibid.*

It is proper to show a witness signatures conceded or proved to be genuine, but this is the limit of comparison. *Ibid.*

EXCEPTIONS, BILL OF.

See "WITNESSES," § 2; "TRIAL," § 3; "APPEAL AND ERROR," § 1.

Questions, which the exceptions do not show were raised in the court below, will not be considered. *Parker* v. *McKannon Bros.*, 96.

When the transcript of evidence is made controlling by the bill of exceptions, it will prevail even in contradiction of the bill. *Roebling's Sons* v. *Barre, etc. Co.*, 131.

A substituted bill of exceptions need not require the furnishing of a transcript referred to in the original bill. *McKinstry* v. *Collins*, 221.

EXECUTION.

See "JUDGMENT," § 1.

EXECUTORS AND ADMINISTRATORS.

See "PARTNERSHIP," § 2.

Neglect to seasonably notify probate court of acceptance, see "ACTIONS," § 2.

§ 1. Allowance and Payment of Claims.

On a claim against a decedent's estate *held* that the charge that, if money is shown into claimant's hands, the burden is on him to account for it, is correct. *Vitty* v. *Peaslee's Est.*, 402.

On a claim against a decedent's estate, a certain writing executed by the decedent *held* admissible as tending to support claimant's contention. *Ibid.*

§ 2. Actions.

An administrator, who sues as such, cannot object to a decree because rendered against him as administrator. *Sowles* v. *Bartwell*, 70.

§ 3. Accounting and Settlement.

Administrators are entitled to credit for paying a debt of the estate with their own note. *Walworth's Est.* v. *Bartholomew's Est.*, 1.

The burden is on the administrator to show that a note belonging to the estate was not collectible. *Ibid.*

Presumption of negligence against an administrator *held* rebutted by the facts. *Ibid.*

Dividends, received by an administrator on stock belonging to the estate after same was wrongfully transferred to him, are chargeable against him. *Ibid.*

An administrator, using funds of the estate for his own profit, will be allowed nothing for his services, and will be charged annual interest. *Ibid.*

An administrator mingling trust funds with his own, though not entitled to compensation for looking after such funds, is entitled to pay for other services. *Ibid.*

On final settlement, an administrator may be credited for his services at the end of every year. *Ibid.*

When delay in settling a deceased administrator's account is not chargeable to him or his representative, it will be settled as of the date of his death, and only simple interest allowed on the balance then found due. *Ibid.*

The expenses in settling a deceased administrator's account, which are necessitated by his fault, fall on his estate. *Ibid.*

FENCES.

See "RAILROADS," § 2.

FINES.

See "CONSTITUTIONAL LAW," § 2.

FOREIGN LAW.

See "MASTER AND SERVANT."

Comity requires us to enforce a foreign law unless it is either criminal or penal, or contrary to pure morals or abstract justice, or its enforcement would be of evil example to our people. *Morrisette v. R. Co.,* 267.

FRAUDS, STATUTE OF.

That the selling agent fails to change his copy of a duplicate order to correspond with that of the buyer, does not render it insufficient to satisfy the Statute of Frauds. *Equitable Mfg. Co. v. Allen,* 22.

GAME LAWS.

No. 94, Acts 1896, *held* not to allow the killing at any time of deer without horns. *State v. Jewett,* 435.

GAMING.

No appeal lies from judgment of a justice of the peace ordering the destruction of a Klondike machine under No. 121, Acts 1896. *State v Klondike Machine,* 426.

GRANTS.

See "PUBLIC LANDS"; "WATER AND WATER COURSES," § 3.

GUARDIAN AND WARD.

A bill to set aside the allowance of a guardian's account for fraud, *held* sufficient. *Scoville v. Brock,* 385.

Bill against orator's former guardian for negligence *held* not objectionable for want of equity. *Ibid.*

As against one who attempts to set aside the allowance of his former guardian for fraud, time does not necessarily begin to run when the confidential relation ends, but only when its influence ceases to operate. *Ibid.*

HIGHWAYS.

Objection that defendant claimed the place where plaintiff, while driving, was injured by stones placed in the highway, *held* no reason for excluding the question, to a witness, what had been the use of the locality by persons with teams. *Luce* v. *Hassam*, 450.

Held no variance between declaration alleging that plaintiff, when injured, was riding in a wagon, and proof that she was riding in a two-wheeled vehicle. *Ibid.*

HUSBAND AND WIFE.

See "PAUPERS."

§ 1. Conveyances, Contracts, and other Transactions, between Husband and Wife.

Wife *held* to be the lawful owner of a note transferred to her by her husband. *Buck* v. *Troy Aqueduct Co.*, 75.

A husband does not become bound in any way to his wife by transferring to her a note, without indorsement. *Ibid.*

§ 2. Disabilities and Privileges of Coverture.

A wife *held* not liable for deceit consisting of a false statement in joint deed of herself and husband of property not her separate estate. *Brunnell* v. *Carr*, 174.

In such case the husband is liable for his deceit. *Ibid.*

When a woman who is the owner and payee of a note marries the maker, she retains every right in respect of the note, except the right to sue her husband in her own name. *Spencer* v. *Stockwell*, 176.

She may transfer such note to a third person, who may sue the husband thereon for the benefit of the wife. *Ibid.*

INHERITANCE TAX.

See "TAXATION," § 2.

INSURANCE.

§ 1. Control and Regulation in General.

Under V. S. 4178 and Nos. 73 and 76, Acts 1902, a foreign Life Ins. Co. *held* entitled, in computing its "reserve liability," to value first year's insurance on one year option policies as *term* insurance. *Bankers' Life Ins. Co.* v. *Fleetwood, et al.*, 297.

Insurance commissioners have not discretion to exact any different valuation. *Ibid.*

§ 2. Action of Policies.

Issue of insured's mental capacity to cancel a fire insurance policy properly submitted to the jury. *McCloskey* v. *Ins. Co.,* 151.

INTEREST.

In assumpsit on book account interest should be computed on annual balances. *Hammond's Admr.* v. *Hammond,* 437.

INTOXICATING LIQUORS.

See "CONSTITUTIONAL LAW," § 2.

§ 1. Offences.

Giving away intoxicating liquor is "furnishing it." *State* v. *Tague,* 118.

§ 2. Criminal Prosecutions.

Complaint for keeping intoxicating liquor for sale without a license, *held* not to justify the inference that respondent was keeping for sale when his license should again be in force. *State* v. *Constantino,* 192.

In a complaint charging respondent with furnishing, selling, and exposing for sale intoxicating liquor without a license, the negation of the license covers all the acts charged. *Ibid.*

JUDGMENT.

See "TRUSTEE PROCESS."

§ 1. By Default.

Judgment by default in action by trustee process *held* interlocutory, and final judgment may be rendered at a subsequent term. *Leonard* v. *Sibley,* 254.

Execution may issue on such final judgment, though liability of trustee not yet determined. *Ibid.*

§ 2. Equitable Relief.

A bill to restrain the enforcement of a foreign judgment *held* not demurrable for want of equity. *Weed* v. *Hunt,* 212.

In a suit to restrain a foreign judgment, orator's allegation that she has no adequate remedy at law, *held* conclusive. *Ibid.*

The facts disclosed by a bill to restrain the enforcement of a foreign judgment, *held* to be a case of both accident and mistake. *Ibid.*

§ 3. Construction and Operation.

An order of the probate court, directing payment of a conditional bequest to a trustee, *held* not conclusive that the beneficiary was not entitled to the fund. *Congregational Church of Chester v. Cutler*, 338.

§ 4. Conclusiveness of Adjudication.

A special verdict is conclusive in a subsequent suit in equity between the same parties. *Sowles v. Sartwell*, 70.

JUSTICE EJECTMENT.

See "LANDLORD AND TENANT," § 2.

JUSTICE OF THE PEACE.

See "GAMING."

KLONDIKE MACHINE.

See "GAMING."

LANDLORD AND TENANT.

See "COVENANTS," § 1.

§ 1. Premises and Enjoyment and Use Thereof.

Notice to repair pursuant to covenant in lease need not state particulars and extent of repairs required. *Foss v. Stanton*, 365.

§ 2. Re-entry and Recovery of Possession by Landlord.

Proceedings in "justice ejectment" *held* available though tenancy be for life, provided created by contract. *Foss v. Stanton*, 365.

§ 3. Renting on Shares.

When a farm is let on shares, though the owner reserves a "lien and ownership" on the products, the parties are tenants in common of the crops. *Sowles v. Martin et al.*, 180; *Hunt v. Rublee*, 448.

In such case the owner may sell produce, upon tenant's default, but she must account to the tenant for his share. *Ibid.*

If, in such case, the tenant has misappropriated the products, the owner may sue in equity for an accounting. *Ibid.*

Assumpsit *held* not to lie between tenants in common of property for the value of plaintiff's interest in part of it. *Ibid.*

LEASES.

See "COVENANTS," § 1; "LANDLORD AND TENANT."

LIMITATION OF ACTIONS.

§ 1. Computation of Period of Limitation.

In respect of the Statute of Limitations the issuing of the writ is the commencement of the action, provided service follows, but not otherwise. *Tracy* v. *Ry. Co.,* 313.

When the writ is issued, and service thereof fails through unavoidable accident, the suit is commenced within the meaning of V. S. 1214. *Ibid.*

An utter failure of service is an insufficient service within the meaning of V. S. 1214. *Ibid.*

Case in which timely service was prevented through mislaying of writ, *held* to fall within V. S. 1214 relative to extension of period of limitation. *Ibid.*

§ 2. Pleading, Evidence, Trial, and Review.

Oral evidence *held* admissible, in an action begun after period of limitation, to show that previous action fell within V. S. 1214, relative to extension of period of limitation. *Tracy* v. *Ry. Co.,* 313.

In assumpsit on book account, evidence *held* not to tend to show that a certain article was delivered in payment of any specific items, so as to prevent its being a general credit, taking the account out of the Statute of Limitations. *Hammond's Admr.* v. *Hammond,* 437.

MASTERS IN CHANCERY.

See "EQUITY."

Review of Findings, see "APPEAL AND ERROR," § 2.

MASTER AND SERVANT.

§ 1. Master's Liability for Injury to Servant.

Foreign law that contributory negligence does not bar recovery but operates only to reduce damages relates to the right of action, not to the remedy. *Morrisette* v. *R. Co.,* 267.

Foreign law relating to contributory negligence *held* not so contrary to public policy that our courts will not enforce it. *Ibid.*

In a suit brought here for injuries received in Canada the right of action is governed by the Canadian law. *Ibid.*

In an action for injuries to a brakeman by striking a switch lantern, plaintiff's counsel *held* entitled to testify to the measurement of one of such lanterns. *Ibid.*

In such action it is proper to allow plaintiff to show, by observations and measurements made after the accident, the position and relative distance of stirrups and grab-irons on cars of same kind as those operated by him. *Ibid.*

In such action rules of the company *held* admissible to show that plaintiff was not required to leave his post, as he did, till after the train had stopped. *Ibid.*

MORTGAGES.

See "SUBROGATION."

Mortgage as a marriage brokerage contract, see "CONTRACTS," § 1; "APPEAL AND ERROR," § 2.

MUNICIPAL CORPORATIONS.

See "TAXATION," § 1.

§ 1. Officers, Agents, and Employes.

Chief of police *held* to be within rule of department forbidding participation in political meetings. *Brownell* v. *Russell*, 326.

Rule forbidding participation by policemen in political meetings *held* not to violate Art. 8 of the Constitution. *Ibid.*

Rule forbidding members of police force to particpiate in political meetings *held* a reasonable exercise of the power to make rules for the government of police force. *Ibid.*

Police officer's violation of rule forbidding participation in political meetings *held* to justify his removal from office. *Ibid.*

When the board of police examiners find that a police officer has violated a rule, they cannot control the effect of their finding by also reporting that they find him not guilty of the charge. *Ibid.*

NEW TRIAL.

Remarks of plaintiff in presence of jurors *held* to entitle defendant to new trial. *Grand Trunk Ry. Co.* v. *Davis*, 187.

Remarks of party in presence of jury which naturally would prejudice in his favor, will be presumed to have been so intended.
Ibid.

OFFICERS.

See "ASSAULT AND BATTERY," § 1; "SHERIFFS AND CONSTABLES."

OFF-SET.

V. S. 1159 prohibits off-set of damages arising from breach of contract
after suit thereon. *Jackson* v. *Hunt,* 284.

PARTIES.

See "PARTNERSHIP," § 2.

In a suit in equity for an accounting between tenants in common,
one who bought part of the common property agreeing to retain
the purchase money till settlement between the co-owners, but
who paid it over in violation of this agreement, is a proper
party defendant. *Sowles* v. *Martin et al.,* 180.

PARTNERSHIP.

§ 1. Rights and Liabilities as to Third Person.

In assumpsit against two as partners, when only one resides in this
State, and neither the firm nor the other partner has property
here, personal service on the resident defendant and substituted
service on the absent defendant gives the court jurisdiction of
neither the firm nor the absent defendant. *People's Nat. Bank*
v. *Hall & Buell,* 280.

In such case, if the action is on a note signed by both defendants,
the writ will not abate, but suit will proceed against the resident
defendant, under V. S. 1174. *Ibid.*

§ 2. Dissolution, Settlement, and Accounting.

Under V. S. 2445, administrator, and not heir of deceased must sue
for accounting. *Mason* v. *Mason's Exr.,* 287.

PAUPERS.

See "ACTIONS," § 1.

A wife cannot gain a settlement different from that of her husband.
Essex v. *Jericho,* 104

PLEADING.

:See "ABATEMENT"; "ANIMALS"; "ASSAULT AND BATTERY," § 1; "BANK-RUPTCY," § 2; "BANKS AND BANKING," § 1; "CHARITIES," § 2; "CORPORATIONS," § 5; "EVIDENCE," § 1; "HIGHWAYS"; "INTOXICAT-ING LIQUOR," § 2; "INSURANCE," § 2; "JUDGMENT," § 2; "PART-NESHIP," § 2; "PARTIES."

In action by receivers, see "CORPORATIONS," § 3.

§ 1. Form and Allegations in General.

When, in a bill in equity, the amount involved is written out in full, and also indicated with the dollar sign, the objection that the dollar sign is not in the English language is frivolous. *Weed* v. *Hunt*, 212.

§ 2. Demurrer.

A defect in form is not reached by general demurrer. *Belknap* v. *Billings*, 54.

§ 3. Motions.

A motion to dismiss goes only to what appears of record. *Tracy* v. *Ry. Co.*, 313.

POLICE.

See "MUNICIPAL CORPORATIONS."

POWERS.

See "WILLS," § 3.

A power involving no trust fails upon the death of the donee. *Cheney's Exr.* v. *Stafford*, 16.

PRESCRIPTION.

See "ADVERSE POSSESSION"; "WATER AND WATER COURSES," § 2.

PRINCIPAL AND AGENT.

See "ALTERATION OF INSTRUMENTS"; "CORPORATIONS," § 5.

PROBATE COURT.

See "JUDGMENTS," § 3.

When heirs are paid different sums, in a partial distribution by the administrator, the probate court should, on final decree, equalize the difference. *Walworth's Est.* v. *Bartholomew's Est.*, 1.

PROPERTY.

The pipes and hydrants of a water system are real property. *Stiles* v. *Newport*, 154.

PUBLIC LANDS.

A grant of land from the state conveys only such interest as the state then has. *Davis* v. *Moyles*, 25.

RAILROADS.

Carriage of passengers, see "CARRIERS." Power of Executive Committee, see "CORPORATIONS," § 5.

§ 1. Receivers.

In computing net earnings of railroad company only actual expenditures can be deducted from gross earnings. *Bell* v. *R. Co.*, 42.

Sums paid for interest and extraordinary repairs should be deducted from gross earnings. *Ibid.*

In computing net earnings of receivership, expenses of litigation *held* not proper deduction from gross earnings. *Ibid.*

Claim for stationery and printing not entitled to preference under V. S. 3803. *Ibid.*

Mandate formerly sent down construed, and *held* to intend formal notice in holding that only such creditors as had no notice of previous action could recover. *Ibid.*

Notice published by orator's solicitors in prior suit *held* without effect as notice to creditors in present suit. *Ibid.*

§ 2. Operation.

The duty to fence the sides of its road is owed by a railroad company to the immediate abutter only. *Delphia* v. *R. Co.*, 84.

Plaintiff *held* guilty of contributory negligence precluding his recovery for injury while crossing a railroad track. *Tracy* v. *Ry. Co.*, 313.

When negligence of plaintiff and defendant are concurrent and operative, there can be no recovery. *Ibid.*

REAL PROPERTY.

See "PROPERTY."

RECEIVERS.

See "RAILROADS," § 1; "BANKS AND BANKING," § 1.

RECITALS.

See "Evidence," § 5.

REPLEVIN.

See "Assault and Battery," § 1.

An officer serving a writ of replevin has no right to deliver the property to the plaintiff before he takes the required bond. *McKinstry* v. *Collins*, 221.

SALES.

See "Estoppel." Requirements of Statute of Frauds, see "Frauds, Statute of."

§ 1. Requisites and Validity of Contract.

A provision added by the buyer to his duplicate order blank, at the time of the sale and with the knowledge of the selling agent, becomes a part of the completed agreement. *Equitable Mfg. Co.* v. *Allen*, 22.

§ 2. Modification or Recission of Contract.

Manual tender by the vendee *held* not necessary to the recission of a sale voidable for vendor's fraud, when the latter refuses to take back the property. *Barrett* v. *Tyler et al.*, 108.

Upon such refusal the vendee may still elect whether he will stand on the contract or on the recission. *Ibid.*

But, after the vendee's refusal to take back the property, the sale of a part thereof by the vendee, determines his election to stand on the contract. *Ibid.*

§ 3. Remedies of Seller.

A buyer is not entitled to refuse to accept the goods on the ground that the invoice accompanying them did not contain the terms of the sale. *Equitable Mfg. Co.* v. *Allen*, 22.

When parties refuse to perform a contract made for a term, the other party may treat it as broken. *Parker* v. *McKannon Bros.*, 96.

In trover for property covered by lien note *held* immaterial that plaintiff had taken additional security on other property. *Kimball* v. *Costa*, 289.

§ 4. Conditional Sales.

A conditional sale note though indicating its amount only in the margin, *held* sufficient memorandum under V. S. 2290. *Kimball v. Costa*, 289.

Lien for price of goods sold conditionally *held* not waived by taking chattel mortgage on other property as additional security. *Ibid.*

SCHOOLS AND SCHOOL DISTRICTS.

In assumpsit for goods sold a school district, certified copy of record of warning of town meeting and of proceedings at said meeting authorizing payment of claim *held* admissible. *Currier* v. *Brighton*, 261.

School district cannot be controlled by directors in matter of paying a debt. *Ibid.*

SHERIFFS AND CONSTABLES.

A sheriff may recover from plaintiff his expenses in keeping attached property which plaintiff released from attachment before termination of suit. *Templeton* v. *Sav. Bank*, 345.

Sheriff's right to recover such expenses and his reasonable charges for securing property after return of writ is not dependent upon such items being indorsed on the writ. *Ibid.*

Such charges may be recovered of the plaintiff before the termination of the suit in which the attachment issued. *Ibid.*

SPECIFIC PERFORMANCE.

See "EVIDENCE," § 6.

Specific performance of option on stock will not be decreed, when orator refused to accept related option on real estate. *Reynolds* v. *Hooker*, 184.

STATUTES AND CONSTITUTIONAL PROVISIONS CITED AND CONSTRUED.

Acts 1797, and 1814 (Religious Societies). *Congregational Church of Chester* v. *Cutler*, 338.

Acts 1896, No. 46 (Inheritance Tax). *In Re Joslyn's Est.*, 88.

Acts 1896, No. 94 (Deer). *State* v *Jewett*, 435.

Acts 1898, No. 123 (Trading Stamps). *State* v. *Dodge*, 197.

Acts 1902, Nos. 73, 76 and 77 (Insurance). *Banker's Life Ins. Co.* v. *Fleetwood*, 297.

Acts 1902 (Intoxicating Liquor). *State* v. *Constantino*, 192.

Rev. St. U. S. § 4747 (Pensions). *Bailey* v. *Bailey*, 264.

V. S. Chap. 140 (Town Lines). *Town of Searsburg v. Town of Woodford,* 370.

V. S. 362 (Exemption from Taxation). *Stiles v. Newport,* 154.

V. S. 1159 (Offset). *Jackson v. Hunt,* 284.

V. S. 1174 (Substituted Service). *People's Nat. Bank v. Hall & Buell,* 280.

V. S. 1214 (Extension of Limitation). *Tracy v. Ry. Co.,* 313.

V. S. 1411 (Judgments). *Leonard v. Sibley,* 254.

V. S. 1472 (Replevin Bond). *McKinstry v. Collins,* 221.

V. S. 1505 (Certified Execution). *Angell v. Fletcher,* 359.

V. S. 1560 (Justice Ejectment). *Foss v. Stanton,* 365.

V. S. 2290 (Conditional Sale). *Kimball v. Costa,* 289.

V. S. 2357-2359 (Neglect of Executor or Custodian). *Richardson v. Fletcher,* 206.

V. S. 2445 (Actions by Administrator). *Mason v. Mason's Exrs.,* 287.

V. S. 2644-2647 (Contracts of Married Women). *Spencer v. Stockwell,* 176.

V. S. 2691 (Alimony). *Carter v. Carter,* 190.

V. S. 3171-3172 (Support of Paupers). *Essex v. Jericho,* 104.

V. S. 3808 (Railroads). *Bell v. R. Co.,* 42.

V. S. 4178 (Insurance). *Bankers' Life Ins. Co. v. Fleetwood,* 297.

V. S. 3874-3877 (Fencing Railroads). *Delphia v. R. Co.,* 84.

V. S. 5366 and V. S. 1111 (Officers' Fees). *Templeton v. Sav. Bank,* 345.

Const. 1777, Preamble (Land Grants). *Davis v. Moyles,* 25.

STOCK.

See "SPECIFIC PERFORMANCE."

STREET RAILROADS.

Carriage of passengers, see "CARRIERS."

SUBROGATION.

The grantee of real estate subject to a mortgage *held* not subrogated to the rights of mortgagee upon payment of the mortgage debt by his grantor. *Deavitt v. Ring,* 216.

TAXATION.

§ 1. Liability of Persons and Property.

Only the property of a municipal corporation which is devoted to a public use is exempt from taxation. *Stiles v. Newport,* 154.

That part of the water system of a village lying without its corporate limits, but employed in public use, is exempt from taxation. *Ibid.*

That part of the water system of a village employed in furnishing water for another municipality *held* not exempt from taxation. *Ibid.*

Last owner of real estate on the first day of April liable for taxes regardless of subsequent conveyances. *Fulton* v. *Aldrich*, 310.

Lien on real estate for taxes not enforceable while last owner on the first day of April in year of assessment has personal property from which the tax can be collected. *Ibid.*

Tax not an incumbrance on real estate till the officer does some official act indicating an intention to hold the land. *Ibid.*

Mortgagees paying taxes after foreclosure, but before expiration of equity of redemption, and before any attempt to hold the land for the taxes, *held* mere volunteers. *Ibid.*

§ 2. Inheritance Tax.

Debts due from nonresidents are not subject to the collateral inheritance tax prescribed by No. 46, Acts 1896. *In Re Joslyn's Est.*, 88.

TENANCY IN COMMON.

See "LANDLORD AND TENANT," § 3.

§ 1. Creation and Existence.

Contract by which plaintiff sold defendant a half interest in a stallion *held* to make them co-owners of the property. *Chase* v. *Soule*, 353.

§ 2. Mutual Rights, Duties, and Liabilities of Co-tenants.

One of two co-owners of personal property cannot sell the other's interest without his consent. *Chase* v. *Soule*, 353.

§ 3. Rights and Liabilities of Co-tenants as to Third Persons.

One tenant in common of real estate may maintain trespass in his own name and recover the entire damage to the common property. *Davis* v. *Moyles*, 25.

TOWNS.

See "CHARITIES," § 1.

The proceeding given by V. S. Chap. 140, for establishing town lines, confines the court to locating the charter line. *Town of Searsburg* v. *Town of Woodford*, 370.

It is doubtful whether the Legislature can confer power upon the judiciary to establish any division line between towns except charter line. *Ibid.*

A town line may be established by prescription, though variant from the original grant. *Ibid.*

The charter of a town may be established by prescription. *Town of Readsboro* v. *Town of Woodford*, 376.

TRADING STAMPS.

See "CONSTITUTIONAL LAW," § 4.

TRANSFERS.

Grant of by street railroad, see "CARRIERS."

TRESPASS.

See "TENANCY IN COMMON," § 3.

TRIAL.

§ 1. Reception of Evidence.

An offer of proof in the alternative must be taken in the view less favorable to the offerer. *Buck* v. *Troy Aqueduct Co.*, 75.

§ 2. Taking Case or Question from Jury.

Though evidence is undisputed, yet, if it affords grounds of opposing inferences of fact, it is for the jury. *Tracy* v. *Ry. Co.*, 313.

When there is no concession that the facts are what the oral evidence tends to show, the question cannot be taken from the jury. *Ibid.*

The purpose of a demurrer to the evidence *held* to be to refer to the court questions of law arising on the facts as ascertained. *Bass* v. *Rublee*, 395.

On overruling a motion for a verdict, no judgment is rendered against the moving party. *Ibid.*

§ 3. Instruction to Jury.

An instruction that negligence could not be presumed from the mere happening of the accident *held* covered by the charge. *Morrisette* v. *R. Co.*, 267.

An exception to a portion of a charge does not cover an objection to the failure to charge. *Ibid.*

In a suit here for injuries received in Canada *held* not error to refuse to instruct the jury that, if plaintiff failed to establish the Canadian law to be settled as alleged and different from the law of Vermont, it need not be considered. *Ibid.*

Exception "to the failure of the court to charge as requested, so far as there was such failure," will not be considered. *Luce* v. *Hassam,* 450.

Exception "to charge as given" *held* too general. *Ibid.*

Counsel must specify the points of the charge to which they except. *Ibid.*

In an action by one of two co-owners of a horse against the other, on an agreement to indemnify plaintiff against loss from refusing an offer to buy the horse, instruction that plaintiff had no right to sell *held* properly refused. *Chase* v. *Soule,* 353.

A party is entitled to have his whole case submitted to the jury, either by a general verdict or by special verdicts. *Coolidge* v. *Ayers,* 405.

Remarks of the court *held* proper, as illustrating the rule in respect of using a deadly weapon in defence. *State* v. *Raymo,* 430.

§ 4. Verdict.

The court may properly submit special verdicts, so that it may appear whether certain instructions, if wrong, are also harmful. *McKinstry* v. *Collins,* 221.

A motion for a verdict is in the nature of a demurrer to the evidence, but the required technicalities of such demurrer do not appertain to a motion for a verdict. *Bass* v. *Rublee,* 395.

TRUSTEE PROCESS.

See "JUDGMENT," § 1.

Judgment for trustee *held* not binding as to any issue between plaintiff and defendant, and hence no estoppel in a subsequent suit, defendant not having been served with process, and not having appeared. *Hilliard* v. *Shoe Co.,* 57.

VENDOR AND PURCHASER.

See "SALES," § 3.

VERDICT.

Conclusiveness of, see "JUDGMENT," § 4.
In civil cases, see "TRIAL," § 4.

WATER AND WATER COURSES.

§ 1. Natural Water Courses.

Whether the use of a stream by riparian owner is reasonable is a question of fact. *Lawrie* v. *Silsby*, 240.

Riparian owners are entitled to a reasonable use of the water. *Ibid.*

§ 2. Appropriation and Prescription.

Nonriparian owners may acquire by prescription the rights of a riparian owner, as against other riparian owners. *Lawrie* v. *Silsby*, 240.

Nonriparian owners, by the use of water from a stream *held* not to acquire prescriptive rights as against upper riparian owners. *Ibid.*

Nonriparian owners *held* to have acquired the right to use of a stream, though use was begun by license. *Ibid.*

§ 3. Conveyances and Contracts.

A grant of a water right construed as one to draw a certain quantity of water without regard to the particular use or place. *Woolen Co.* v. *Bugbee*, 61.

A water right granted "not to be used for any purpose to the injury of any machinery now in use," is subject to the water right then used to operate said machinery. *Ibid.*

In such grant a reference to an existing use *held* a measure of quantity merely. *Ibid.*

WILLS.

See "CHARITIES," § 1; "WITNESSES," § 1. Neglect of custodian, see "ACTION," § 2.

§ 1. Testamentary Capacity.

Evidence of a testator's mental condition during long period preceding execution of will, there being no indication of any marked change therein, *held* competent on question of testamentary capacity. *In Re Wheelock's Will*, 235.

Letters of testator are admissible to show his knowledge of the contents of his will. *Ibid.*

An adjudication that one is *non compos* is *prima facie* evidence of lack of testamentary capacity. *Ibid.*

§ 2. Requisites and Validity.

Held that the facts disclosed by uncontradicted testimony tended to show testator's knowledge of the nature and contents of his will at time of its execution. *In Re Mather's Will,* 209.

§ 3. Construction.

A will authorizing the sale of "building lots" does not give the right to sell a lot on which a building stood in testatrix's life time. *Cheney's Exr.* v. *Stafford,* 16.

Of two inconsistent provisions of a will, the last will prevail. *Ibid.*

A will directing the devisee of the life use of certain property to pay the mortgage thereon out of other property, creates a vested right in the final beneficiaries of the mortgaged property to have this done. *Ibid.*

A condition attached to a bequest construed and *held* a condition subsequent. *Congregational Church of Chester* v. *Cutler,* 338.

In an action to construe a conditional bequest to a church, the latter's officers *held* properly permitted to state what their intention was as to performing the condition. *Ibid.*

Life tenant under will, who temporarily waived her rights, *held* not entitled to an equitable lien on interest of remainderman. *Hare* v. *Congregational Soc.,* 362.

Will *held* to give defendant a vested remainder, subject to be divested by the exercise of power of sale by life tenant, but which could not be divested in any other manner. *Ibid.*

WITNESSES.

See "'APPEAL AND ERROR," § 1.

§ 1. Competency.

The proponent of a will, who is also a legatee but is not an attesting witness, *held* competent to testify to its execution. *In Re Wheelock's Will,* 235.

§ 2. Credibility, Impeachment, Contradiction and Corroboration.

Impeaching evidence is rightly excluded when proper foundation has not been laid. *McKinstry* v. *Collins,* 221.

In an action for an assault, evidence of the circumstances in which plaintiff pleaded guilty of an assault on defendant is admissible. *Ibid.*